# BATMAN™

## ARKHAM UNHINGED™

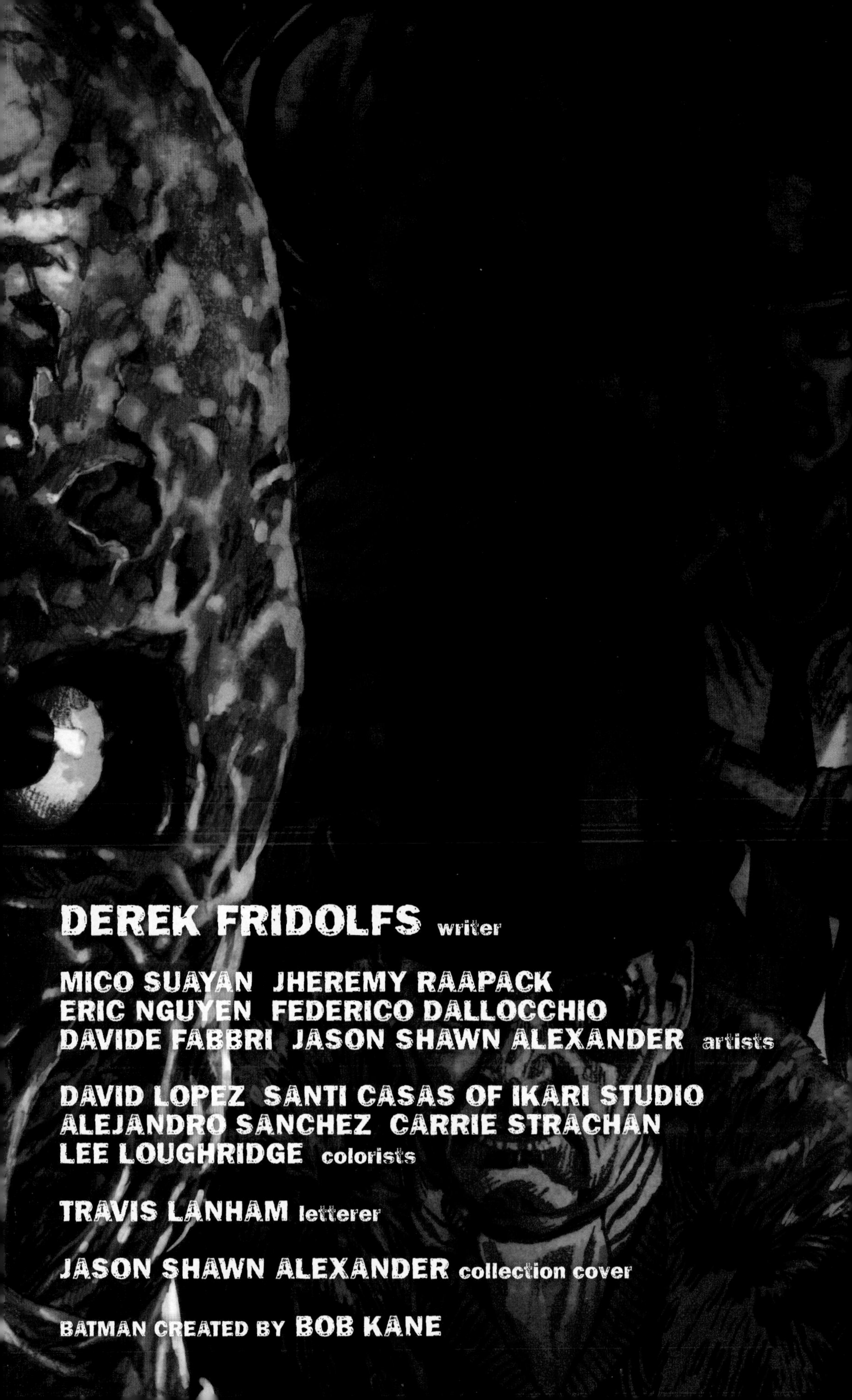

**DEREK FRIDOLFS** writer

**MICO SUAYAN JHEREMY RAAPACK**
**ERIC NGUYEN FEDERICO DALLOCCHIO**
**DAVIDE FABBRI JASON SHAWN ALEXANDER** artists

**DAVID LOPEZ SANTI CASAS OF IKARI STUDIO**
**ALEJANDRO SANCHEZ CARRIE STRACHAN**
**LEE LOUGHRIDGE** colorists

**TRAVIS LANHAM** letterer

**JASON SHAWN ALEXANDER** collection cover

BATMAN CREATED BY **BOB KANE**

Jim Chadwick Editor – Original Series
Sarah Gaydos Assistant Editor – Original Series
Robin Wildman Editor
Robbin Brosterman Design Director – Books
Louis Prandi Publication Design

Hank Kanalz Senior VP – Vertigo and Integrated Publishing

Diane Nelson President
Dan DiDio and Jim Lee Co-Publishers
Geoff Johns Chief Creative Officer
John Rood Executive VP – Sales, Marketing and Business Development
Amy Genkins Senior VP – Business and Legal Affairs
Nairi Gardiner Senior VP – Finance
Jeff Boison VP – Publishing Planning
Mark Chiarello VP – Art Direction and Design
John Cunningham VP – Marketing
Terri Cunningham VP – Editorial Administration
Alison Gill Senior VP – Manufacturing and Operations
Jay Kogan VP – Business and Legal Affairs, Publishing
Jack Mahan VP – Business Affairs, Talent
Nick Napolitano VP – Manufacturing Administration
Courtney Simmons Senior VP – Publicity
Bob Wayne Senior VP – Sales

BATMAN: ARKHAM UNHINGED VOLUME 3



DC Comics, 1700 Broadway, New York, NY 10019
A Warner Bros. Entertainment Company.
Printed by RR Donnelley, Salem, VA, USA. 11/29/13. First Printing.
ISBN: 978-1-4012-4305-0

Library of Congress Cataloging-in-Publication Data

Fridolfs, Derek, author.
Batman : Arkham Unhinged. Volume 3 / Derek Fridolfs ; [illustrated by] Jason Shawn Alexander.
pages cm
ISBN 978-1-4012-4305-0 (hardback)
1. Graphic novels. I. Alexander, Jason Shawn, illustrator. II. Title.
PN6728.B36F77 2014
741.5'973—dc23
2013035967

SUSTAINABLE FORESTRY INITIATIVE
Certified Chain of Custody
At Least 20% Certified Forest Content
www.sfiprogram.org
SFI-01042
APPLIES TO TEXT STOCK ONLY

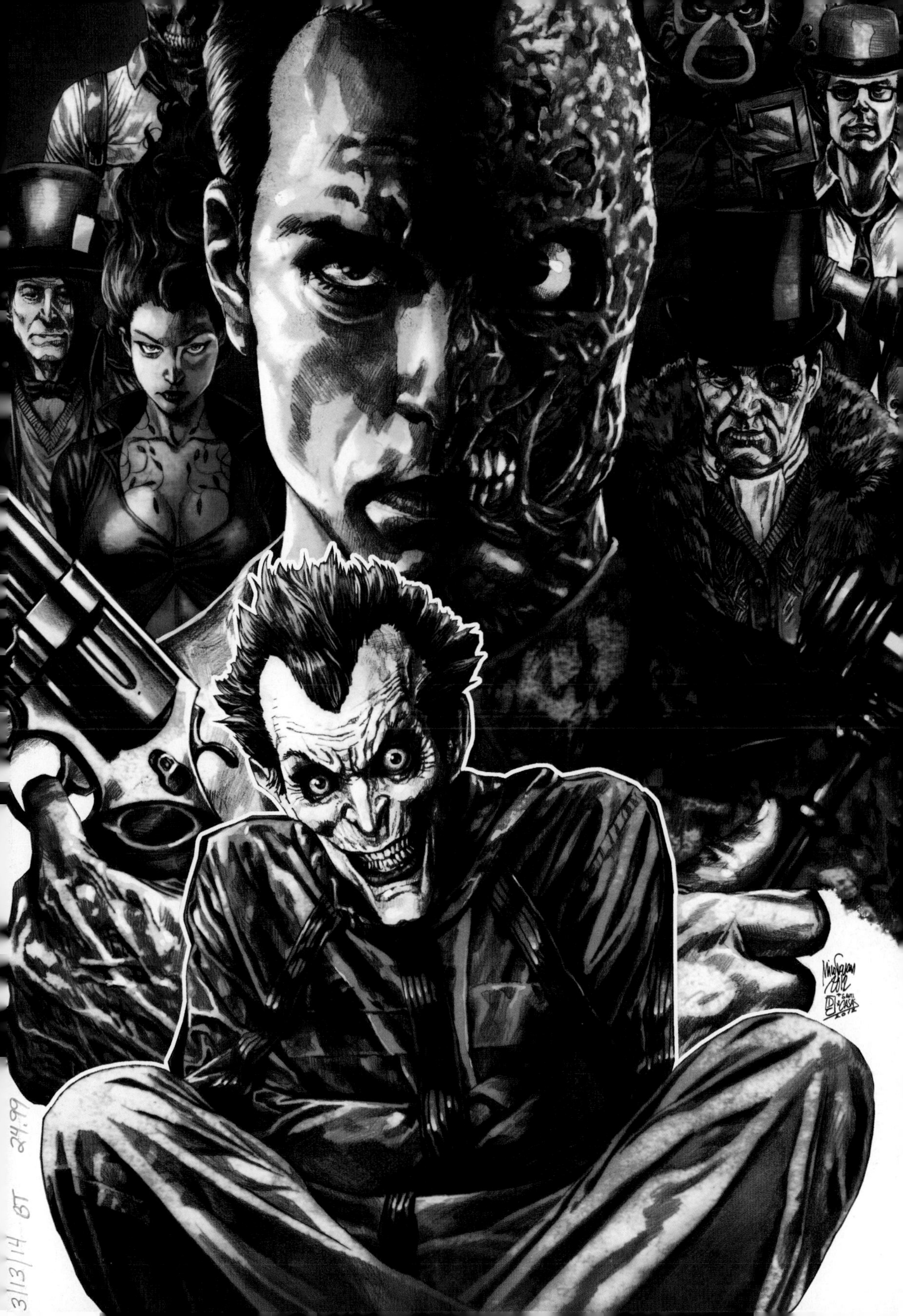

# CLOWN COURT


WRITTEN BY: DEREK FRIDOLFS

ART AND COVER BY: MICO SUAYAN

INTERIOR AND COVER COLORS BY:
DAVID LOPEZ & SANTI CASAS OF IKARI STUDIO

LETTERS BY: TRAVIS LANHAM


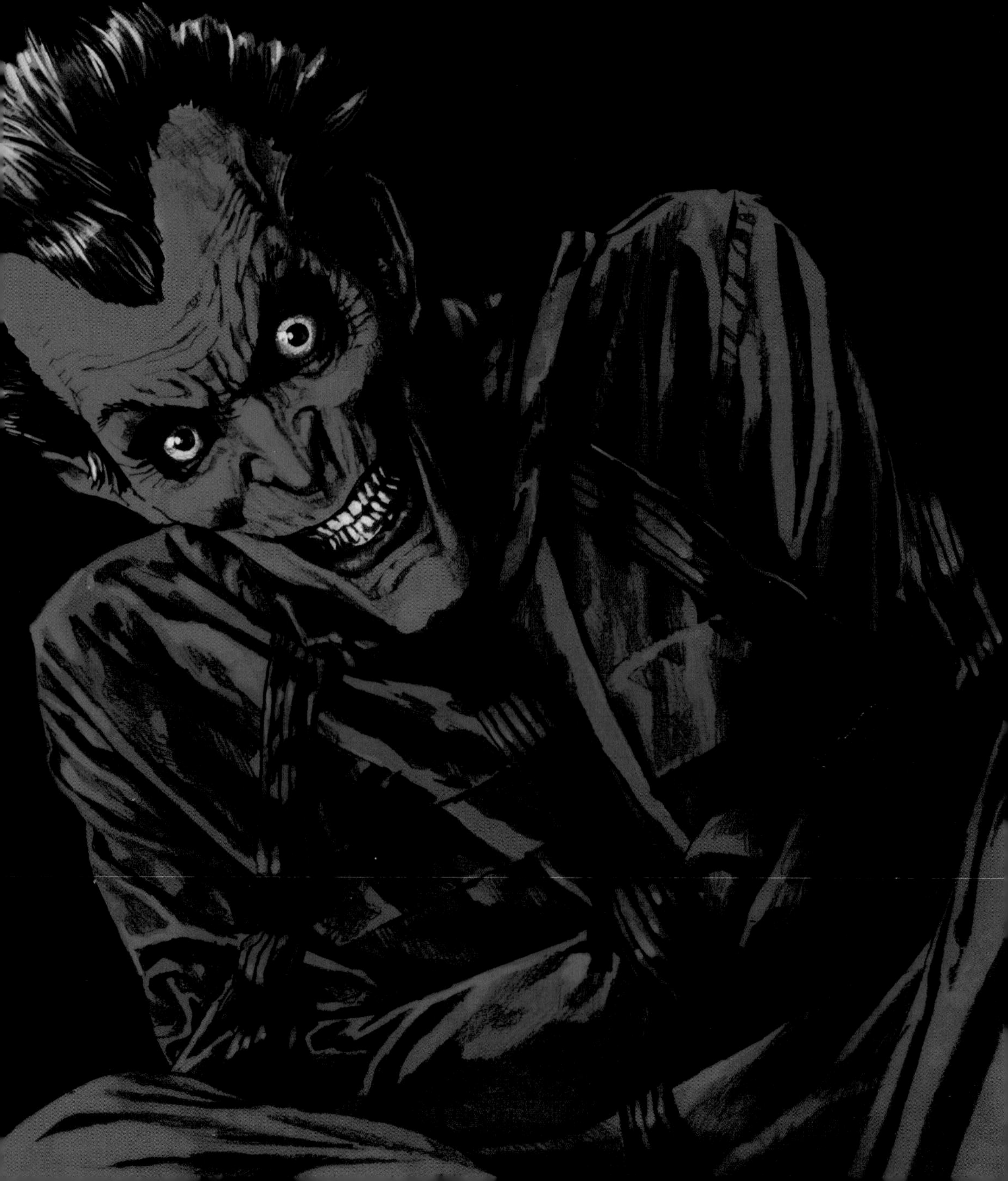

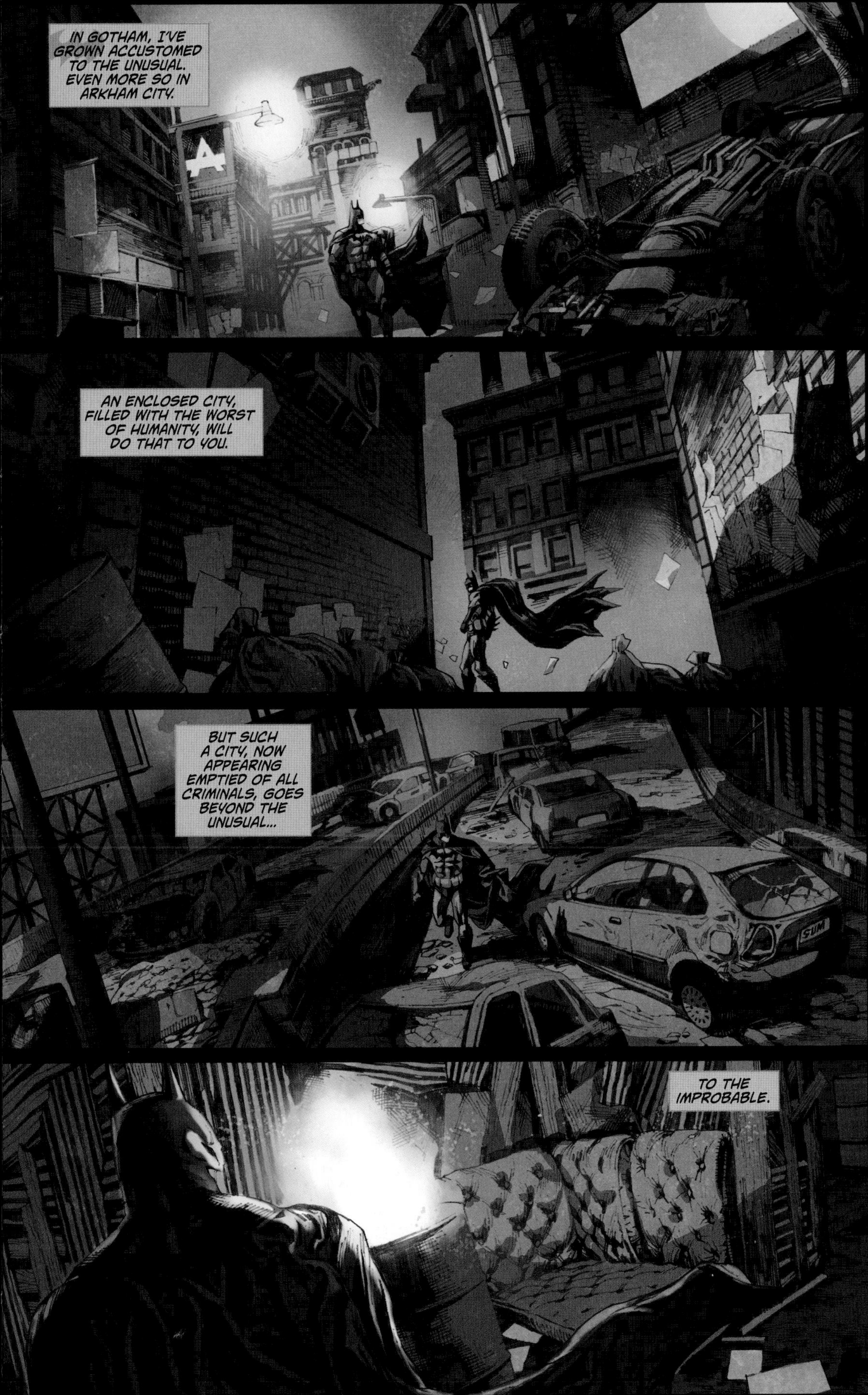
IN GOTHAM, I'VE GROWN ACCUSTOMED TO THE UNUSUAL. EVEN MORE SO IN ARKHAM CITY.
AN ENCLOSED CITY, FILLED WITH THE WORST OF HUMANITY, WILL DO THAT TO YOU.
BUT SUCH A CITY, NOW APPEARING EMPTIED OF ALL CRIMINALS, GOES BEYOND THE UNUSUAL...
SUM
TO THE IMPROBABLE.

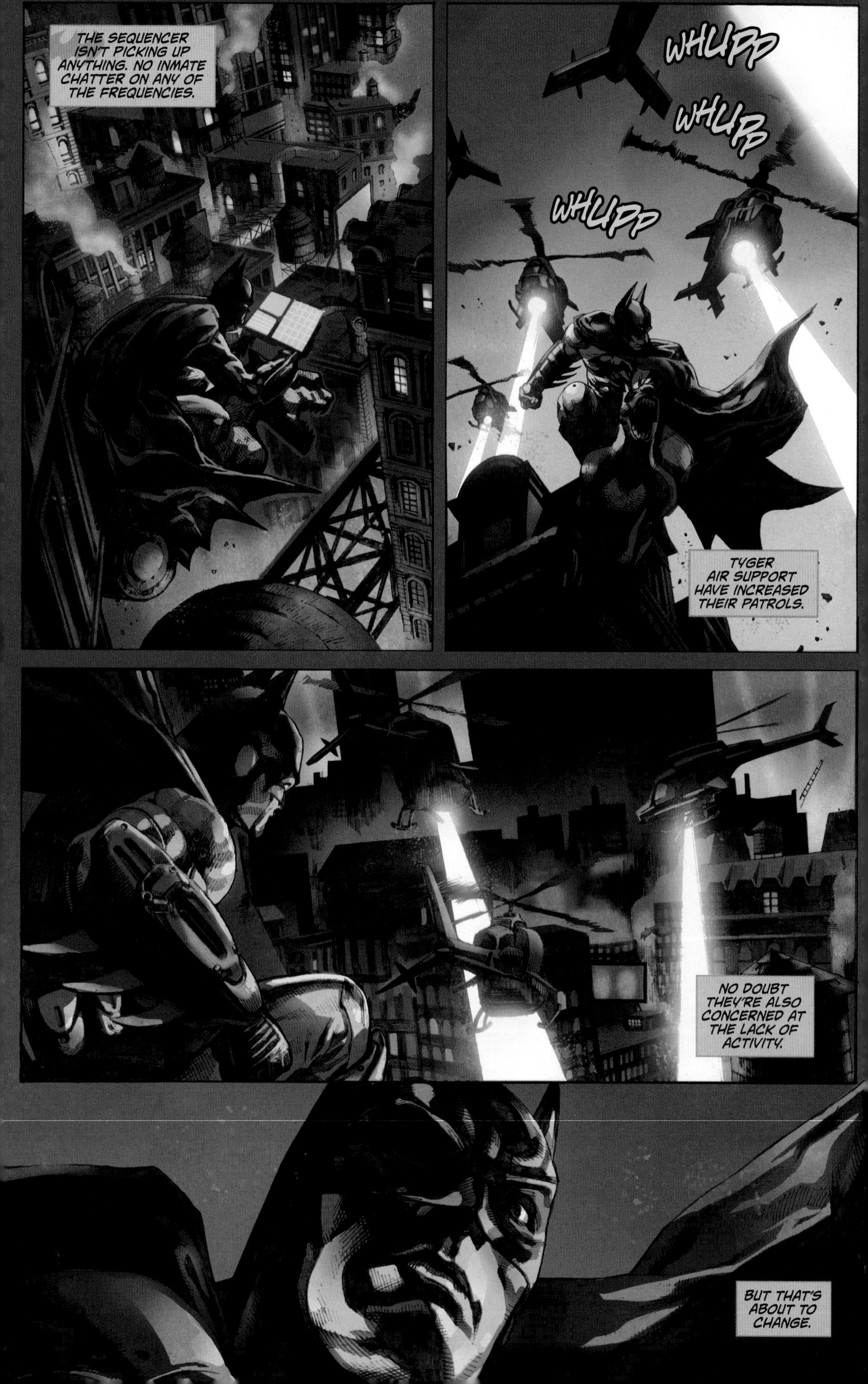
THE SEQUENCER ISN'T PICKING UP ANYTHING. NO INMATE CHATTER ON ANY OF THE FREQUENCIES.
WHUPP
WHUPP
WHUPP
TYGER AIR SUPPORT HAVE INCREASED THEIR PATROLS.
NO DOUBT THEY'RE ALSO CONCERNED AT THE LACK OF ACTIVITY.
BUT THAT'S ABOUT TO CHANGE.

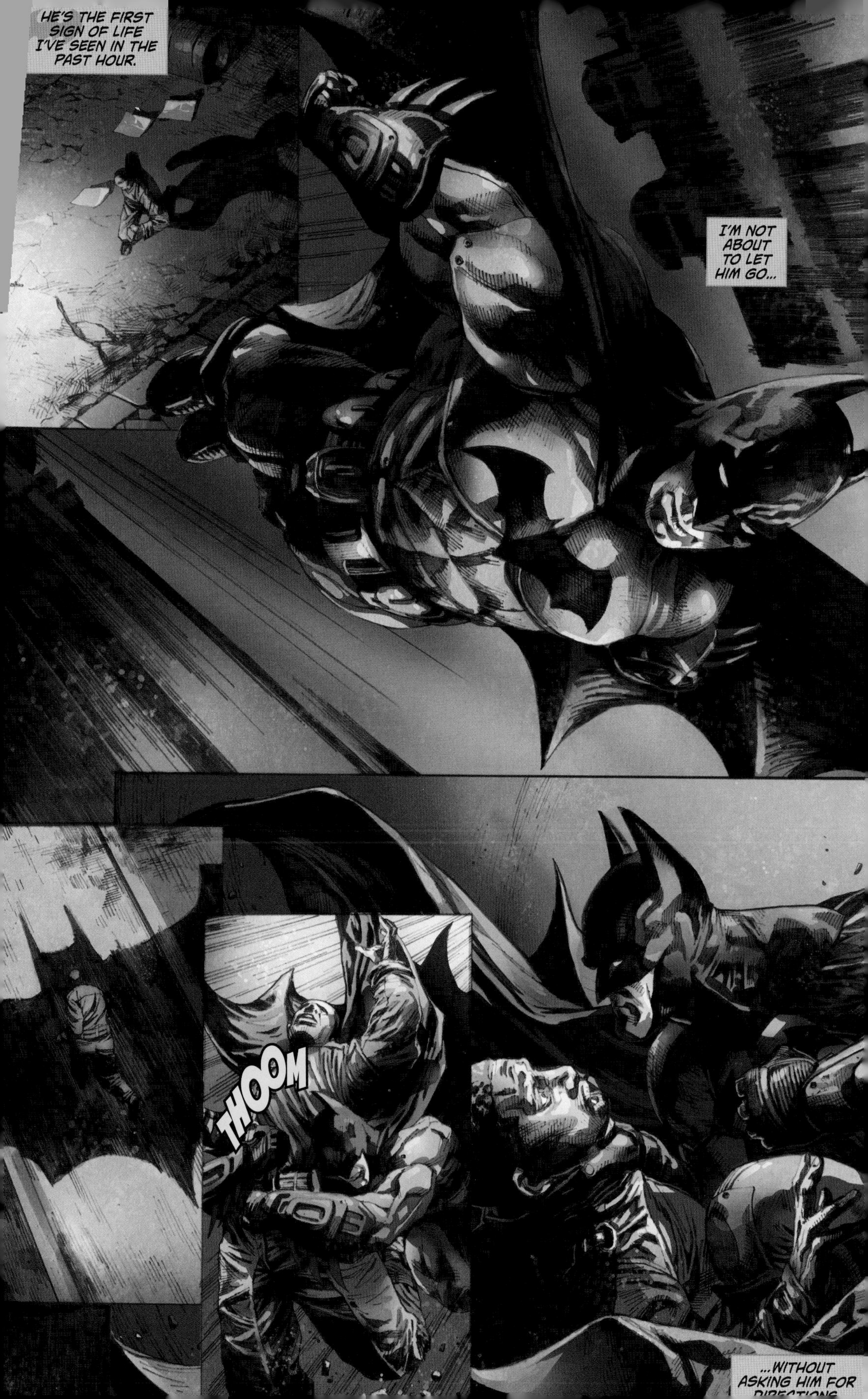
HE'S THE FIRST SIGN OF LIFE I'VE SEEN IN THE PAST HOUR.
I'M NOT ABOUT TO LET HIM GO...
THOOM
...WITHOUT ASKING HIM FOR

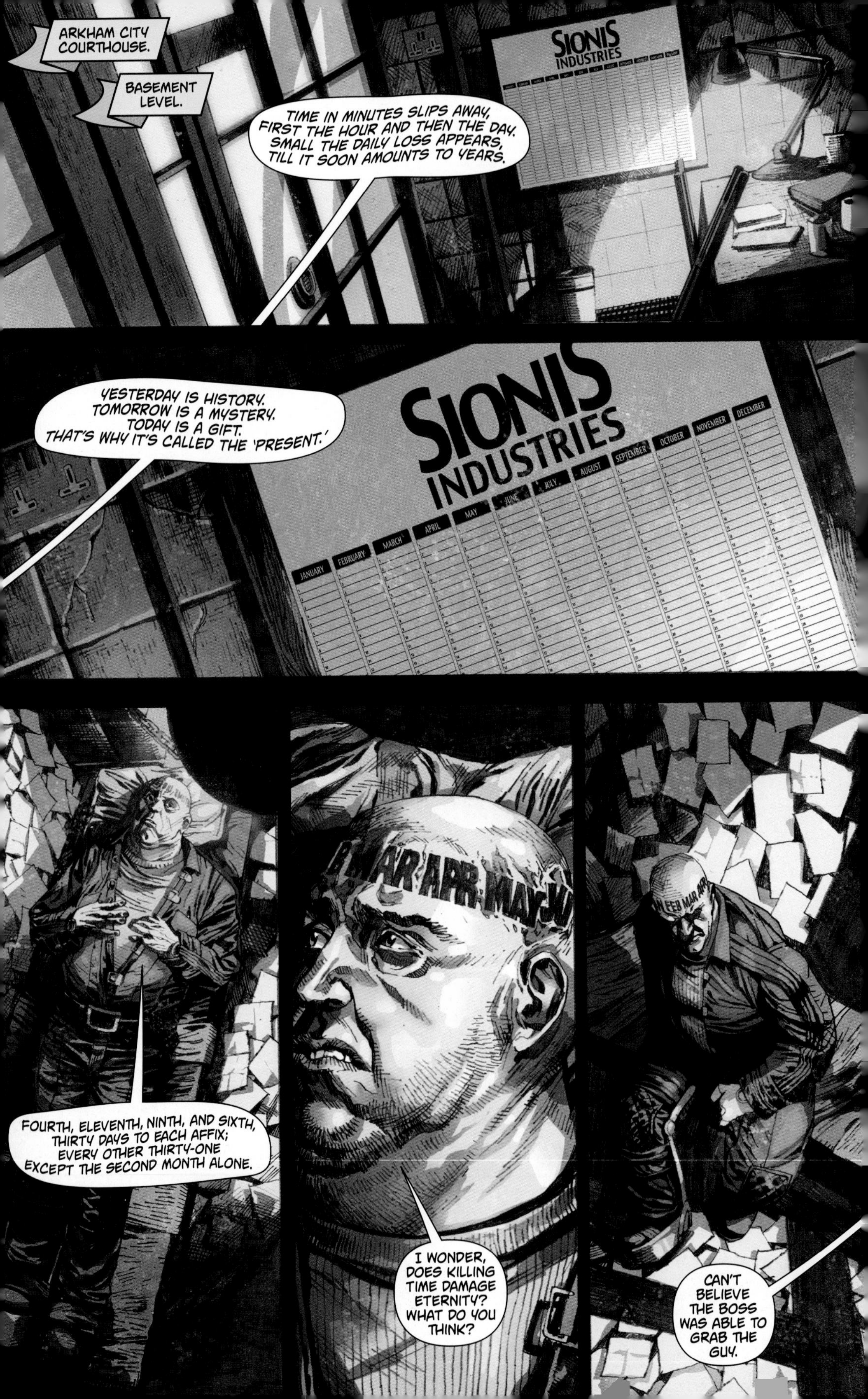
ARKHAM CITY COURTHOUSE.
BASEMENT LEVEL.
TIME IN MINUTES SLIPS AWAY, FIRST THE HOUR AND THEN THE DAY. SMALL THE DAILY LOSS APPEARS, TILL IT SOON AMOUNTS TO YEARS.
SIONIS INDUSTRIES
YESTERDAY IS HISTORY. TOMORROW IS A MYSTERY. TODAY IS A GIFT. THAT'S WHY IT'S CALLED THE 'PRESENT.'
SIONIS INDUSTRIES
JANUARY FEBRUARY MARCH APRIL MAY JUNE JULY AUGUST SEPTEMBER OCTOBER NOVEMBER DECEMBER
FOURTH, ELEVENTH, NINTH, AND SIXTH, THIRTY DAYS TO EACH AFFIX; EVERY OTHER THIRTY-ONE EXCEPT THE SECOND MONTH ALONE.
I WONDER, DOES KILLING TIME DAMAGE ETERNITY? WHAT DO YOU THINK?
CAN'T BELIEVE THE BOSS WAS ABLE TO GRAB THE GUY.

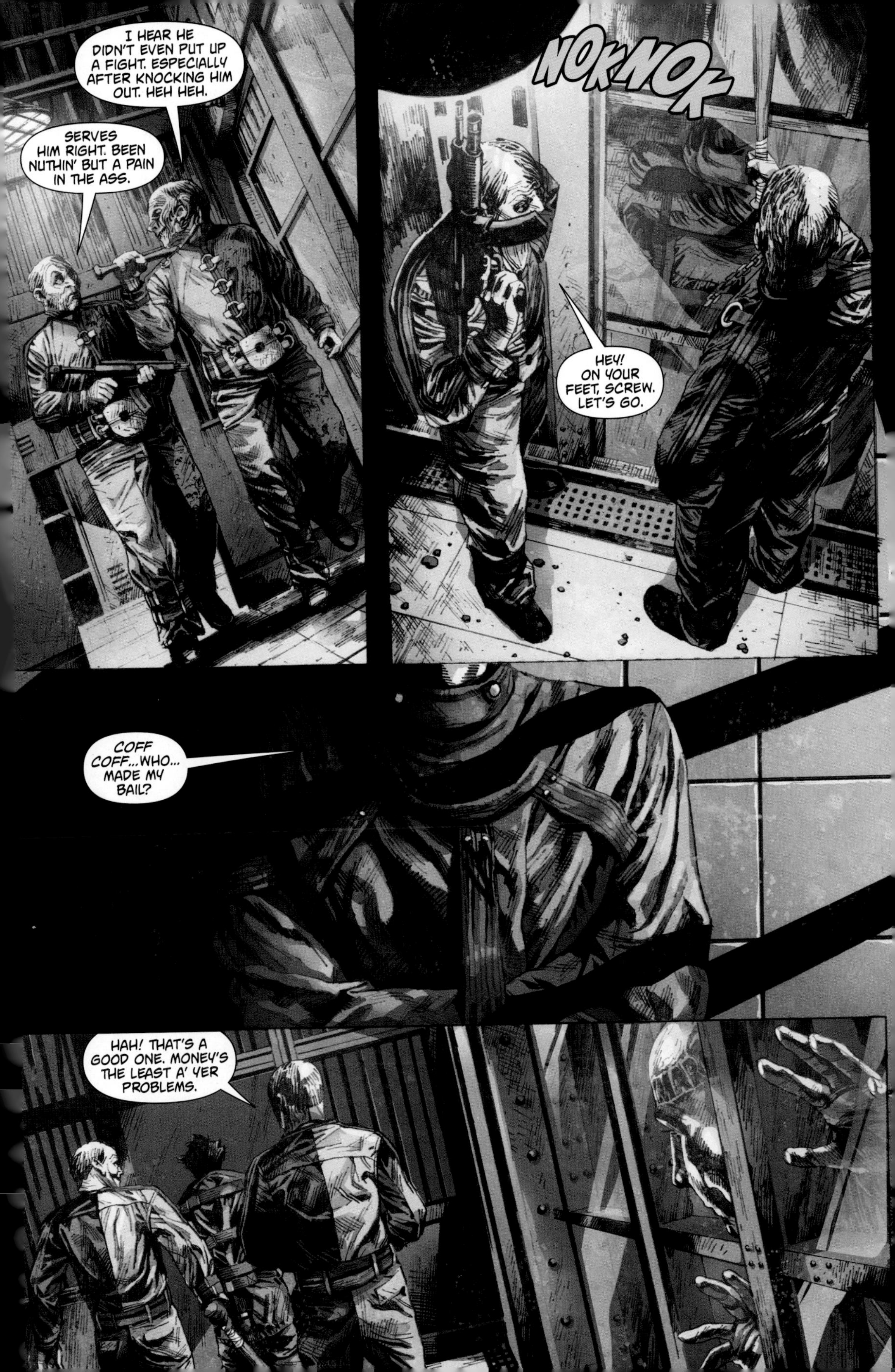
I HEAR HE DIDN'T EVEN PUT UP A FIGHT. ESPECIALLY AFTER KNOCKING HIM OUT. HEH HEH.
SERVES HIM RIGHT. BEEN NUTHIN' BUT A PAIN IN THE ASS.
NOKNOK
HEY! ON YOUR FEET, SCREW. LET'S GO.
COFF COFF...WHO... MADE MY BAIL?
HAH! THAT'S A GOOD ONE. MONEY'S THE LEAST A' YER PROBLEMS.

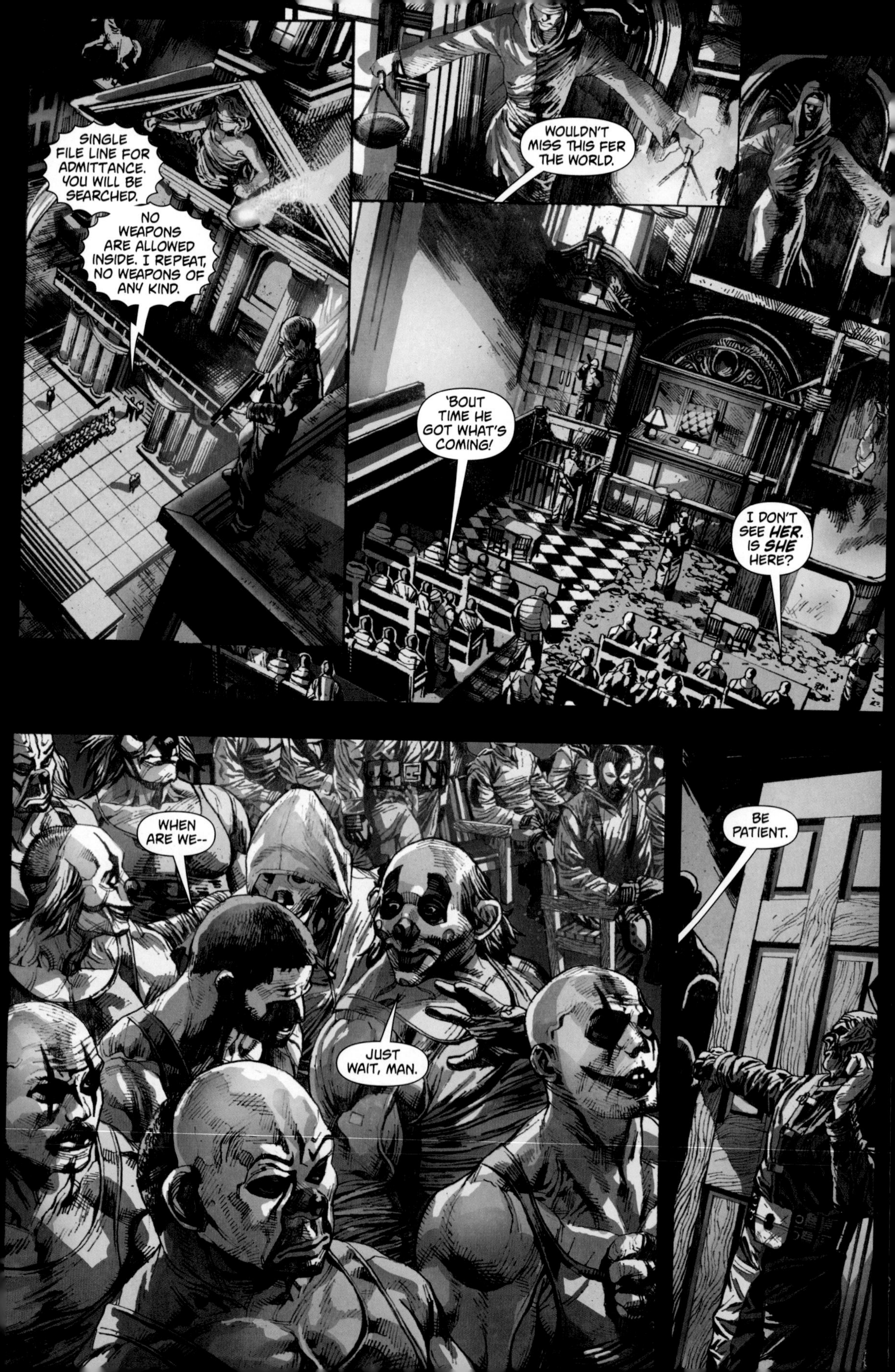
SINGLE FILE LINE FOR ADMITTANCE. YOU WILL BE SEARCHED.
NO WEAPONS ARE ALLOWED INSIDE. I REPEAT, NO WEAPONS OF ANY KIND.
WOULDN'T MISS THIS FER THE WORLD.
'BOUT TIME HE GOT WHAT'S COMING!
I DON'T SEE *HER*. IS *SHE* HERE?
WHEN ARE WE--
JUST WAIT, MAN.
BE PATIENT.

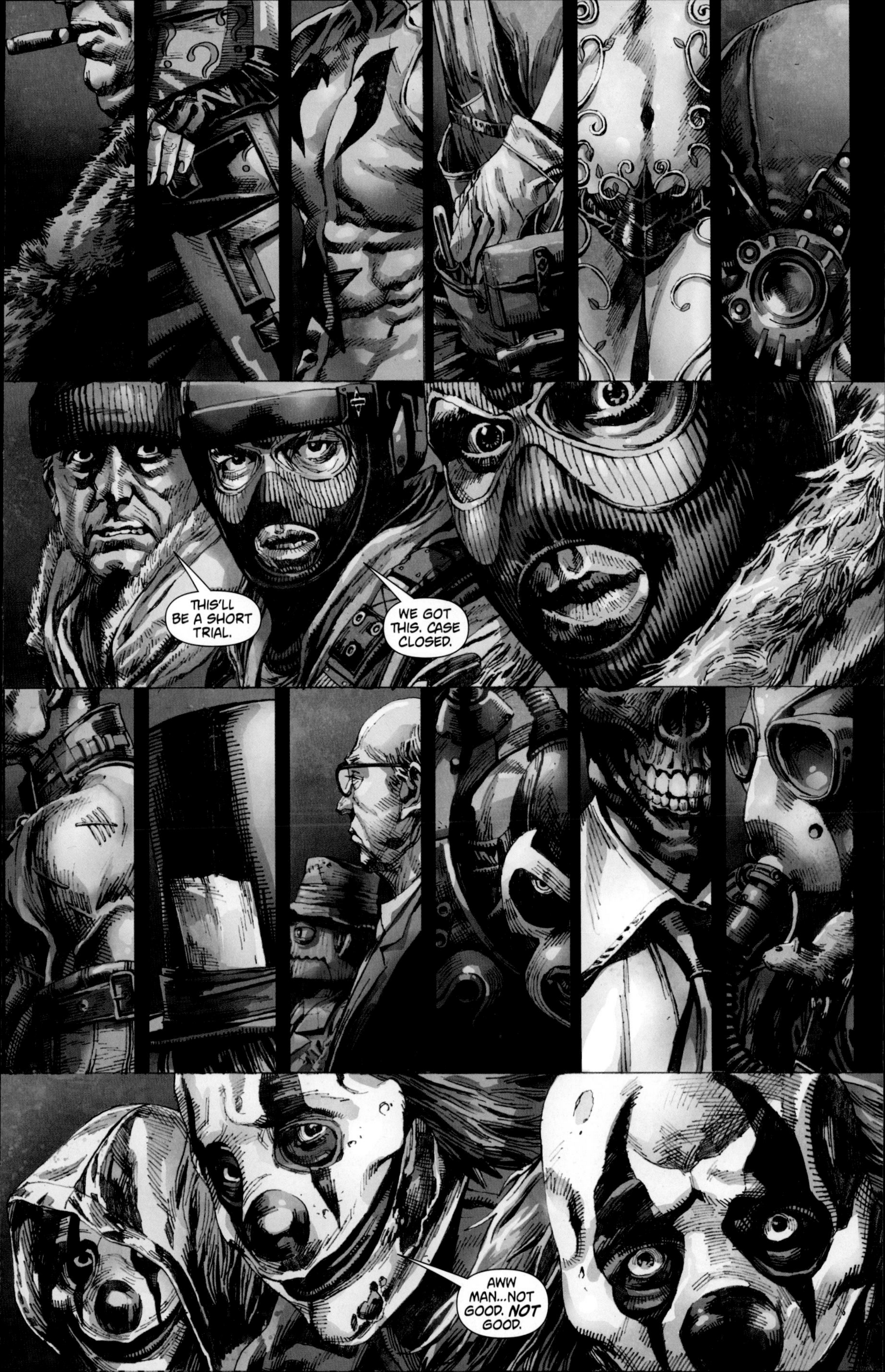
THIS'LL BE A SHORT TRIAL.
WE GOT THIS. CASE CLOSED.
AWW MAN...NOT GOOD. **NOT** GOOD.

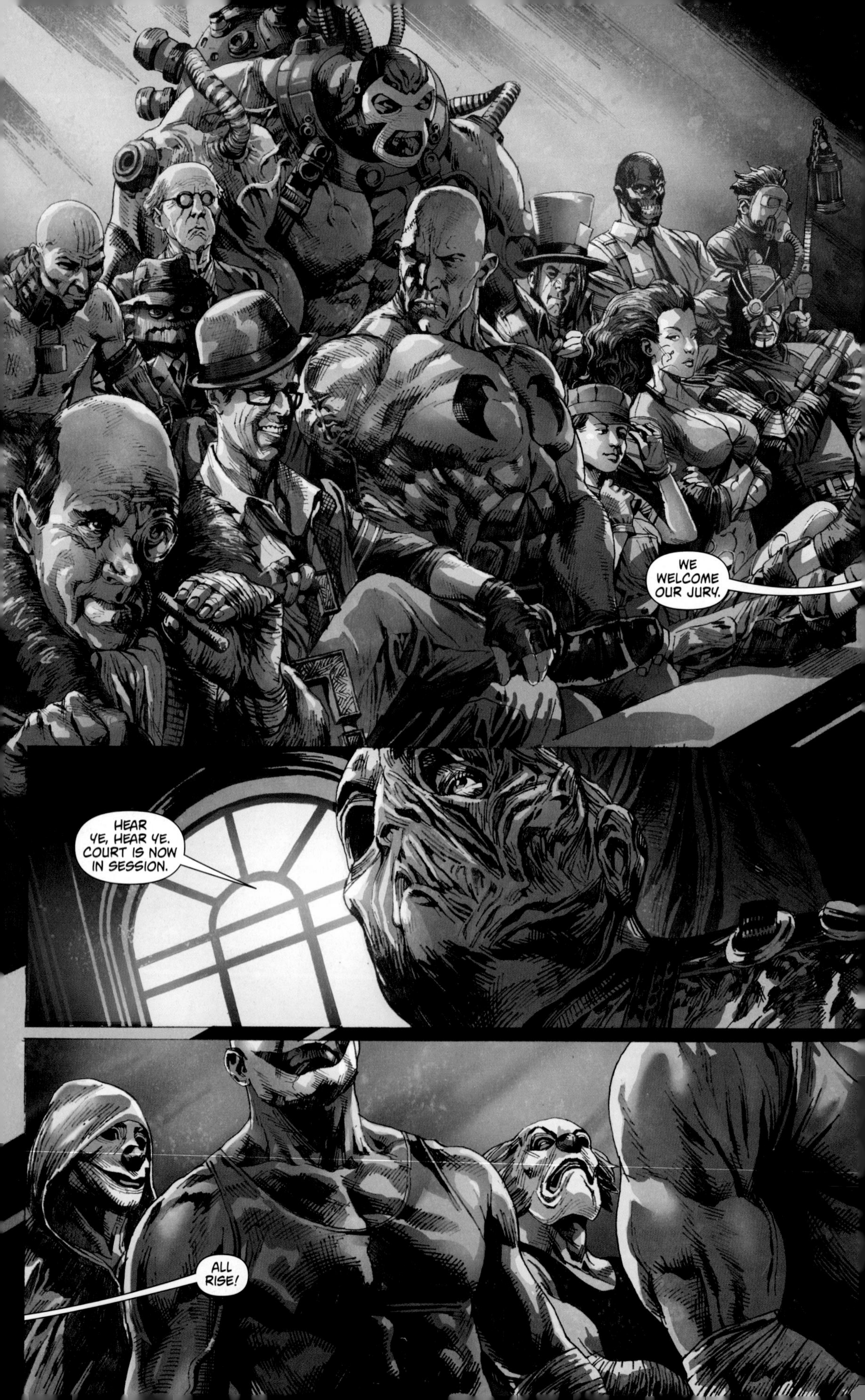
WE WELCOME OUR JURY.
HEAR YE, HEAR YE. COURT IS NOW IN SESSION.
ALL RISE!

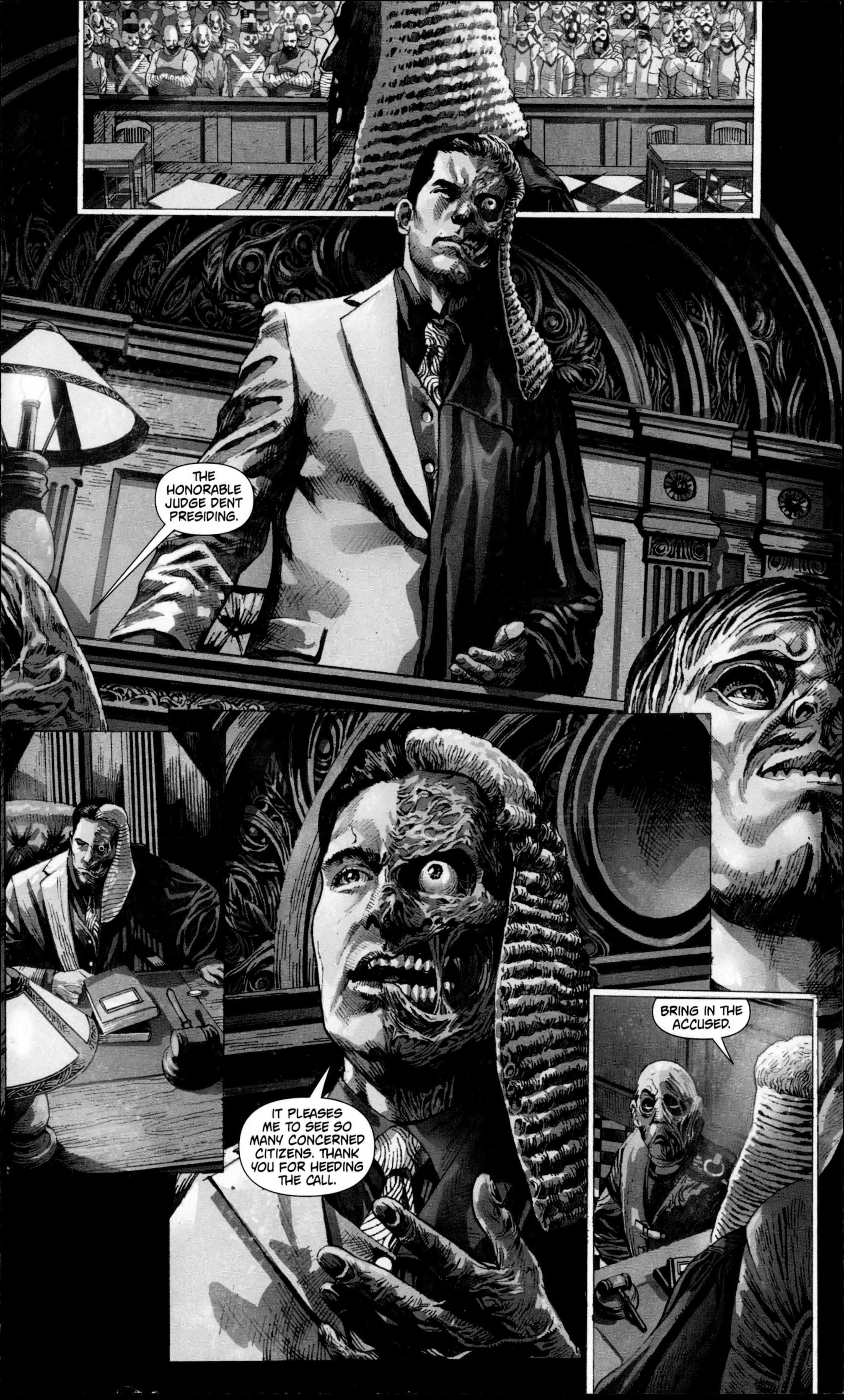
THE HONORABLE JUDGE DENT PRESIDING.
IT PLEASES ME TO SEE SO MANY CONCERNED CITIZENS. THANK YOU FOR HEEDING THE CALL.
BRING IN THE ACCUSED.

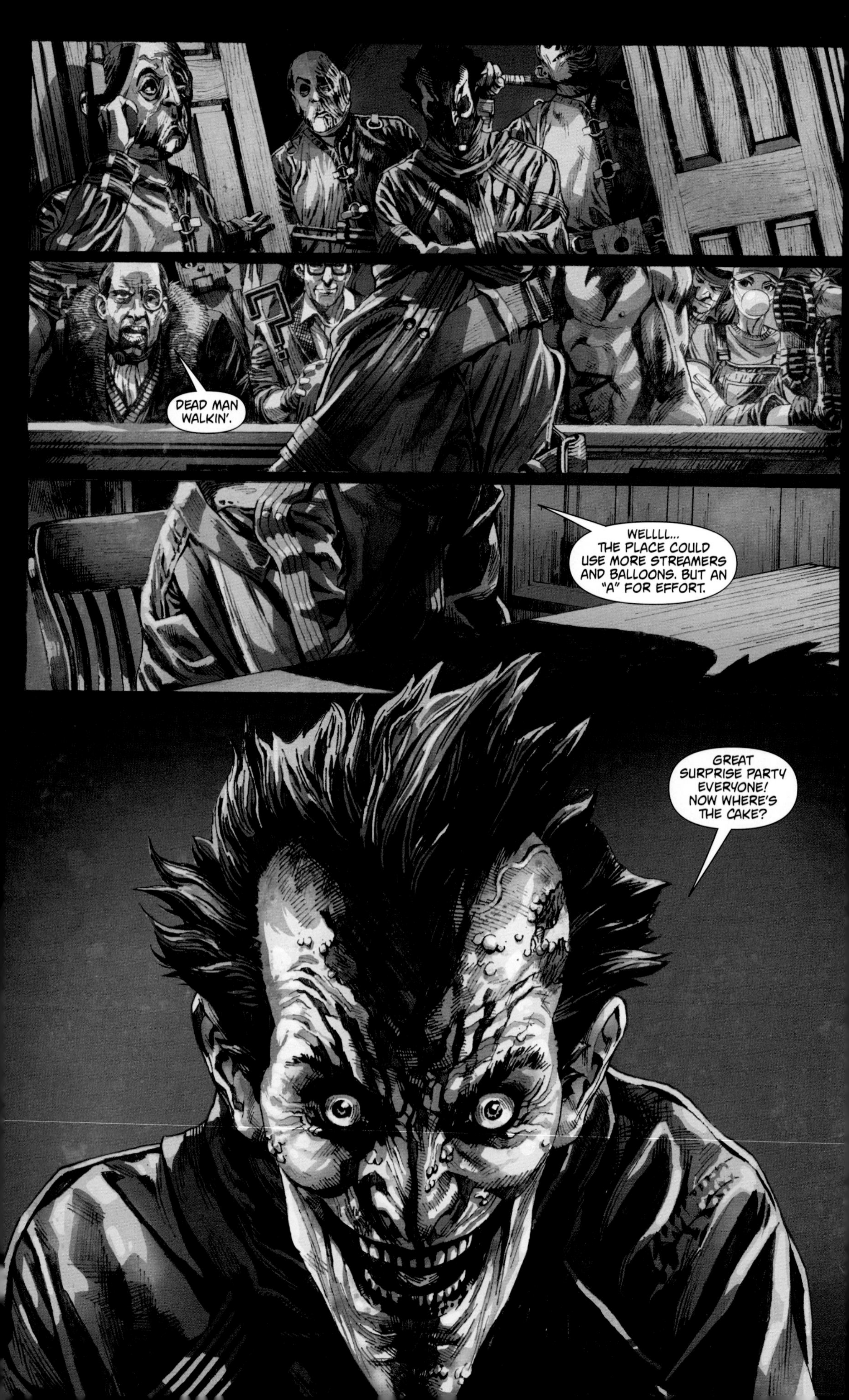
DEAD MAN WALKIN'.
WELLLL... THE PLACE COULD USE MORE STREAMERS AND BALLOONS. BUT AN "A" FOR EFFORT.
GREAT SURPRISE PARTY EVERYONE! NOW WHERE'S THE CAKE?

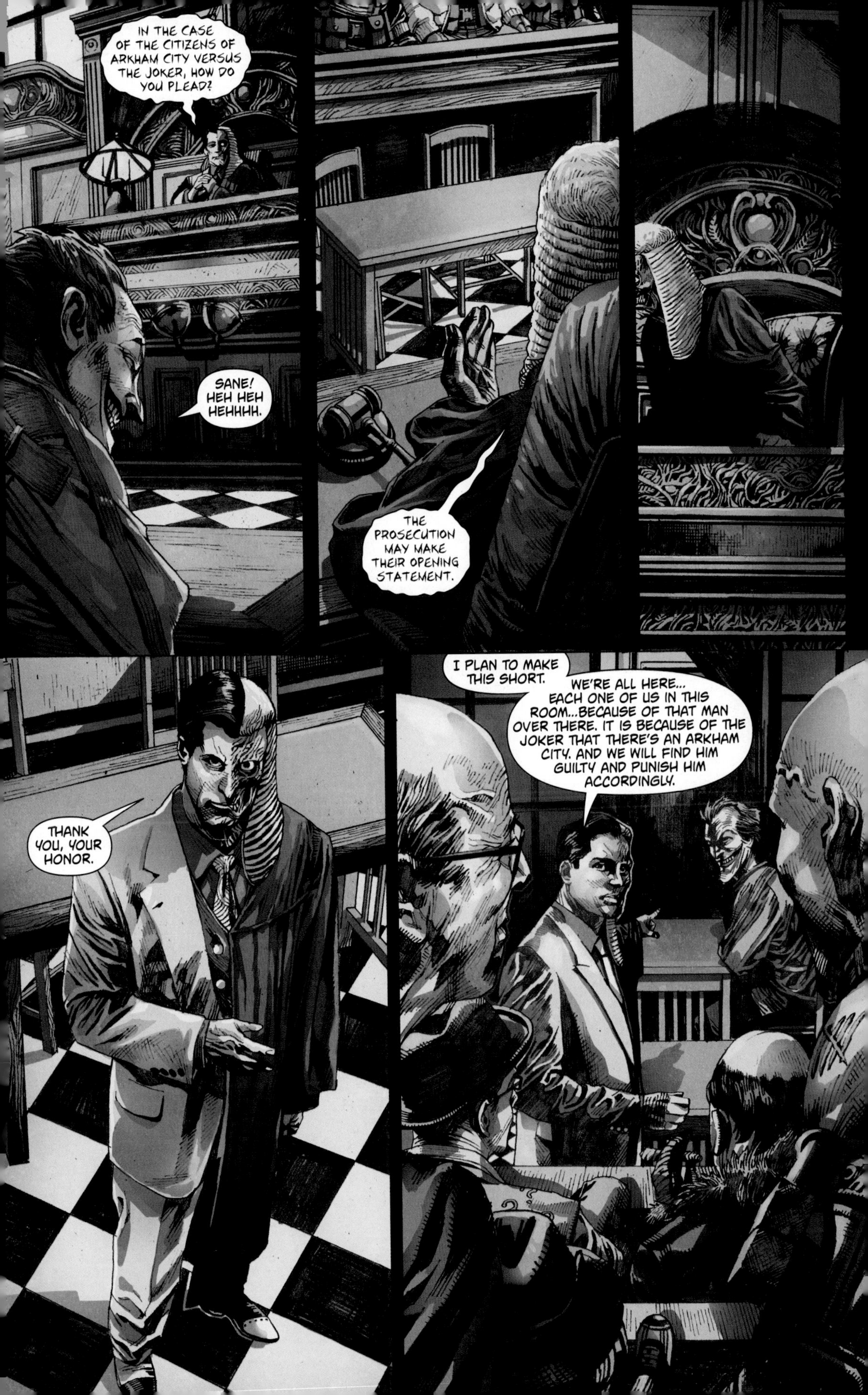
IN THE CASE OF THE CITIZENS OF ARKHAM CITY VERSUS THE JOKER, HOW DO YOU PLEAD?
SANE! HEH HEH HEHHHH.
THE PROSECUTION MAY MAKE THEIR OPENING STATEMENT.
THANK YOU, YOUR HONOR.
I PLAN TO MAKE THIS SHORT.
WE'RE ALL HERE... EACH ONE OF US IN THIS ROOM...BECAUSE OF THAT MAN OVER THERE. IT IS BECAUSE OF THE JOKER THAT THERE'S AN ARKHAM CITY. AND WE WILL FIND HIM GUILTY AND PUNISH HIM ACCORDINGLY.

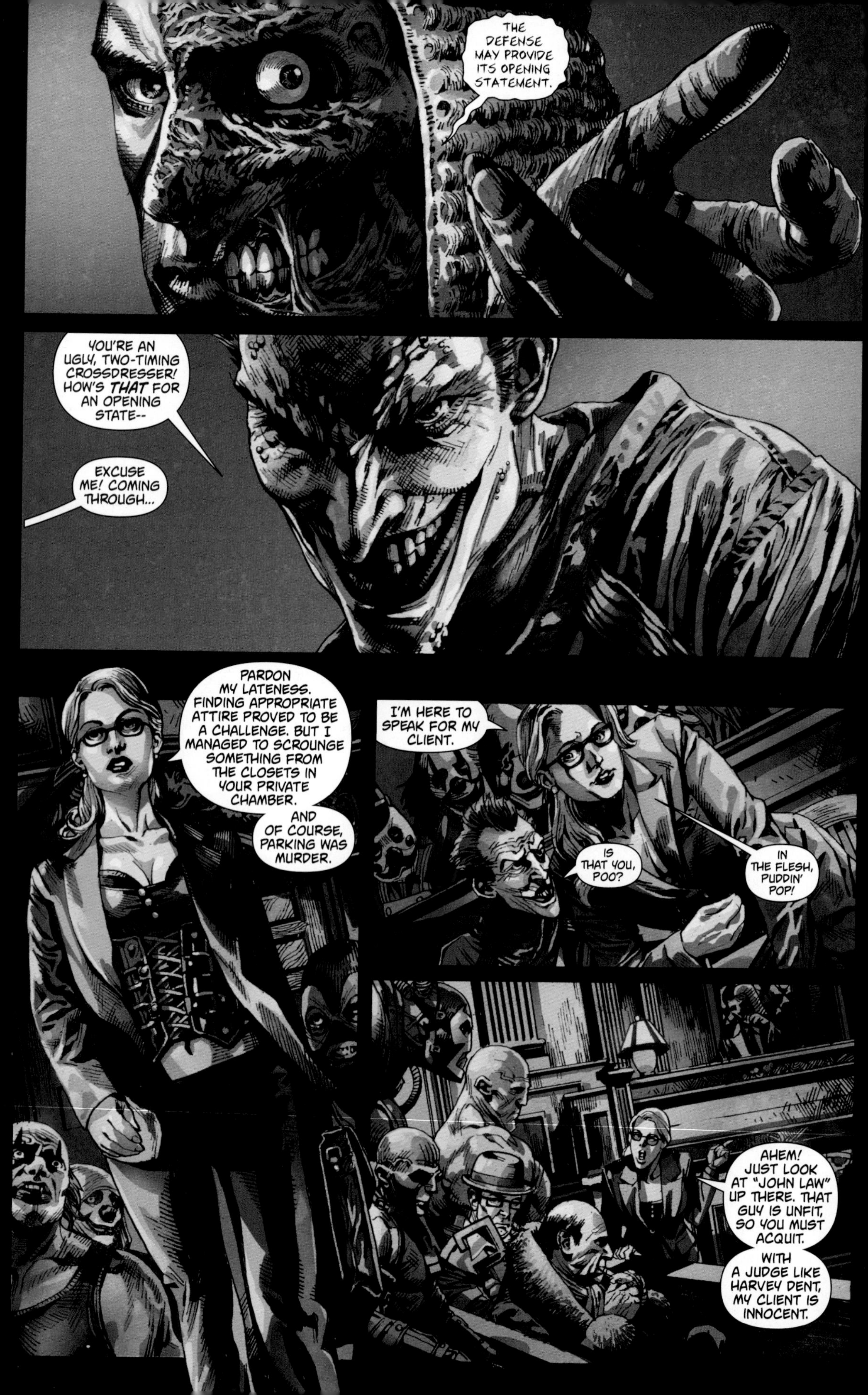
THE DEFENSE MAY PROVIDE ITS OPENING STATEMENT.
YOU'RE AN UGLY, TWO-TIMING CROSSDRESSER! HOW'S *THAT* FOR AN OPENING STATE--
EXCUSE ME! COMING THROUGH...
PARDON MY LATENESS. FINDING APPROPRIATE ATTIRE PROVED TO BE A CHALLENGE. BUT I MANAGED TO SCROUNGE SOMETHING FROM THE CLOSETS IN YOUR PRIVATE CHAMBER.
AND OF COURSE, PARKING WAS MURDER.
I'M HERE TO SPEAK FOR MY CLIENT.
IS THAT YOU, POO?
IN THE FLESH, PUDDIN' POP!
AHEM! JUST LOOK AT "JOHN LAW" UP THERE. THAT GUY IS UNFIT, SO YOU MUST ACQUIT.
WITH A JUDGE LIKE HARVEY DENT, MY CLIENT IS INNOCENT.

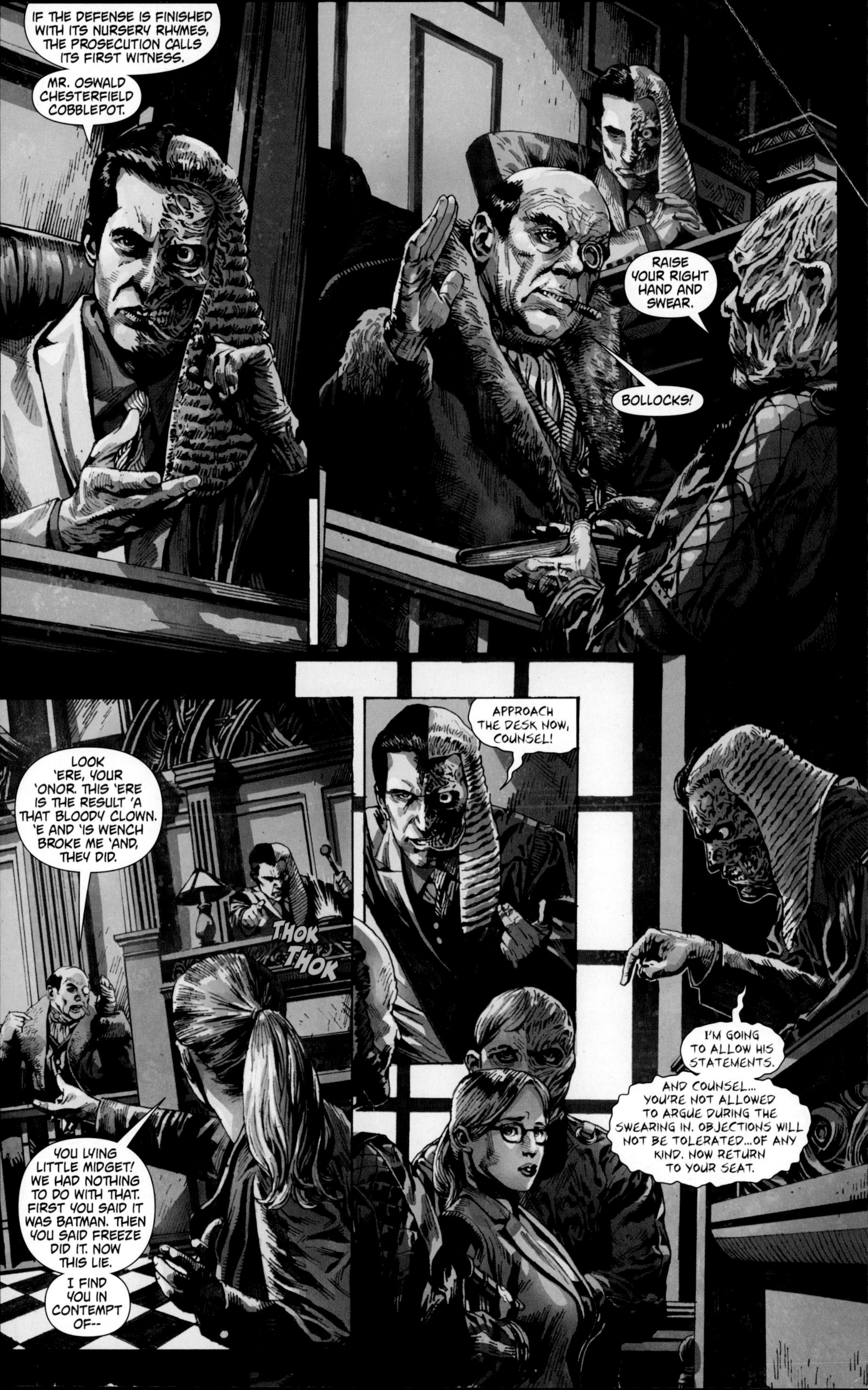
IF THE DEFENSE IS FINISHED WITH ITS NURSERY RHYMES, THE PROSECUTION CALLS ITS FIRST WITNESS.
MR. OSWALD CHESTERFIELD COBBLEPOT.
RAISE YOUR RIGHT HAND AND SWEAR.
BOLLOCKS!
LOOK 'ERE, YOUR 'ONOR. THIS 'ERE IS THE RESULT 'A THAT BLOODY CLOWN. 'E AND 'IS WENCH BROKE ME 'AND, THEY DID.
THOK THOK
YOU LYING LITTLE MIDGET! WE HAD NOTHING TO DO WITH THAT. FIRST YOU SAID IT WAS BATMAN. THEN YOU SAID FREEZE DID IT. NOW THIS LIE.
I FIND YOU IN CONTEMPT OF--
APPROACH THE DESK NOW, COUNSEL!
I'M GOING TO ALLOW HIS STATEMENTS.
AND COUNSEL... YOU'RE NOT ALLOWED TO ARGUE DURING THE SWEARING IN. OBJECTIONS WILL NOT BE TOLERATED...OF ANY KIND. NOW RETURN TO YOUR SEAT.

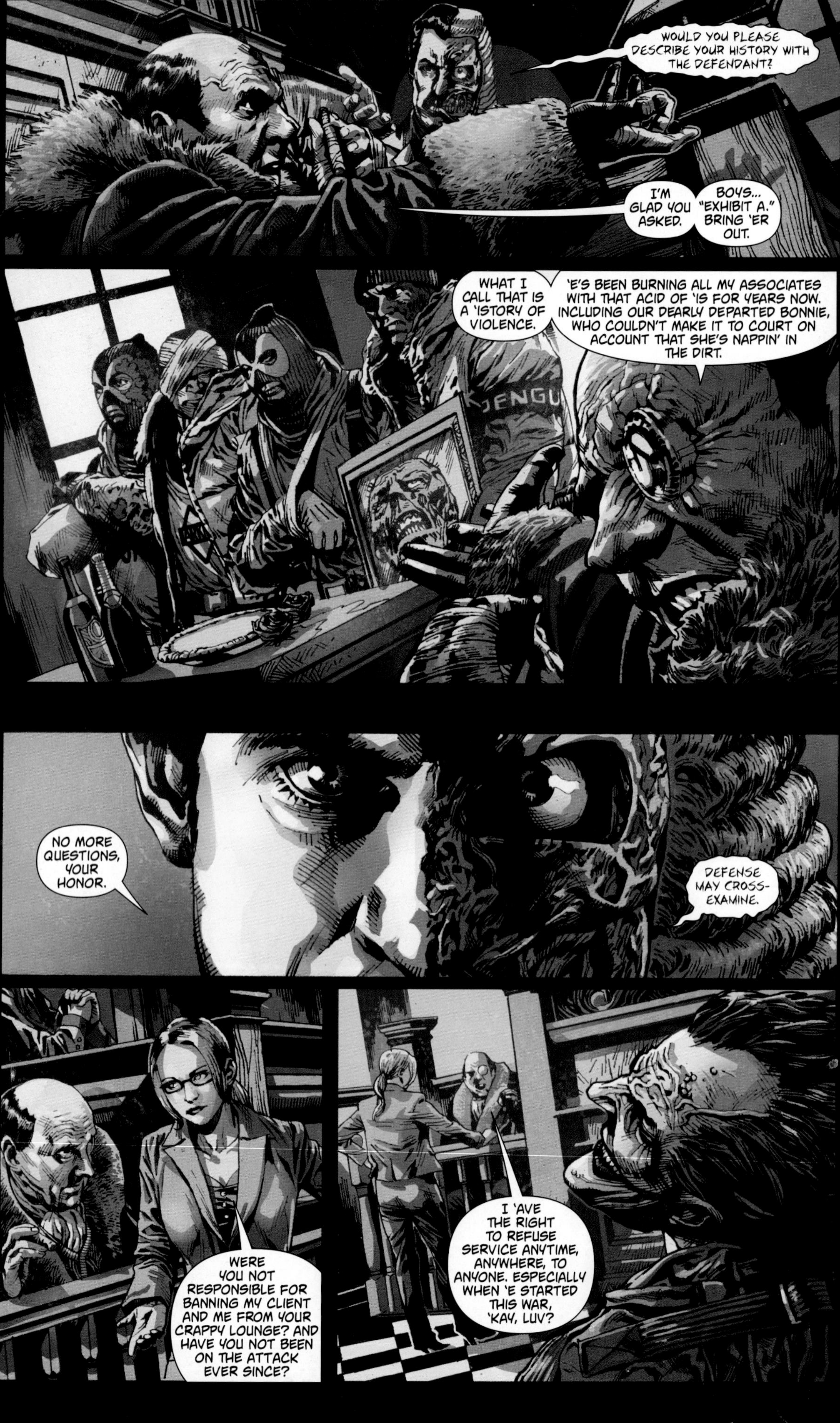
WOULD YOU PLEASE DESCRIBE YOUR HISTORY WITH THE DEFENDANT?
I'M GLAD YOU ASKED.
BOYS... "EXHIBIT A." BRING 'ER OUT.
WHAT I CALL THAT IS A 'ISTORY OF VIOLENCE.
'E'S BEEN BURNING ALL MY ASSOCIATES WITH THAT ACID OF 'IS FOR YEARS NOW. INCLUDING OUR DEARLY DEPARTED BONNIE, WHO COULDN'T MAKE IT TO COURT ON ACCOUNT THAT SHE'S NAPPIN' IN THE DIRT.
NO MORE QUESTIONS, YOUR HONOR.
DEFENSE MAY CROSS-EXAMINE.
WERE YOU NOT RESPONSIBLE FOR BANNING MY CLIENT AND ME FROM YOUR CRAPPY LOUNGE? AND HAVE YOU NOT BEEN ON THE ATTACK EVER SINCE?
I 'AVE THE RIGHT TO REFUSE SERVICE ANYTIME, ANYWHERE, TO ANYONE. ESPECIALLY WHEN 'E STARTED THIS WAR, 'KAY, LUV?

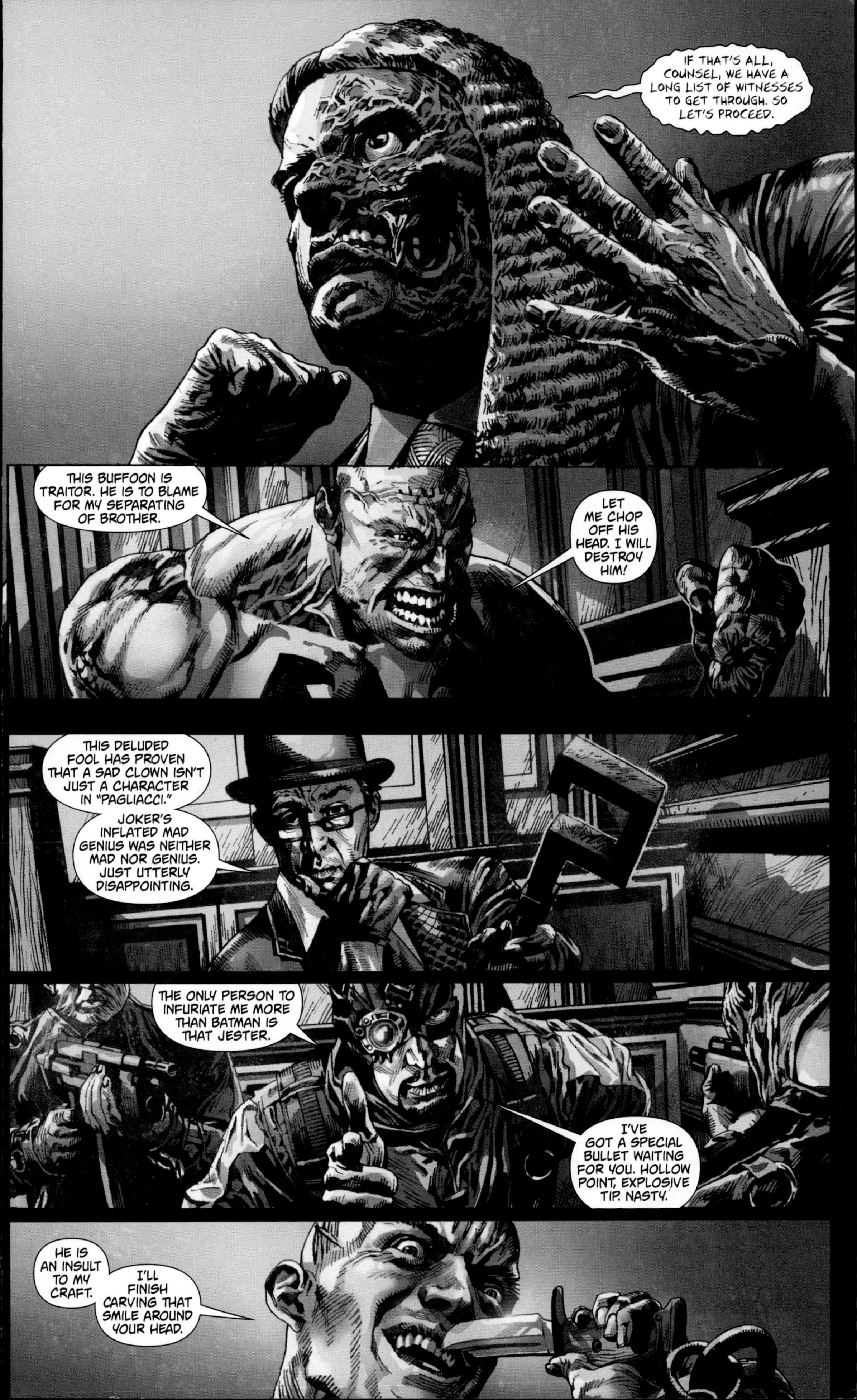
IF THAT'S ALL, COUNSEL, WE HAVE A LONG LIST OF WITNESSES TO GET THROUGH. SO LET'S PROCEED.
THIS BUFFOON IS TRAITOR. HE IS TO BLAME FOR MY SEPARATING OF BROTHER.
LET ME CHOP OFF HIS HEAD. I WILL DESTROY HIM!
THIS DELUDED FOOL HAS PROVEN THAT A SAD CLOWN ISN'T JUST A CHARACTER IN "PAGLIACCI."
JOKER'S INFLATED MAD GENIUS WAS NEITHER MAD NOR GENIUS. JUST UTTERLY DISAPPOINTING.
THE ONLY PERSON TO INFURIATE ME MORE THAN BATMAN IS THAT JESTER.
I'VE GOT A SPECIAL BULLET WAITING FOR YOU. HOLLOW POINT, EXPLOSIVE TIP. NASTY.
HE IS AN INSULT TO MY CRAFT.
I'LL FINISH CARVING THAT SMILE AROUND YOUR HEAD.

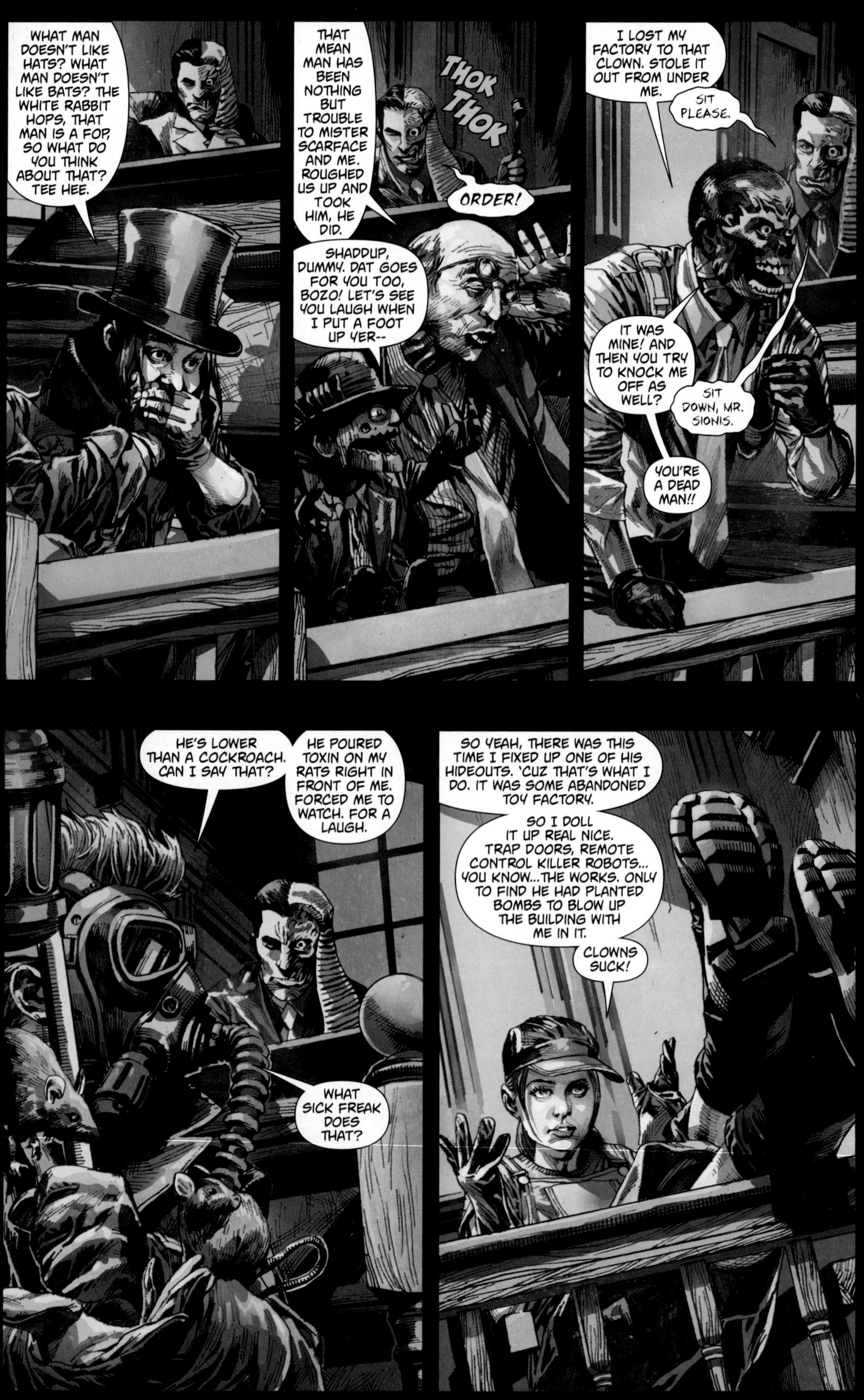
WHAT MAN DOESN'T LIKE HATS? WHAT MAN DOESN'T LIKE BATS? THE WHITE RABBIT HOPS, THAT MAN IS A FOP, SO WHAT DO YOU THINK ABOUT THAT? TEE HEE.
THAT MEAN MAN HAS BEEN NOTHING BUT TROUBLE TO MISTER SCARFACE AND ME. ROUGHED US UP AND TOOK HIM, HE DID.
THOK THOK
ORDER!
SHADDUP, DUMMY. DAT GOES FOR YOU TOO, BOZO! LET'S SEE YOU LAUGH WHEN I PUT A FOOT UP YER--
I LOST MY FACTORY TO THAT CLOWN. STOLE IT OUT FROM UNDER ME.
SIT PLEASE.
IT WAS MINE! AND THEN YOU TRY TO KNOCK ME OFF AS WELL?
SIT DOWN, MR. SIONIS.
YOU'RE A DEAD MAN!!
HE'S LOWER THAN A COCKROACH. CAN I SAY THAT?
HE POURED TOXIN ON MY RATS RIGHT IN FRONT OF ME. FORCED ME TO WATCH. FOR A LAUGH.
WHAT SICK FREAK DOES THAT?
SO YEAH, THERE WAS THIS TIME I FIXED UP ONE OF HIS HIDEOUTS. 'CUZ THAT'S WHAT I DO. IT WAS SOME ABANDONED TOY FACTORY.
SO I DOLL IT UP REAL NICE. TRAP DOORS, REMOTE CONTROL KILLER ROBOTS... YOU KNOW...THE WORKS. ONLY TO FIND HE HAD PLANTED BOMBS TO BLOW UP THE BUILDING WITH ME IN IT.
CLOWNS SUCK!

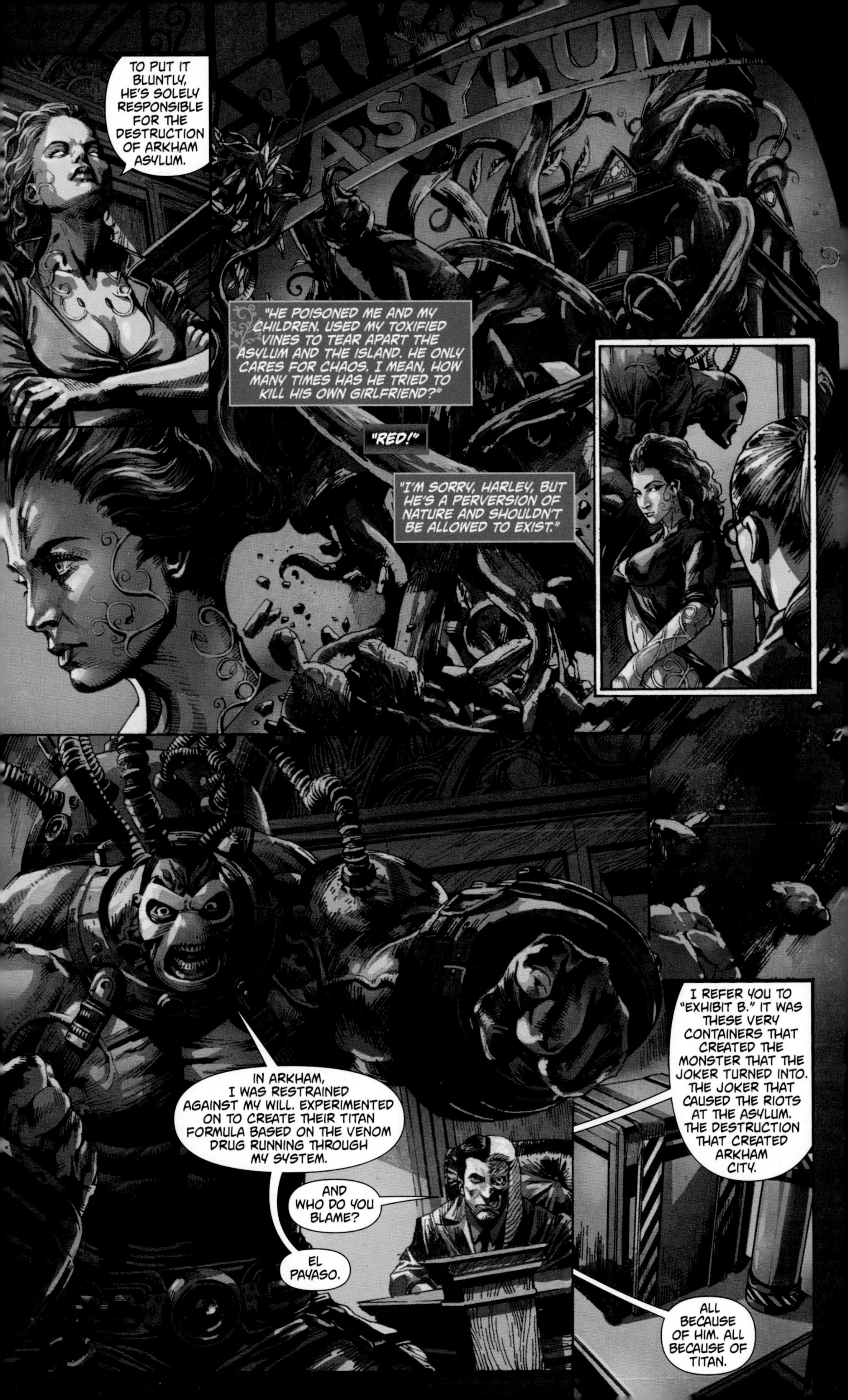
TO PUT IT BLUNTLY, HE'S SOLELY RESPONSIBLE FOR THE DESTRUCTION OF ARKHAM ASYLUM.
ASYLUM
"HE POISONED ME AND MY CHILDREN. USED MY TOXIFIED VINES TO TEAR APART THE ASYLUM AND THE ISLAND. HE ONLY CARES FOR CHAOS. I MEAN, HOW MANY TIMES HAS HE TRIED TO KILL HIS OWN GIRLFRIEND?"
"RED!"
"I'M SORRY, HARLEY, BUT HE'S A PERVERSION OF NATURE AND SHOULDN'T BE ALLOWED TO EXIST."
IN ARKHAM, I WAS RESTRAINED AGAINST MY WILL. EXPERIMENTED ON TO CREATE THEIR TITAN FORMULA BASED ON THE VENOM DRUG RUNNING THROUGH MY SYSTEM.
AND WHO DO YOU BLAME?
EL PAYASO.
I REFER YOU TO "EXHIBIT B." IT WAS THESE VERY CONTAINERS THAT CREATED THE MONSTER THAT THE JOKER TURNED INTO. THE JOKER THAT CAUSED THE RIOTS AT THE ASYLUM. THE DESTRUCTION THAT CREATED ARKHAM CITY.
ALL BECAUSE OF HIM. ALL BECAUSE OF TITAN.

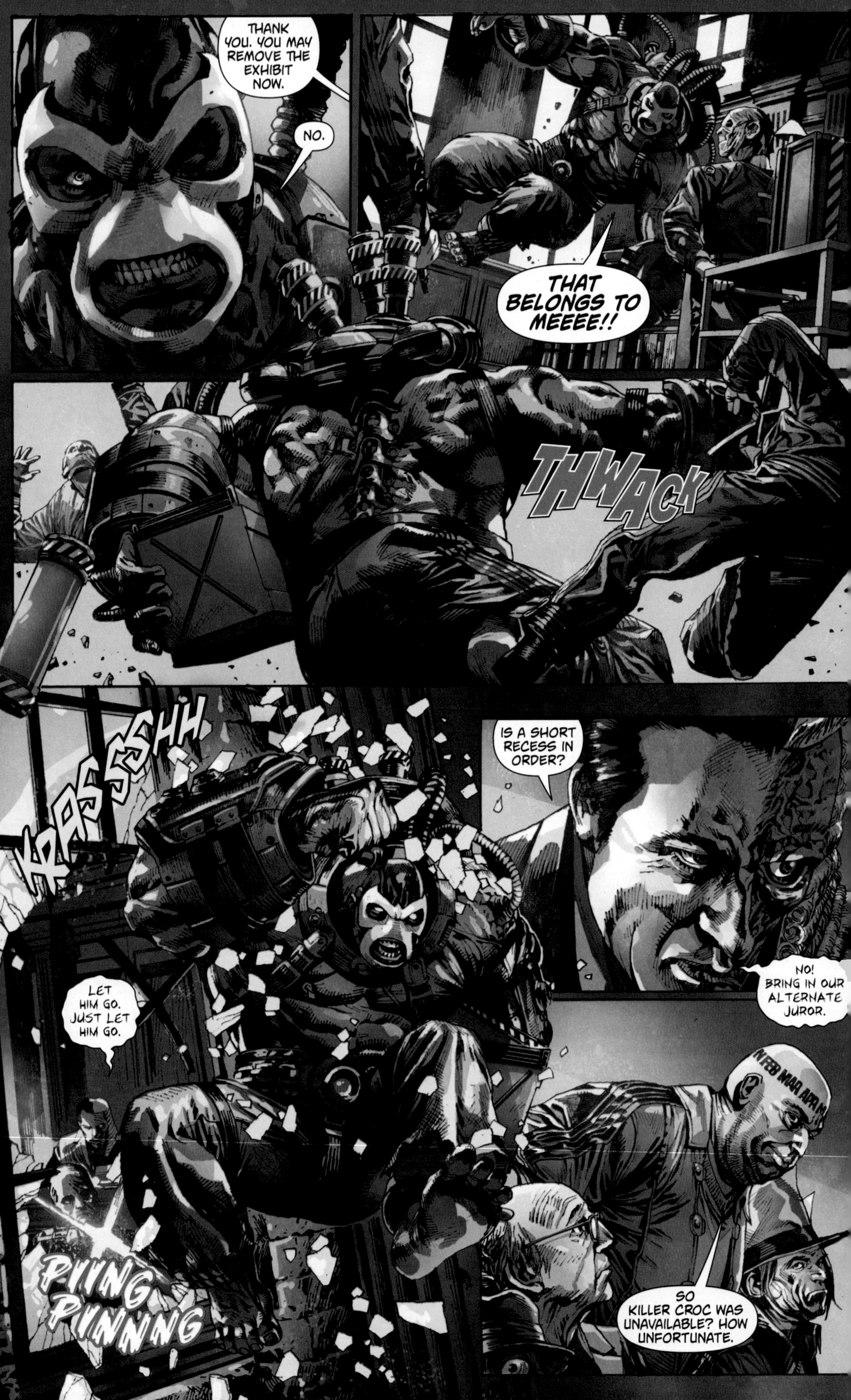
THANK YOU. YOU MAY REMOVE THE EXHIBIT NOW.
NO.
THAT BELONGS TO MEEEE!!
THWACK
KRASSSHH
IS A SHORT RECESS IN ORDER?
NO! BRING IN OUR ALTERNATE JUROR.
LET HIM GO. JUST LET HIM GO.
PIING PINNNG
SO KILLER CROC WAS UNAVAILABLE? HOW UNFORTUNATE.

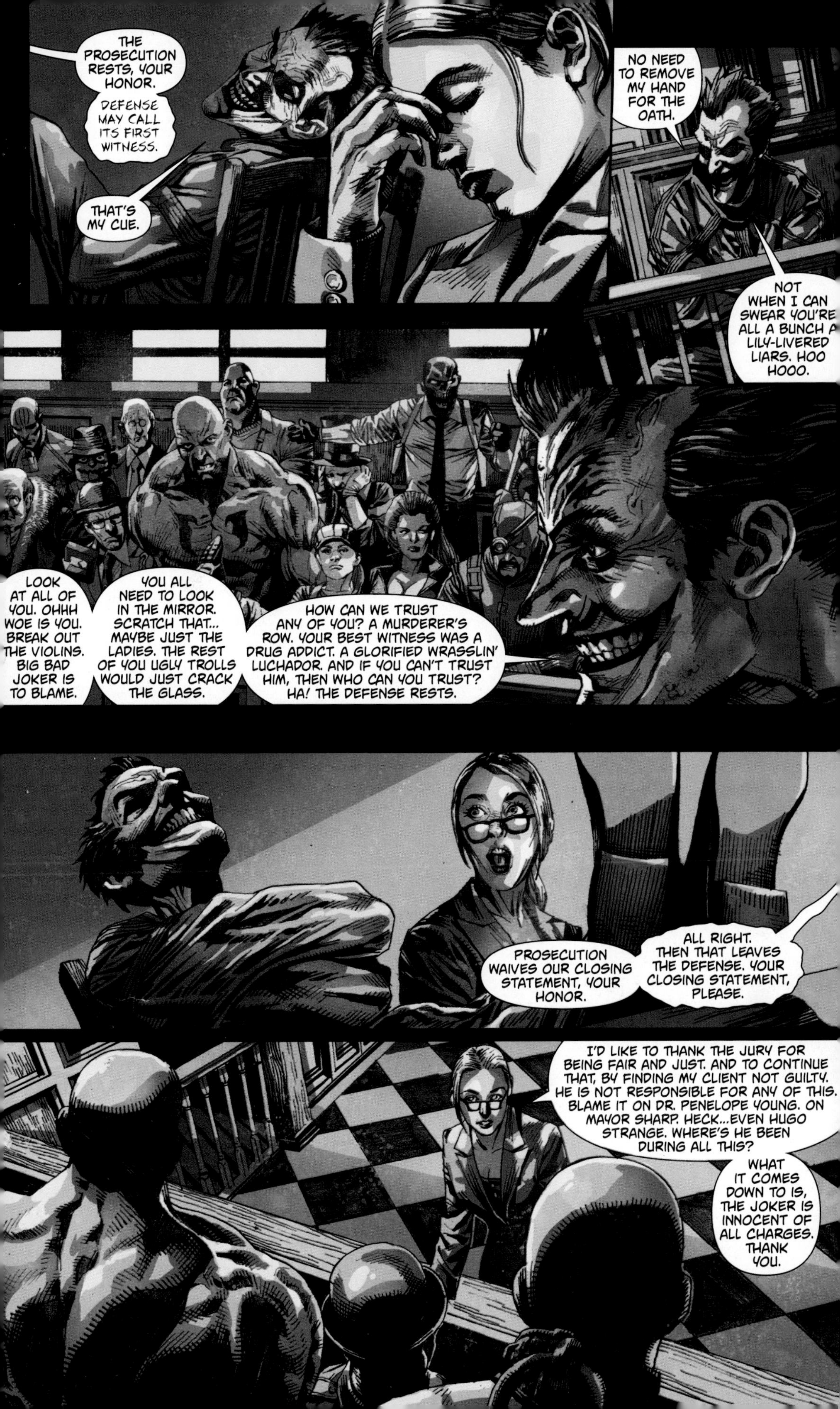
THE PROSECUTION RESTS, YOUR HONOR.
DEFENSE MAY CALL ITS FIRST WITNESS.
THAT'S MY CUE.
NO NEED TO REMOVE MY HAND FOR THE OATH.
NOT WHEN I CAN SWEAR YOU'RE ALL A BUNCH A LILY-LIVERED LIARS. HOO HOOO.
LOOK AT ALL OF YOU. OHHH WOE IS YOU. BREAK OUT THE VIOLINS. BIG BAD JOKER IS TO BLAME.
YOU ALL NEED TO LOOK IN THE MIRROR. SCRATCH THAT... MAYBE JUST THE LADIES. THE REST OF YOU UGLY TROLLS WOULD JUST CRACK THE GLASS.
HOW CAN WE TRUST ANY OF YOU? A MURDERER'S ROW. YOUR BEST WITNESS WAS A DRUG ADDICT. A GLORIFIED WRASSLIN' LUCHADOR. AND IF YOU CAN'T TRUST HIM, THEN WHO CAN YOU TRUST? HA! THE DEFENSE RESTS.
PROSECUTION WAIVES OUR CLOSING STATEMENT, YOUR HONOR.
ALL RIGHT. THEN THAT LEAVES THE DEFENSE. YOUR CLOSING STATEMENT, PLEASE.
I'D LIKE TO THANK THE JURY FOR BEING FAIR AND JUST. AND TO CONTINUE THAT, BY FINDING MY CLIENT NOT GUILTY. HE IS NOT RESPONSIBLE FOR ANY OF THIS. BLAME IT ON DR. PENELOPE YOUNG. ON MAYOR SHARP. HECK...EVEN HUGO STRANGE. WHERE'S HE BEEN DURING ALL THIS?
WHAT IT COMES DOWN TO IS, THE JOKER IS INNOCENT OF ALL CHARGES. THANK YOU.

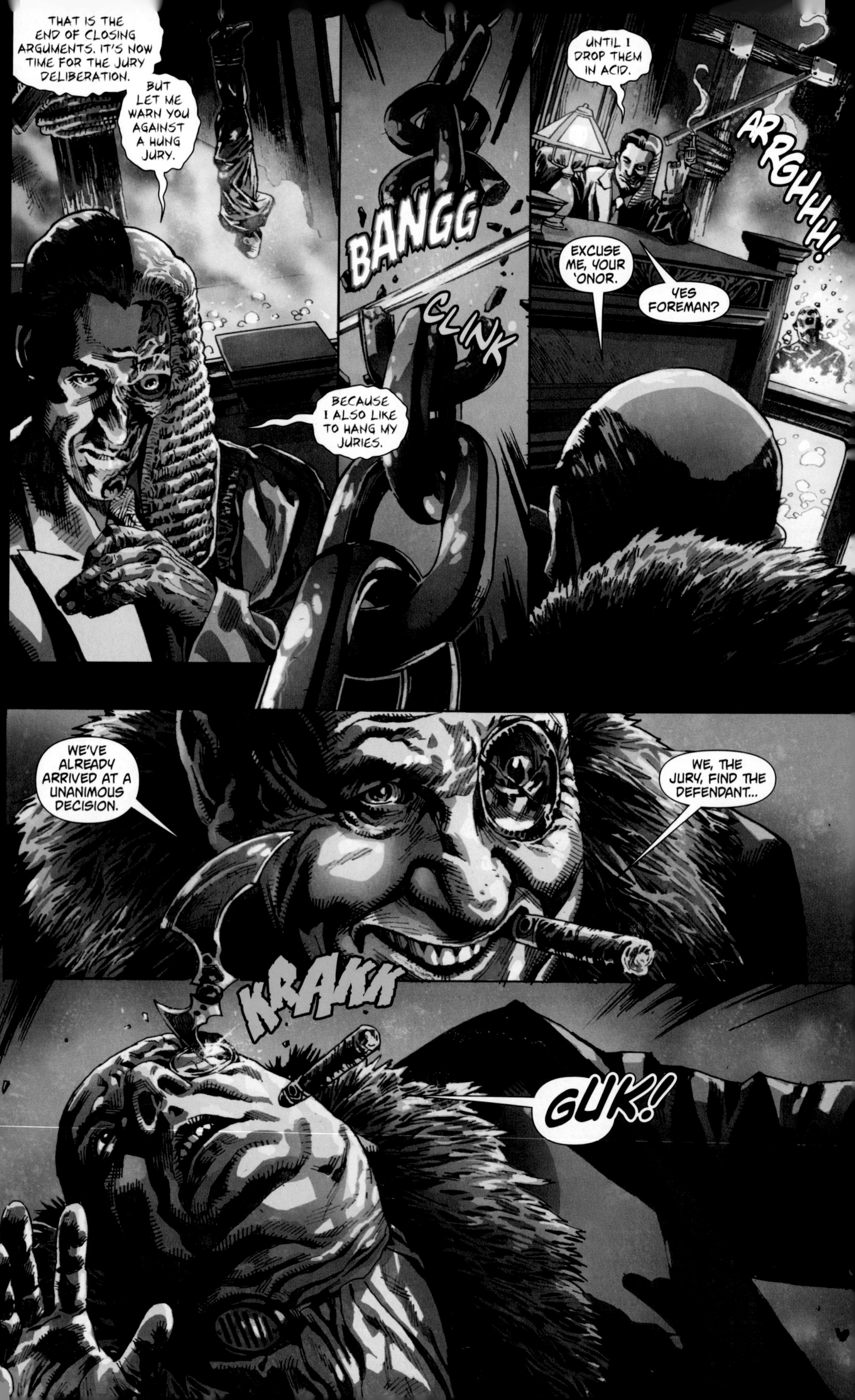

THAT IS THE END OF CLOSING ARGUMENTS. IT'S NOW TIME FOR THE JURY DELIBERATION.
BUT LET ME WARN YOU AGAINST A HUNG JURY.
BANGG
CLINK
BECAUSE I ALSO LIKE TO HANG MY JURIES.
UNTIL I DROP THEM IN ACID.
ARRGHHH!
EXCUSE ME, YOUR 'ONOR.
YES FOREMAN?
WE'VE ALREADY ARRIVED AT A UNANIMOUS DECISION.
WE, THE JURY, FIND THE DEFENDANT...
KRAKK
GUK!

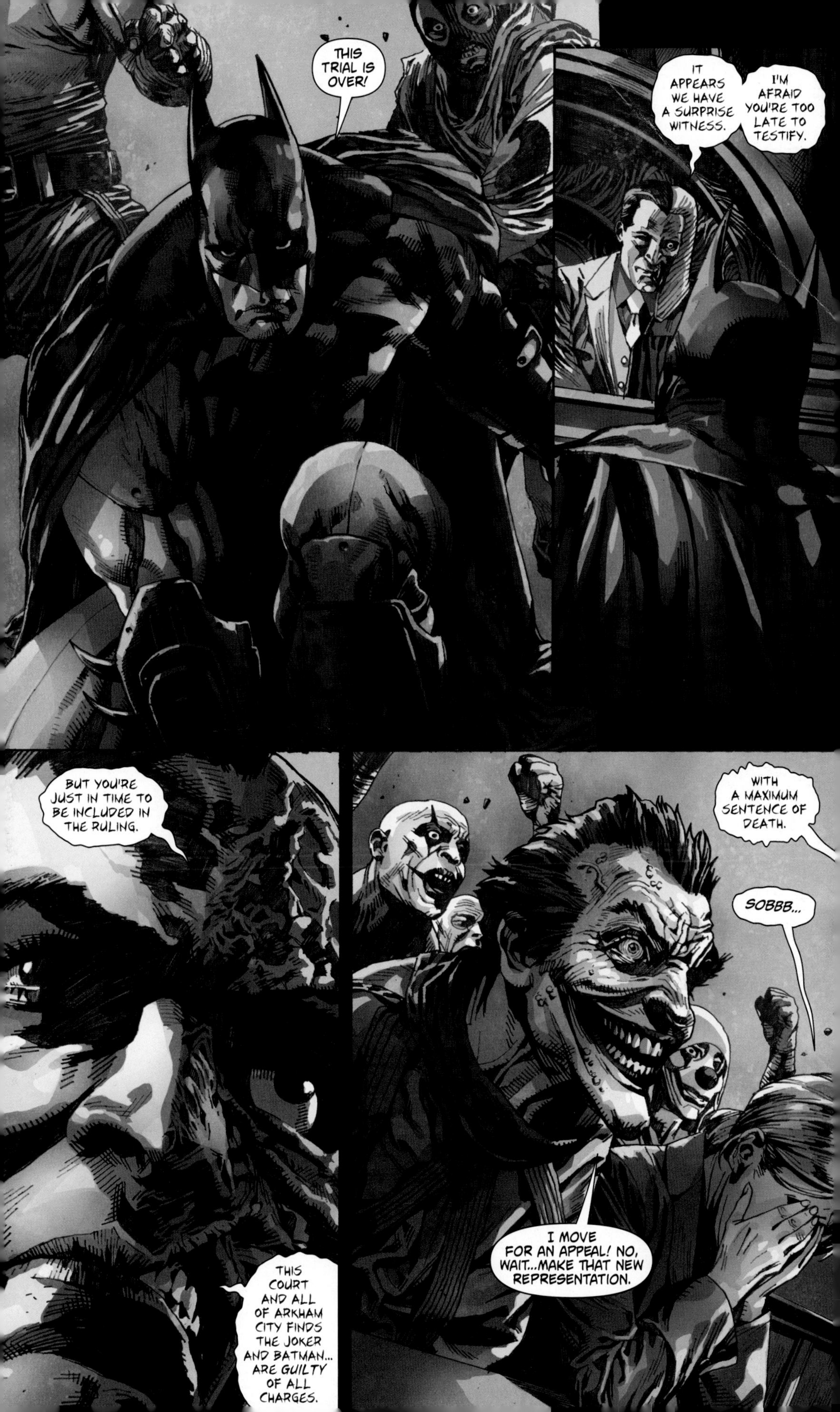
THIS TRIAL IS OVER!
IT APPEARS WE HAVE A SURPRISE WITNESS.
I'M AFRAID YOU'RE TOO LATE TO TESTIFY.
BUT YOU'RE JUST IN TIME TO BE INCLUDED IN THE RULING.
THIS COURT AND ALL OF ARKHAM CITY FINDS THE JOKER AND BATMAN... ARE GUILTY OF ALL CHARGES.
WITH A MAXIMUM SENTENCE OF DEATH.
SOBBB...
I MOVE FOR AN APPEAL! NO, WAIT...MAKE THAT NEW REPRESENTATION.

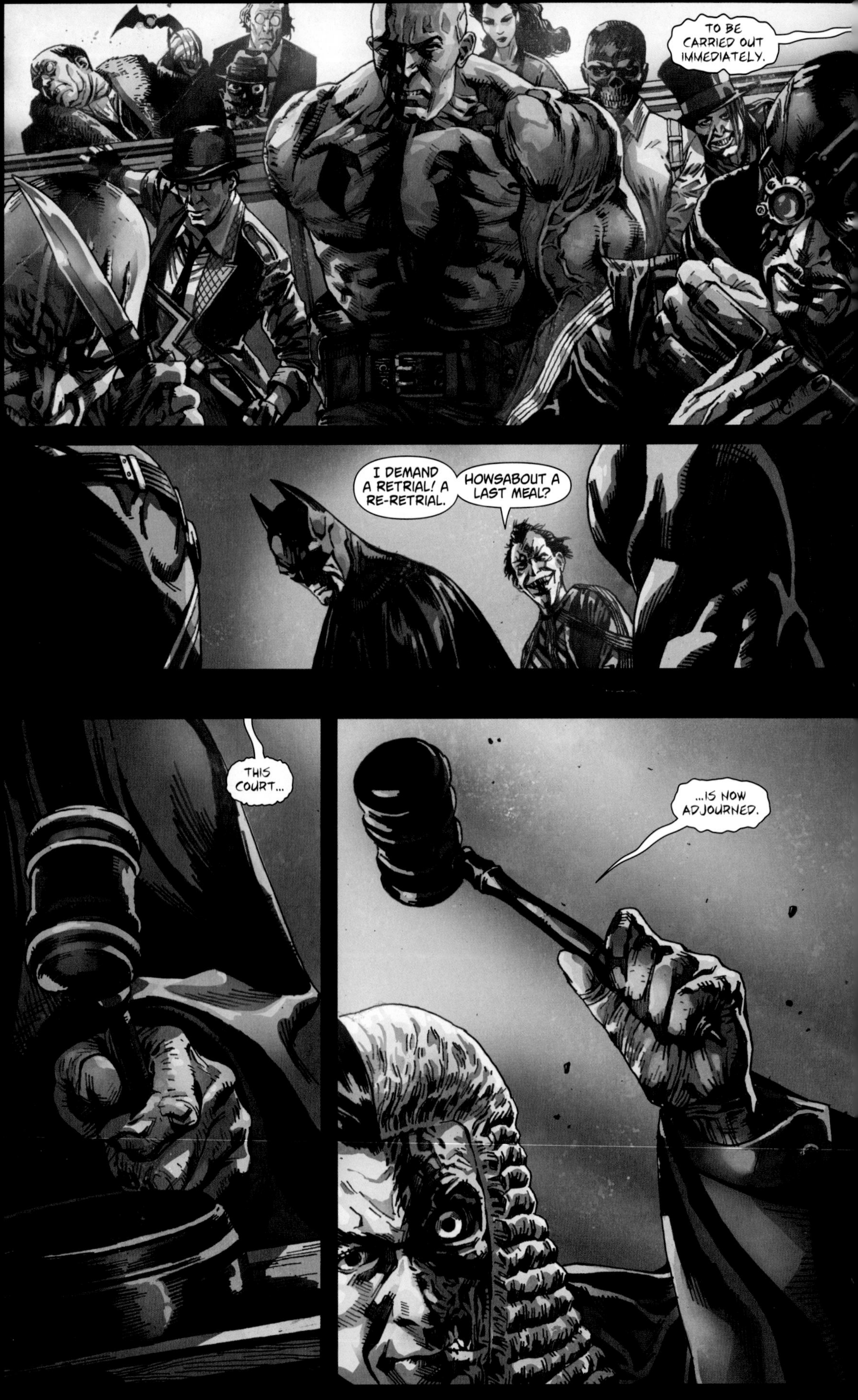
TO BE CARRIED OUT IMMEDIATELY.
I DEMAND A RETRIAL! A RE-RETRIAL.
HOWSABOUT A LAST MEAL?
THIS COURT...
...IS NOW ADJOURNED.

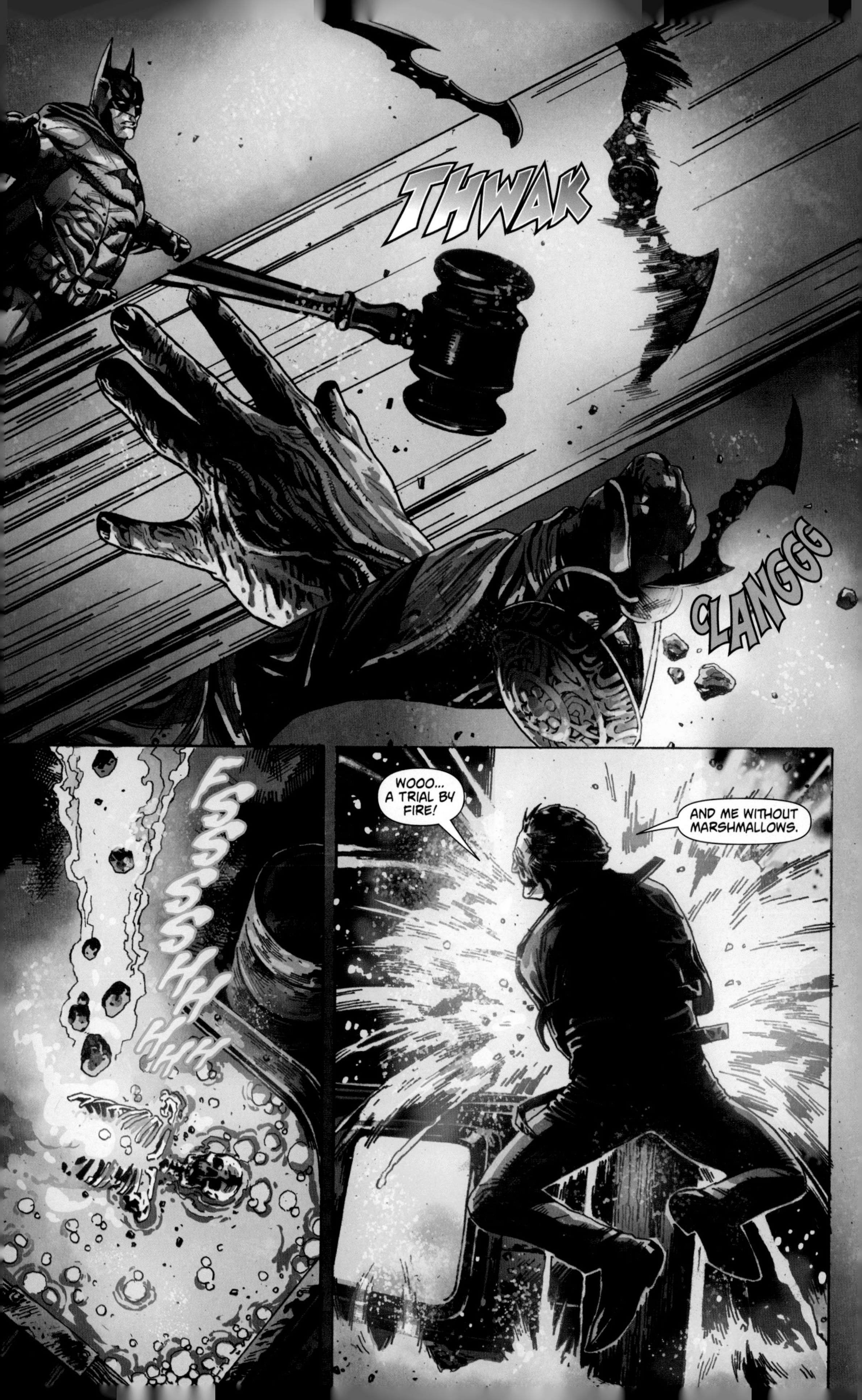
THWAK
CLANGGG
FSSSSSSHHHHH
WOOO... A TRIAL BY FIRE!
AND ME WITHOUT MARSHMALLOWS.

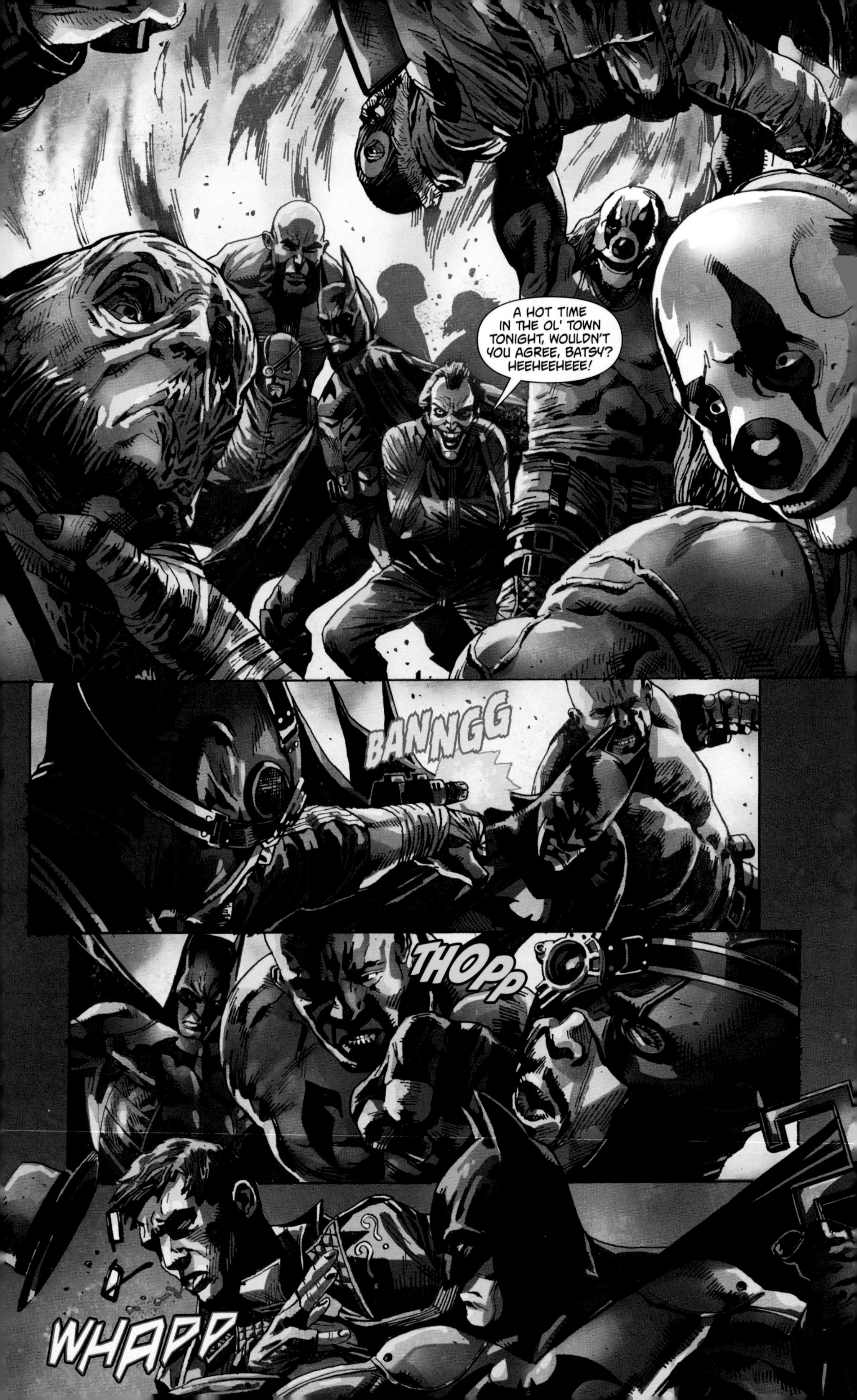
A HOT TIME IN THE OL' TOWN TONIGHT, WOULDN'T YOU AGREE, BATSY? HEEHEEHEEE!
BANNGG
THOPP
WHAPP

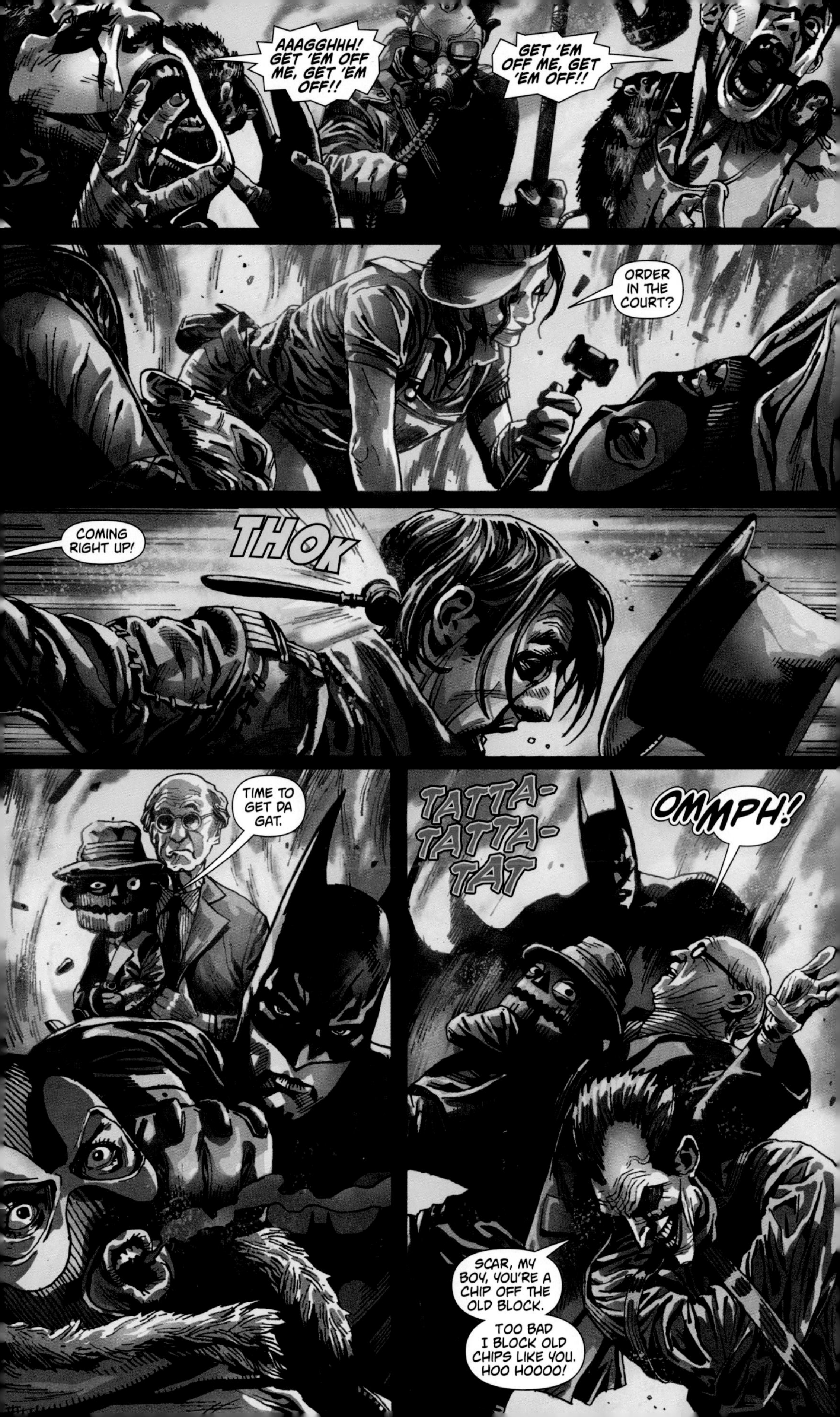
AAAGGHHH! GET 'EM OFF ME, GET 'EM OFF!!
GET 'EM OFF ME, GET 'EM OFF!!
ORDER IN THE COURT?
COMING RIGHT UP!
THOK
TIME TO GET DA GAT.
TATTA-TATTA-TAT
OMMPH!
SCAR, MY BOY, YOU'RE A CHIP OFF THE OLD BLOCK.
TOO BAD I BLOCK OLD CHIPS LIKE YOU. HOO HOOOO!

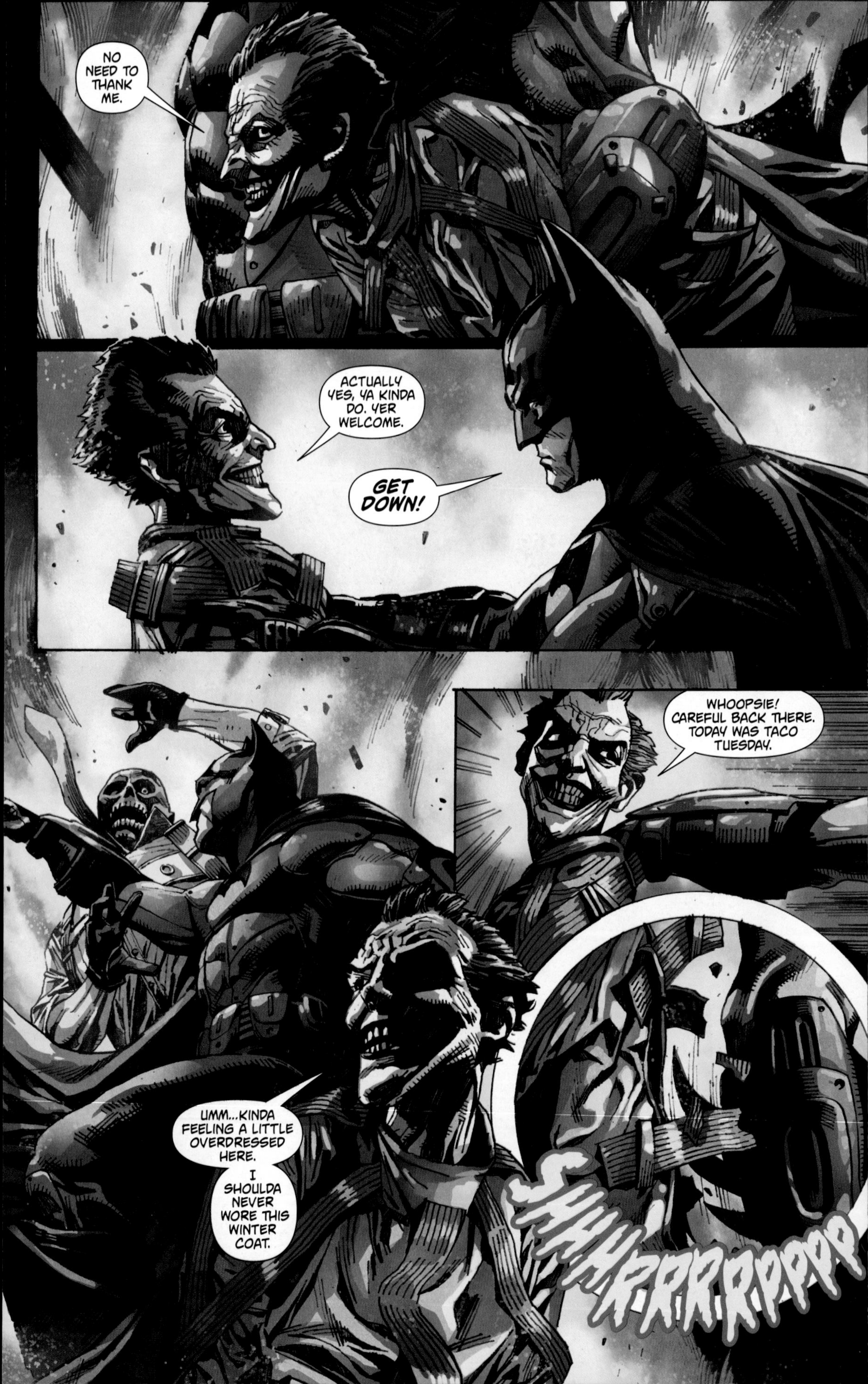
NO NEED TO THANK ME.
ACTUALLY YES, YA KINDA DO. YER WELCOME.
GET DOWN!
WHOOPSIE! CAREFUL BACK THERE. TODAY WAS TACO TUESDAY.
SHHHRRRRRPPPP
UMM...KINDA FEELING A LITTLE OVERDRESSED HERE.
I SHOULDA NEVER WORE THIS WINTER COAT.

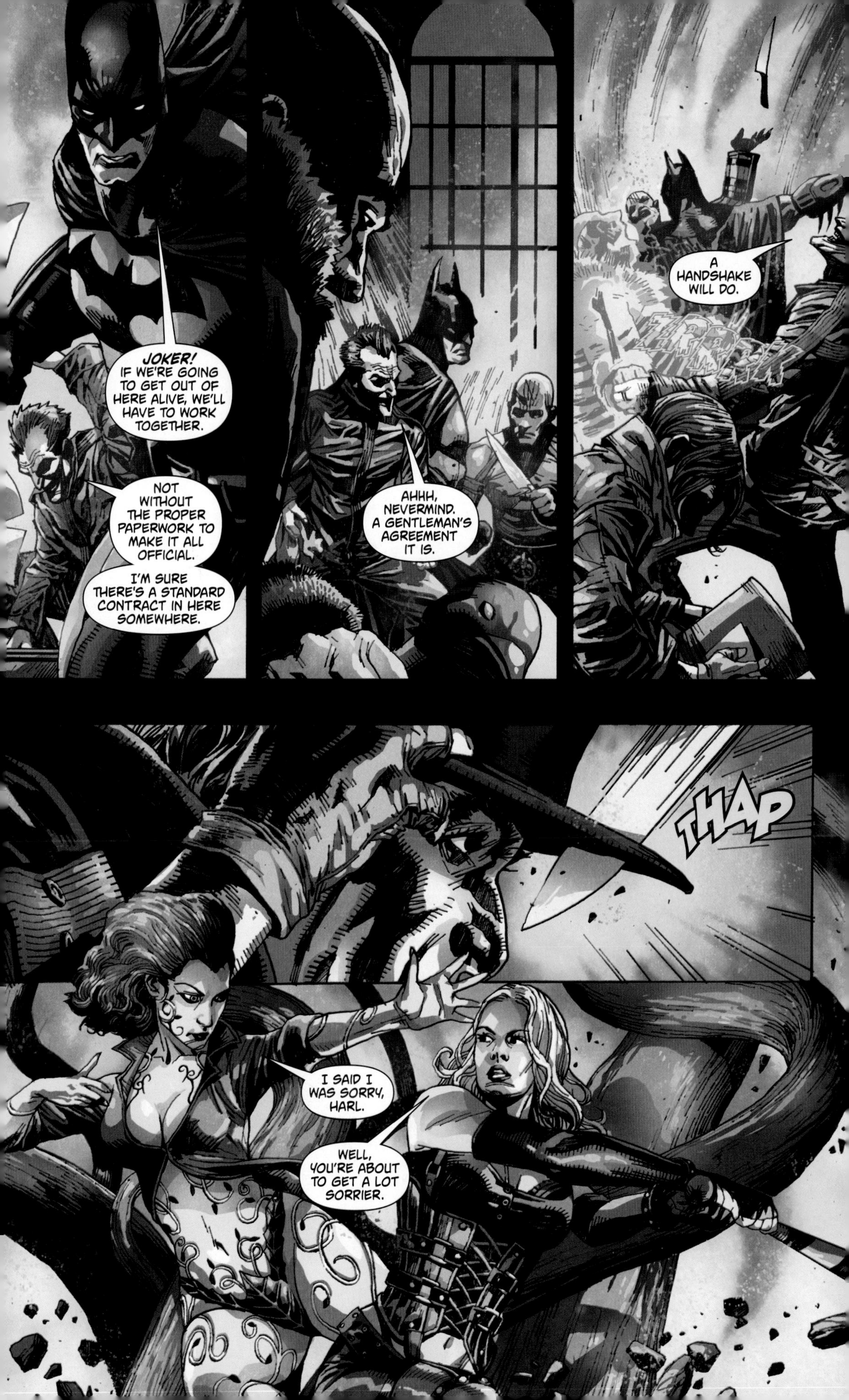
JOKER! IF WE'RE GOING TO GET OUT OF HERE ALIVE, WE'LL HAVE TO WORK TOGETHER.
NOT WITHOUT THE PROPER PAPERWORK TO MAKE IT ALL OFFICIAL.
I'M SURE THERE'S A STANDARD CONTRACT IN HERE SOMEWHERE.
AHHH, NEVERMIND. A GENTLEMAN'S AGREEMENT IT IS.
A HANDSHAKE WILL DO.
THAP
I SAID I WAS SORRY, HARL.
WELL, YOU'RE ABOUT TO GET A LOT SORRIER.

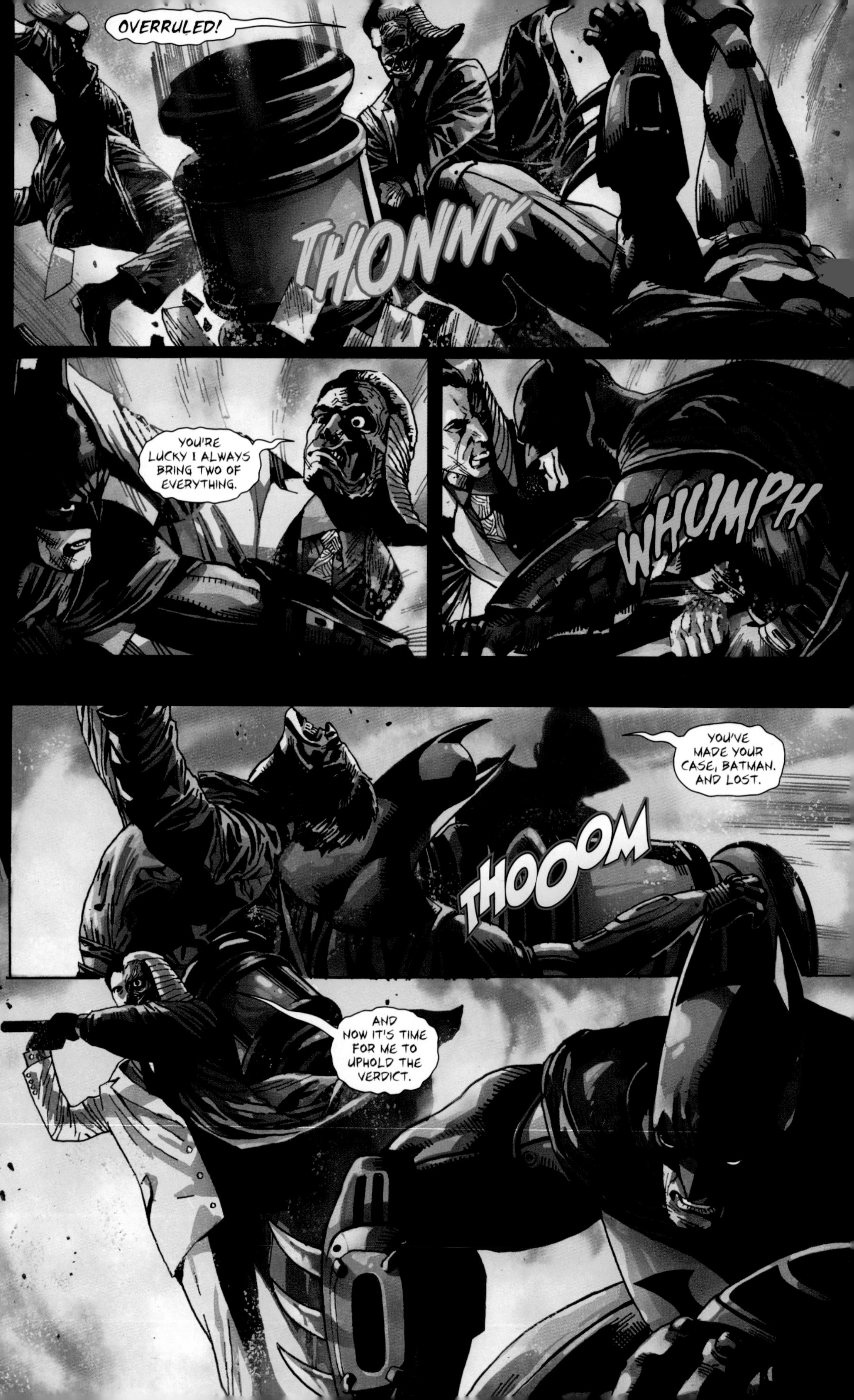
OVERRULED!
THONNK
YOU'RE LUCKY I ALWAYS BRING TWO OF EVERYTHING.
WHUMPH
YOU'VE MADE YOUR CASE, BATMAN. AND LOST.
THOOOM
AND NOW IT'S TIME FOR ME TO UPHOLD THE VERDICT.

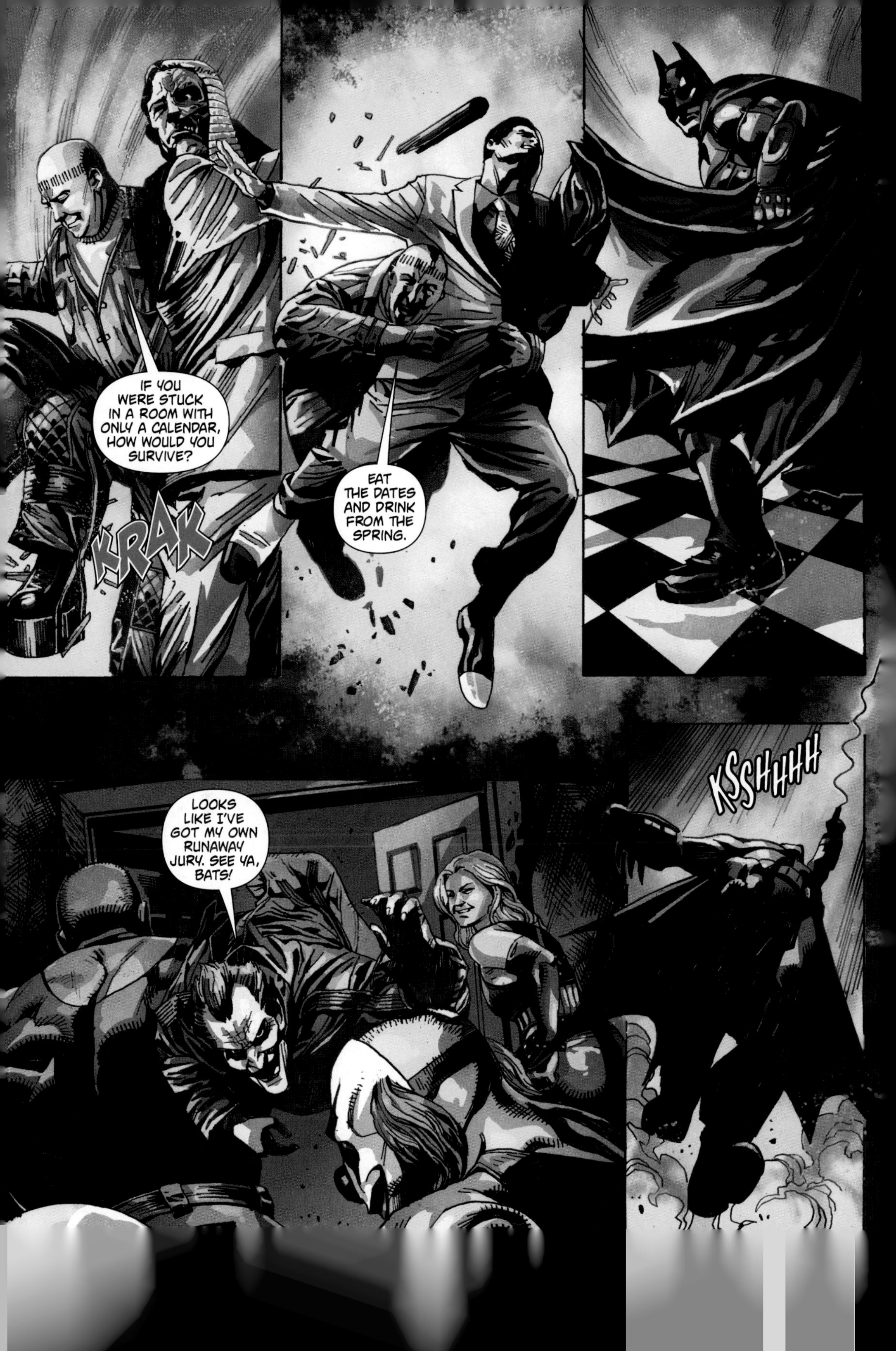
IF YOU WERE STUCK IN A ROOM WITH ONLY A CALENDAR, HOW WOULD YOU SURVIVE?
KRAK
EAT THE DATES AND DRINK FROM THE SPRING.
LOOKS LIKE I'VE GOT MY OWN RUNAWAY JURY. SEE YA, BATS!
KSSHHHH

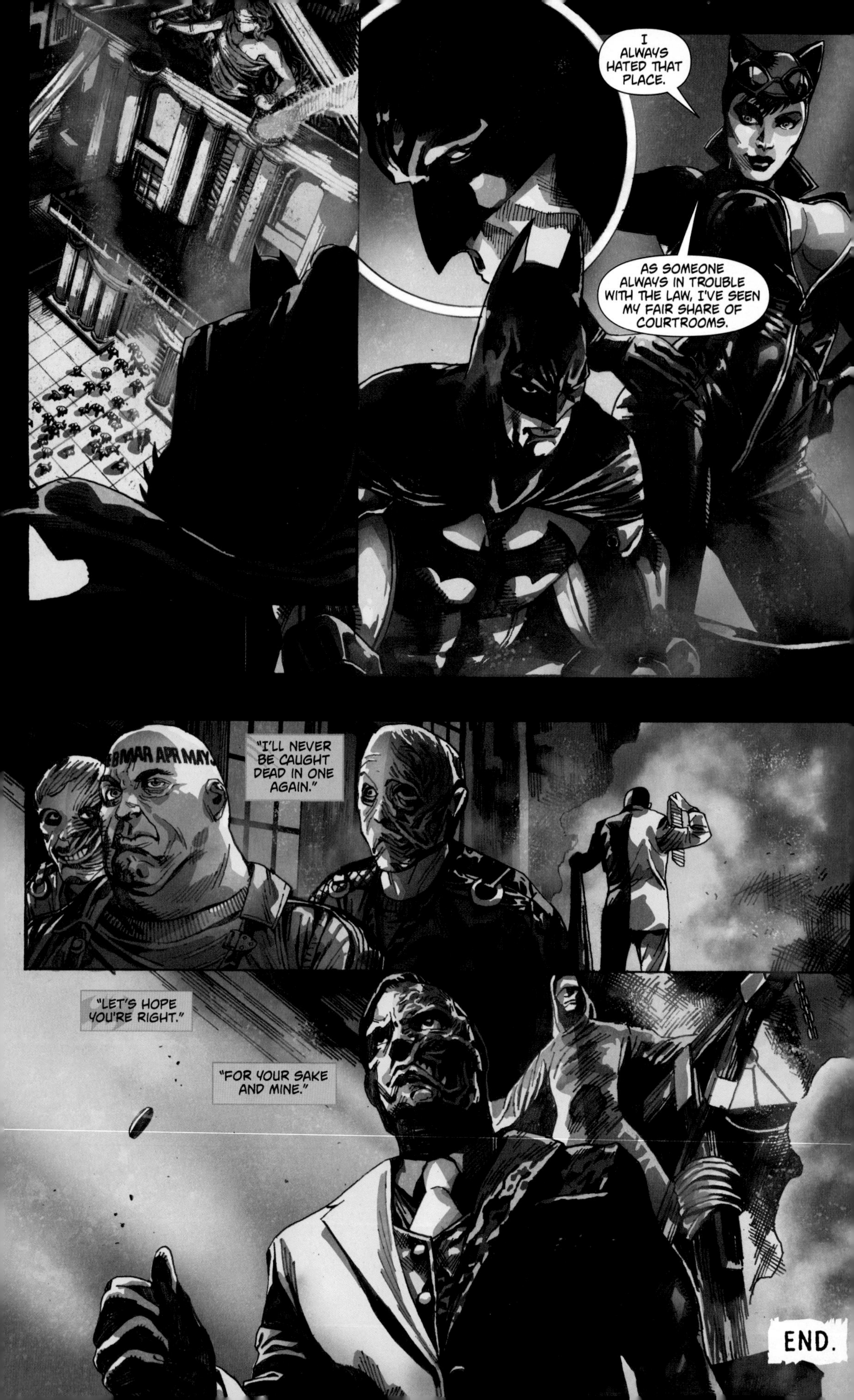

I ALWAYS HATED THAT PLACE.
AS SOMEONE ALWAYS IN TROUBLE WITH THE LAW, I'VE SEEN MY FAIR SHARE OF COURTROOMS.
FEB MAR APR MAY
"I'LL NEVER BE CAUGHT DEAD IN ONE AGAIN."
"LET'S HOPE YOU'RE RIGHT."
"FOR YOUR SAKE AND MINE."
END.

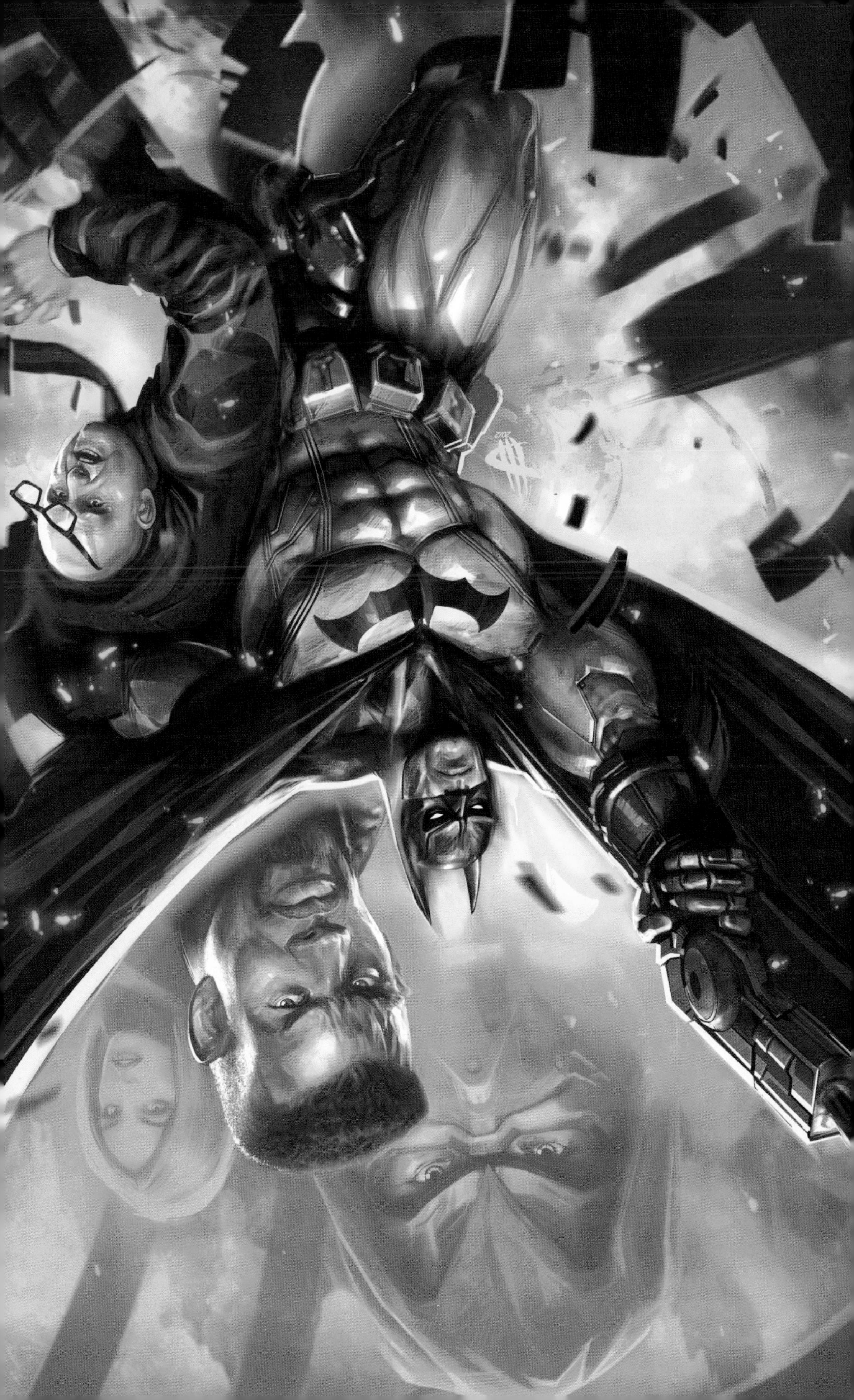

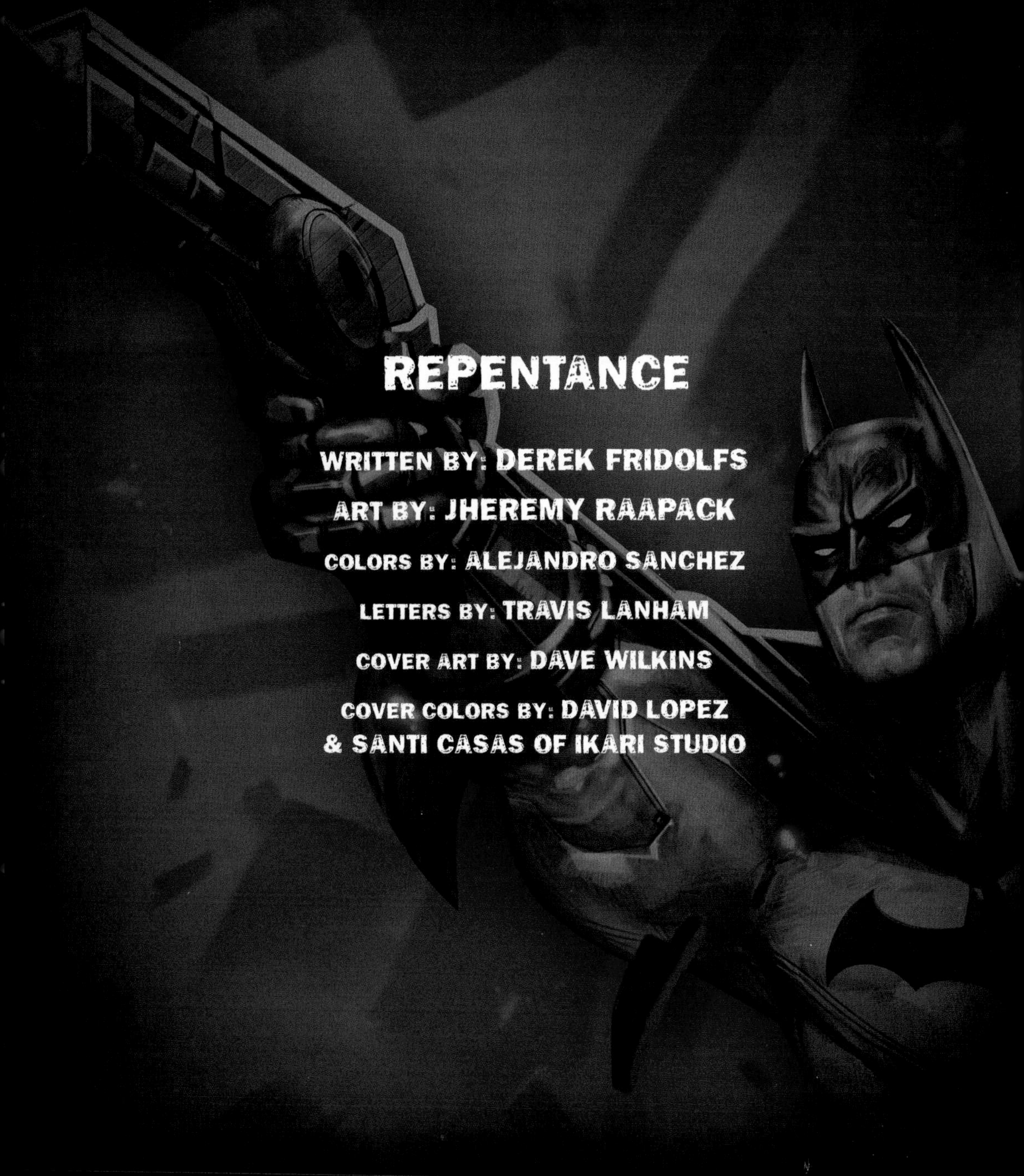

# REPENTANCE

WRITTEN BY: DEREK FRIDOLFS

ART BY: JHEREMY RAAPACK

COLORS BY: ALEJANDRO SANCHEZ

LETTERS BY: TRAVIS LANHAM

COVER ART BY: DAVE WILKINS

COVER COLORS BY: DAVID LOPEZ
& SANTI CASAS OF IKARI STUDIO

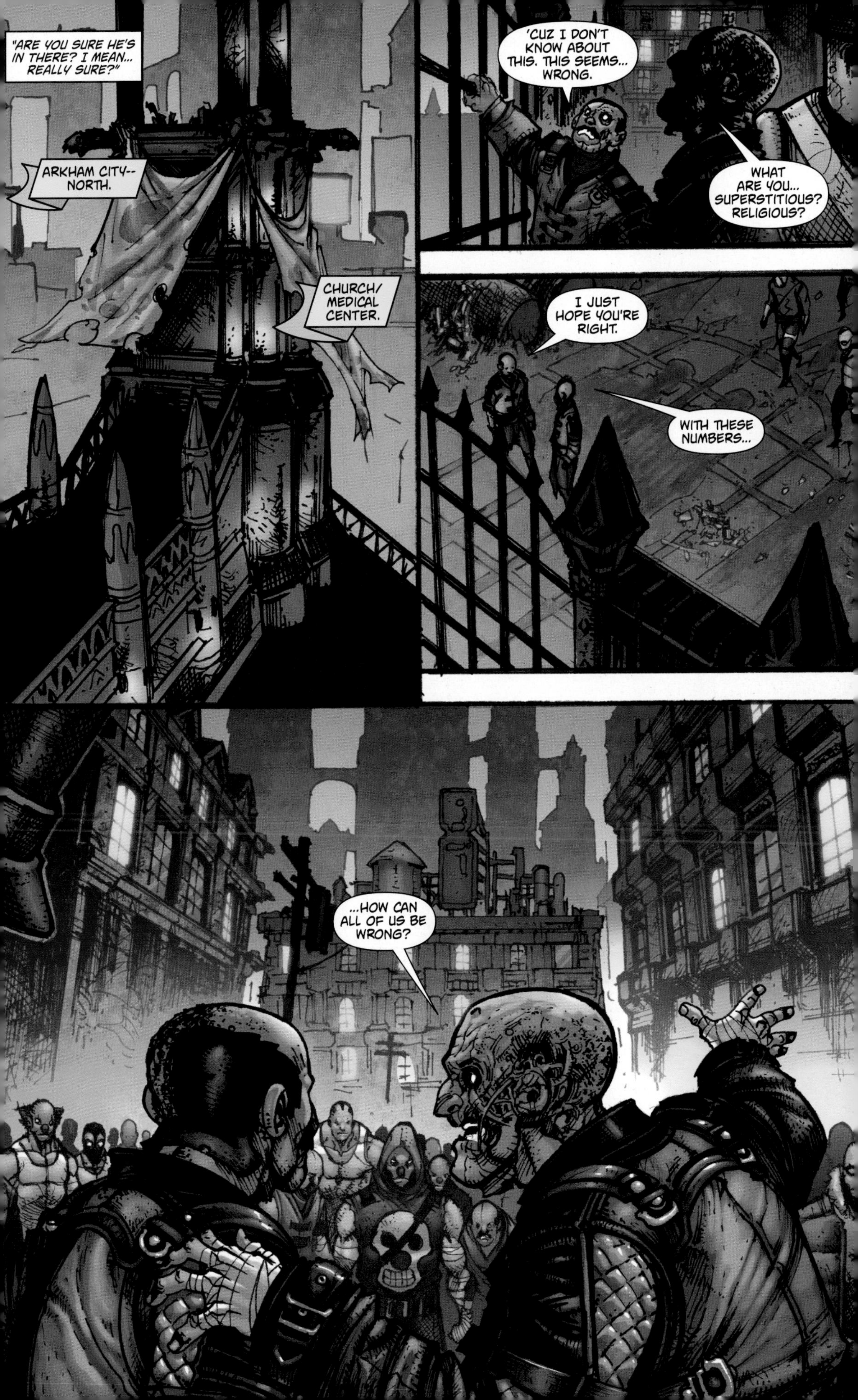
"ARE YOU SURE HE'S IN THERE? I MEAN... REALLY SURE?"
ARKHAM CITY-- NORTH.
CHURCH/ MEDICAL CENTER.
'CUZ I DON'T KNOW ABOUT THIS. THIS SEEMS... WRONG.
WHAT ARE YOU... SUPERSTITIOUS? RELIGIOUS?
I JUST HOPE YOU'RE RIGHT.
WITH THESE NUMBERS...
...HOW CAN ALL OF US BE WRONG?

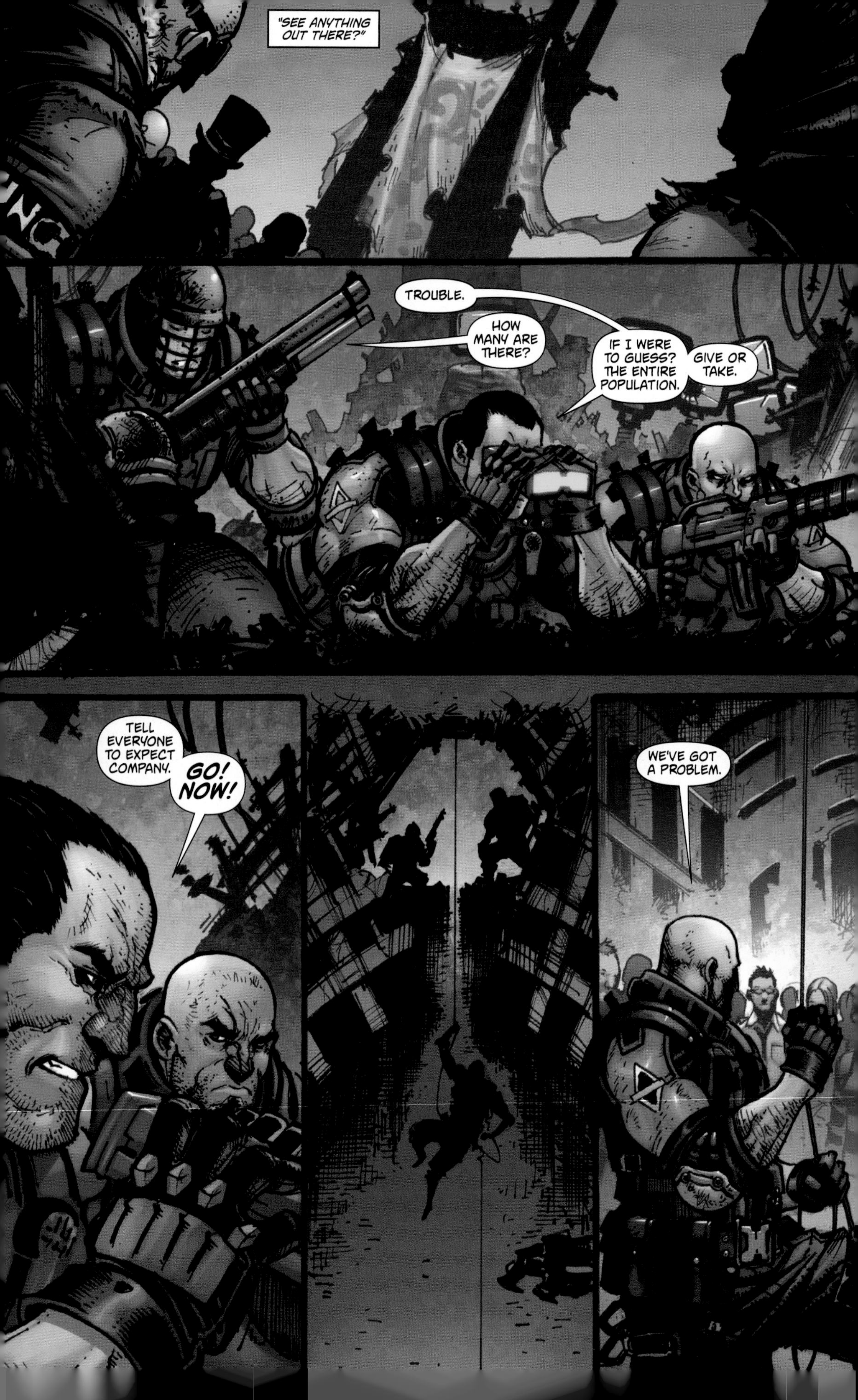
"SEE ANYTHING OUT THERE?"
TROUBLE.
HOW MANY ARE THERE?
IF I WERE TO GUESS? THE ENTIRE POPULATION.
GIVE OR TAKE.
TELL EVERYONE TO EXPECT COMPANY.
GO! NOW!
WE'VE GOT A PROBLEM.

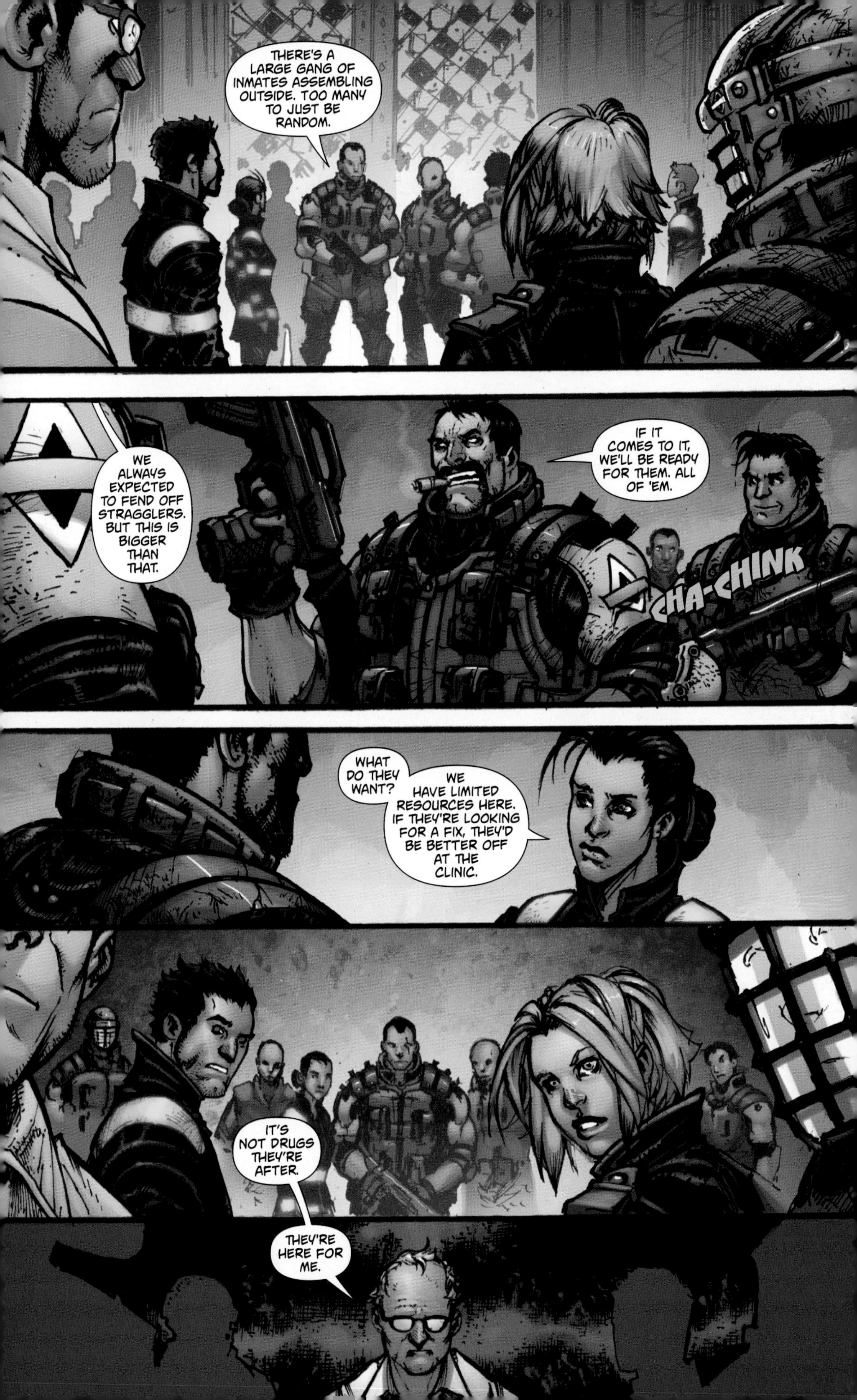
THERE'S A LARGE GANG OF INMATES ASSEMBLING OUTSIDE. TOO MANY TO JUST BE RANDOM.
WE ALWAYS EXPECTED TO FEND OFF STRAGGLERS. BUT THIS IS BIGGER THAN THAT.
IF IT COMES TO IT, WE'LL BE READY FOR THEM. ALL OF 'EM.
CHA-CHINK
WHAT DO THEY WANT?
WE HAVE LIMITED RESOURCES HERE. IF THEY'RE LOOKING FOR A FIX, THEY'D BE BETTER OFF AT THE CLINIC.
IT'S NOT DRUGS THEY'RE AFTER.
THEY'RE HERE FOR ME.

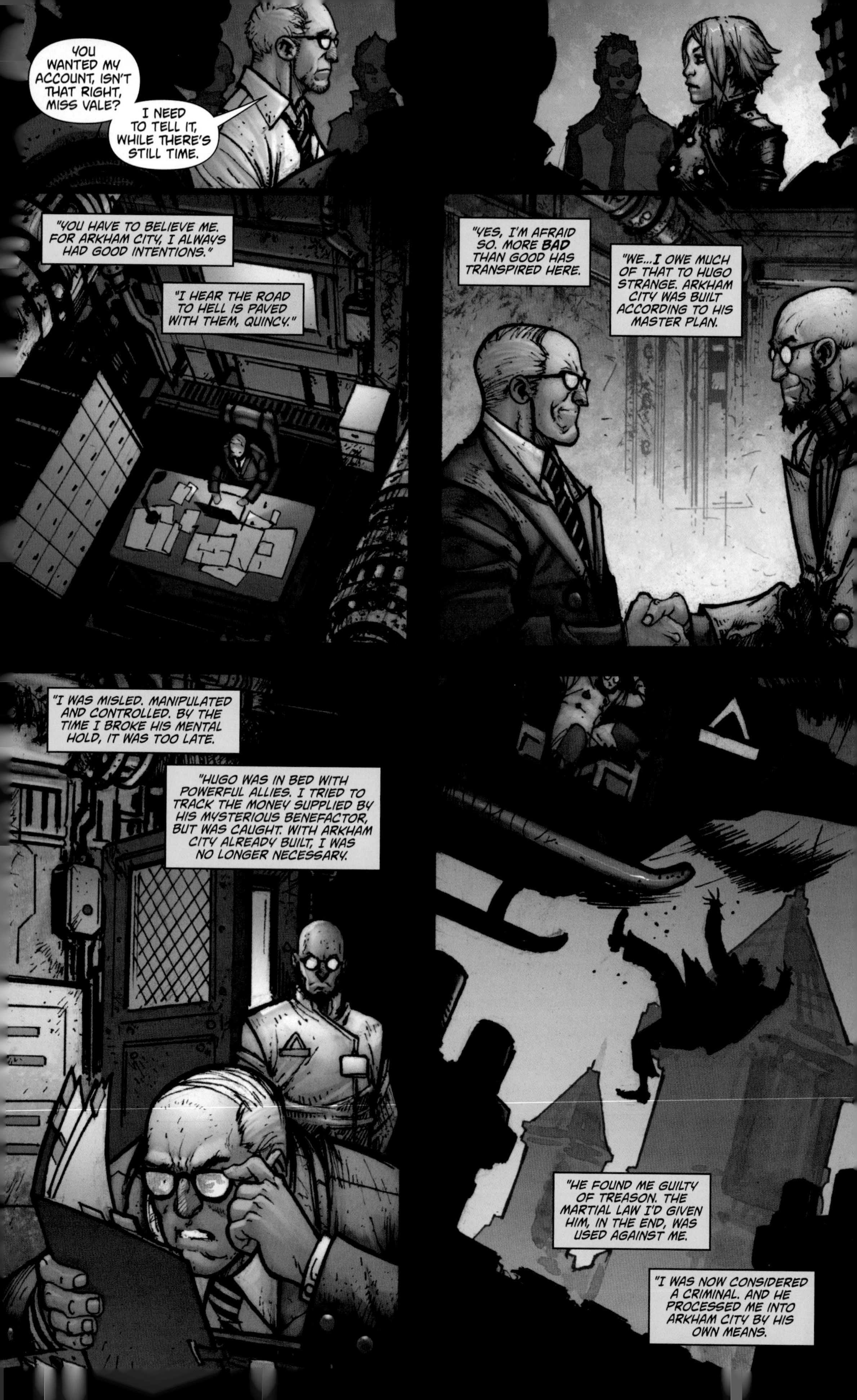
YOU WANTED MY ACCOUNT, ISN'T THAT RIGHT, MISS VALE?
I NEED TO TELL IT, WHILE THERE'S STILL TIME.
"YOU HAVE TO BELIEVE ME. FOR ARKHAM CITY, I ALWAYS HAD GOOD INTENTIONS."
"I HEAR THE ROAD TO HELL IS PAVED WITH THEM, QUINCY."
"YES, I'M AFRAID SO. MORE BAD THAN GOOD HAS TRANSPIRED HERE.
"WE...I OWE MUCH OF THAT TO HUGO STRANGE. ARKHAM CITY WAS BUILT ACCORDING TO HIS MASTER PLAN.
"I WAS MISLED. MANIPULATED AND CONTROLLED. BY THE TIME I BROKE HIS MENTAL HOLD, IT WAS TOO LATE.
"HUGO WAS IN BED WITH POWERFUL ALLIES. I TRIED TO TRACK THE MONEY SUPPLIED BY HIS MYSTERIOUS BENEFACTOR, BUT WAS CAUGHT. WITH ARKHAM CITY ALREADY BUILT, I WAS NO LONGER NECESSARY.
"HE FOUND ME GUILTY OF TREASON. THE MARTIAL LAW I'D GIVEN HIM, IN THE END, WAS USED AGAINST ME.
"I WAS NOW CONSIDERED A CRIMINAL. AND HE PROCESSED ME INTO ARKHAM CITY BY HIS OWN MEANS.

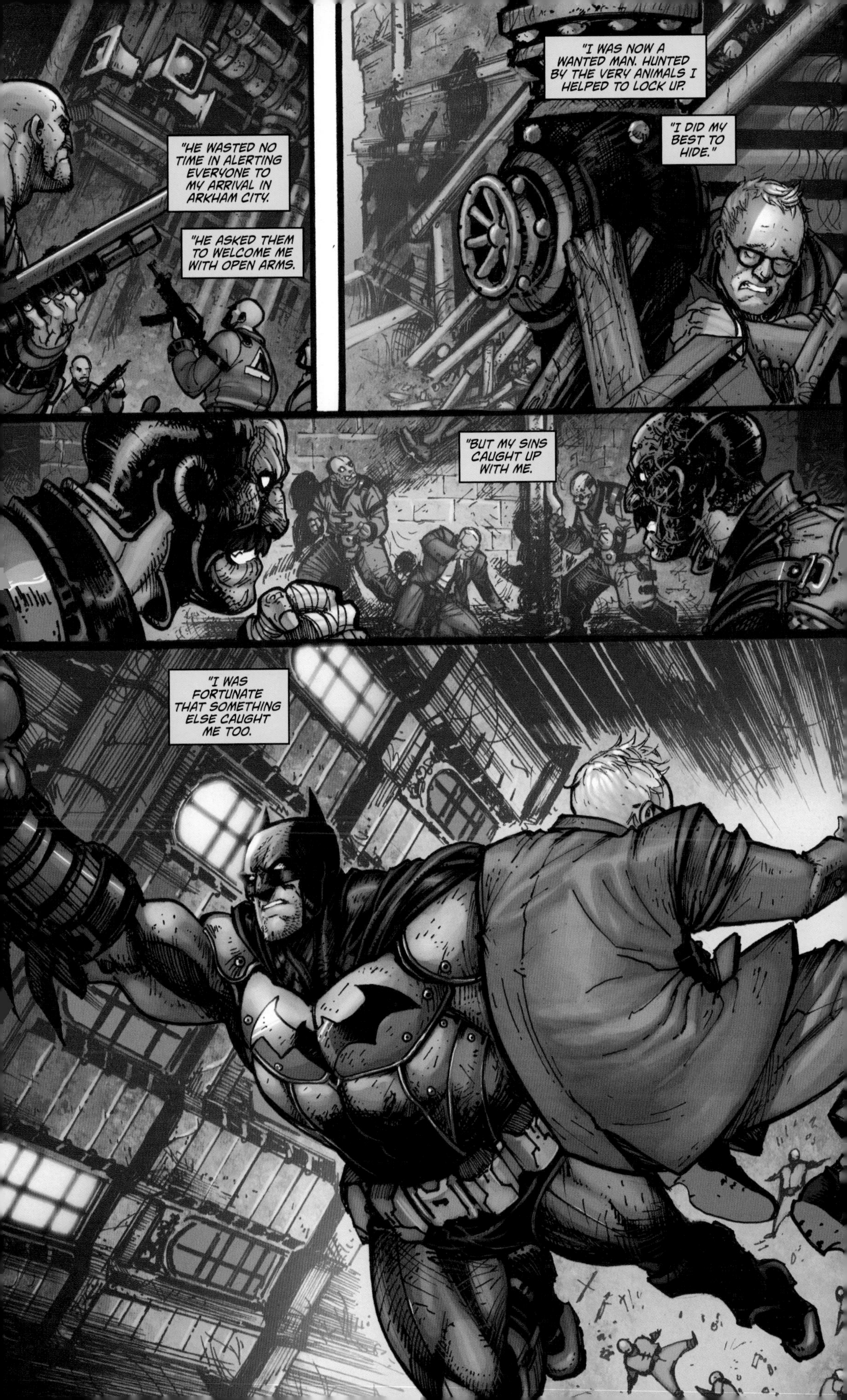
"HE WASTED NO TIME IN ALERTING EVERYONE TO MY ARRIVAL IN ARKHAM CITY.
"HE ASKED THEM TO WELCOME ME WITH OPEN ARMS.
"I WAS NOW A WANTED MAN. HUNTED BY THE VERY ANIMALS I HELPED TO LOCK UP.
"I DID MY BEST TO HIDE."
"BUT MY SINS CAUGHT UP WITH ME.
"I WAS FORTUNATE THAT SOMETHING ELSE CAUGHT ME TOO.

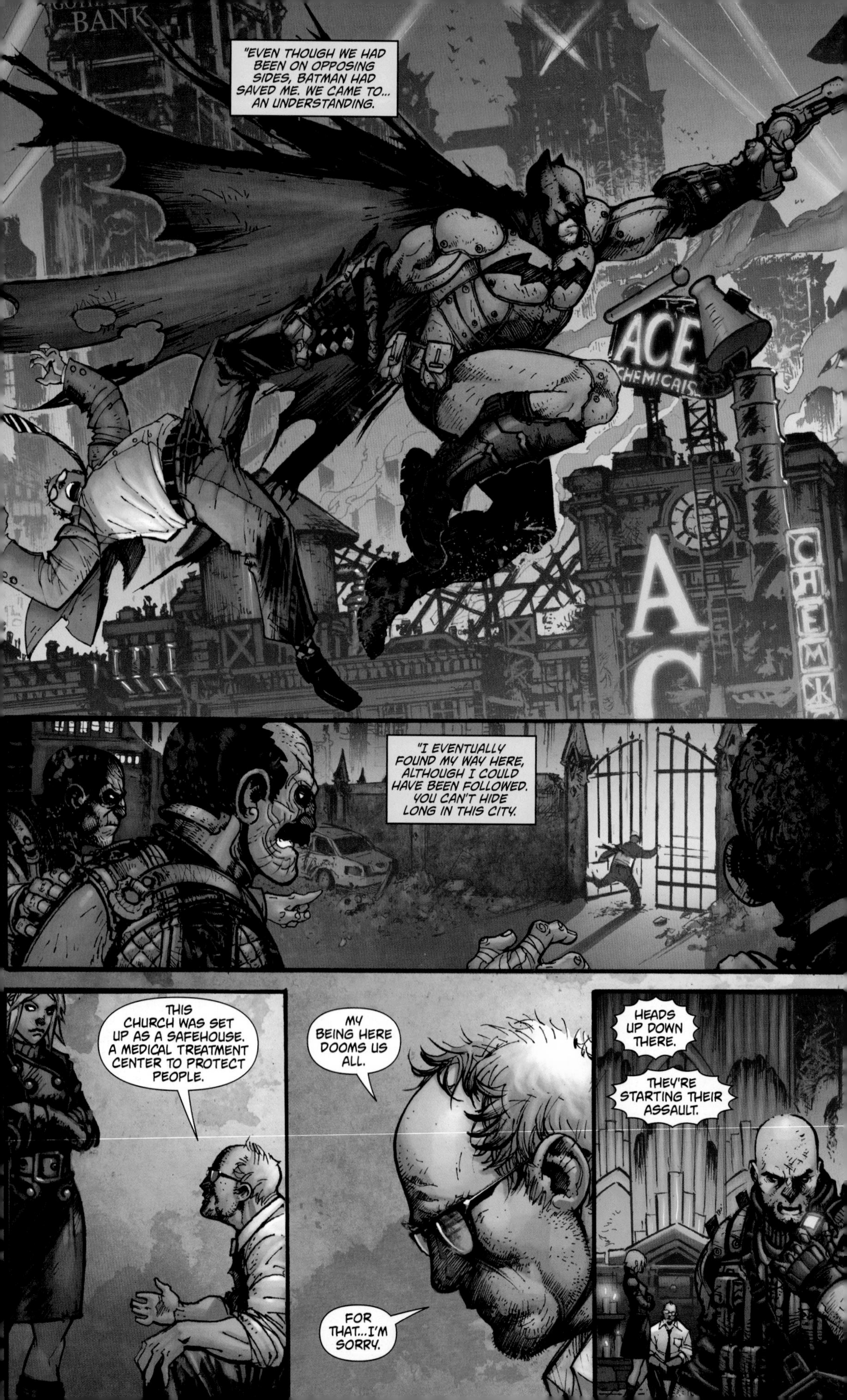
"EVEN THOUGH WE HAD BEEN ON OPPOSING SIDES, BATMAN HAD SAVED ME. WE CAME TO... AN UNDERSTANDING.
ACE CHEMICALS
BANK
"I EVENTUALLY FOUND MY WAY HERE, ALTHOUGH I COULD HAVE BEEN FOLLOWED. YOU CAN'T HIDE LONG IN THIS CITY.
THIS CHURCH WAS SET UP AS A SAFEHOUSE. A MEDICAL TREATMENT CENTER TO PROTECT PEOPLE.
MY BEING HERE DOOMS US ALL.
FOR THAT...I'M SORRY.
HEADS UP DOWN THERE.
THEY'RE STARTING THEIR ASSAULT.

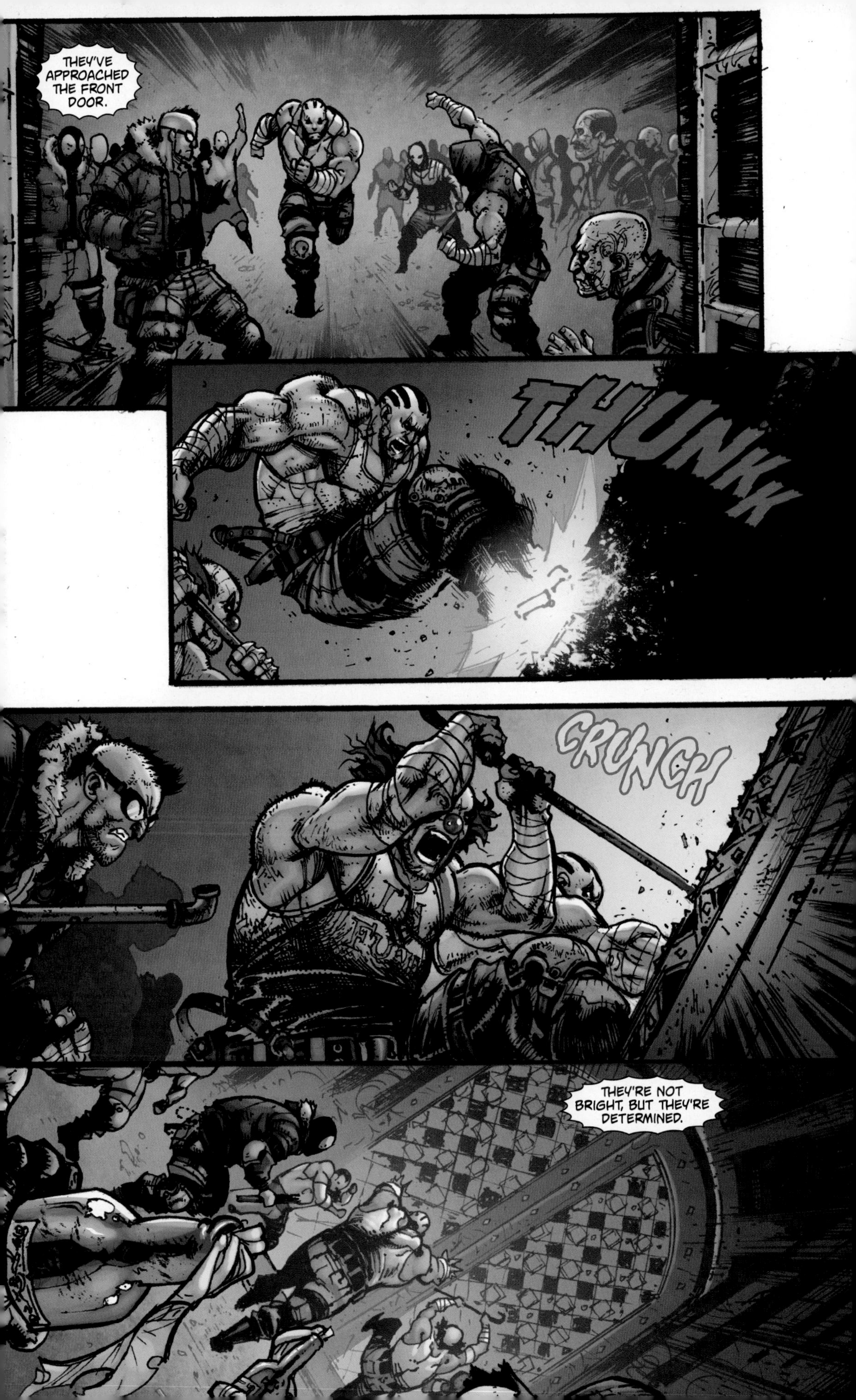
THEY'VE APPROACHED THE FRONT DOOR.
THUNKK
CRUNCH
THEY'RE NOT BRIGHT, BUT THEY'RE DETERMINED.

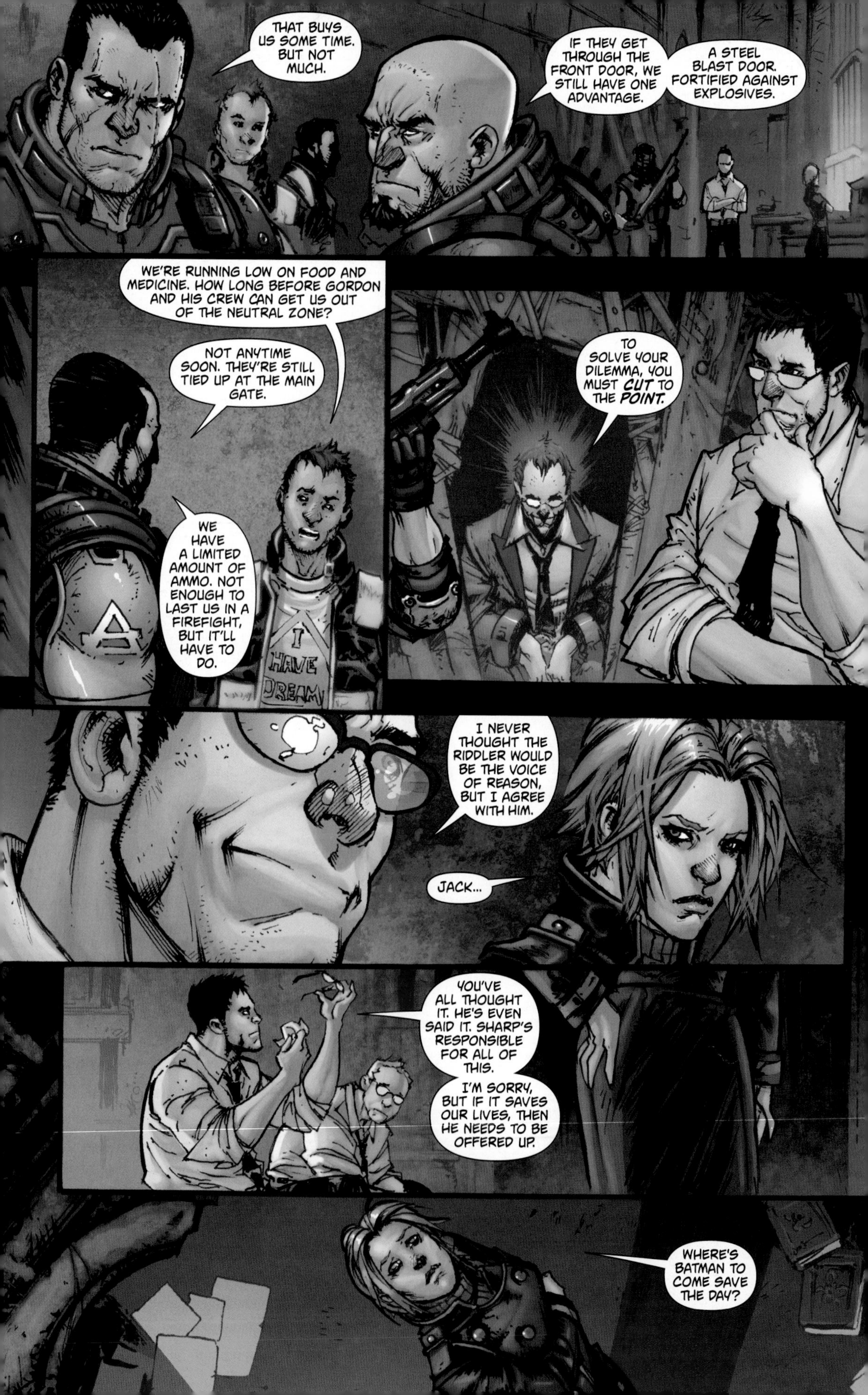
THAT BUYS US SOME TIME. BUT NOT MUCH.
IF THEY GET THROUGH THE FRONT DOOR, WE STILL HAVE ONE ADVANTAGE.
A STEEL BLAST DOOR. FORTIFIED AGAINST EXPLOSIVES.
WE'RE RUNNING LOW ON FOOD AND MEDICINE. HOW LONG BEFORE GORDON AND HIS CREW CAN GET US OUT OF THE NEUTRAL ZONE?
NOT ANYTIME SOON. THEY'RE STILL TIED UP AT THE MAIN GATE.
WE HAVE A LIMITED AMOUNT OF AMMO. NOT ENOUGH TO LAST US IN A FIREFIGHT, BUT IT'LL HAVE TO DO.
I HAVE DREAM
TO SOLVE YOUR DILEMMA, YOU MUST CUT TO THE POINT.
I NEVER THOUGHT THE RIDDLER WOULD BE THE VOICE OF REASON, BUT I AGREE WITH HIM.
JACK...
YOU'VE ALL THOUGHT IT. HE'S EVEN SAID IT. SHARP'S RESPONSIBLE FOR ALL OF THIS.
I'M SORRY, BUT IF IT SAVES OUR LIVES, THEN HE NEEDS TO BE OFFERED UP.
WHERE'S BATMAN TO COME SAVE THE DAY?

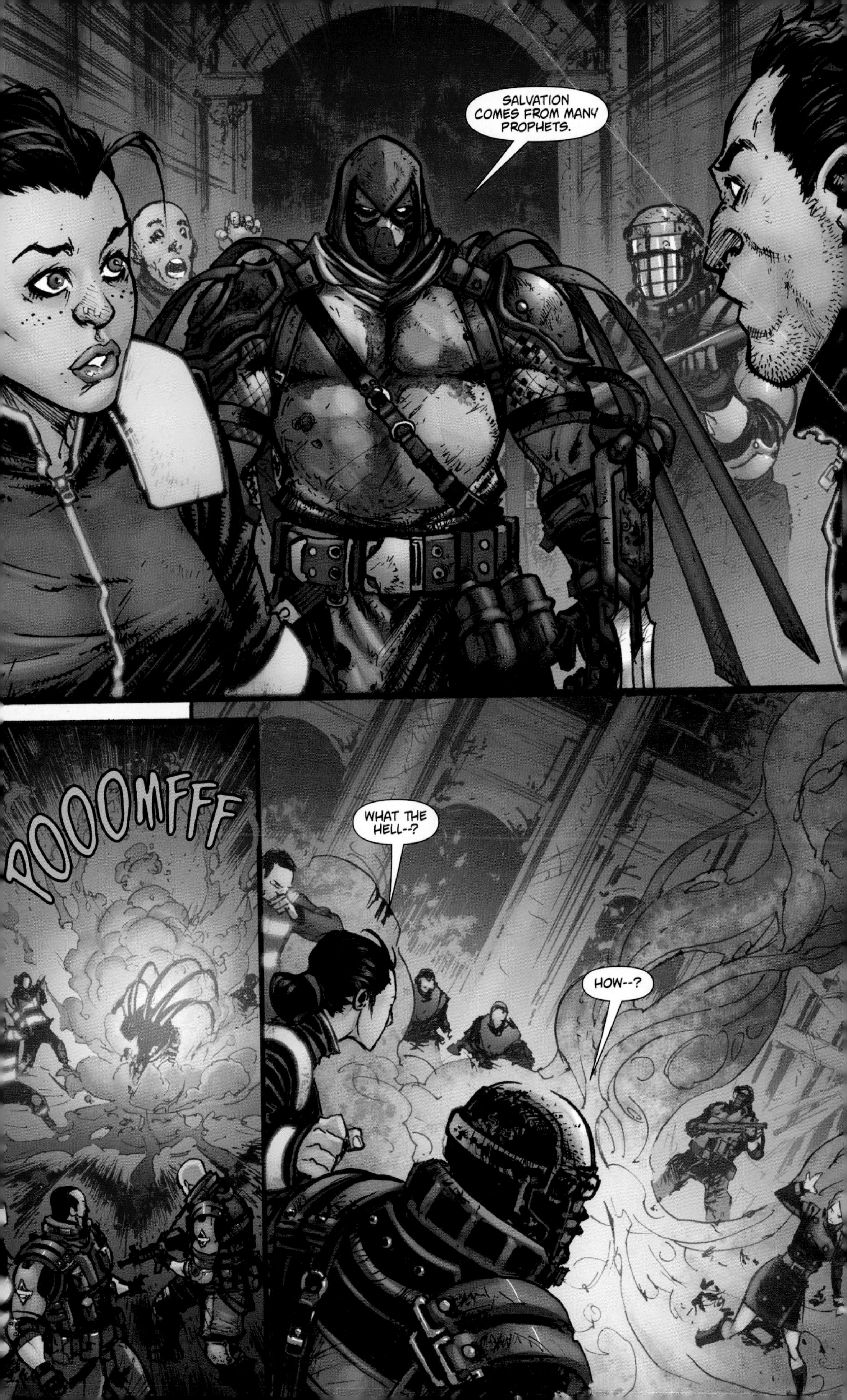
SALVATION COMES FROM MANY PROPHETS.
POOOMFFF
WHAT THE HELL--?
HOW--?

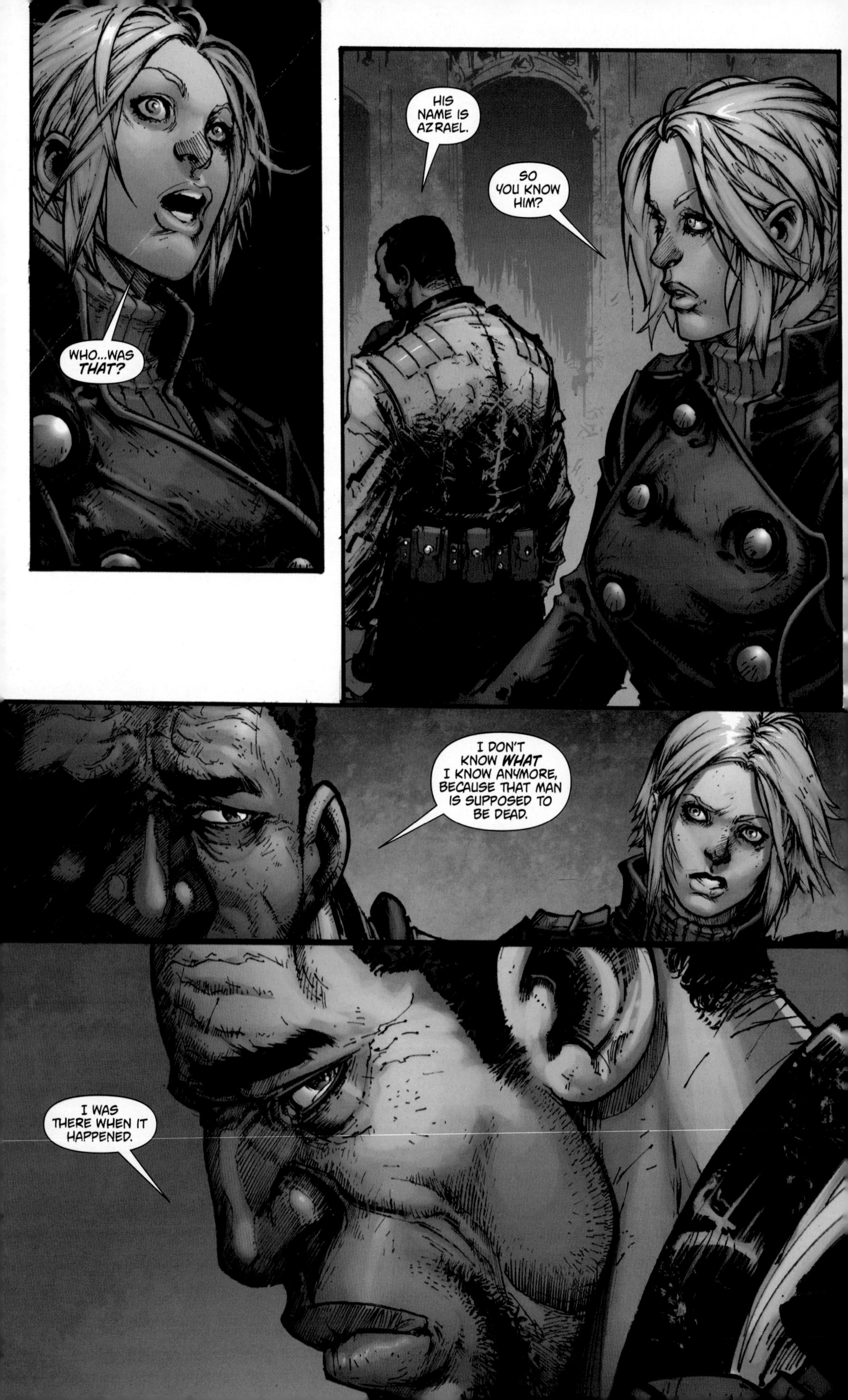
WHO...WAS THAT?
HIS NAME IS AZRAEL.
SO YOU KNOW HIM?
I DON'T KNOW WHAT I KNOW ANYMORE, BECAUSE THAT MAN IS SUPPOSED TO BE DEAD.
I WAS THERE WHEN IT HAPPENED.

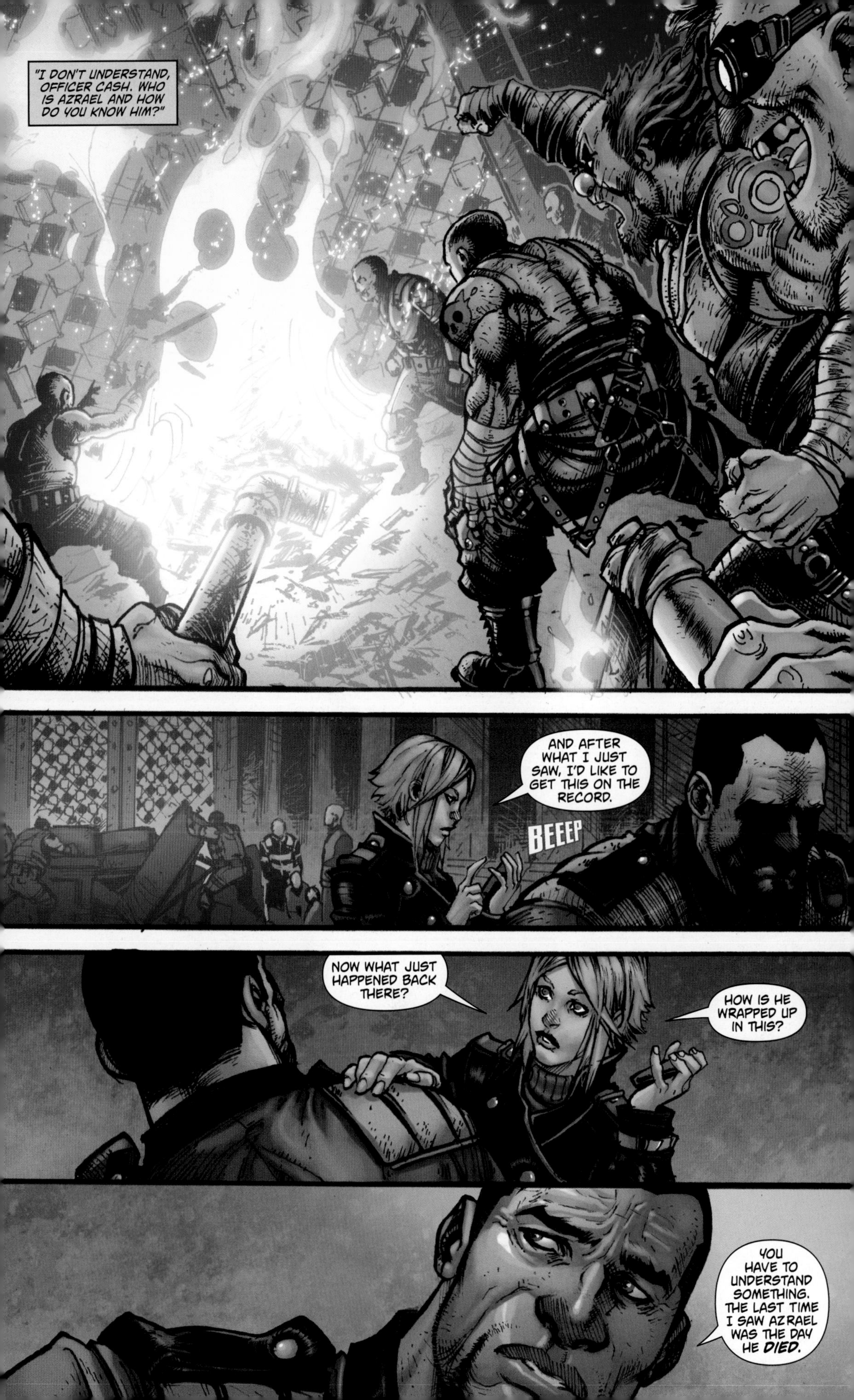
"I DON'T UNDERSTAND, OFFICER CASH. WHO IS AZRAEL AND HOW DO YOU KNOW HIM?"
AND AFTER WHAT I JUST SAW, I'D LIKE TO GET THIS ON THE RECORD.
BEEEP
NOW WHAT JUST HAPPENED BACK THERE?
HOW IS HE WRAPPED UP IN THIS?
YOU HAVE TO UNDERSTAND SOMETHING. THE LAST TIME I SAW AZRAEL WAS THE DAY HE DIED.

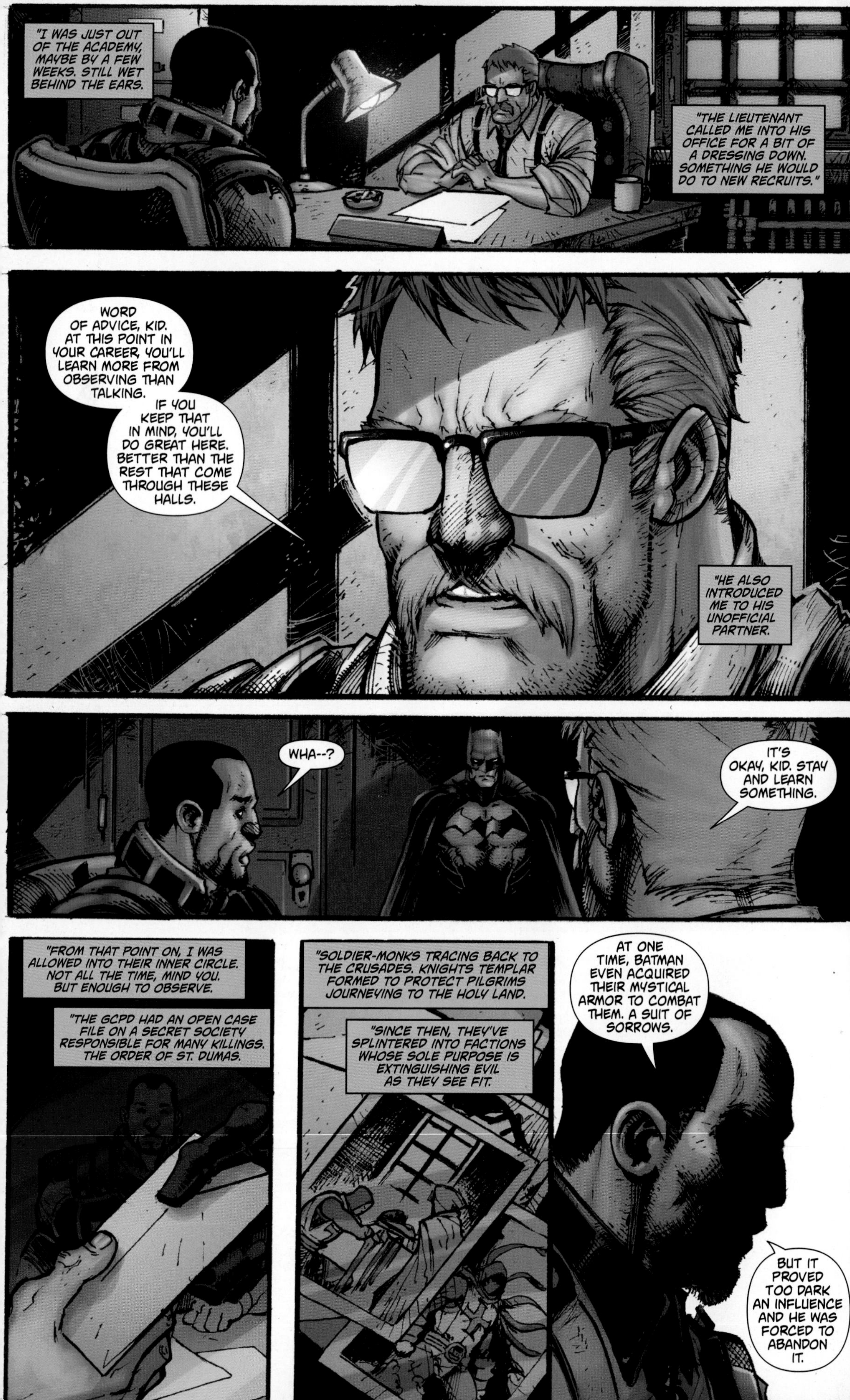
"I WAS JUST OUT OF THE ACADEMY, MAYBE BY A FEW WEEKS. STILL WET BEHIND THE EARS.
"THE LIEUTENANT CALLED ME INTO HIS OFFICE FOR A BIT OF A DRESSING DOWN. SOMETHING HE WOULD DO TO NEW RECRUITS."
WORD OF ADVICE, KID. AT THIS POINT IN YOUR CAREER, YOU'LL LEARN MORE FROM OBSERVING THAN TALKING.
IF YOU KEEP THAT IN MIND, YOU'LL DO GREAT HERE. BETTER THAN THE REST THAT COME THROUGH THESE HALLS.
"HE ALSO INTRODUCED ME TO HIS UNOFFICIAL PARTNER.
WHA--?
IT'S OKAY, KID. STAY AND LEARN SOMETHING.
"FROM THAT POINT ON, I WAS ALLOWED INTO THEIR INNER CIRCLE. NOT ALL THE TIME, MIND YOU. BUT ENOUGH TO OBSERVE.
"THE GCPD HAD AN OPEN CASE FILE ON A SECRET SOCIETY RESPONSIBLE FOR MANY KILLINGS. THE ORDER OF ST. DUMAS.
"SOLDIER-MONKS TRACING BACK TO THE CRUSADES. KNIGHTS TEMPLAR FORMED TO PROTECT PILGRIMS JOURNEYING TO THE HOLY LAND.
"SINCE THEN, THEY'VE SPLINTERED INTO FACTIONS WHOSE SOLE PURPOSE IS EXTINGUISHING EVIL AS THEY SEE FIT.
AT ONE TIME, BATMAN EVEN ACQUIRED THEIR MYSTICAL ARMOR TO COMBAT THEM. A SUIT OF SORROWS.
BUT IT PROVED TOO DARK AN INFLUENCE AND HE WAS FORCED TO ABANDON IT.

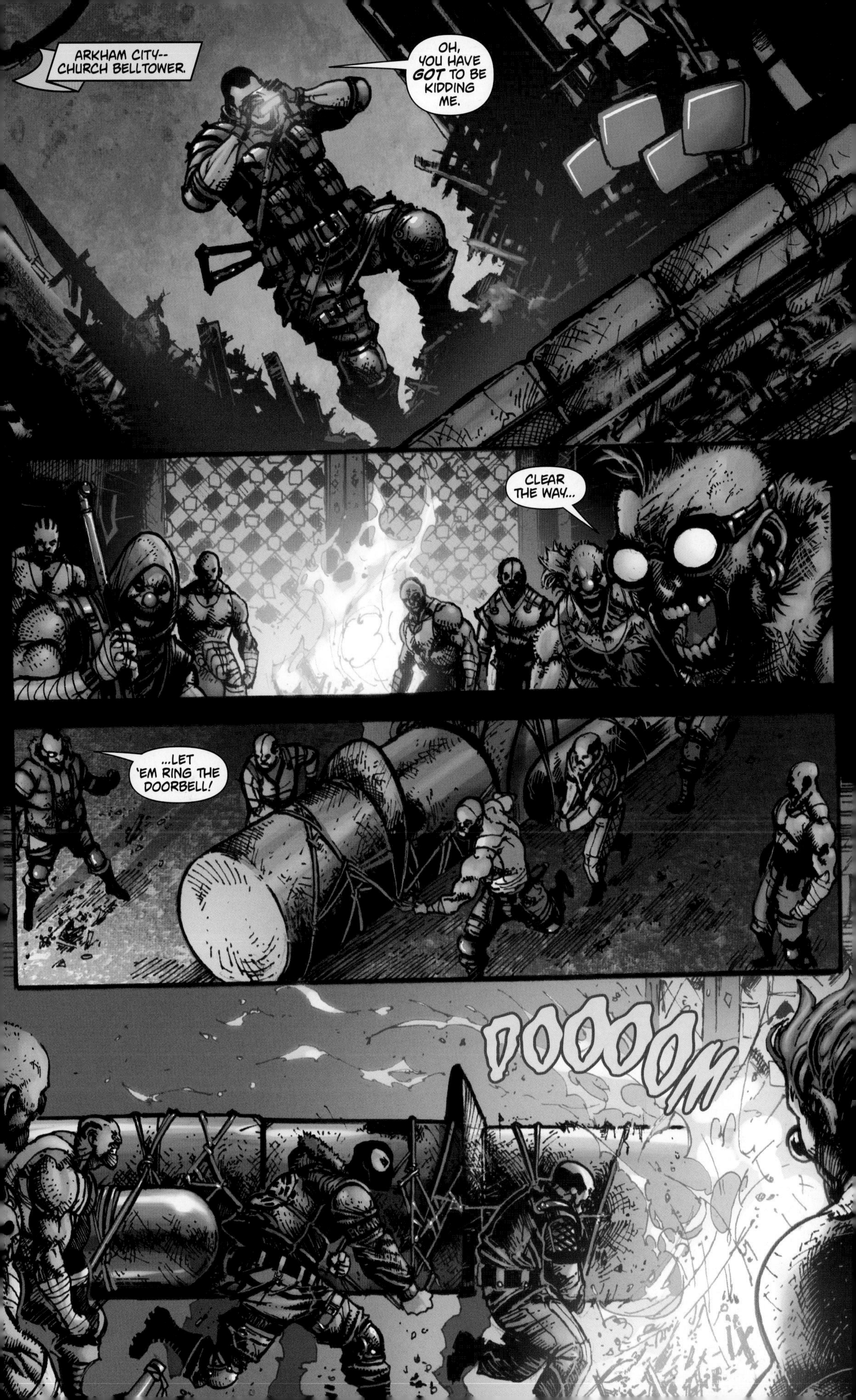
ARKHAM CITY--
CHURCH BELLTOWER.
OH, YOU HAVE **GOT** TO BE KIDDING ME.
CLEAR THE WAY...
...LET 'EM RING THE DOORBELL!
DOOOOOM

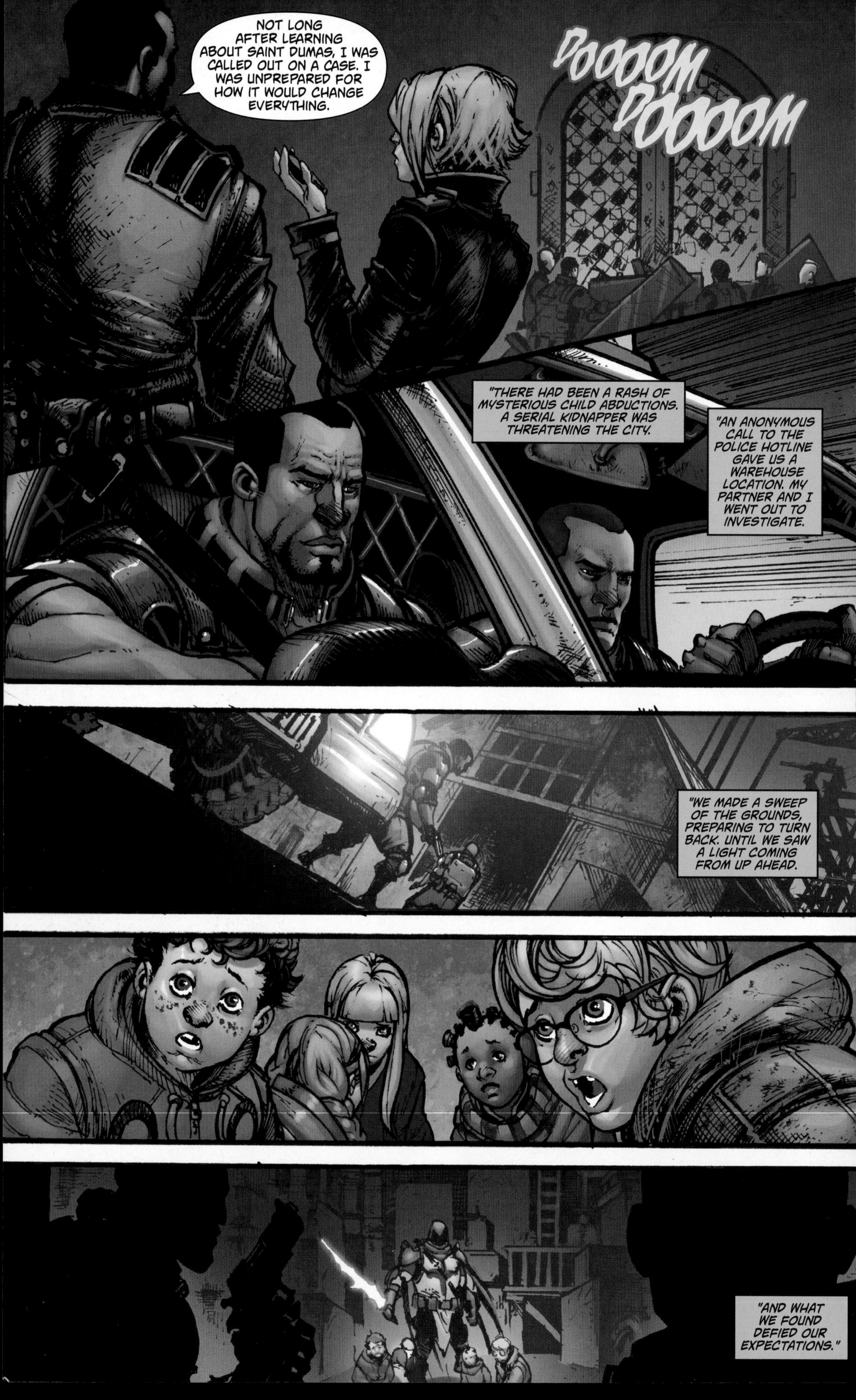
NOT LONG AFTER LEARNING ABOUT SAINT DUMAS, I WAS CALLED OUT ON A CASE. I WAS UNPREPARED FOR HOW IT WOULD CHANGE EVERYTHING.
DOOOOM DOOOOM
"THERE HAD BEEN A RASH OF MYSTERIOUS CHILD ABDUCTIONS. A SERIAL KIDNAPPER WAS THREATENING THE CITY.
"AN ANONYMOUS CALL TO THE POLICE HOTLINE GAVE US A WAREHOUSE LOCATION. MY PARTNER AND I WENT OUT TO INVESTIGATE.
"WE MADE A SWEEP OF THE GROUNDS, PREPARING TO TURN BACK. UNTIL WE SAW A LIGHT COMING FROM UP AHEAD.
"AND WHAT WE FOUND DEFIED OUR EXPECTATIONS."

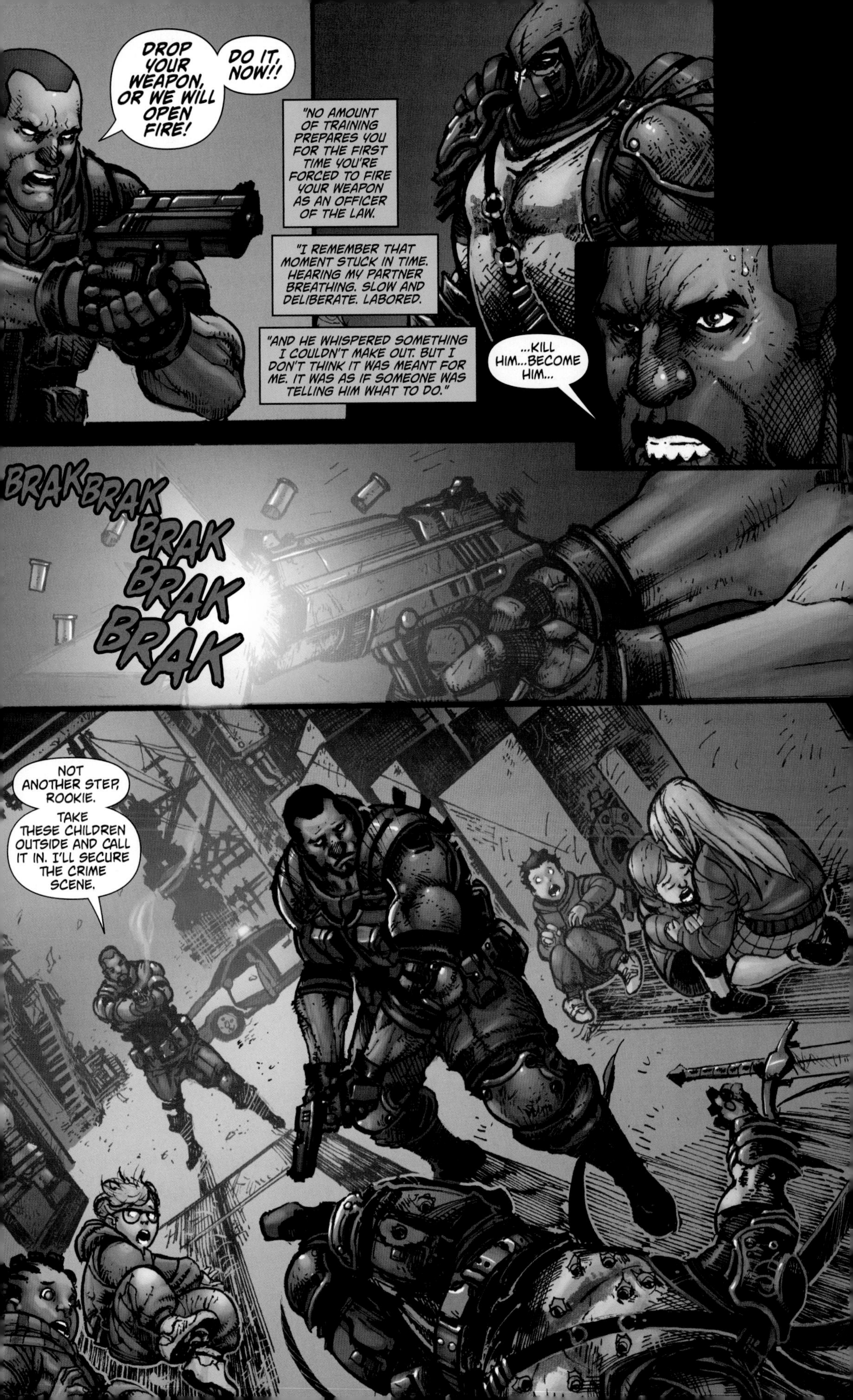
DROP YOUR WEAPON, OR WE WILL OPEN FIRE!
DO IT, NOW!!
"NO AMOUNT OF TRAINING PREPARES YOU FOR THE FIRST TIME YOU'RE FORCED TO FIRE YOUR WEAPON AS AN OFFICER OF THE LAW.
"I REMEMBER THAT MOMENT STUCK IN TIME. HEARING MY PARTNER BREATHING. SLOW AND DELIBERATE. LABORED.
"AND HE WHISPERED SOMETHING I COULDN'T MAKE OUT. BUT I DON'T THINK IT WAS MEANT FOR ME. IT WAS AS IF SOMEONE WAS TELLING HIM WHAT TO DO."
...KILL HIM...BECOME HIM...
BRAK BRAK BRAK BRAK BRAK
NOT ANOTHER STEP, ROOKIE.
TAKE THESE CHILDREN OUTSIDE AND CALL IT IN. I'LL SECURE THE CRIME SCENE.

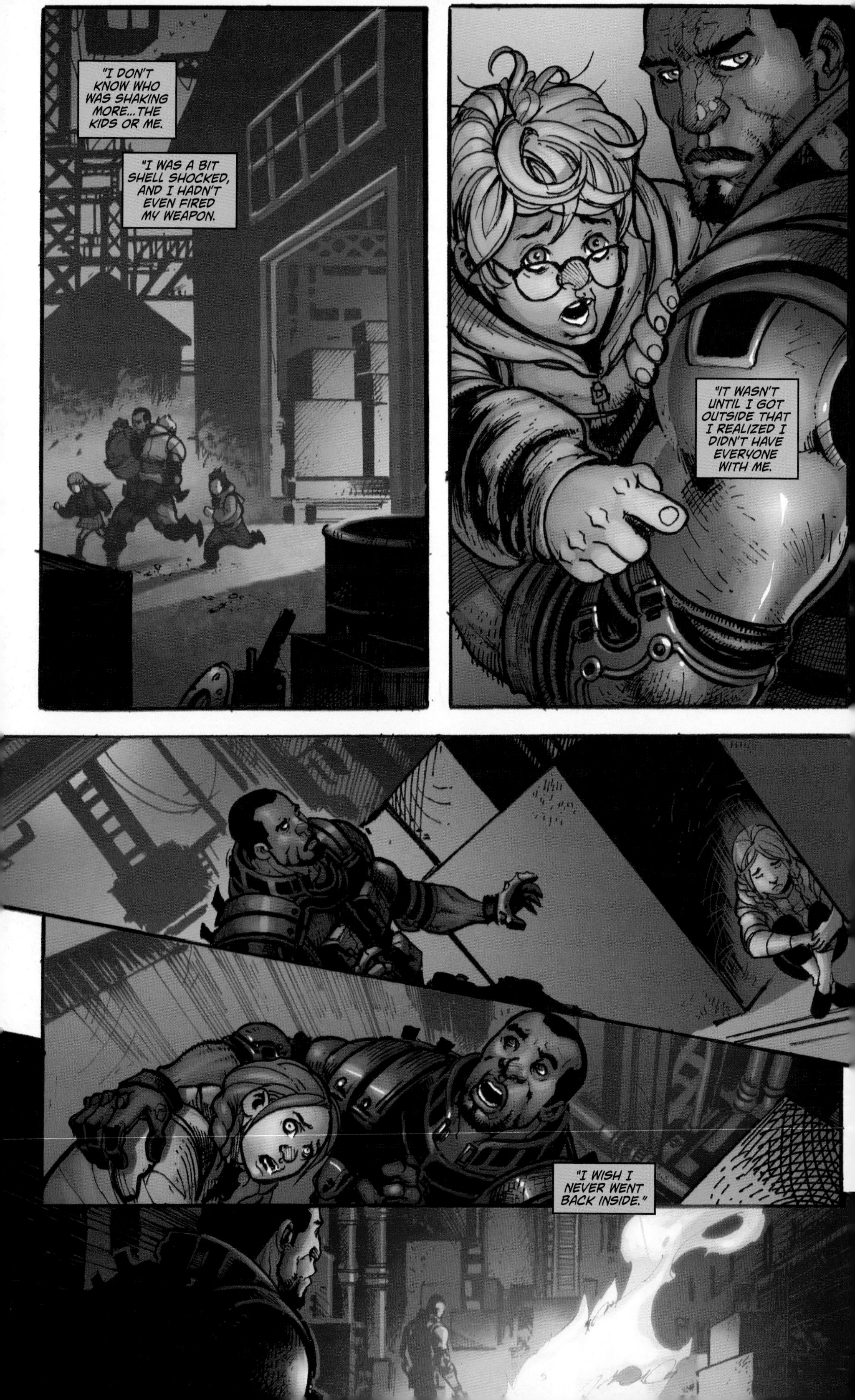
"I DON'T KNOW WHO WAS SHAKING MORE...THE KIDS OR ME.
"I WAS A BIT SHELL SHOCKED, AND I HADN'T EVEN FIRED MY WEAPON.
"IT WASN'T UNTIL I GOT OUTSIDE THAT I REALIZED I DIDN'T HAVE EVERYONE WITH ME.
"I WISH I NEVER WENT BACK INSIDE."

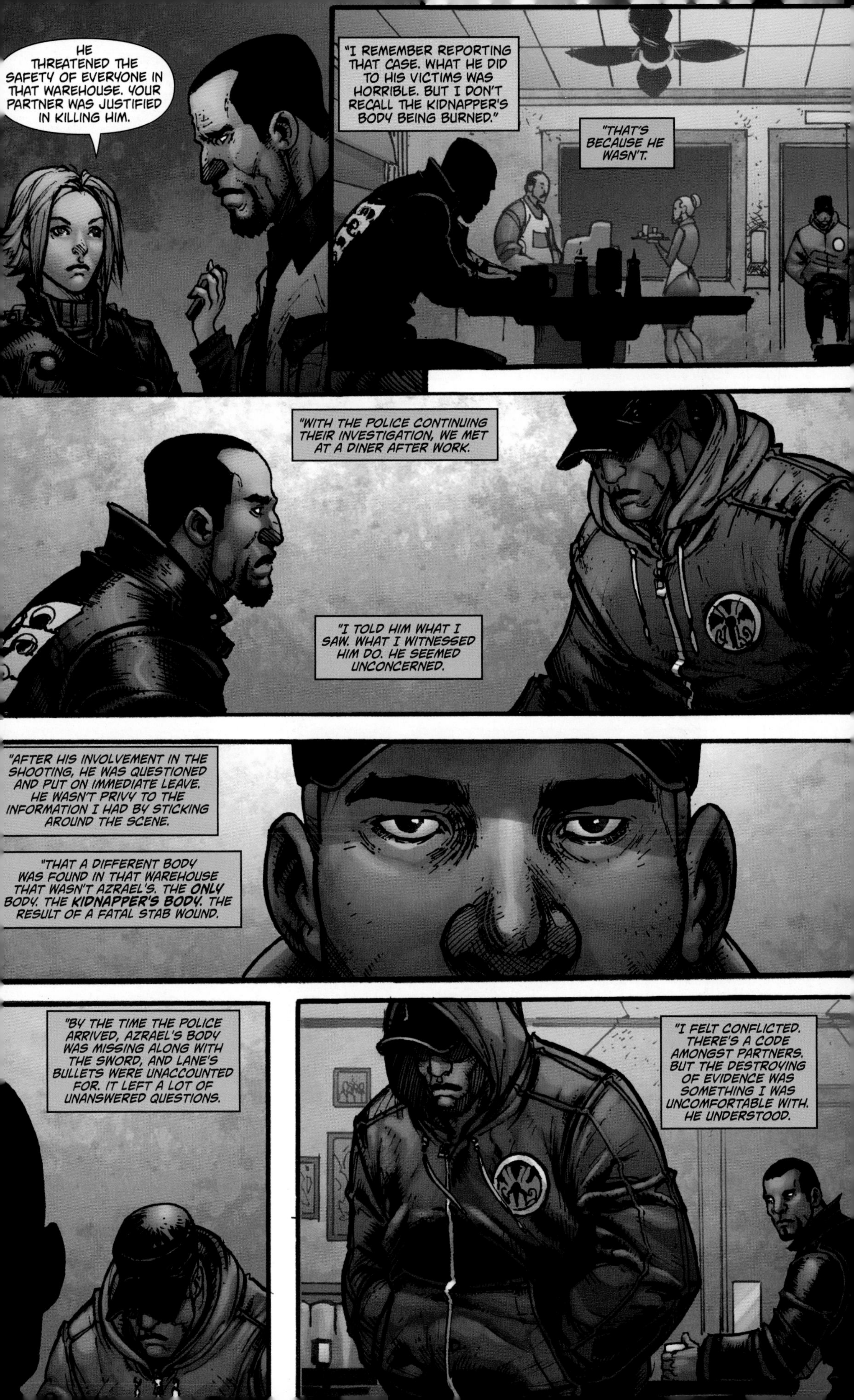
HE THREATENED THE SAFETY OF EVERYONE IN THAT WAREHOUSE. YOUR PARTNER WAS JUSTIFIED IN KILLING HIM.
"I REMEMBER REPORTING THAT CASE. WHAT HE DID TO HIS VICTIMS WAS HORRIBLE. BUT I DON'T RECALL THE KIDNAPPER'S BODY BEING BURNED."
"THAT'S BECAUSE HE WASN'T.
"WITH THE POLICE CONTINUING THEIR INVESTIGATION, WE MET AT A DINER AFTER WORK.
"I TOLD HIM WHAT I SAW. WHAT I WITNESSED HIM DO. HE SEEMED UNCONCERNED.
"AFTER HIS INVOLVEMENT IN THE SHOOTING, HE WAS QUESTIONED AND PUT ON IMMEDIATE LEAVE. HE WASN'T PRIVY TO THE INFORMATION I HAD BY STICKING AROUND THE SCENE.
"THAT A DIFFERENT BODY WAS FOUND IN THAT WAREHOUSE THAT WASN'T AZRAEL'S. THE ONLY BODY. THE KIDNAPPER'S BODY. THE RESULT OF A FATAL STAB WOUND.
"BY THE TIME THE POLICE ARRIVED, AZRAEL'S BODY WAS MISSING ALONG WITH THE SWORD, AND LANE'S BULLETS WERE UNACCOUNTED FOR. IT LEFT A LOT OF UNANSWERED QUESTIONS.
"I FELT CONFLICTED. THERE'S A CODE AMONGST PARTNERS. BUT THE DESTROYING OF EVIDENCE WAS SOMETHING I WAS UNCOMFORTABLE WITH. HE UNDERSTOOD.

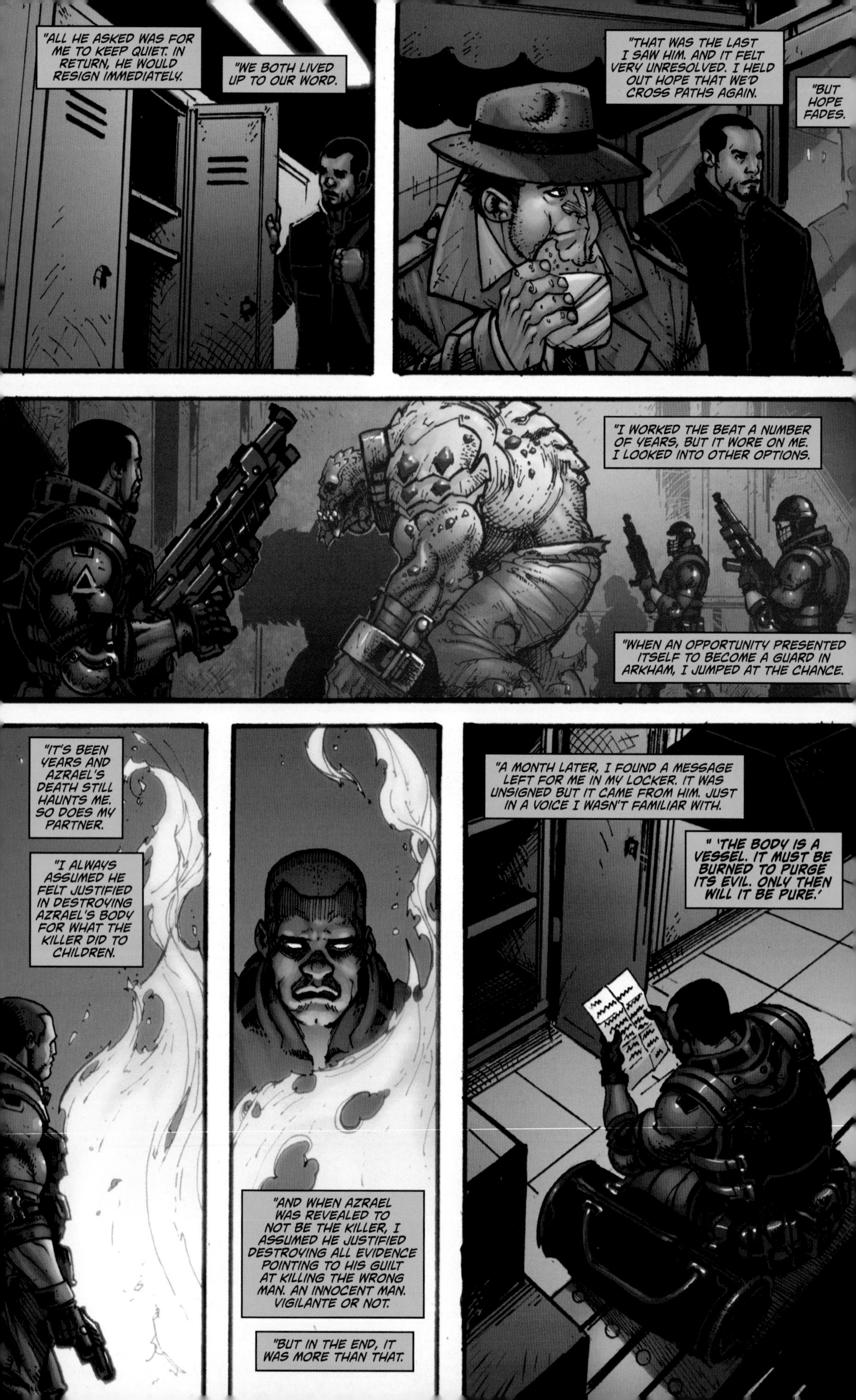
"ALL HE ASKED WAS FOR ME TO KEEP QUIET. IN RETURN, HE WOULD RESIGN IMMEDIATELY.
"WE BOTH LIVED UP TO OUR WORD.
"THAT WAS THE LAST I SAW HIM. AND IT FELT VERY UNRESOLVED. I HELD OUT HOPE THAT WE'D CROSS PATHS AGAIN.
"BUT HOPE FADES.
"I WORKED THE BEAT A NUMBER OF YEARS, BUT IT WORE ON ME. I LOOKED INTO OTHER OPTIONS.
"WHEN AN OPPORTUNITY PRESENTED ITSELF TO BECOME A GUARD IN ARKHAM, I JUMPED AT THE CHANCE.
"IT'S BEEN YEARS AND AZRAEL'S DEATH STILL HAUNTS ME. SO DOES MY PARTNER.
"I ALWAYS ASSUMED HE FELT JUSTIFIED IN DESTROYING AZRAEL'S BODY FOR WHAT THE KILLER DID TO CHILDREN.
"AND WHEN AZRAEL WAS REVEALED TO NOT BE THE KILLER, I ASSUMED HE JUSTIFIED DESTROYING ALL EVIDENCE POINTING TO HIS GUILT AT KILLING THE WRONG MAN. AN INNOCENT MAN. VIGILANTE OR NOT.
"BUT IN THE END, IT WAS MORE THAN THAT.
"A MONTH LATER, I FOUND A MESSAGE LEFT FOR ME IN MY LOCKER. IT WAS UNSIGNED BUT IT CAME FROM HIM. JUST IN A VOICE I WASN'T FAMILIAR WITH.
" 'THE BODY IS A VESSEL. IT MUST BE BURNED TO PURGE ITS EVIL. ONLY THEN WILL IT BE PURE.'

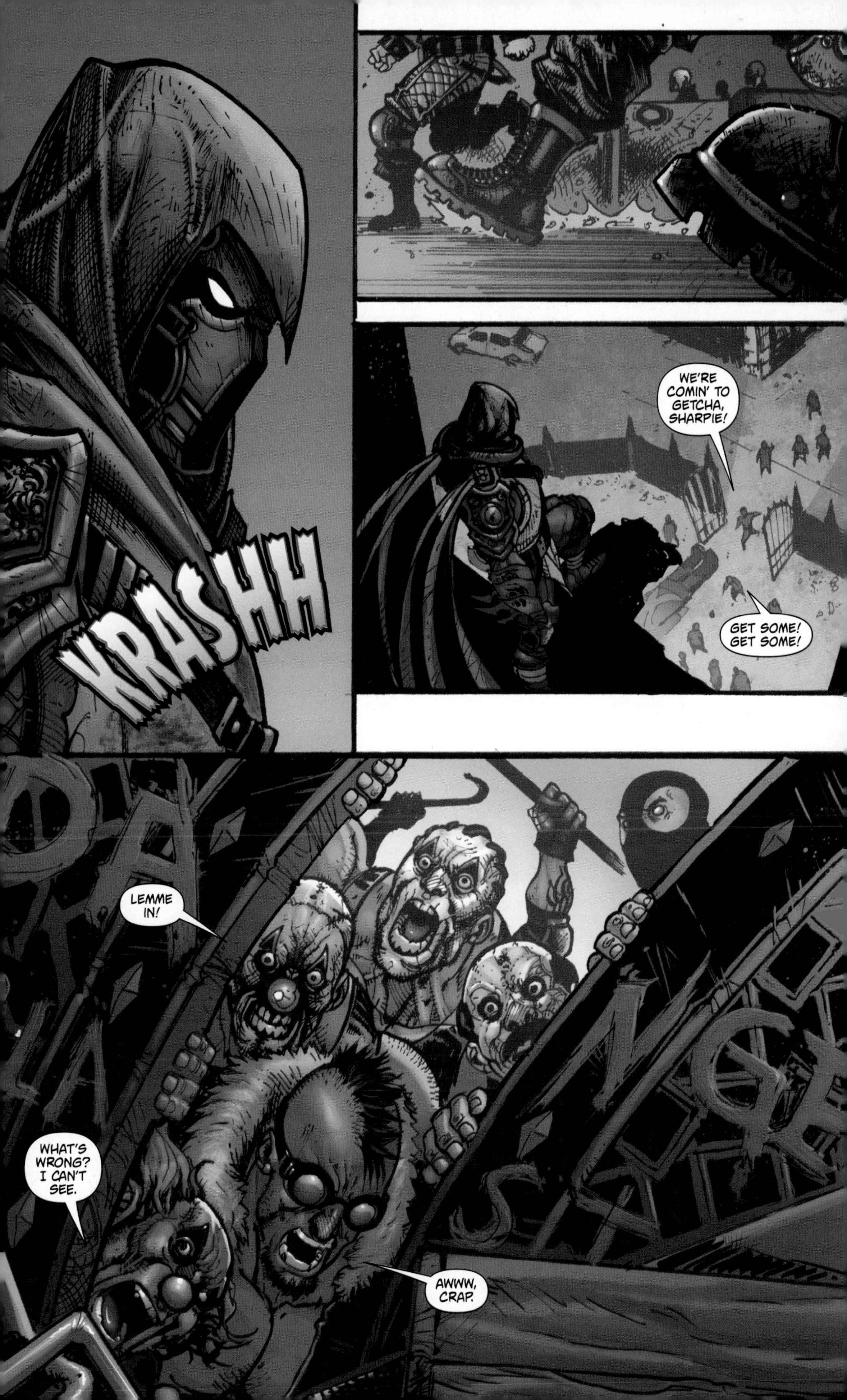
KRASHH
WE'RE COMIN' TO GETCHA, SHARPIE!
GET SOME! GET SOME!
LEMME IN!
WHAT'S WRONG? I CAN'T SEE.
AWWW, CRAP.

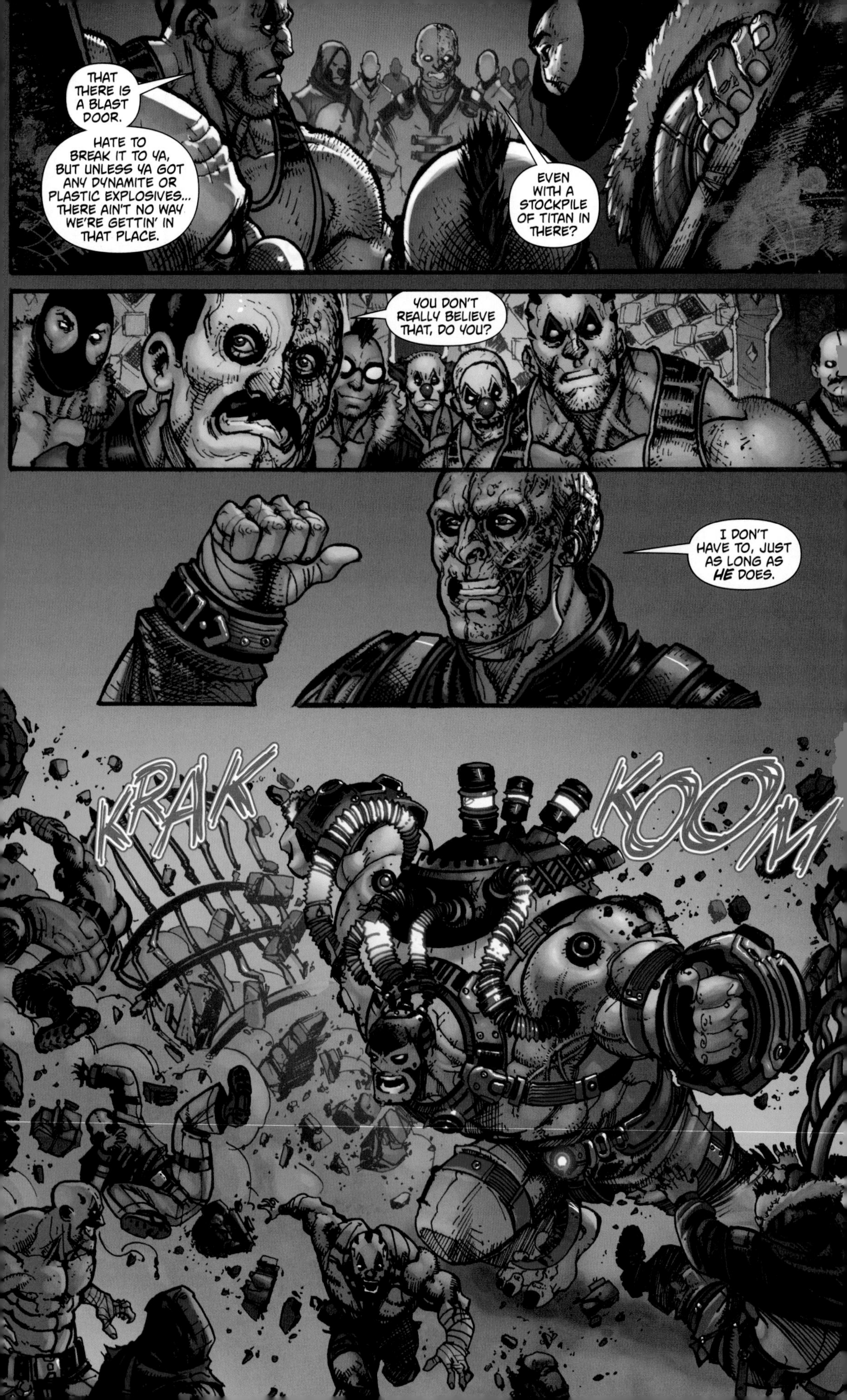
THAT THERE IS A BLAST DOOR.
HATE TO BREAK IT TO YA, BUT UNLESS YA GOT ANY DYNAMITE OR PLASTIC EXPLOSIVES... THERE AIN'T NO WAY WE'RE GETTIN' IN THAT PLACE.
EVEN WITH A STOCKPILE OF TITAN IN THERE?
YOU DON'T REALLY BELIEVE THAT, DO YOU?
I DON'T HAVE TO, JUST AS LONG AS **HE** DOES.
KRAK
KOOM

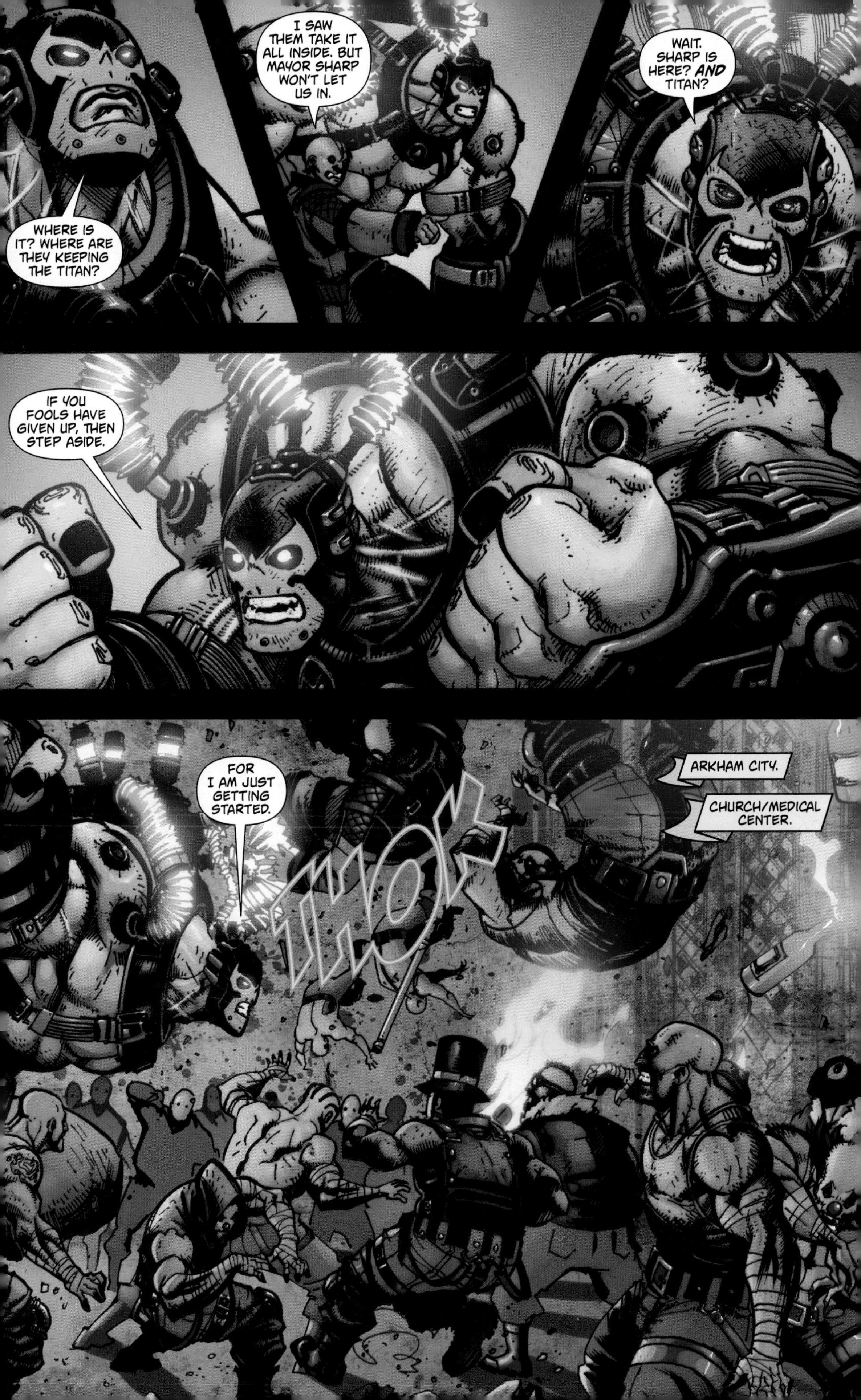
WHERE IS IT? WHERE ARE THEY KEEPING THE TITAN?
I SAW THEM TAKE IT ALL INSIDE. BUT MAYOR SHARP WON'T LET US IN.
WAIT. SHARP IS HERE? AND TITAN?
IF YOU FOOLS HAVE GIVEN UP, THEN STEP ASIDE.
ARKHAM CITY.
CHURCH/MEDICAL CENTER.
FOR I AM JUST GETTING STARTED.
THOK

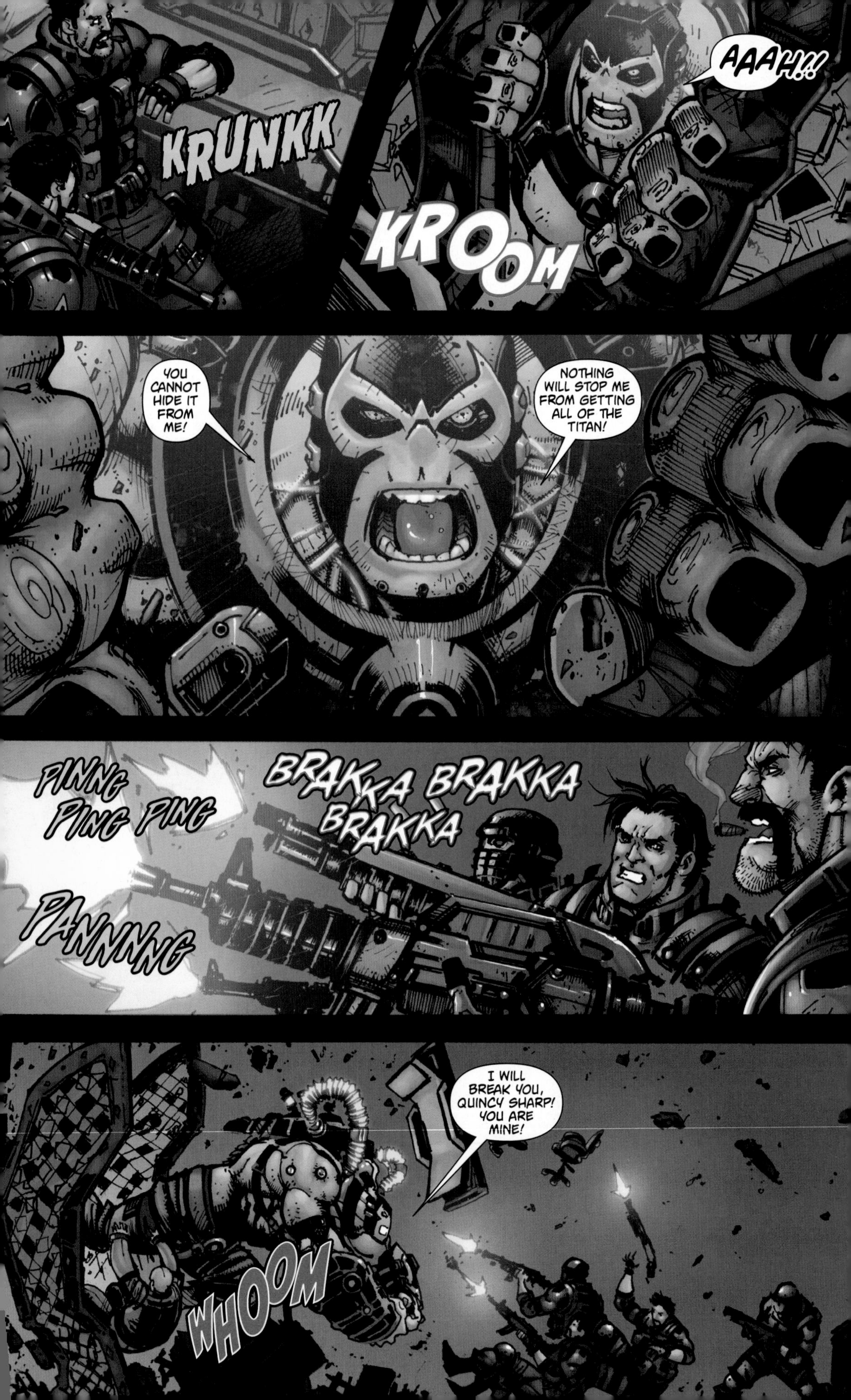
KRUNKK
AAAH!!
KROOM
YOU CANNOT HIDE IT FROM ME!
NOTHING WILL STOP ME FROM GETTING ALL OF THE TITAN!
PINNG PING PING
BRAKKA BRAKKA BRAKKA
PANNNNG
I WILL BREAK YOU, QUINCY SHARP! YOU ARE MINE!
WHOOM

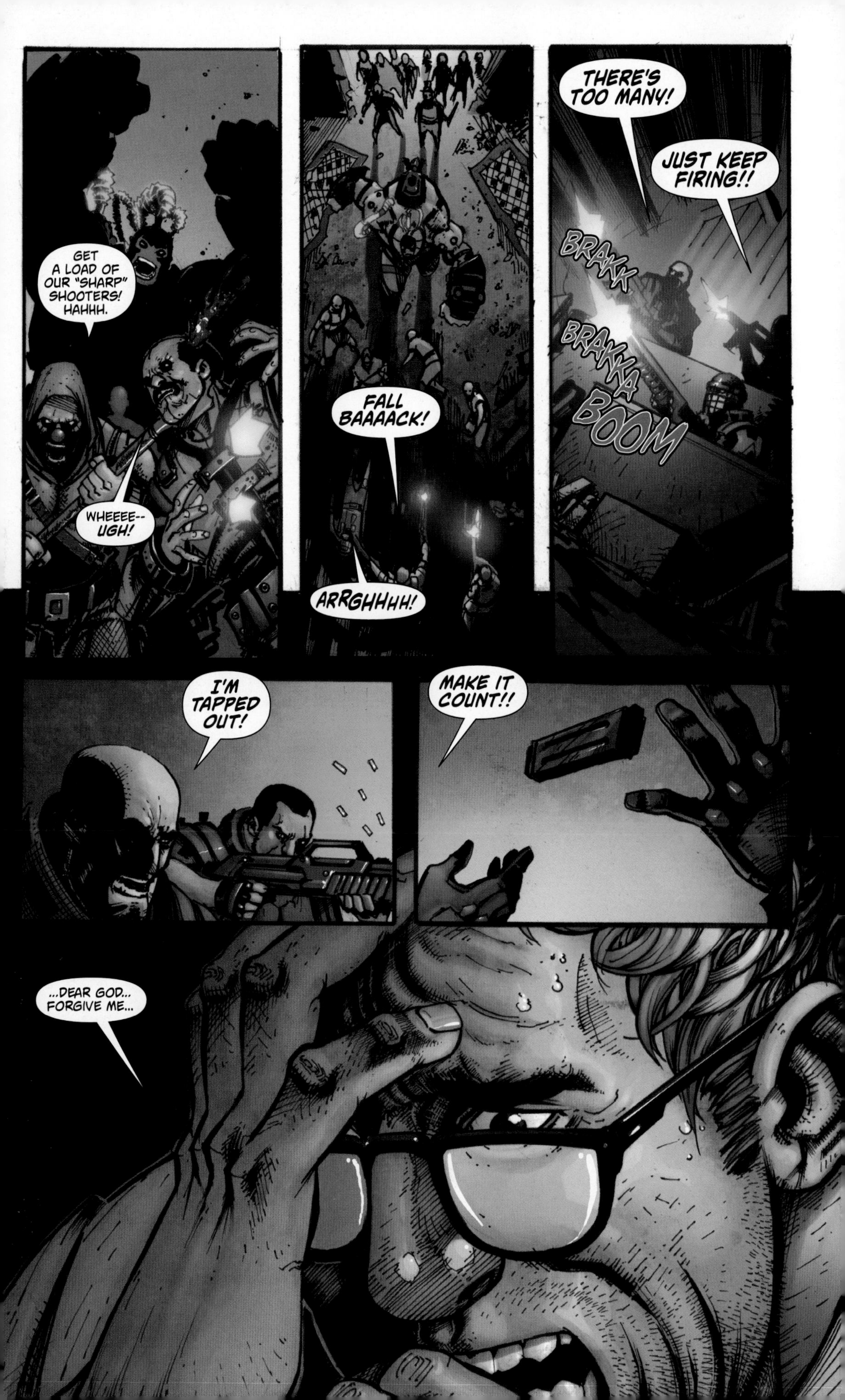
GET A LOAD OF OUR "SHARP" SHOOTERS! HAHHH.
WHEEEE-- UGH!
FALL BAAAACK!
ARRGHHHH!
THERE'S TOO MANY!
JUST KEEP FIRING!!
BRAKK
BRAKKA BOOM
I'M TAPPED OUT!
MAKE IT COUNT!!
...DEAR GOD... FORGIVE ME...

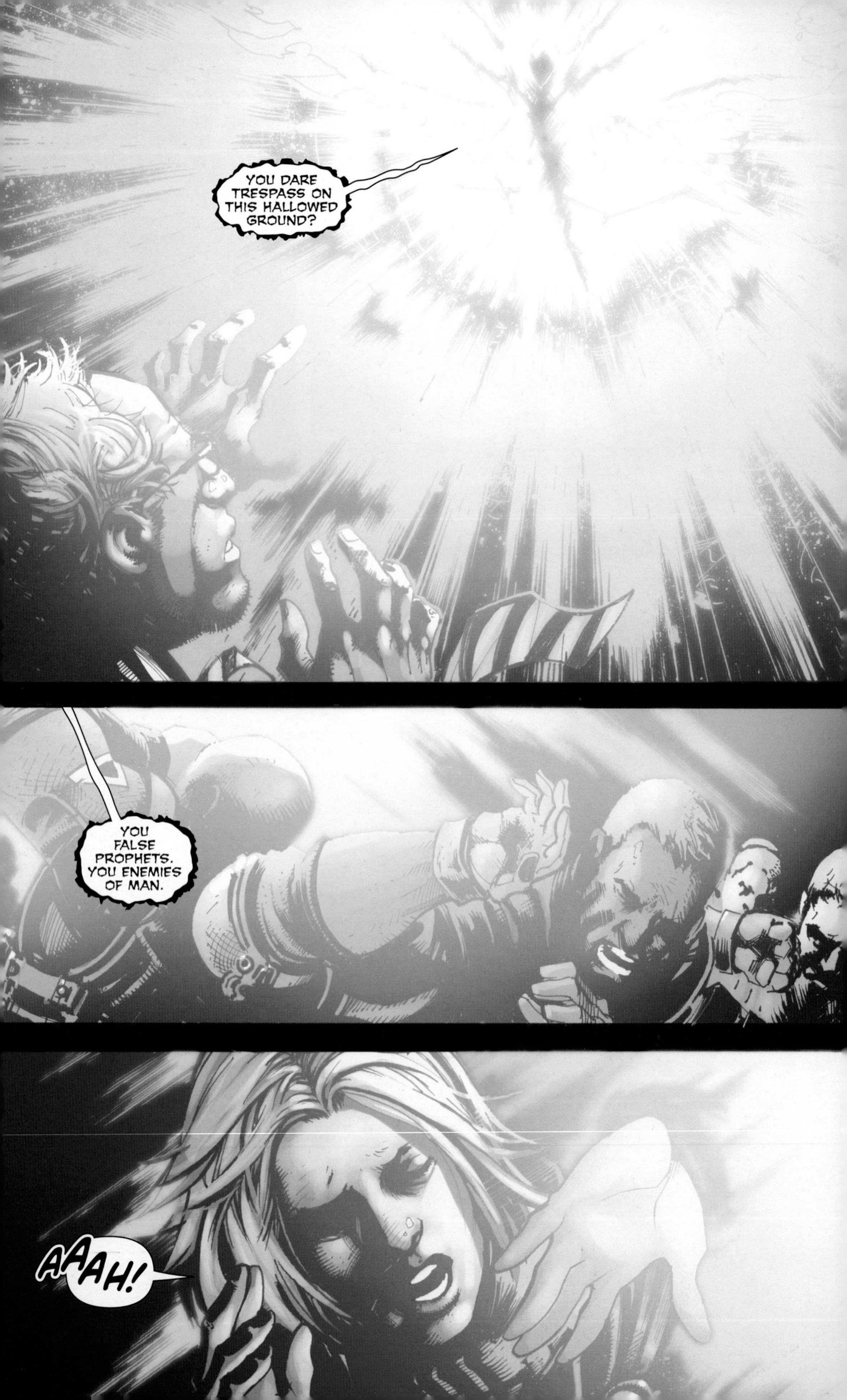
YOU DARE TRESPASS ON THIS HALLOWED GROUND?
YOU FALSE PROPHETS. YOU ENEMIES OF MAN.
AAAH!

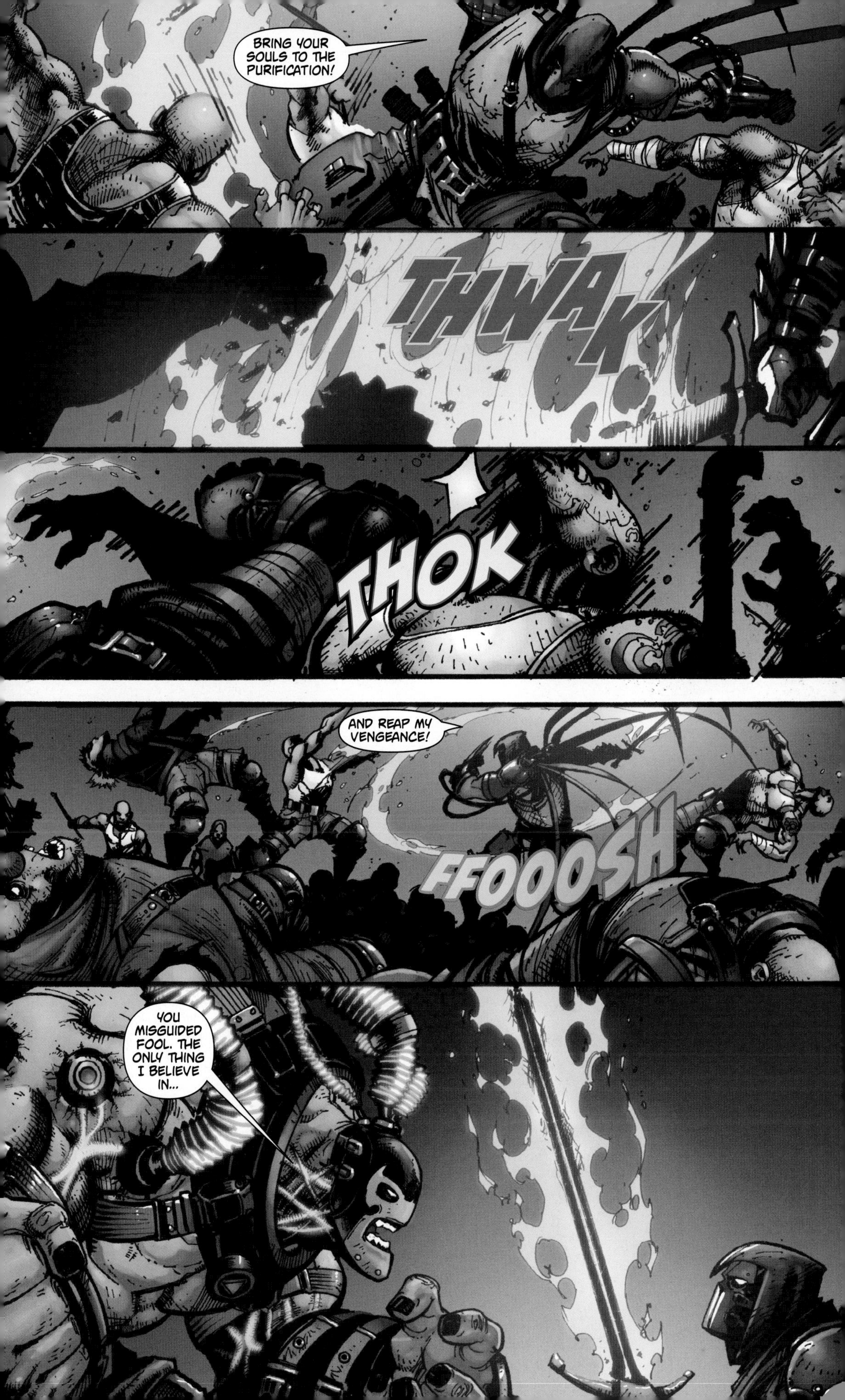
BRING YOUR SOULS TO THE PURIFICATION!
THWAK
THOK
AND REAP MY VENGEANCE!
FFOOOSH
YOU MISGUIDED FOOL. THE ONLY THING I BELIEVE IN...

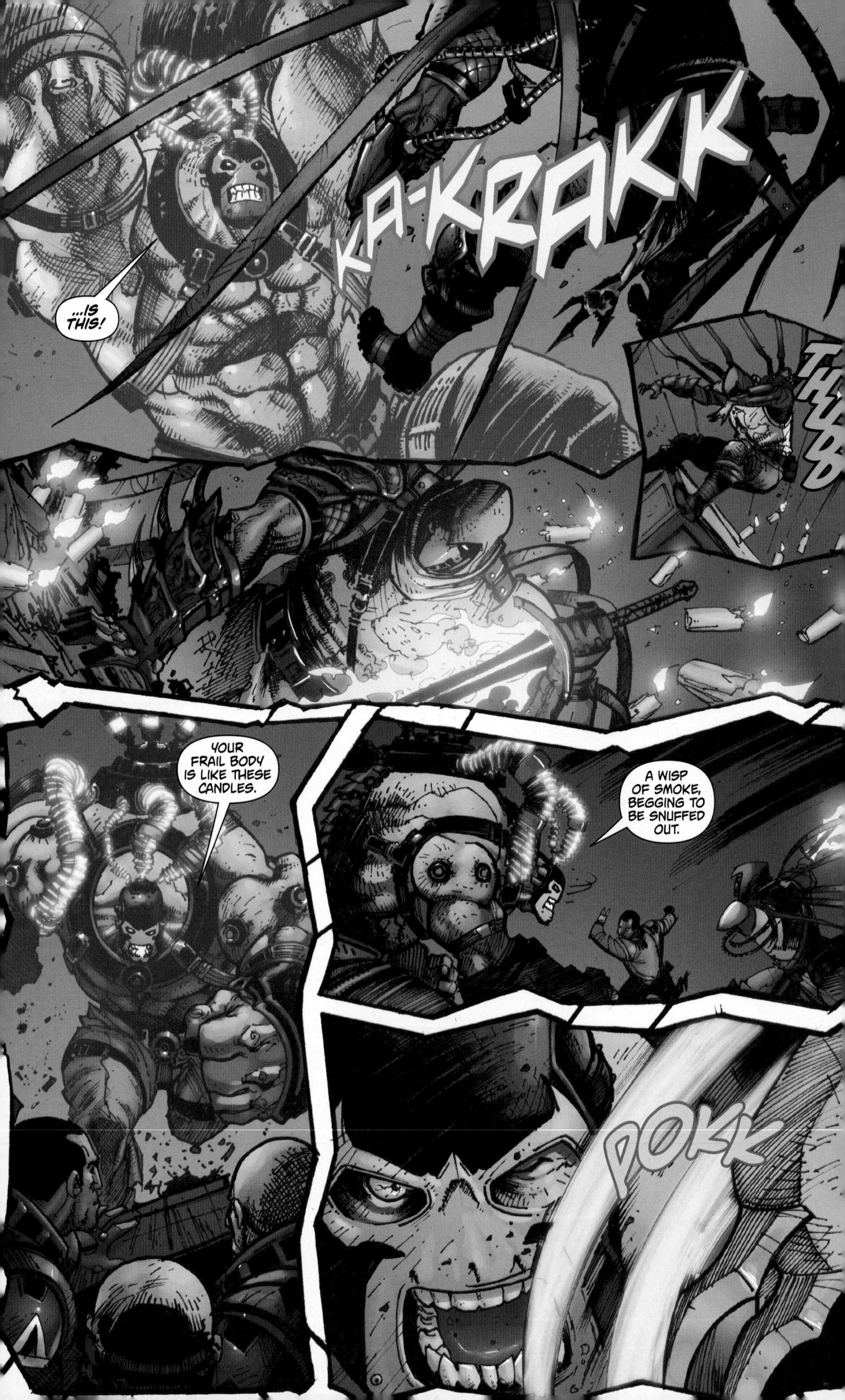
KA-KRAKK
...IS THIS!
YOUR FRAIL BODY IS LIKE THESE CANDLES.
A WISP OF SMOKE, BEGGING TO BE SNUFFED OUT.
POKK

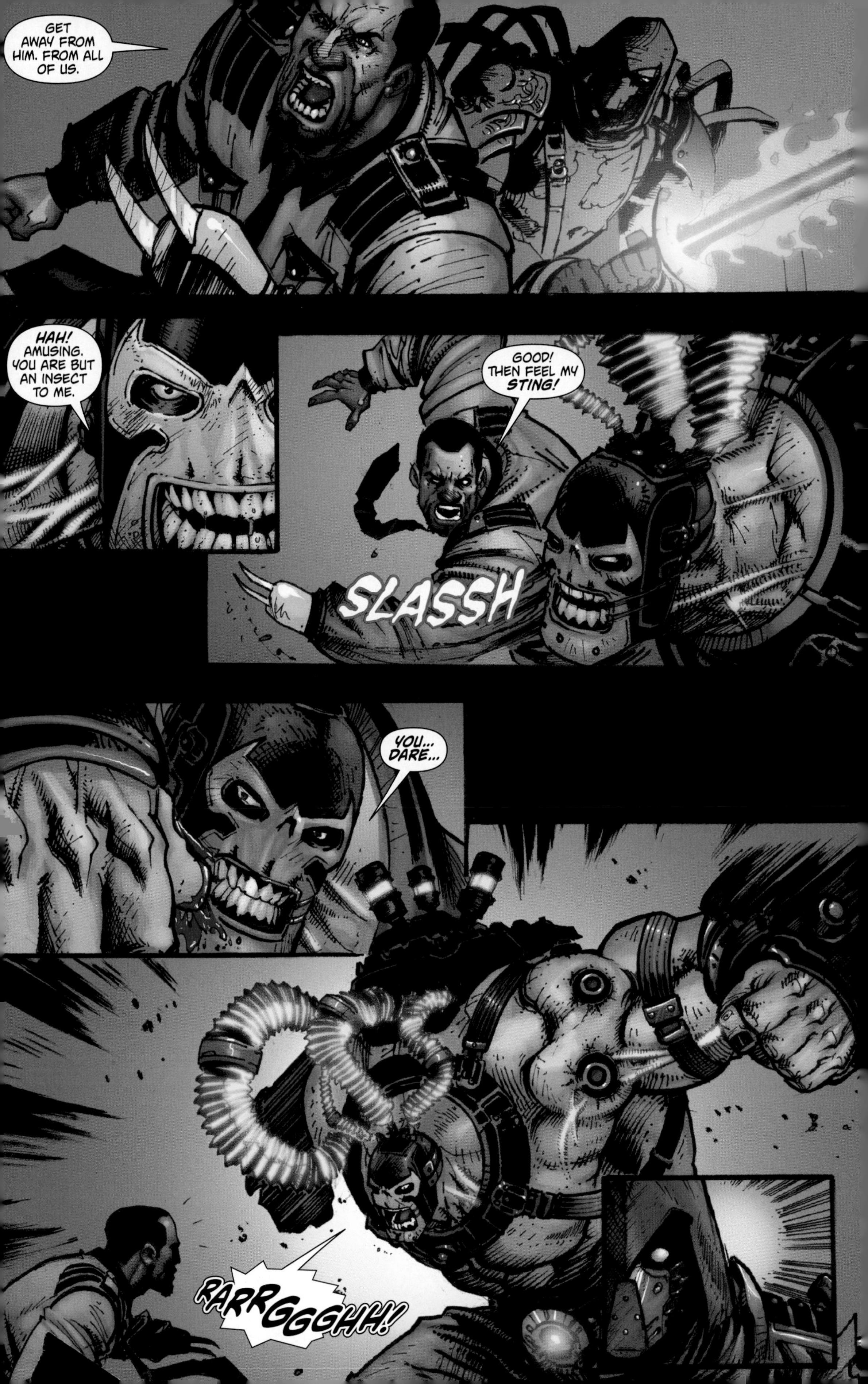
GET AWAY FROM HIM. FROM ALL OF US.
HAH! AMUSING. YOU ARE BUT AN INSECT TO ME.
GOOD! THEN FEEL MY STING!
SLASSH
YOU... DARE...
RARRGGGHH!

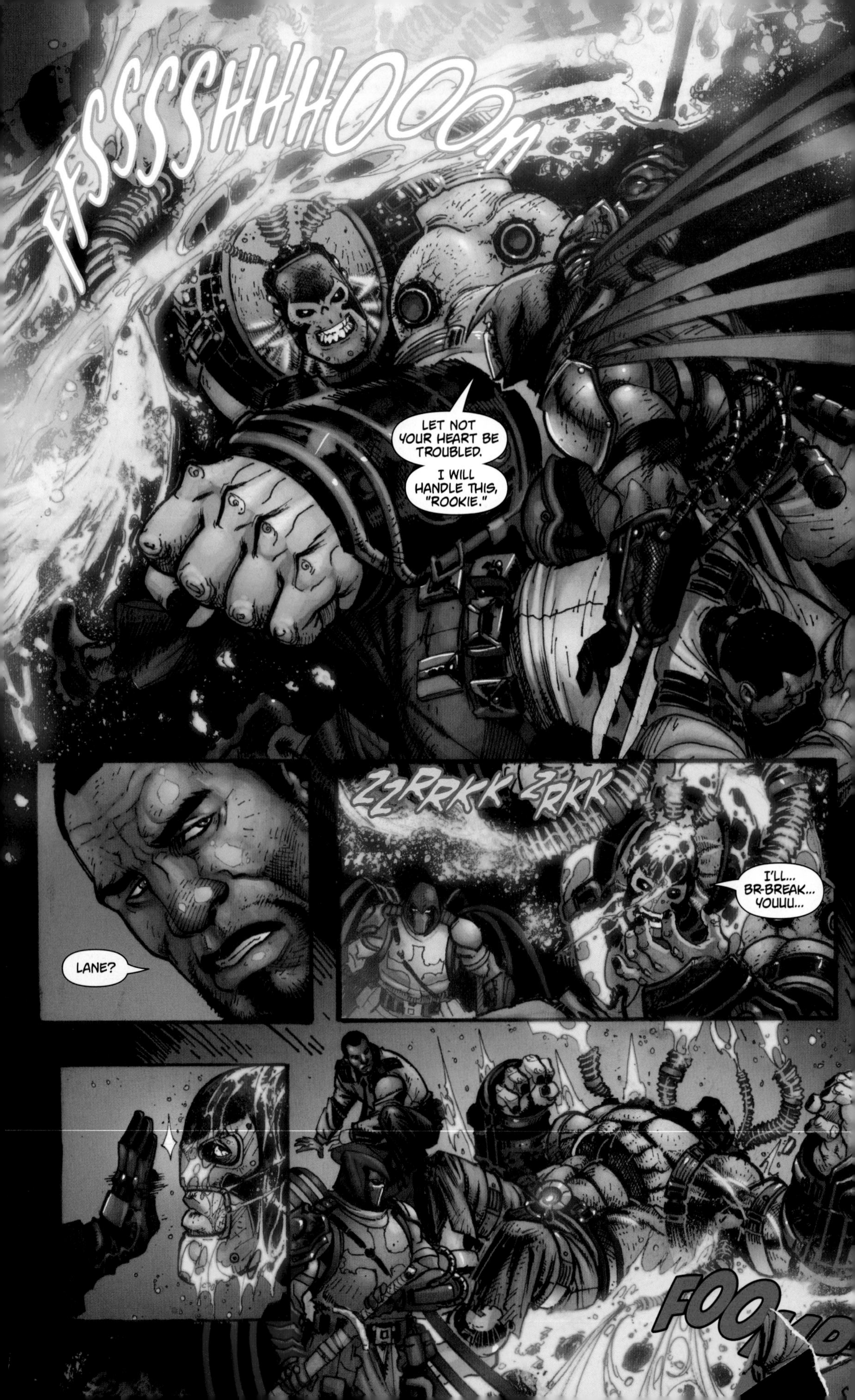
FFSSSSHHHOOOm
LET NOT YOUR HEART BE TROUBLED.
I WILL HANDLE THIS, "ROOKIE."
LANE?
ZZRRKK ZRKK
I'LL... BR-BREAK... YOUUU...
FOO

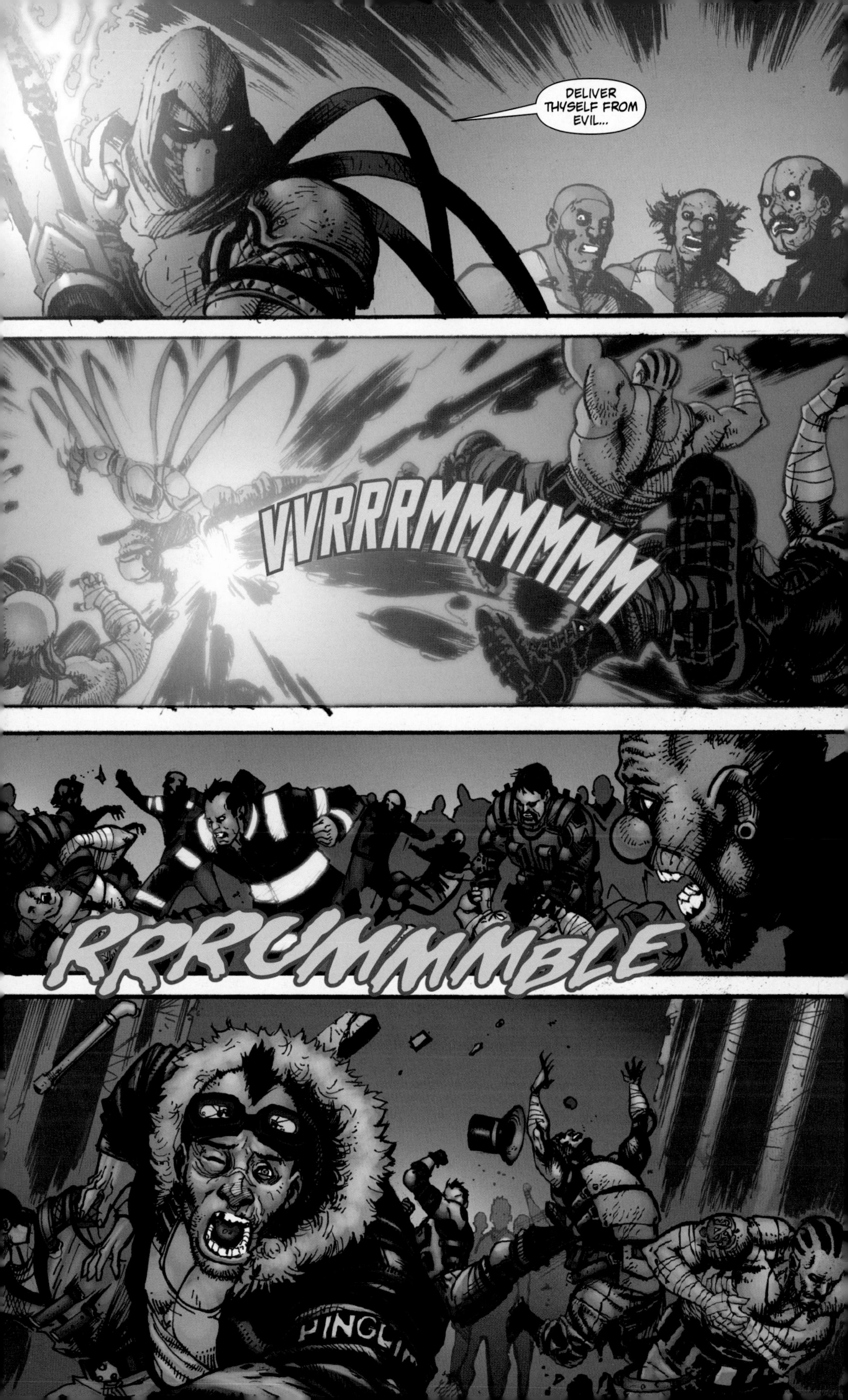
DELIVER THYSELF FROM EVIL...
VVRRRMMMMMM
RRRUMMMBLE
PINGU

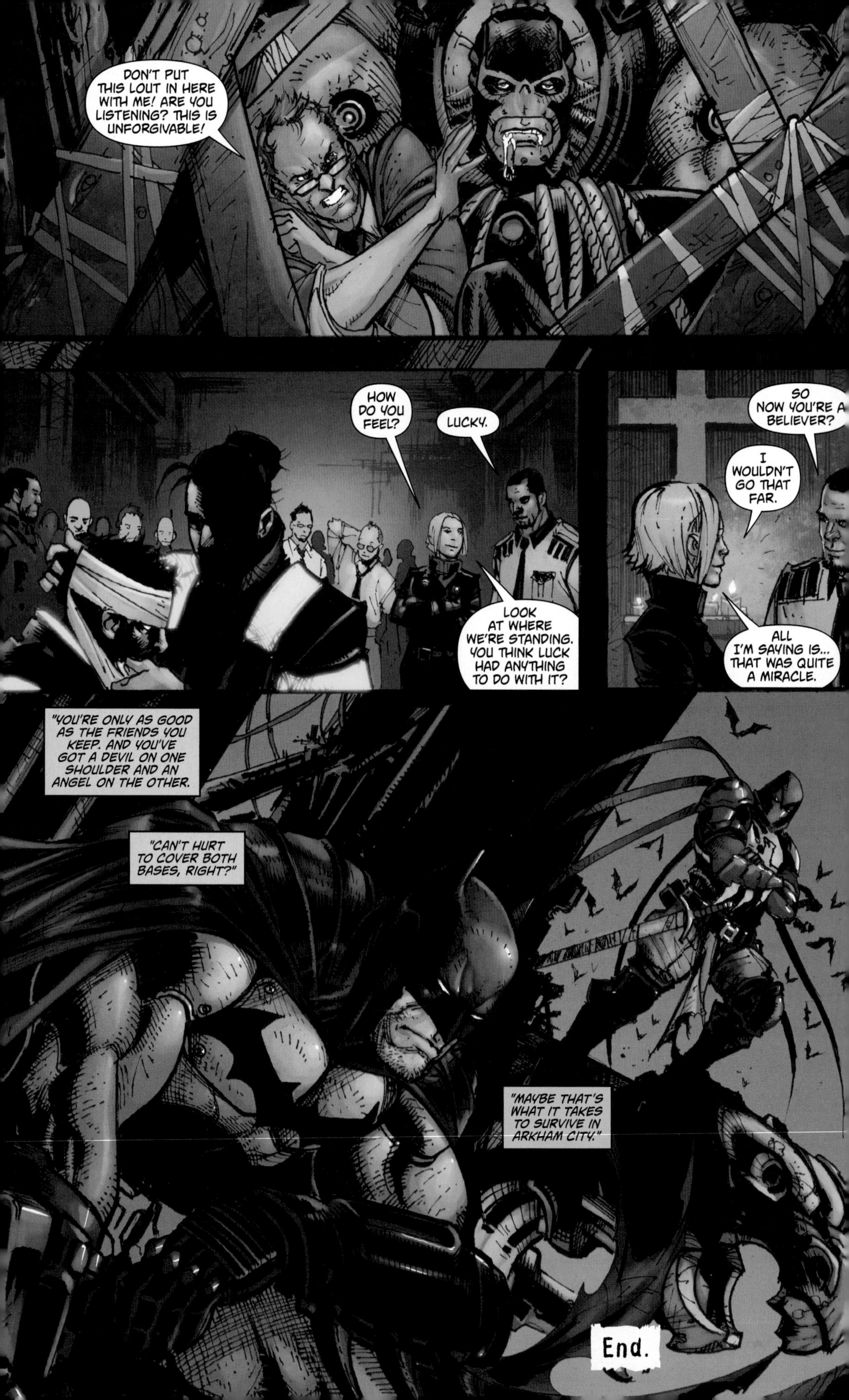
DON'T PUT THIS LOUT IN HERE WITH ME! ARE YOU LISTENING? THIS IS UNFORGIVABLE!
HOW DO YOU FEEL?
LUCKY.
LOOK AT WHERE WE'RE STANDING. YOU THINK LUCK HAD ANYTHING TO DO WITH IT?
SO NOW YOU'RE A BELIEVER?
I WOULDN'T GO THAT FAR.
ALL I'M SAYING IS... THAT WAS QUITE A MIRACLE.
"YOU'RE ONLY AS GOOD AS THE FRIENDS YOU KEEP. AND YOU'VE GOT A DEVIL ON ONE SHOULDER AND AN ANGEL ON THE OTHER.
"CAN'T HURT TO COVER BOTH BASES, RIGHT?"
"MAYBE THAT'S WHAT IT TAKES TO SURVIVE IN ARKHAM CITY."
End.

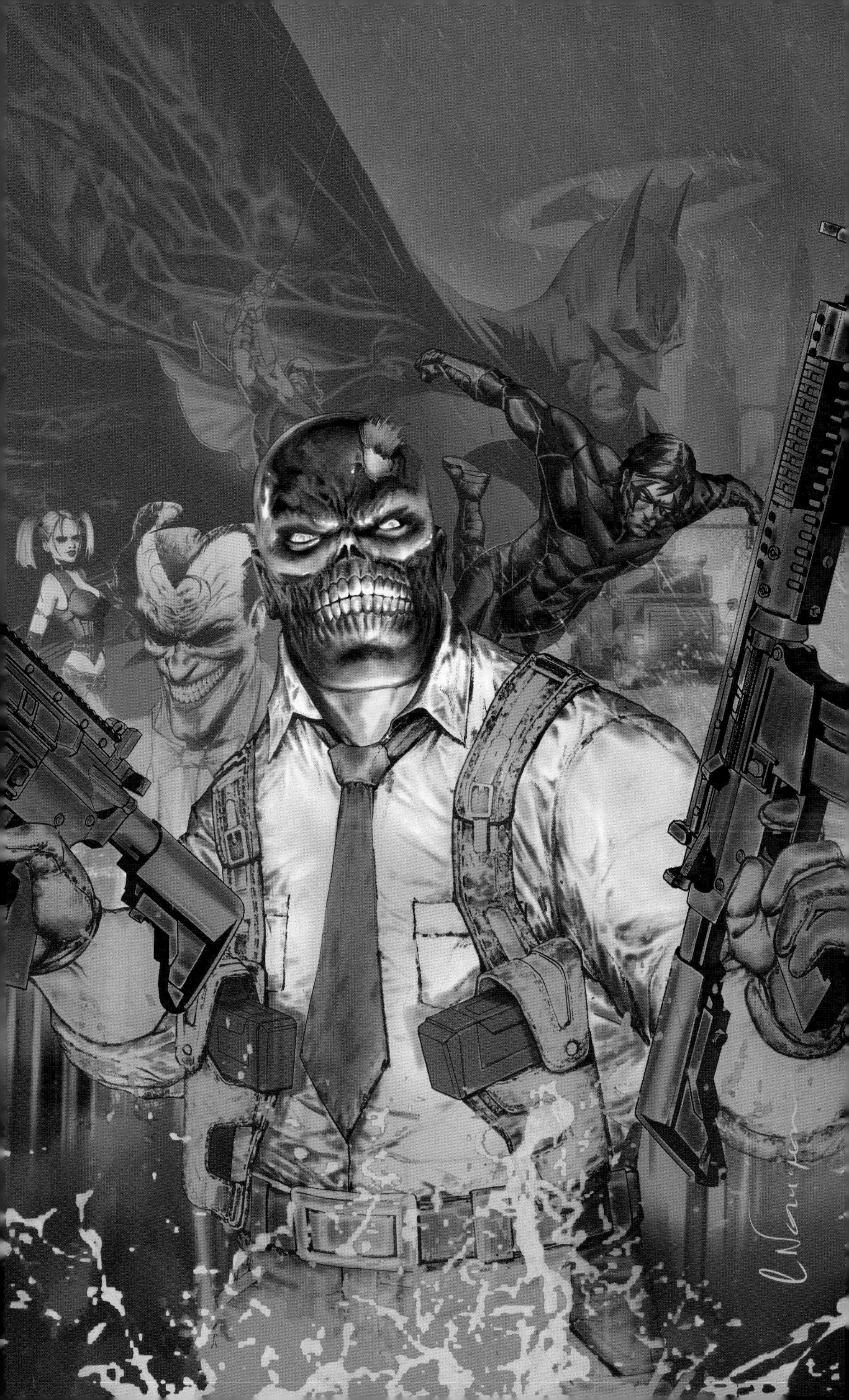

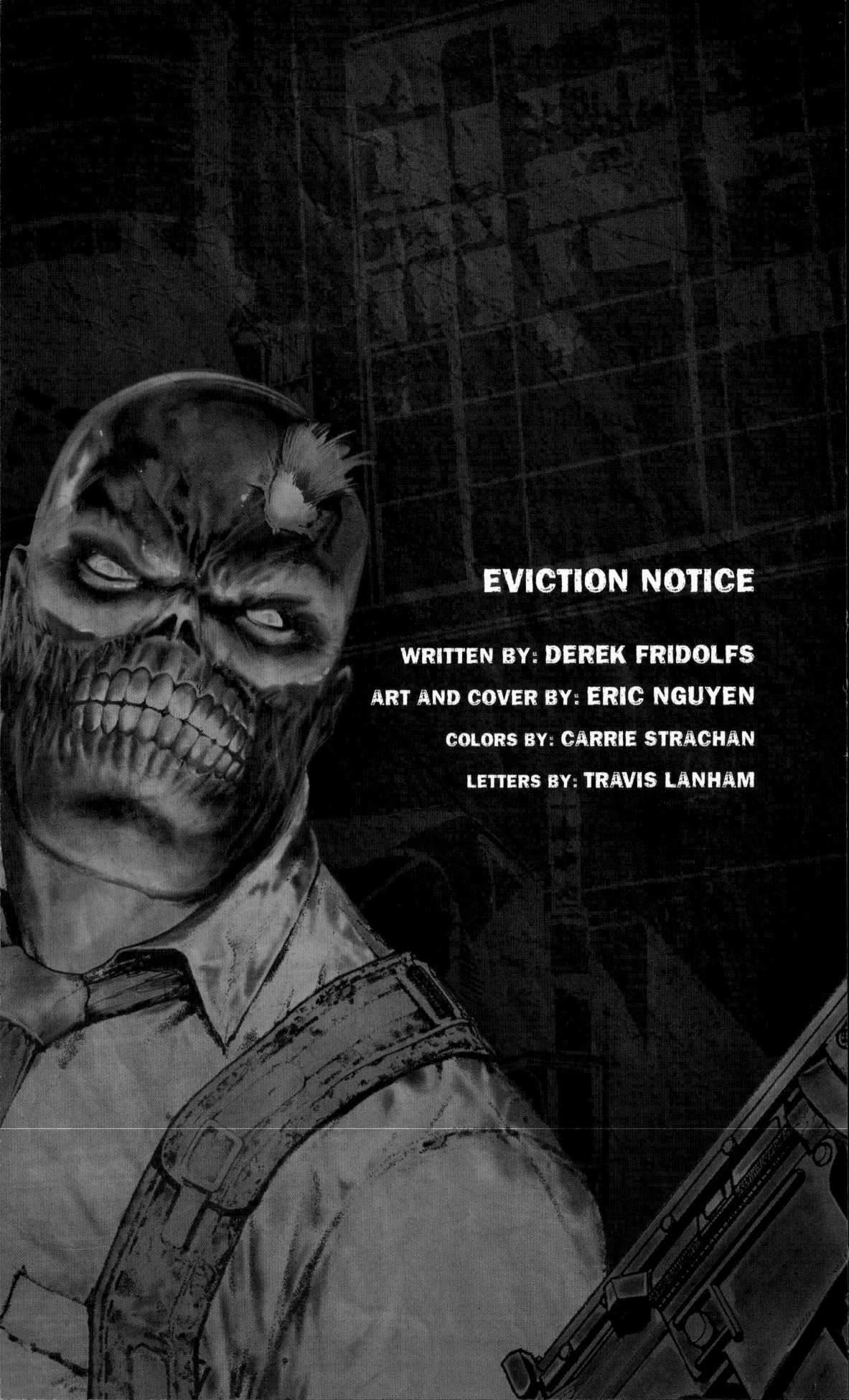

# EVICTION NOTICE

WRITTEN BY: **DEREK FRIDOLFS**

ART AND COVER BY: **ERIC NGUYEN**

COLORS BY: **CARRIE STRACHAN**

LETTERS BY: **TRAVIS LANHAM**

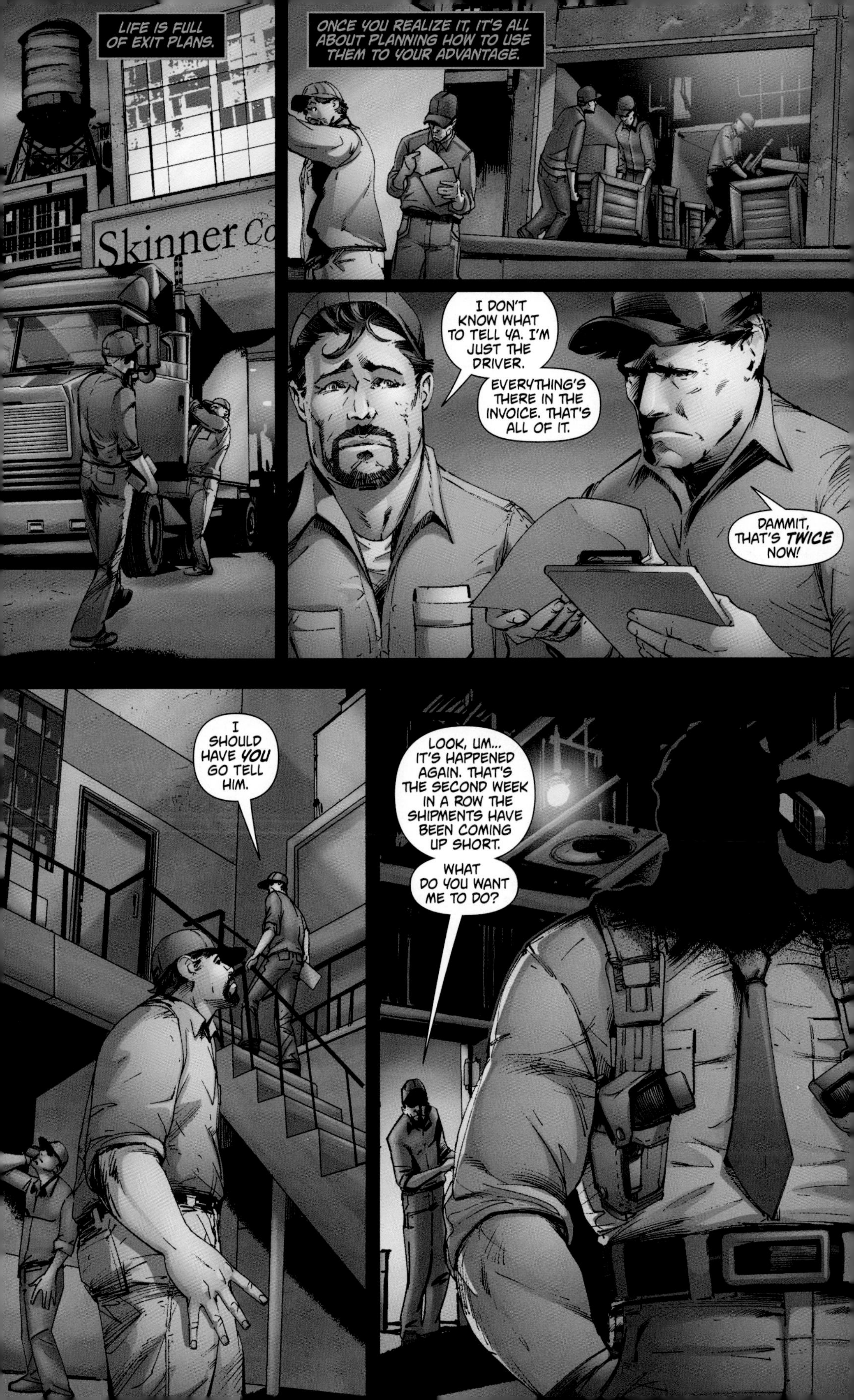
LIFE IS FULL OF EXIT PLANS.
Skinner Co
ONCE YOU REALIZE IT, IT'S ALL ABOUT PLANNING HOW TO USE THEM TO YOUR ADVANTAGE.
I DON'T KNOW WHAT TO TELL YA. I'M JUST THE DRIVER.
EVERYTHING'S THERE IN THE INVOICE. THAT'S ALL OF IT.
DAMMIT, THAT'S TWICE NOW!
I SHOULD HAVE YOU GO TELL HIM.
LOOK, UM... IT'S HAPPENED AGAIN. THAT'S THE SECOND WEEK IN A ROW THE SHIPMENTS HAVE BEEN COMING UP SHORT.
WHAT DO YOU WANT ME TO DO?

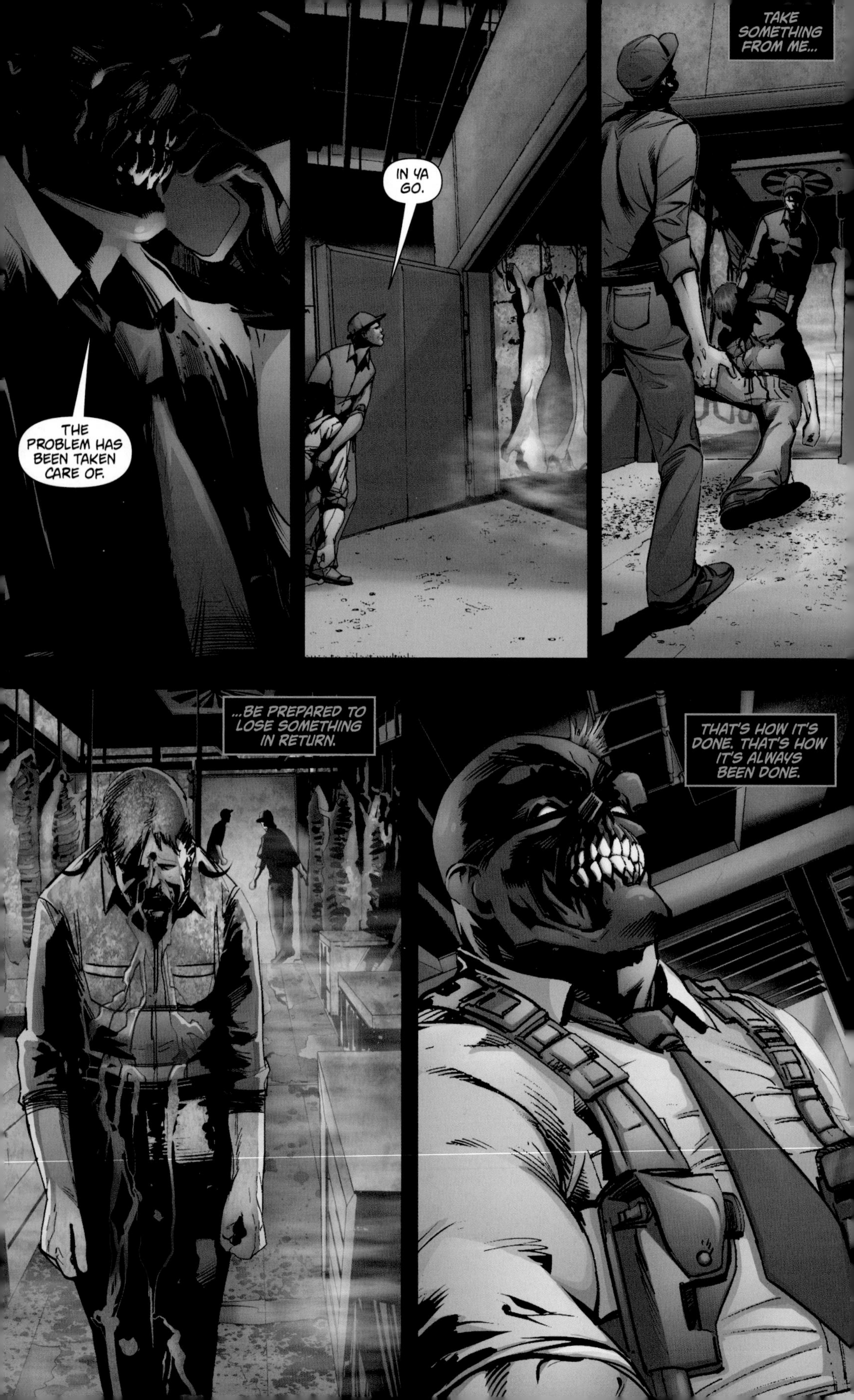
THE PROBLEM HAS BEEN TAKEN CARE OF.
IN YA GO.
TAKE SOMETHING FROM ME...
...BE PREPARED TO LOSE SOMETHING IN RETURN.
THAT'S HOW IT'S DONE. THAT'S HOW IT'S ALWAYS BEEN DONE.

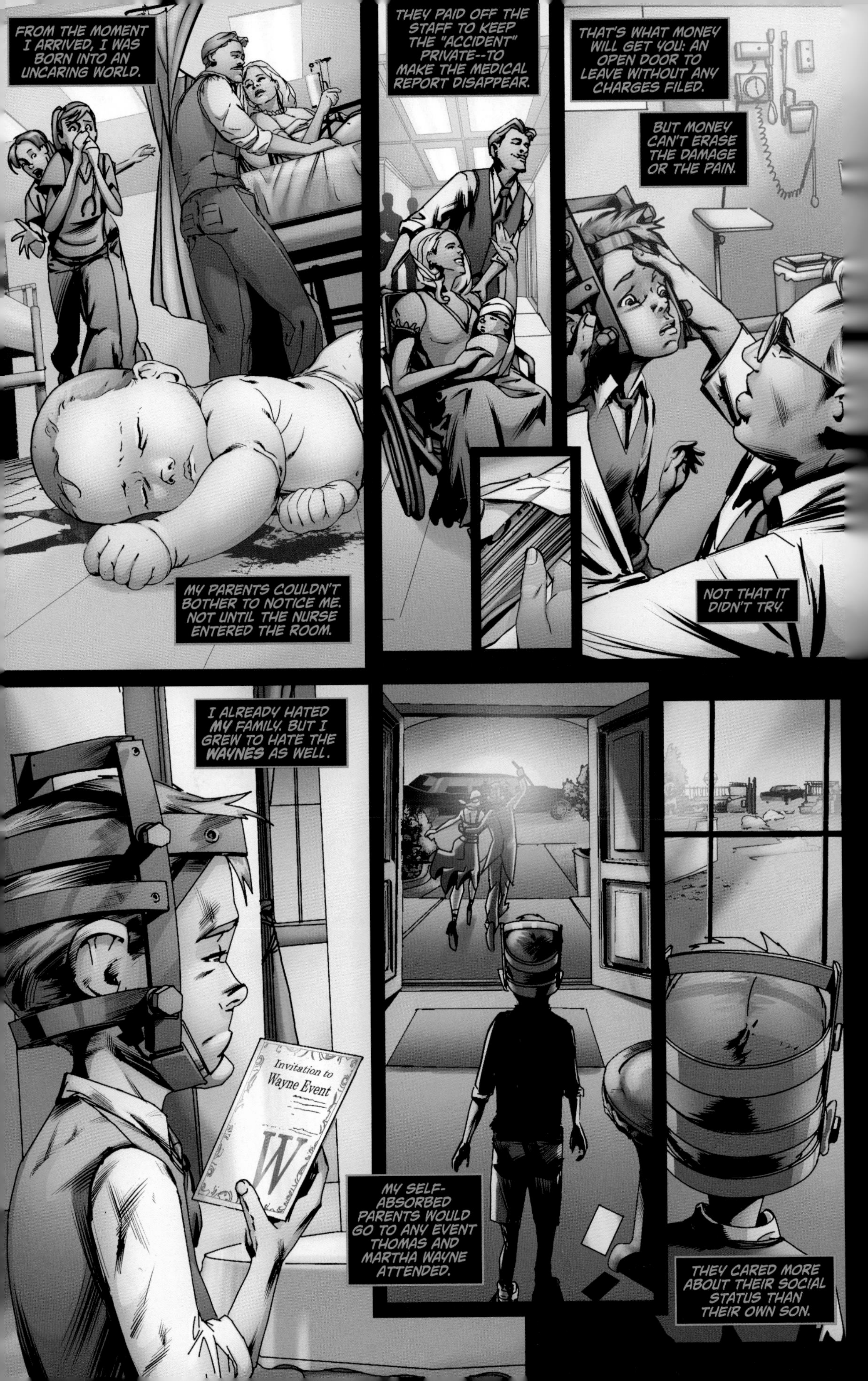
FROM THE MOMENT I ARRIVED, I WAS BORN INTO AN UNCARING WORLD.
MY PARENTS COULDN'T BOTHER TO NOTICE ME. NOT UNTIL THE NURSE ENTERED THE ROOM.
THEY PAID OFF THE STAFF TO KEEP THE "ACCIDENT" PRIVATE--TO MAKE THE MEDICAL REPORT DISAPPEAR.
THAT'S WHAT MONEY WILL GET YOU: AN OPEN DOOR TO LEAVE WITHOUT ANY CHARGES FILED.
BUT MONEY CAN'T ERASE THE DAMAGE OR THE PAIN.
NOT THAT IT DIDN'T TRY.
I ALREADY HATED MY FAMILY. BUT I GREW TO HATE THE WAYNES AS WELL.
Invitation to Wayne Event
W
MY SELF-ABSORBED PARENTS WOULD GO TO ANY EVENT THOMAS AND MARTHA WAYNE ATTENDED.
THEY CARED MORE ABOUT THEIR SOCIAL STATUS THAN THEIR OWN SON.

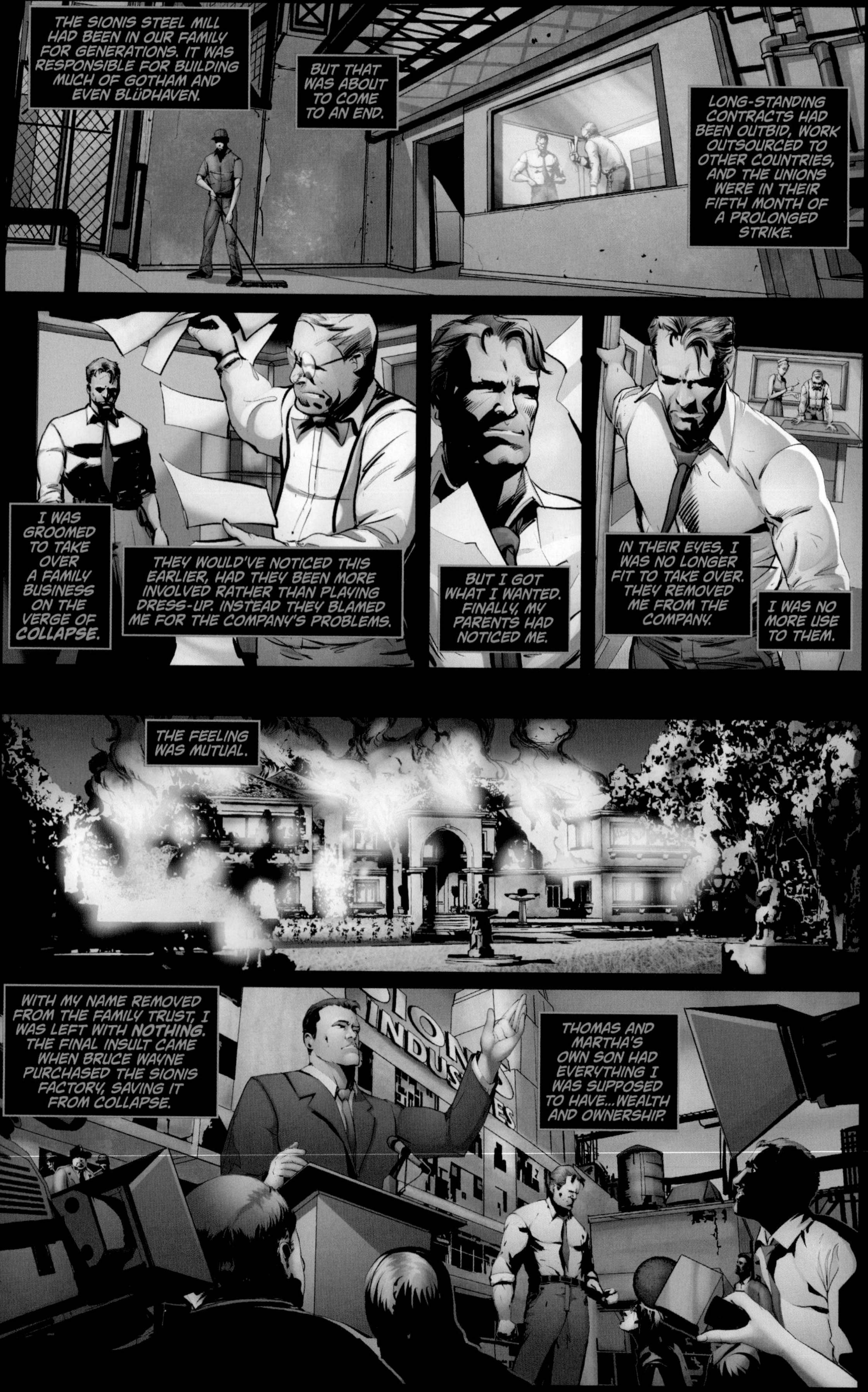
THE SIONIS STEEL MILL HAD BEEN IN OUR FAMILY FOR GENERATIONS. IT WAS RESPONSIBLE FOR BUILDING MUCH OF GOTHAM AND EVEN BLÜDHAVEN.
BUT THAT WAS ABOUT TO COME TO AN END.
LONG-STANDING CONTRACTS HAD BEEN OUTBID, WORK OUTSOURCED TO OTHER COUNTRIES, AND THE UNIONS WERE IN THEIR FIFTH MONTH OF A PROLONGED STRIKE.
I WAS GROOMED TO TAKE OVER A FAMILY BUSINESS ON THE VERGE OF COLLAPSE.
THEY WOULD'VE NOTICED THIS EARLIER, HAD THEY BEEN MORE INVOLVED RATHER THAN PLAYING DRESS-UP. INSTEAD THEY BLAMED ME FOR THE COMPANY'S PROBLEMS.
BUT I GOT WHAT I WANTED. FINALLY, MY PARENTS HAD NOTICED ME.
IN THEIR EYES, I WAS NO LONGER FIT TO TAKE OVER. THEY REMOVED ME FROM THE COMPANY.
I WAS NO MORE USE TO THEM.
THE FEELING WAS MUTUAL.
WITH MY NAME REMOVED FROM THE FAMILY TRUST, I WAS LEFT WITH NOTHING. THE FINAL INSULT CAME WHEN BRUCE WAYNE PURCHASED THE SIONIS FACTORY, SAVING IT FROM COLLAPSE.
THOMAS AND MARTHA'S OWN SON HAD EVERYTHING I WAS SUPPOSED TO HAVE...WEALTH AND OWNERSHIP.

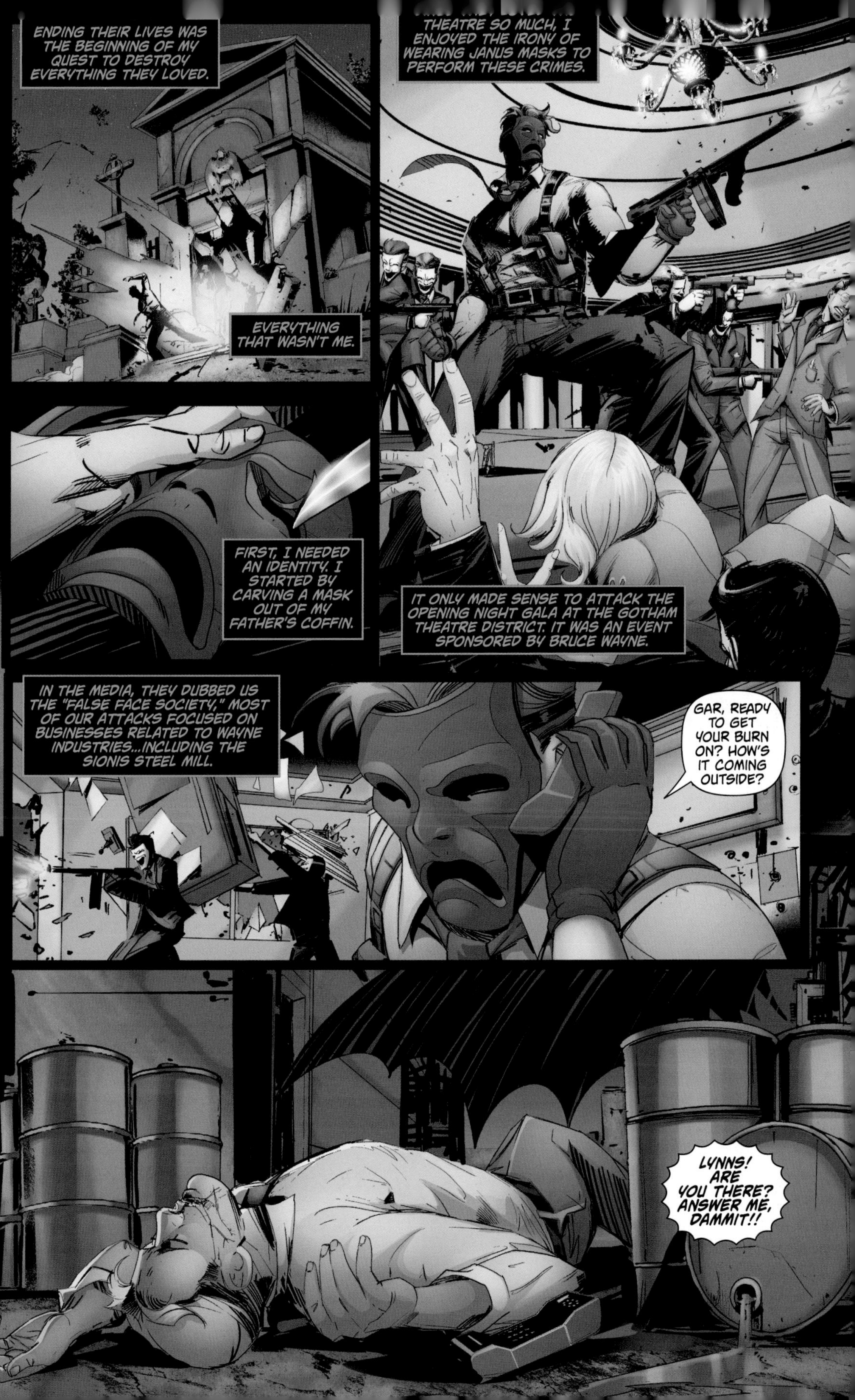

ENDING THEIR LIVES WAS THE BEGINNING OF MY QUEST TO DESTROY EVERYTHING THEY LOVED.
EVERYTHING THAT WASN'T ME.
THEATRE SO MUCH, I ENJOYED THE IRONY OF WEARING JANUS MASKS TO PERFORM THESE CRIMES.
FIRST, I NEEDED AN IDENTITY. I STARTED BY CARVING A MASK OUT OF MY FATHER'S COFFIN.
IT ONLY MADE SENSE TO ATTACK THE OPENING NIGHT GALA AT THE GOTHAM THEATRE DISTRICT. IT WAS AN EVENT SPONSORED BY BRUCE WAYNE.
IN THE MEDIA, THEY DUBBED US THE "FALSE FACE SOCIETY," MOST OF OUR ATTACKS FOCUSED ON BUSINESSES RELATED TO WAYNE INDUSTRIES...INCLUDING THE SIONIS STEEL MILL.
GAR, READY TO GET YOUR BURN ON? HOW'S IT COMING OUTSIDE?
LYNNS! ARE YOU THERE? ANSWER ME, DAMMIT!!

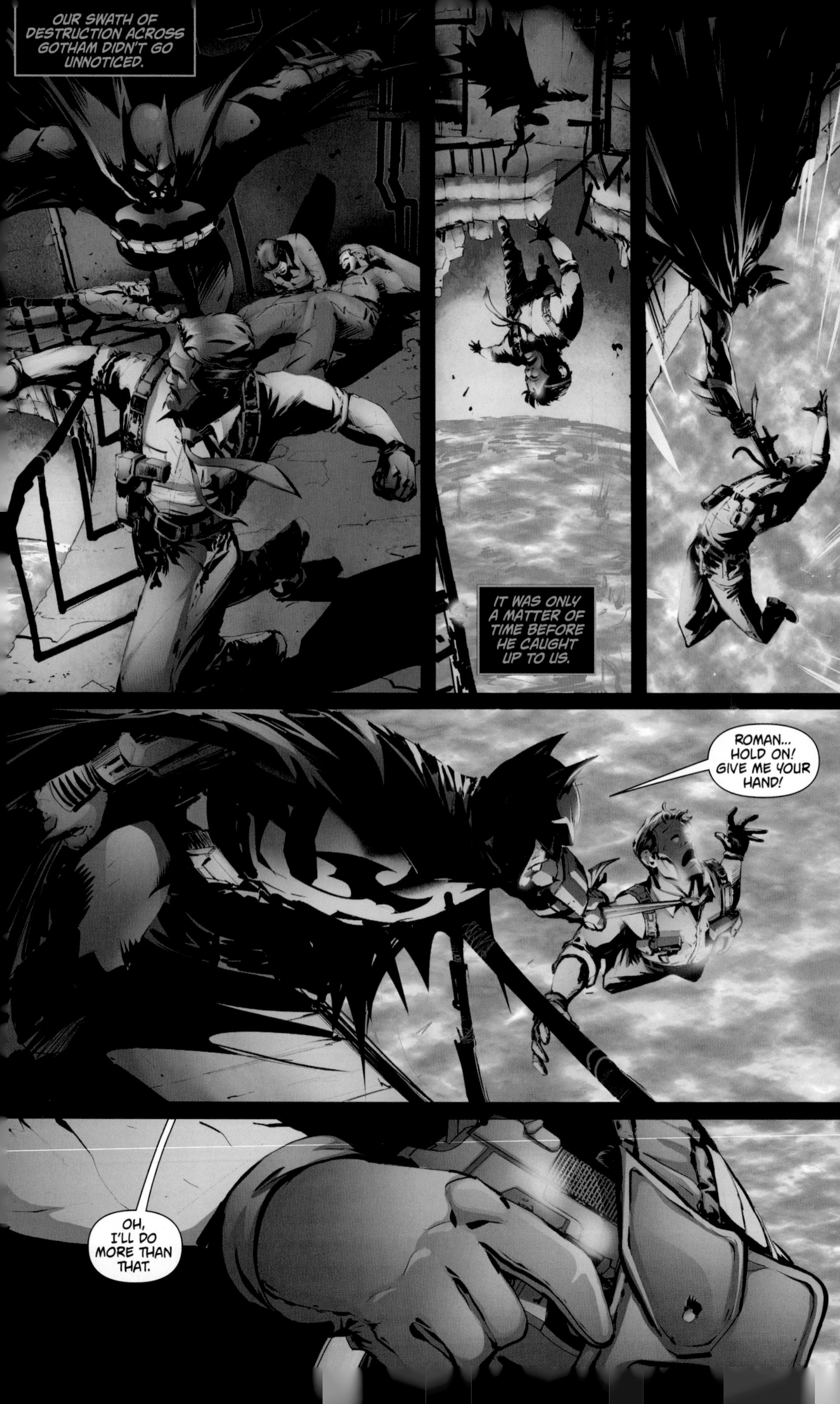
OUR SWATH OF DESTRUCTION ACROSS GOTHAM DIDN'T GO UNNOTICED.
IT WAS ONLY A MATTER OF TIME BEFORE HE CAUGHT UP TO US.
ROMAN... HOLD ON! GIVE ME YOUR HAND!
OH, I'LL DO MORE THAN THAT.

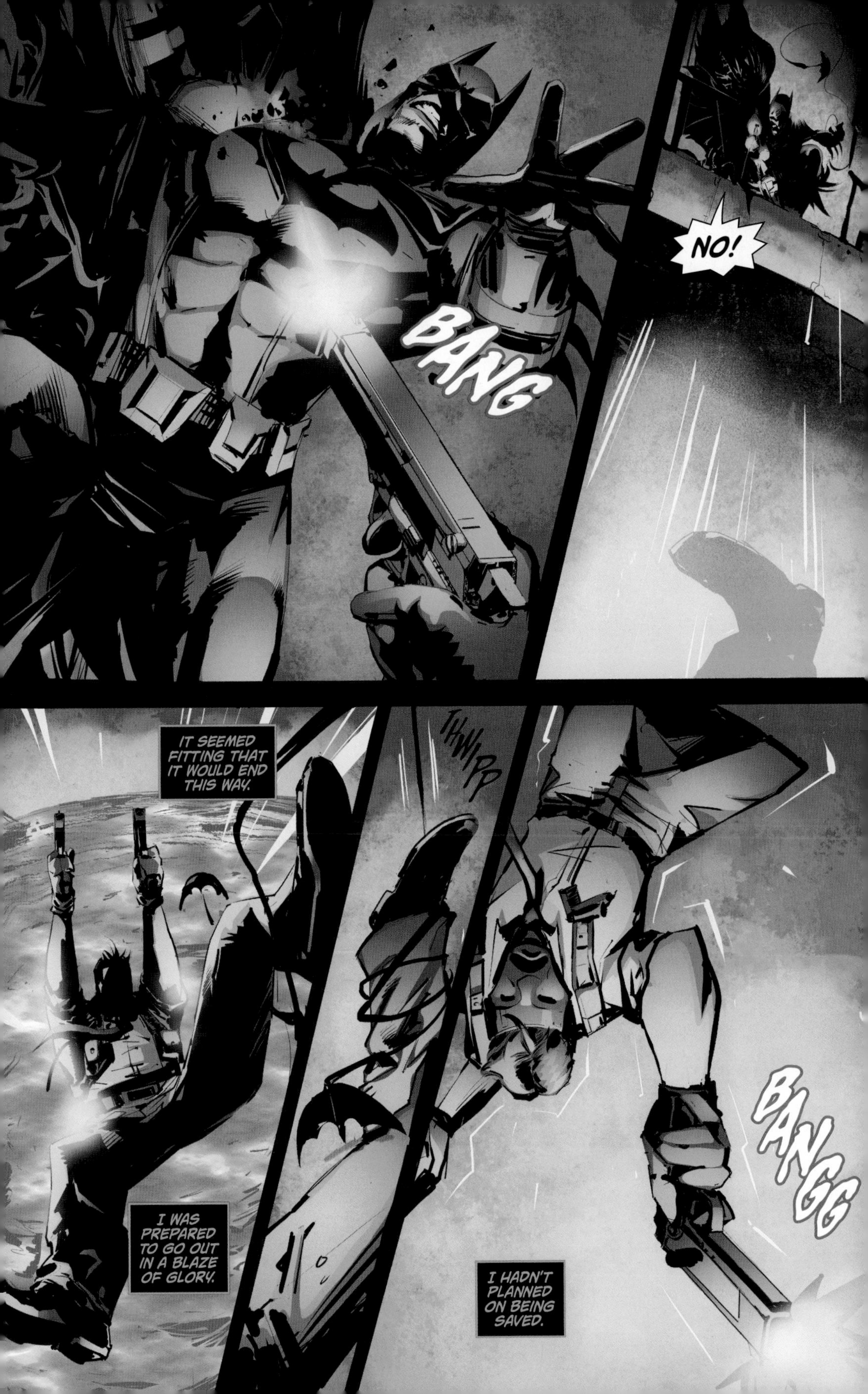
BANG
NO!
IT SEEMED FITTING THAT IT WOULD END THIS WAY.
THWIPP
I WAS PREPARED TO GO OUT IN A BLAZE OF GLORY.
I HADN'T PLANNED ON BEING SAVED.
BANGG

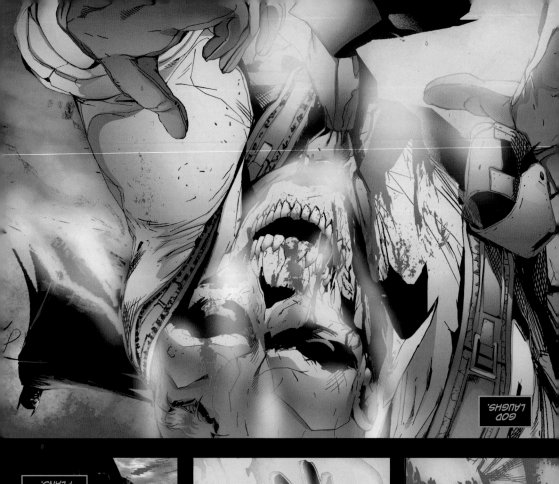

GOD LAUGHS,

BUT YOU KNOW WHAT THEY SAY ABOUT MAKING PLANS.

UAAARGHH!

BA-DOOM

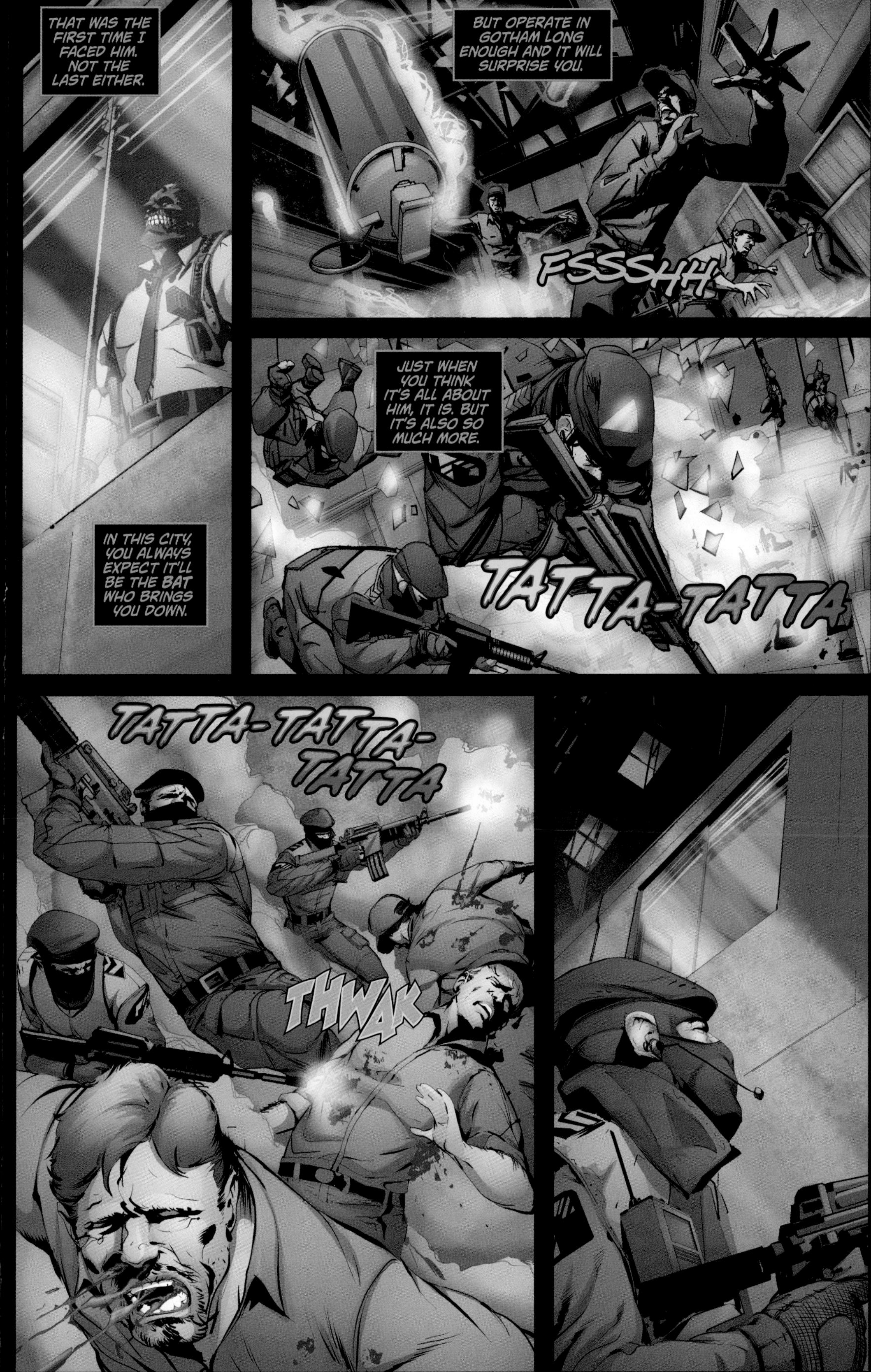
THAT WAS THE FIRST TIME I FACED HIM. NOT THE LAST EITHER.
BUT OPERATE IN GOTHAM LONG ENOUGH AND IT WILL SURPRISE YOU.
FSSSHH
IN THIS CITY, YOU ALWAYS EXPECT IT'LL BE THE BAT WHO BRINGS YOU DOWN.
JUST WHEN YOU THINK IT'S ALL ABOUT HIM, IT IS. BUT IT'S ALSO SO MUCH MORE.
TATTA-TATTA
TATTA-TATTA-TATTA
THWAK

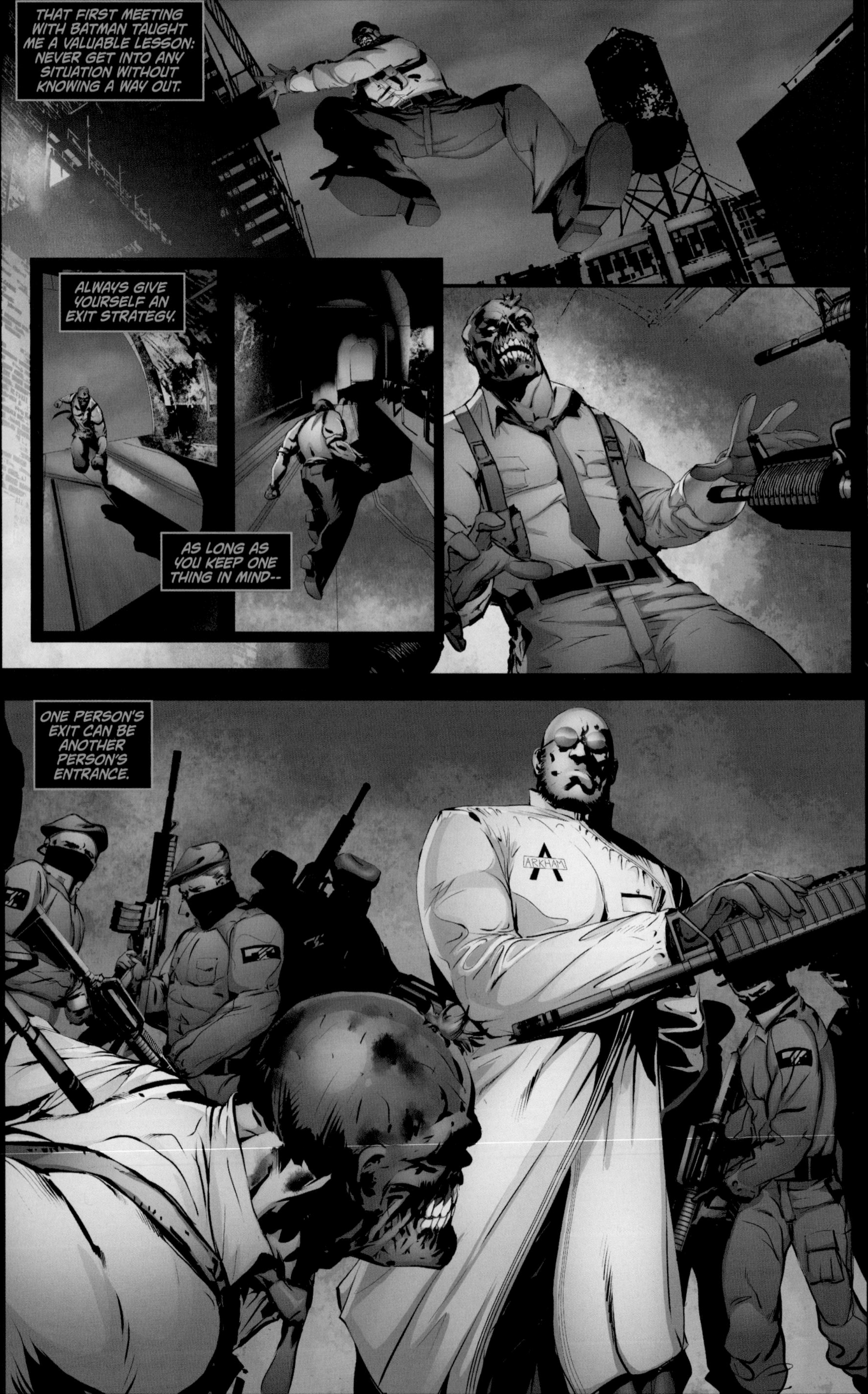
THAT FIRST MEETING WITH BATMAN TAUGHT ME A VALUABLE LESSON: NEVER GET INTO ANY SITUATION WITHOUT KNOWING A WAY OUT.
ALWAYS GIVE YOURSELF AN EXIT STRATEGY.
AS LONG AS YOU KEEP ONE THING IN MIND--
ONE PERSON'S EXIT CAN BE ANOTHER PERSON'S ENTRANCE.
ARKHAM

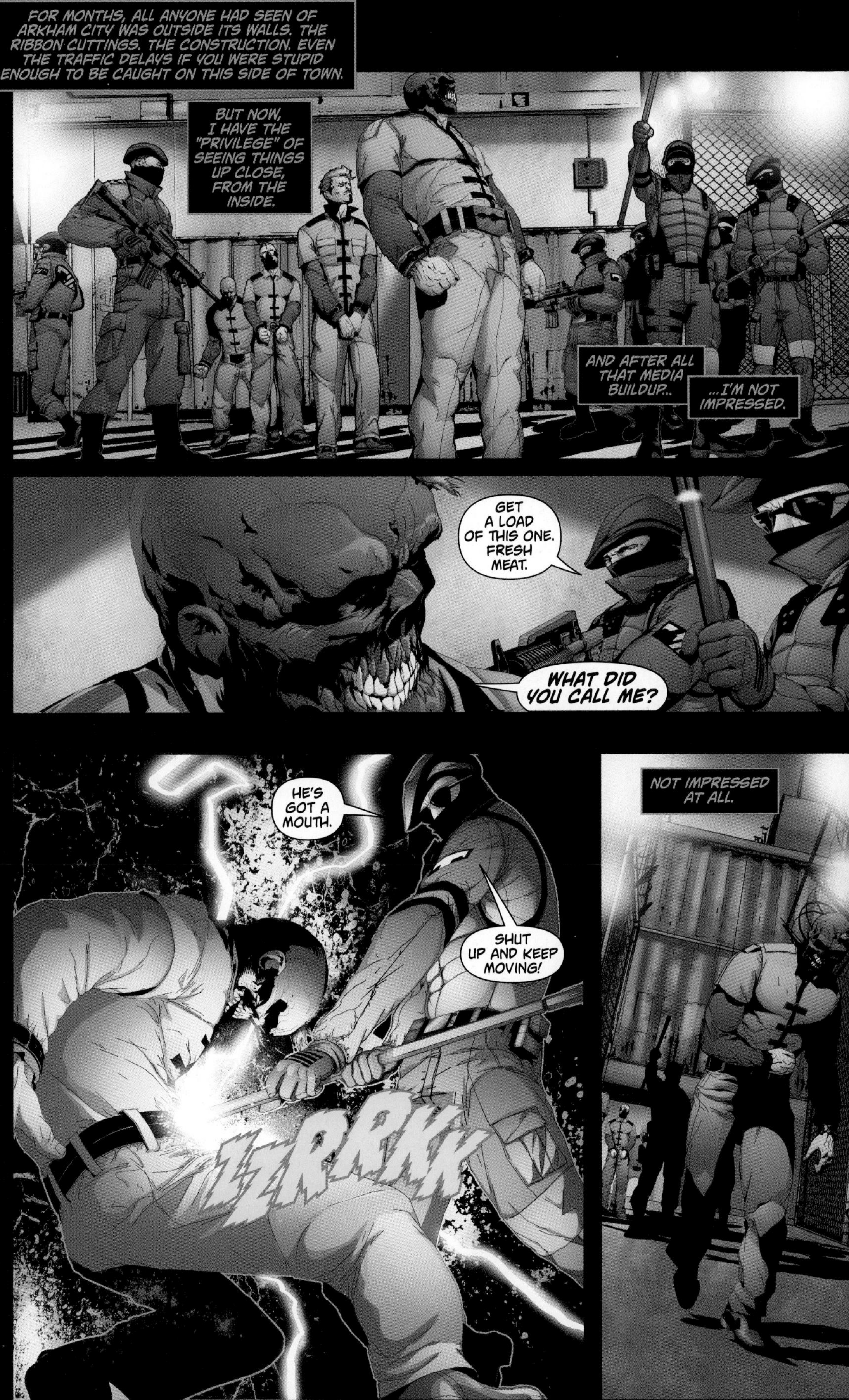
FOR MONTHS, ALL ANYONE HAD SEEN OF ARKHAM CITY WAS OUTSIDE ITS WALLS. THE RIBBON CUTTINGS. THE CONSTRUCTION. EVEN THE TRAFFIC DELAYS IF YOU WERE STUPID ENOUGH TO BE CAUGHT ON THIS SIDE OF TOWN.
BUT NOW, I HAVE THE "PRIVILEGE" OF SEEING THINGS UP CLOSE, FROM THE INSIDE.
AND AFTER ALL THAT MEDIA BUILDUP...
...I'M NOT IMPRESSED.
GET A LOAD OF THIS ONE. FRESH MEAT.
WHAT DID YOU CALL ME?
HE'S GOT A MOUTH.
SHUT UP AND KEEP MOVING!
ZZRRKK
NOT IMPRESSED AT ALL.

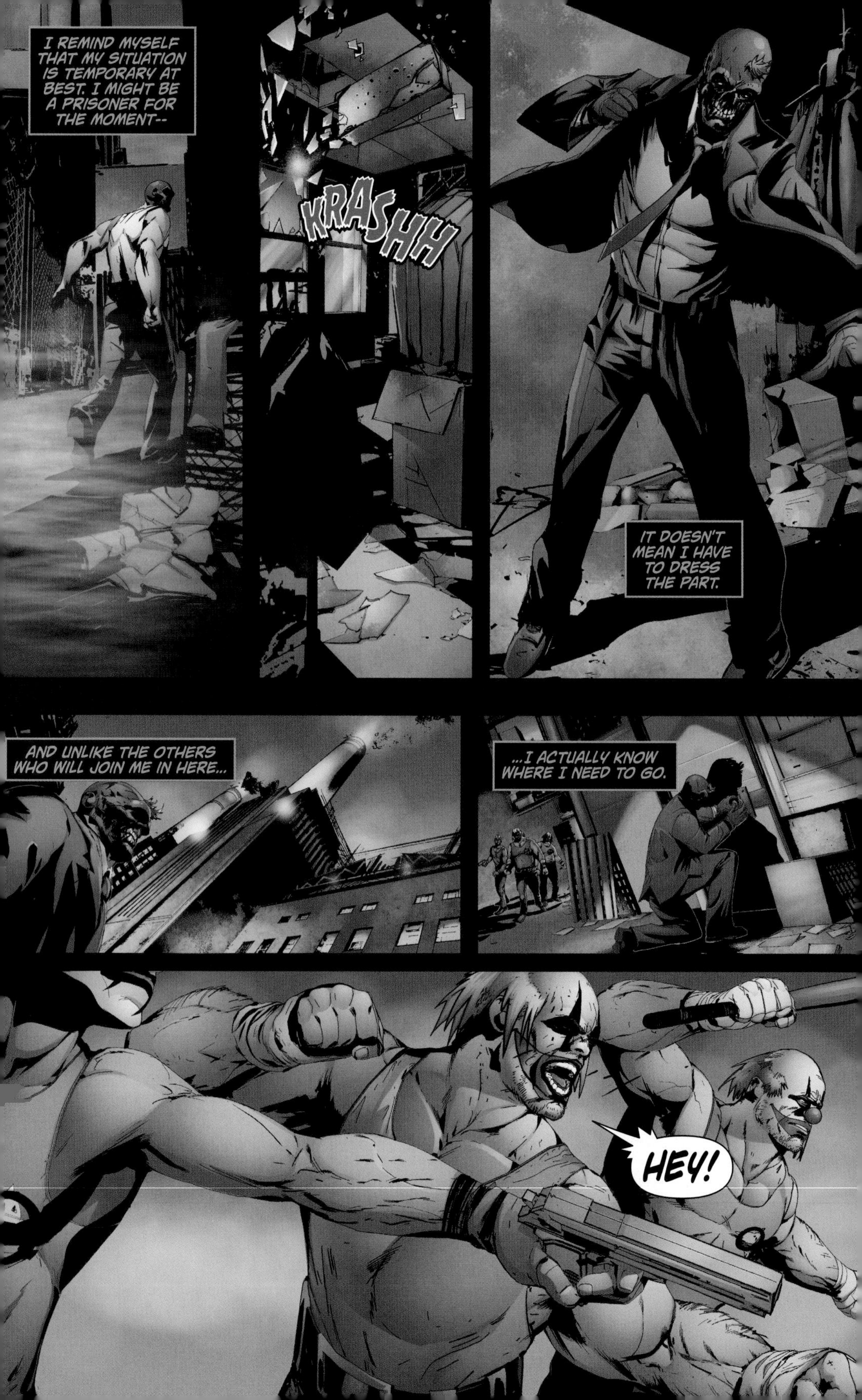
I REMIND MYSELF THAT MY SITUATION IS TEMPORARY AT BEST. I MIGHT BE A PRISONER FOR THE MOMENT--
KRASHH
IT DOESN'T MEAN I HAVE TO DRESS THE PART.
AND UNLIKE THE OTHERS WHO WILL JOIN ME IN HERE...
...I ACTUALLY KNOW WHERE I NEED TO GO.
HEY!

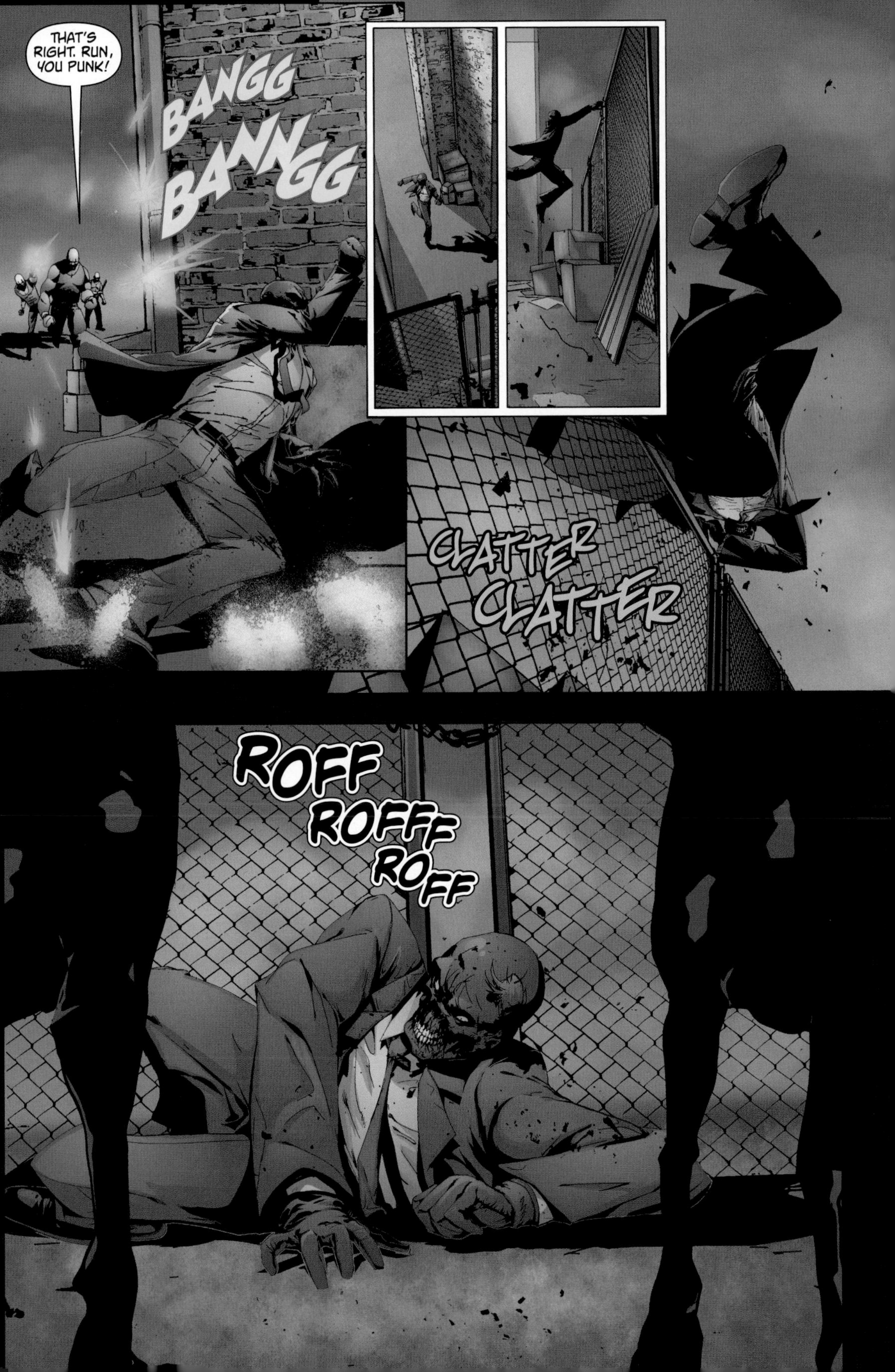
THAT'S RIGHT. RUN, YOU PUNK!
BANGG
BANNGG
CLATTER
CLATTER
ROFF
ROFFF
ROFF

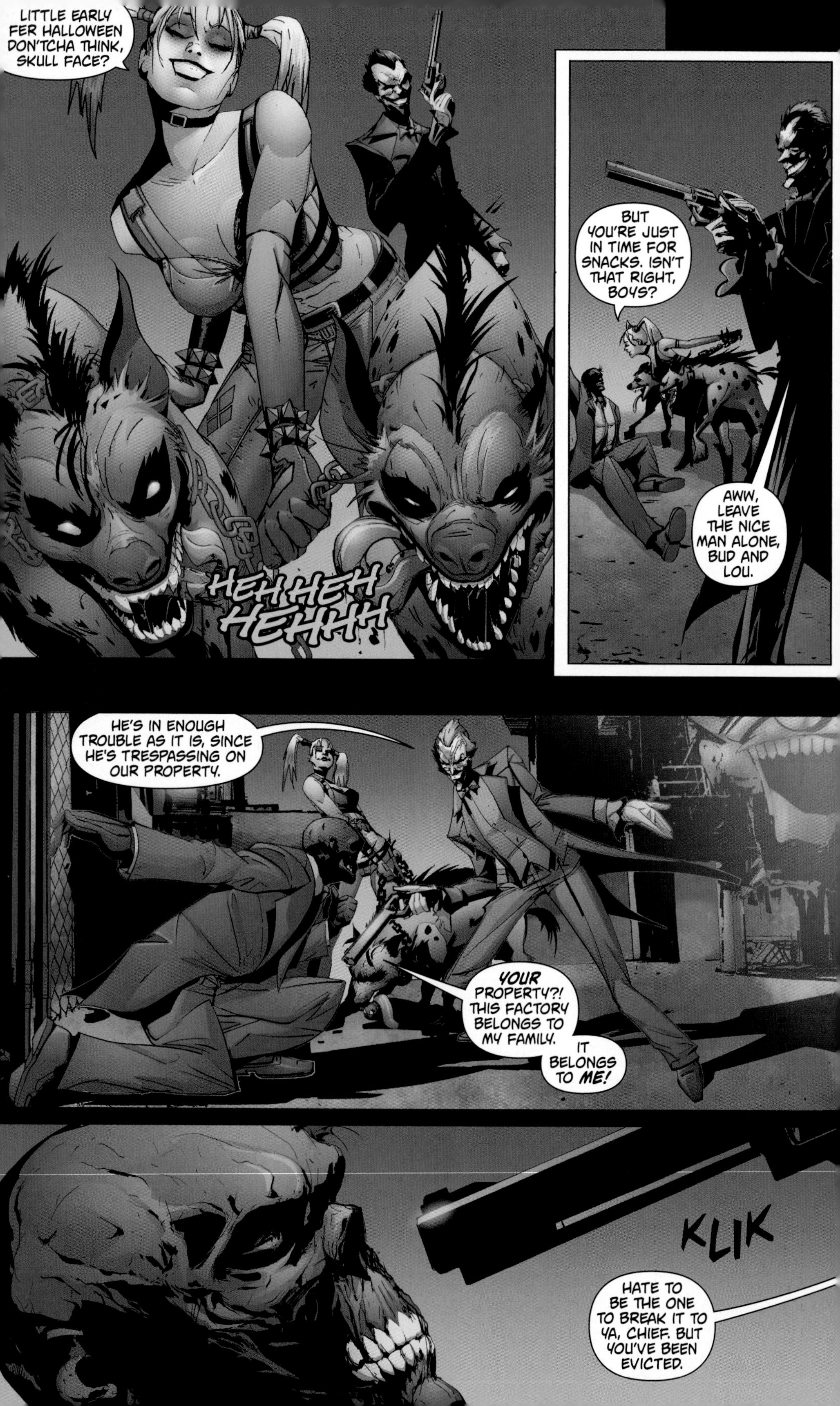
LITTLE EARLY FER HALLOWEEN DON'TCHA THINK, SKULL FACE?
HEH HEH HEHHH
BUT YOU'RE JUST IN TIME FOR SNACKS. ISN'T THAT RIGHT, BOYS?
AWW, LEAVE THE NICE MAN ALONE, BUD AND LOU.
HE'S IN ENOUGH TROUBLE AS IT IS, SINCE HE'S TRESPASSING ON OUR PROPERTY.
YOUR PROPERTY?! THIS FACTORY BELONGS TO MY FAMILY.
IT BELONGS TO ME!
KLIK
HATE TO BE THE ONE TO BREAK IT TO YA, CHIEF. BUT YOU'VE BEEN EVICTED.

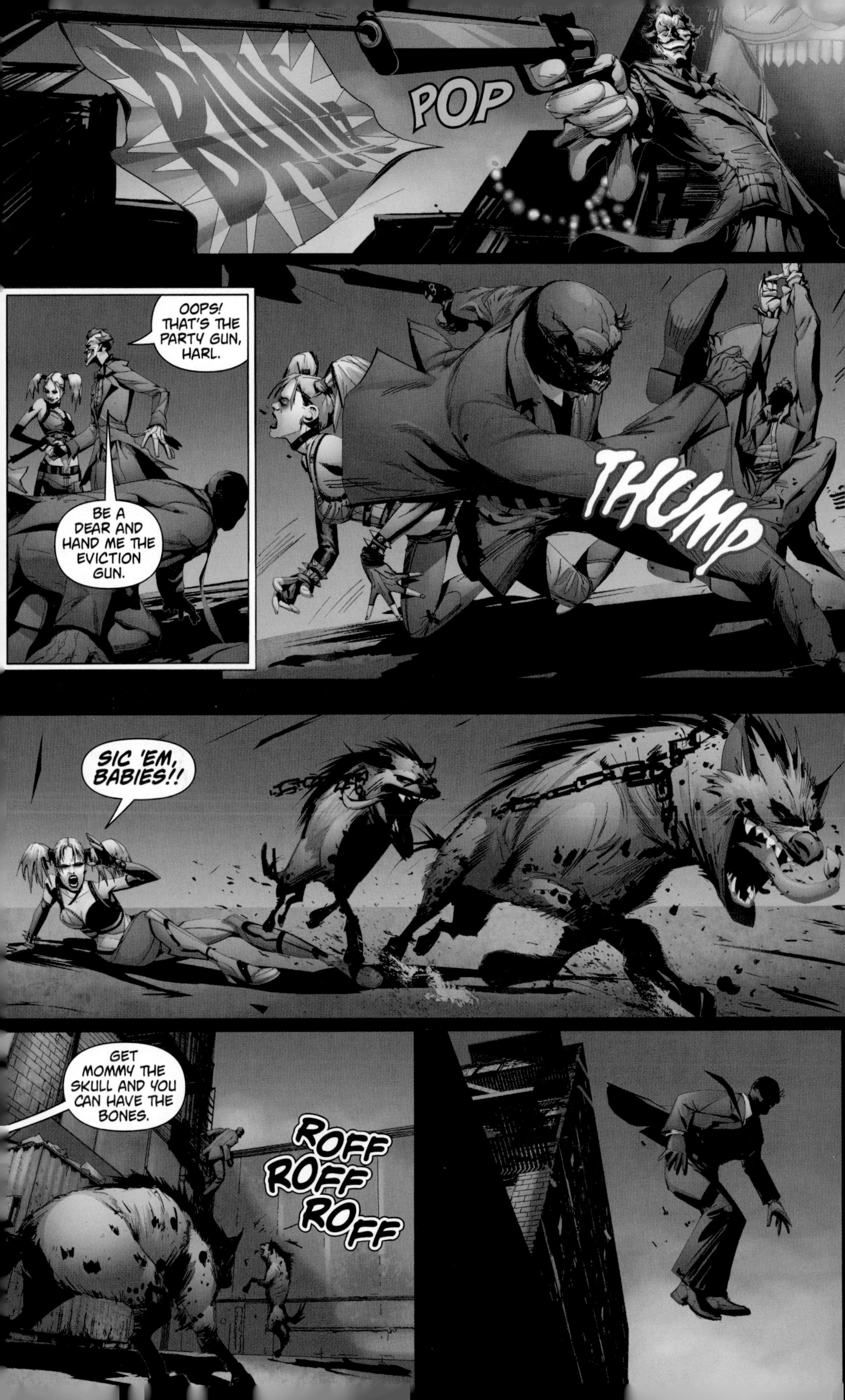
POP
OOPS! THAT'S THE PARTY GUN, HARL.
BE A DEAR AND HAND ME THE EVICTION GUN.
THUMP
SIC 'EM, BABIES!!
GET MOMMY THE SKULL AND YOU CAN HAVE THE BONES.
ROFF ROFF ROFF

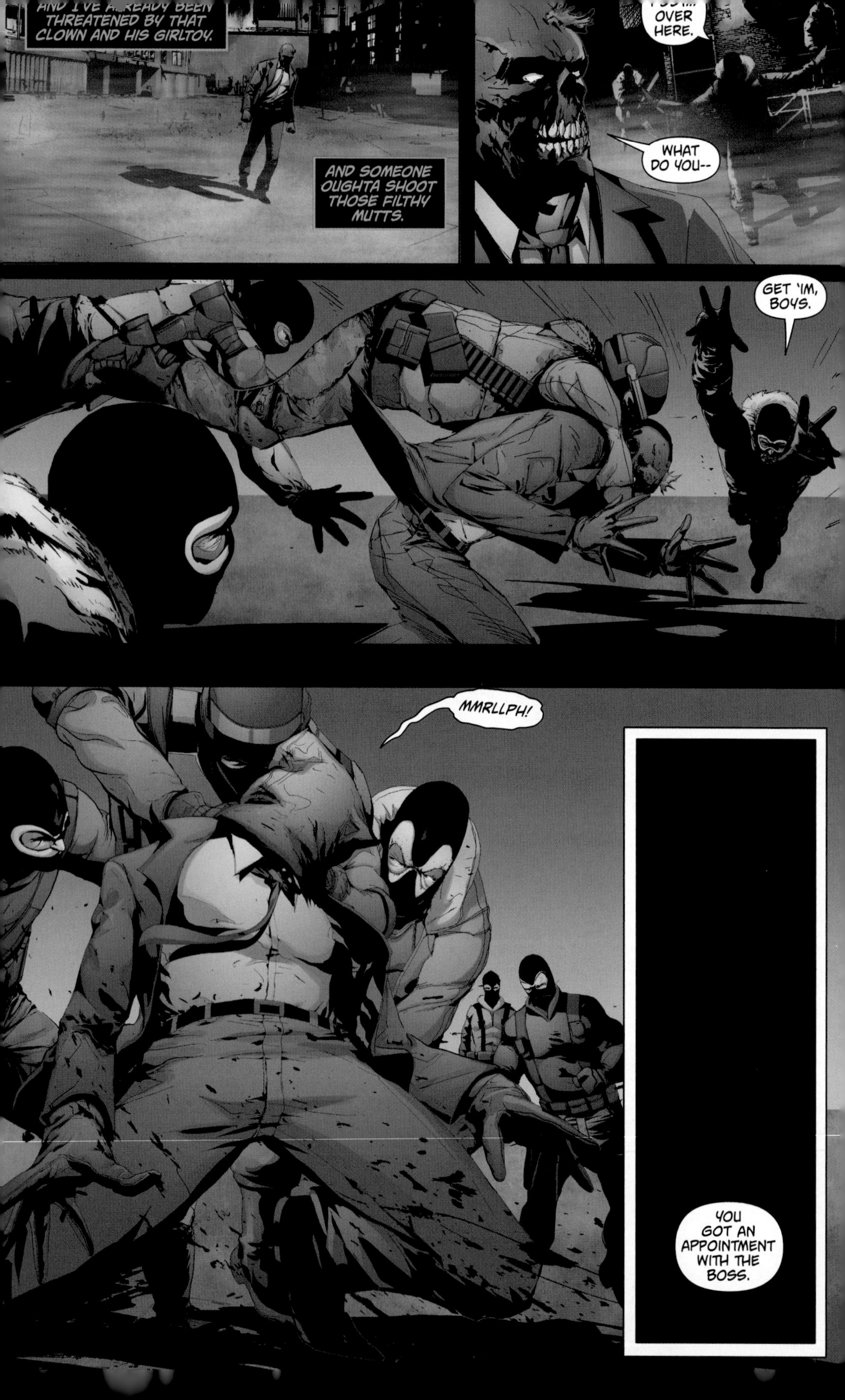
THREATENED BY THAT CLOWN AND HIS GIRLTOY.
AND SOMEONE OUGHTA SHOOT THOSE FILTHY MUTTS.
OVER HERE.
WHAT DO YOU--
GET 'IM, BOYS.
MMRLLPH!
YOU GOT AN APPOINTMENT WITH THE BOSS.

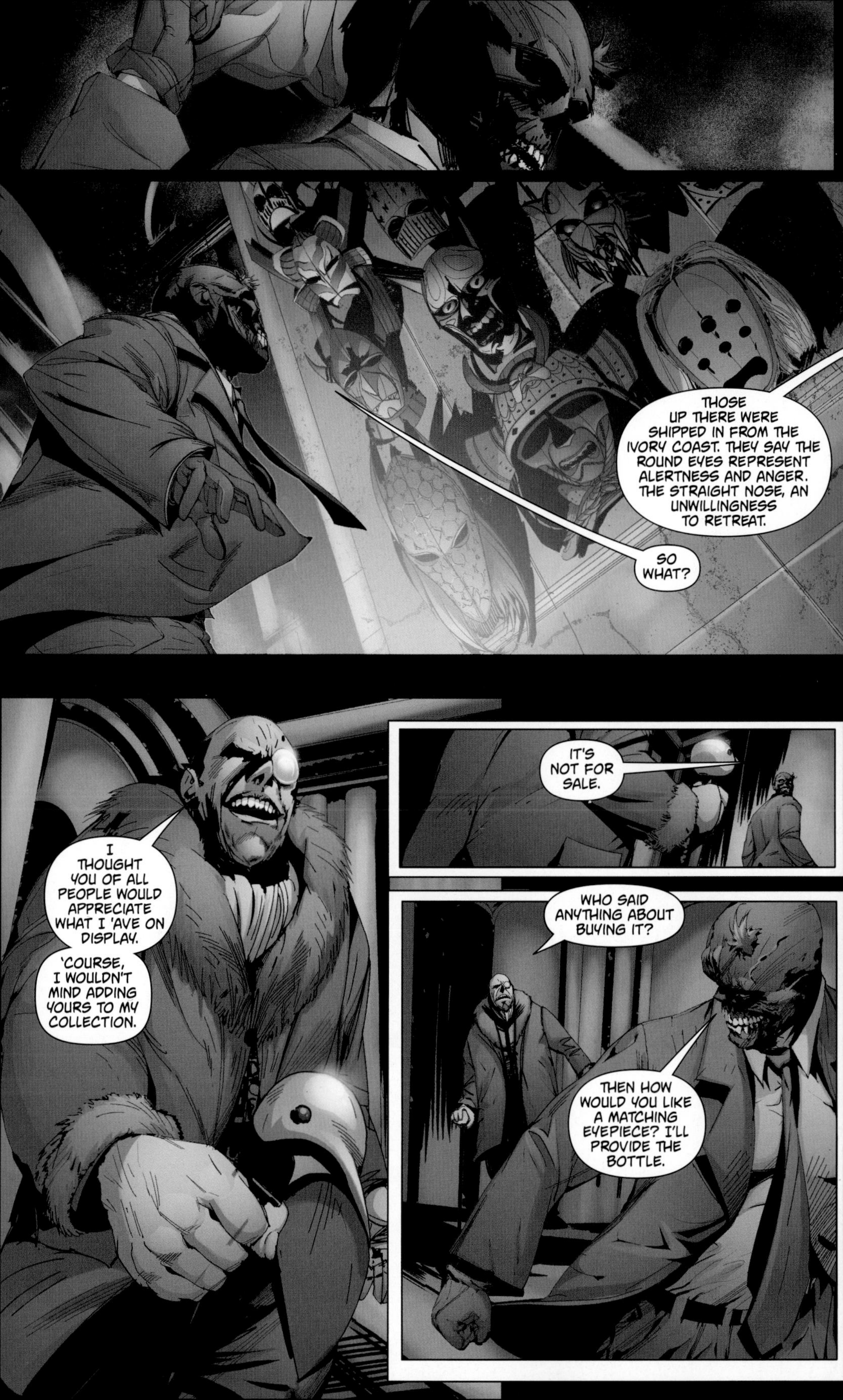
THOSE UP THERE WERE SHIPPED IN FROM THE IVORY COAST. THEY SAY THE ROUND EYES REPRESENT ALERTNESS AND ANGER. THE STRAIGHT NOSE, AN UNWILLINGNESS TO RETREAT.
SO WHAT?
I THOUGHT YOU OF ALL PEOPLE WOULD APPRECIATE WHAT I 'AVE ON DISPLAY.
'COURSE, I WOULDN'T MIND ADDING YOURS TO MY COLLECTION.
IT'S NOT FOR SALE.
WHO SAID ANYTHING ABOUT BUYING IT?
THEN HOW WOULD YOU LIKE A MATCHING EYEPIECE? I'LL PROVIDE THE BOTTLE.

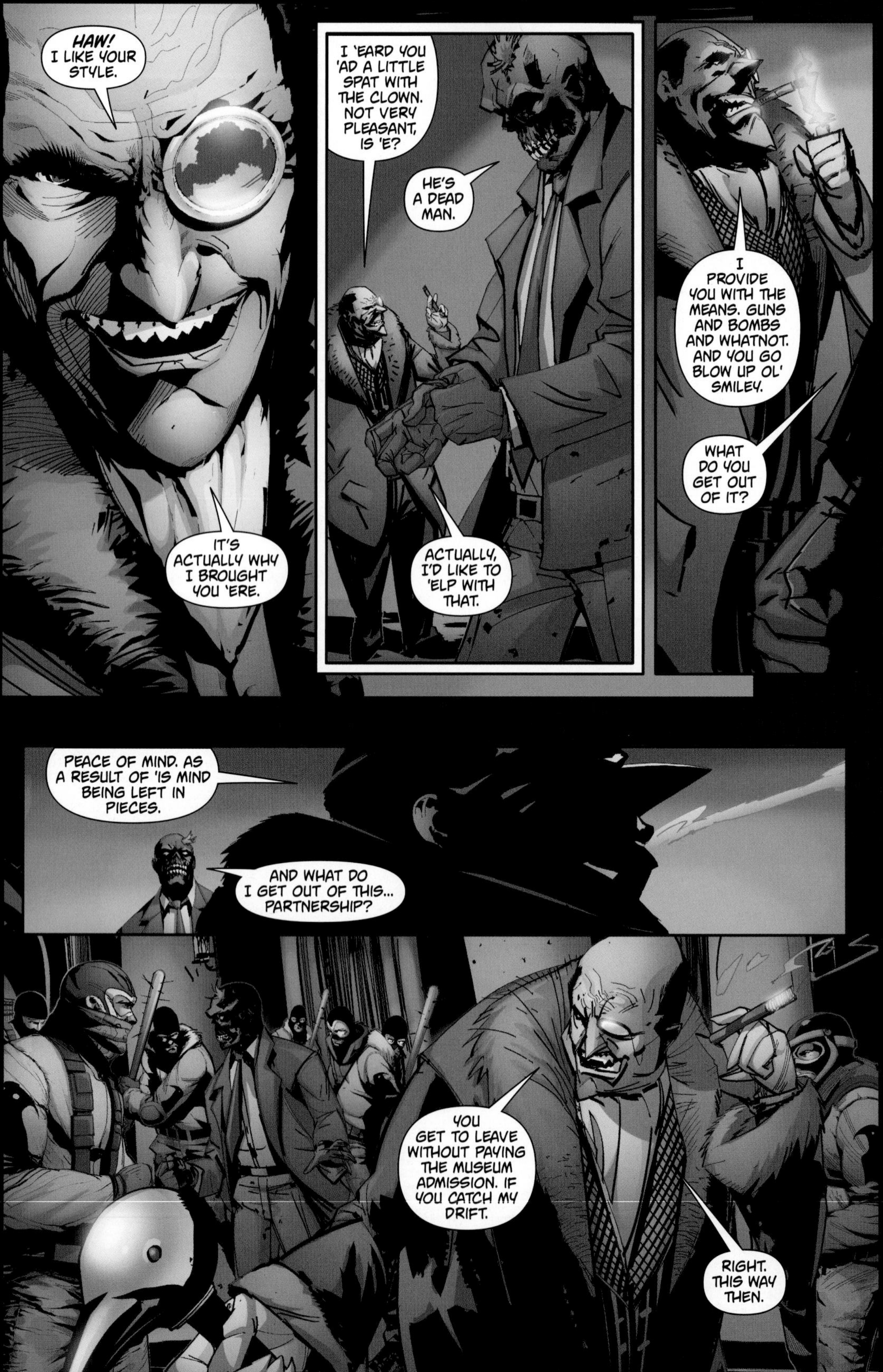
HAW! I LIKE YOUR STYLE.
IT'S ACTUALLY WHY I BROUGHT YOU 'ERE.
I 'EARD YOU 'AD A LITTLE SPAT WITH THE CLOWN. NOT VERY PLEASANT, IS 'E?
HE'S A DEAD MAN.
ACTUALLY, I'D LIKE TO 'ELP WITH THAT.
I PROVIDE YOU WITH THE MEANS. GUNS AND BOMBS AND WHATNOT. AND YOU GO BLOW UP OL' SMILEY.
WHAT DO YOU GET OUT OF IT?
PEACE OF MIND. AS A RESULT OF 'IS MIND BEING LEFT IN PIECES.
AND WHAT DO I GET OUT OF THIS... PARTNERSHIP?
YOU GET TO LEAVE WITHOUT PAYING THE MUSEUM ADMISSION. IF YOU CATCH MY DRIFT.
RIGHT. THIS WAY THEN.

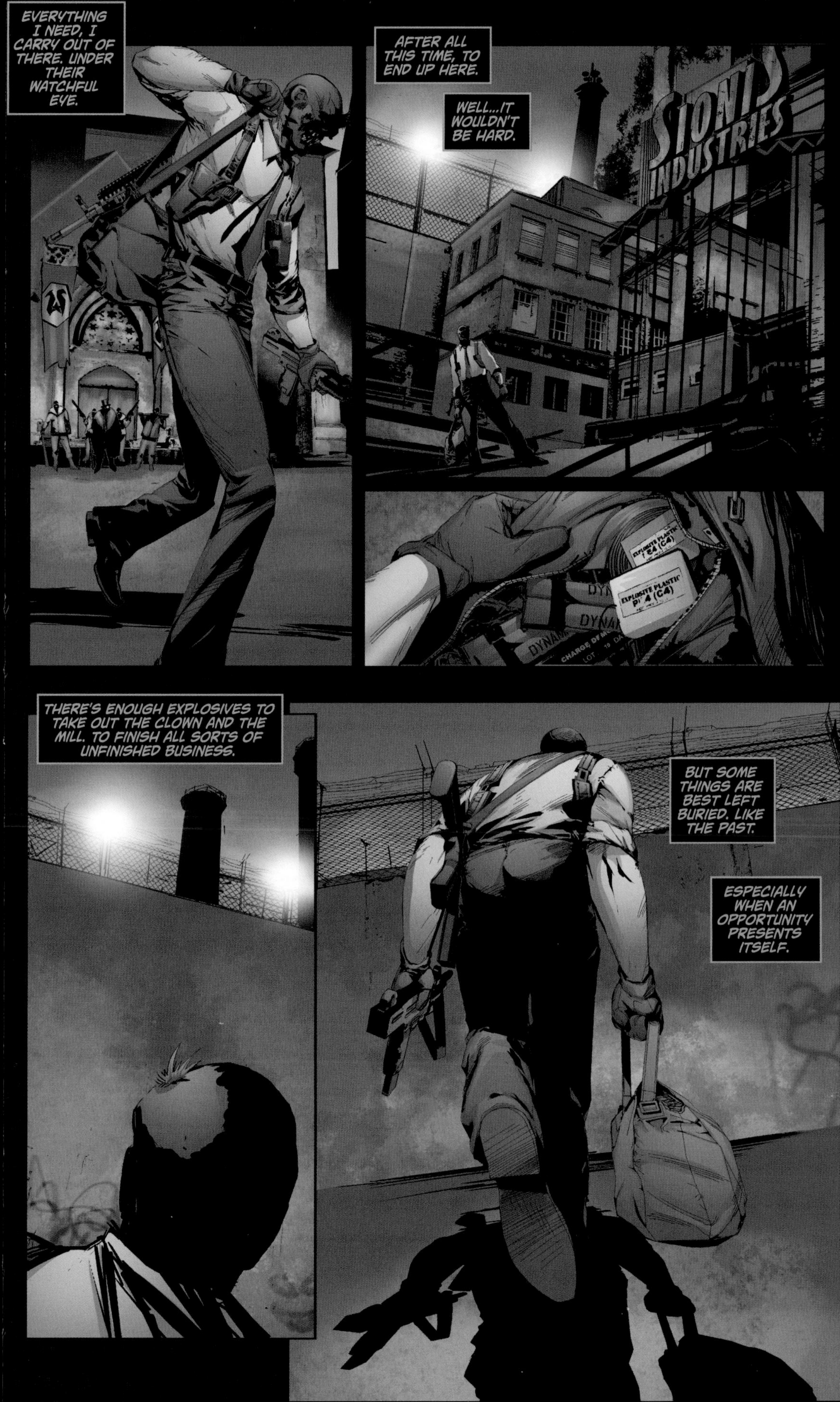
EVERYTHING I NEED, I CARRY OUT OF THERE. UNDER THEIR WATCHFUL EYE.
AFTER ALL THIS TIME, TO END UP HERE.
WELL...IT WOULDN'T BE HARD.
SIONIS INDUSTRIES
EXPLOSIVE PLASTIC
EXPLOSIVE PLASTIC
THERE'S ENOUGH EXPLOSIVES TO TAKE OUT THE CLOWN AND THE MILL. TO FINISH ALL SORTS OF UNFINISHED BUSINESS.
BUT SOME THINGS ARE BEST LEFT BURIED. LIKE THE PAST.
ESPECIALLY WHEN AN OPPORTUNITY PRESENTS ITSELF.

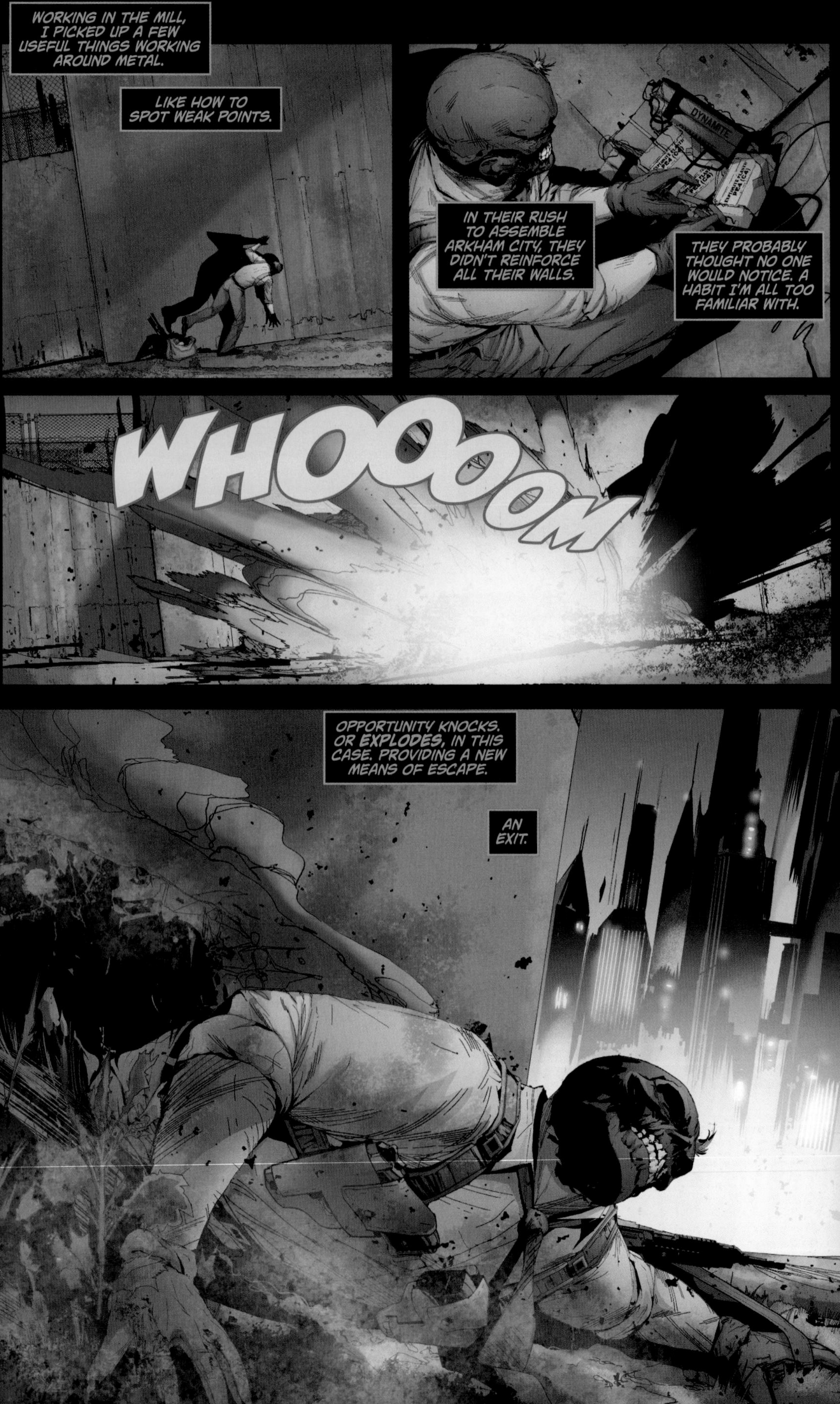
WORKING IN THE MILL, I PICKED UP A FEW USEFUL THINGS WORKING AROUND METAL.
LIKE HOW TO SPOT WEAK POINTS.
DYNAMITE
IN THEIR RUSH TO ASSEMBLE ARKHAM CITY, THEY DIDN'T REINFORCE ALL THEIR WALLS.
THEY PROBABLY THOUGHT NO ONE WOULD NOTICE. A HABIT I'M ALL TOO FAMILIAR WITH.
WHOOOOOM
OPPORTUNITY KNOCKS. OR **EXPLODES**, IN THIS CASE. PROVIDING A NEW MEANS OF ESCAPE.
AN EXIT.

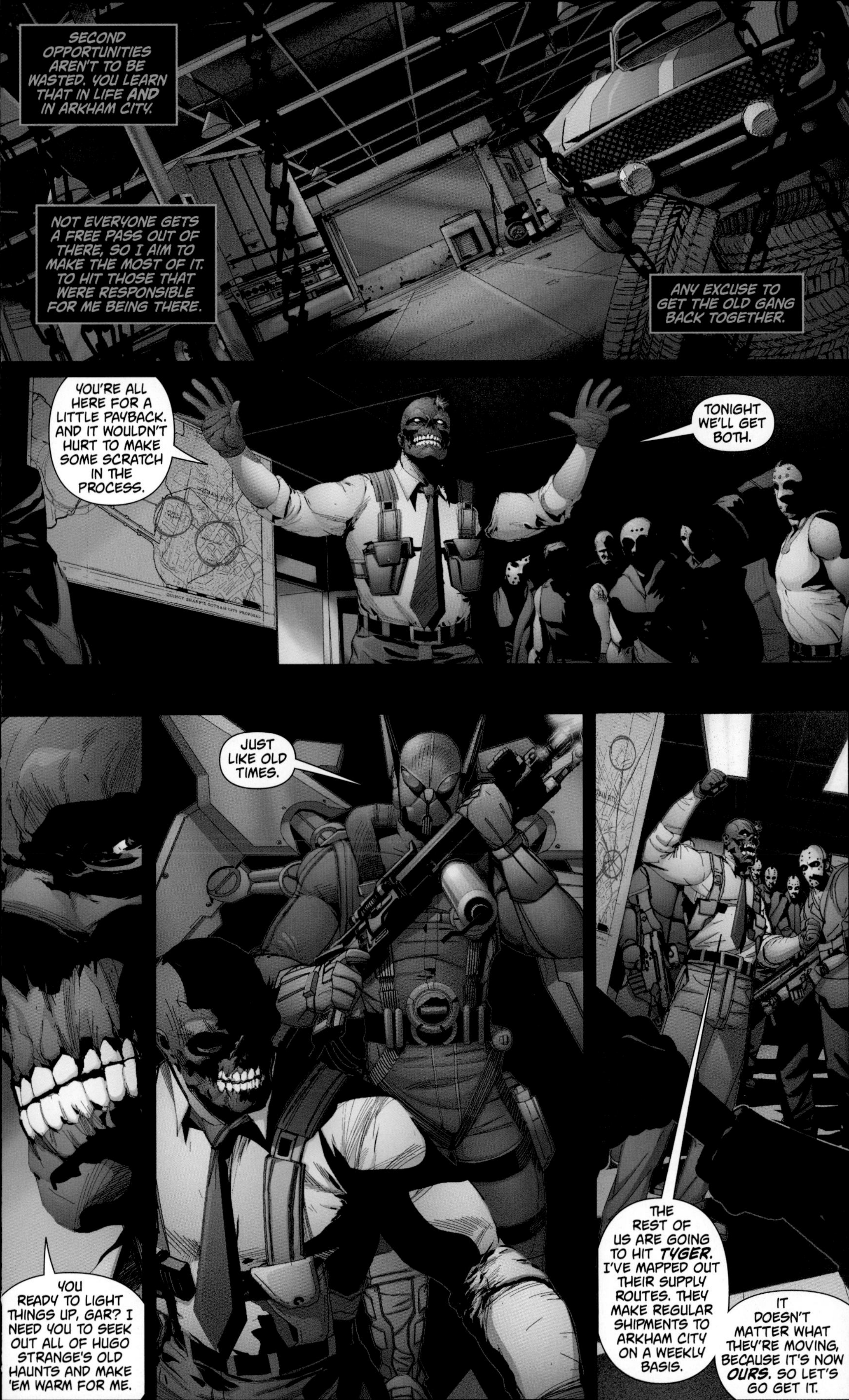
SECOND OPPORTUNITIES AREN'T TO BE WASTED. YOU LEARN THAT IN LIFE AND IN ARKHAM CITY.
NOT EVERYONE GETS A FREE PASS OUT OF THERE, SO I AIM TO MAKE THE MOST OF IT. TO HIT THOSE THAT WERE RESPONSIBLE FOR ME BEING THERE.
ANY EXCUSE TO GET THE OLD GANG BACK TOGETHER.
YOU'RE ALL HERE FOR A LITTLE PAYBACK. AND IT WOULDN'T HURT TO MAKE SOME SCRATCH IN THE PROCESS.
TONIGHT WE'LL GET BOTH.
YOU READY TO LIGHT THINGS UP, GAR? I NEED YOU TO SEEK OUT ALL OF HUGO STRANGE'S OLD HAUNTS AND MAKE 'EM WARM FOR ME.
JUST LIKE OLD TIMES.
THE REST OF US ARE GOING TO HIT **TYGER**. I'VE MAPPED OUT THEIR SUPPLY ROUTES. THEY MAKE REGULAR SHIPMENTS TO ARKHAM CITY ON A WEEKLY BASIS.
IT DOESN'T MATTER WHAT THEY'RE MOVING, BECAUSE IT'S NOW **OURS**. SO LET'S GO GET IT.

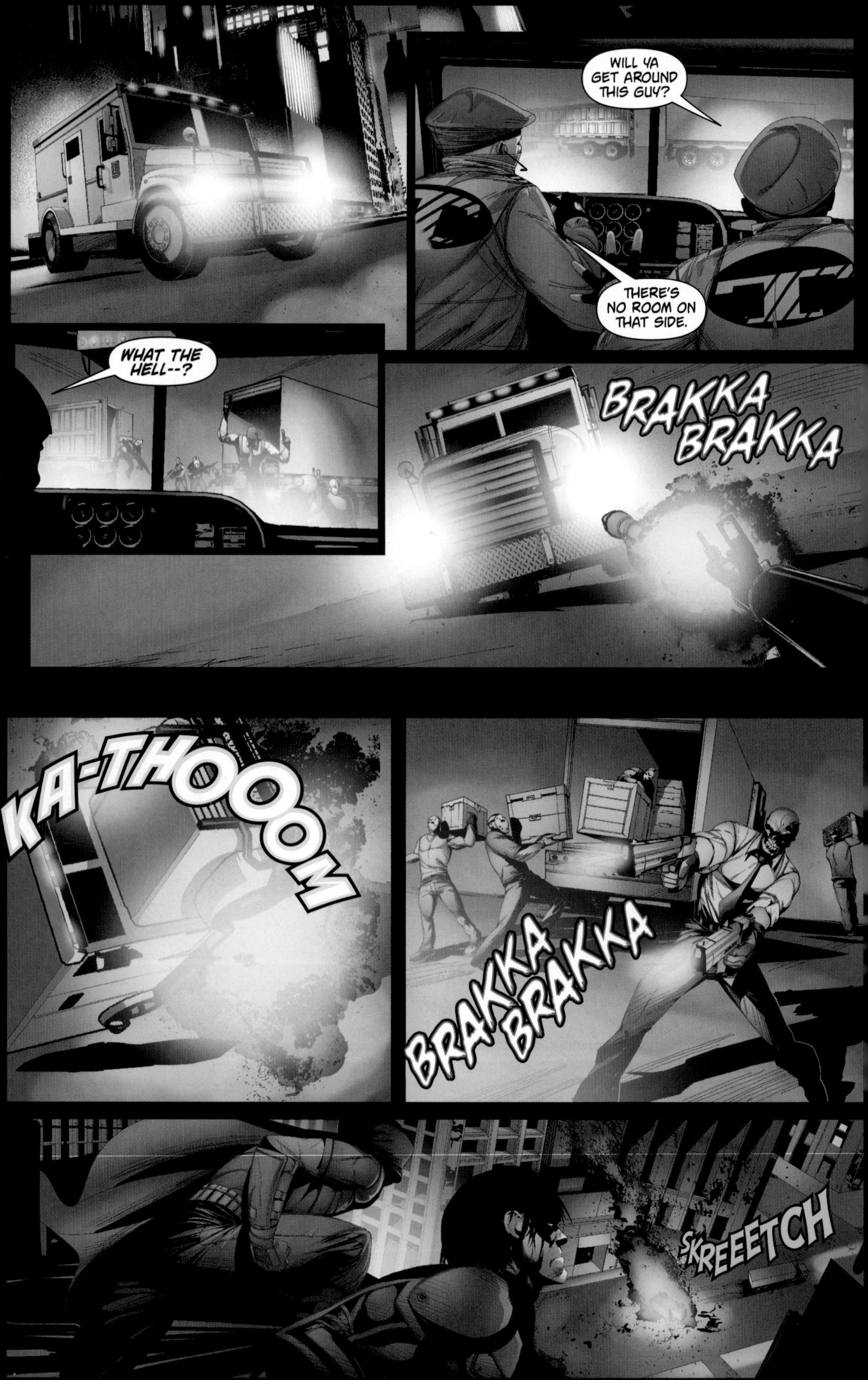
WILL YA GET AROUND THIS GUY?
THERE'S NO ROOM ON THAT SIDE.
WHAT THE HELL--?
BRAKKA BRAKKA
KA-THOOOM
BRAKKA BRAKKA
SKREEETCH

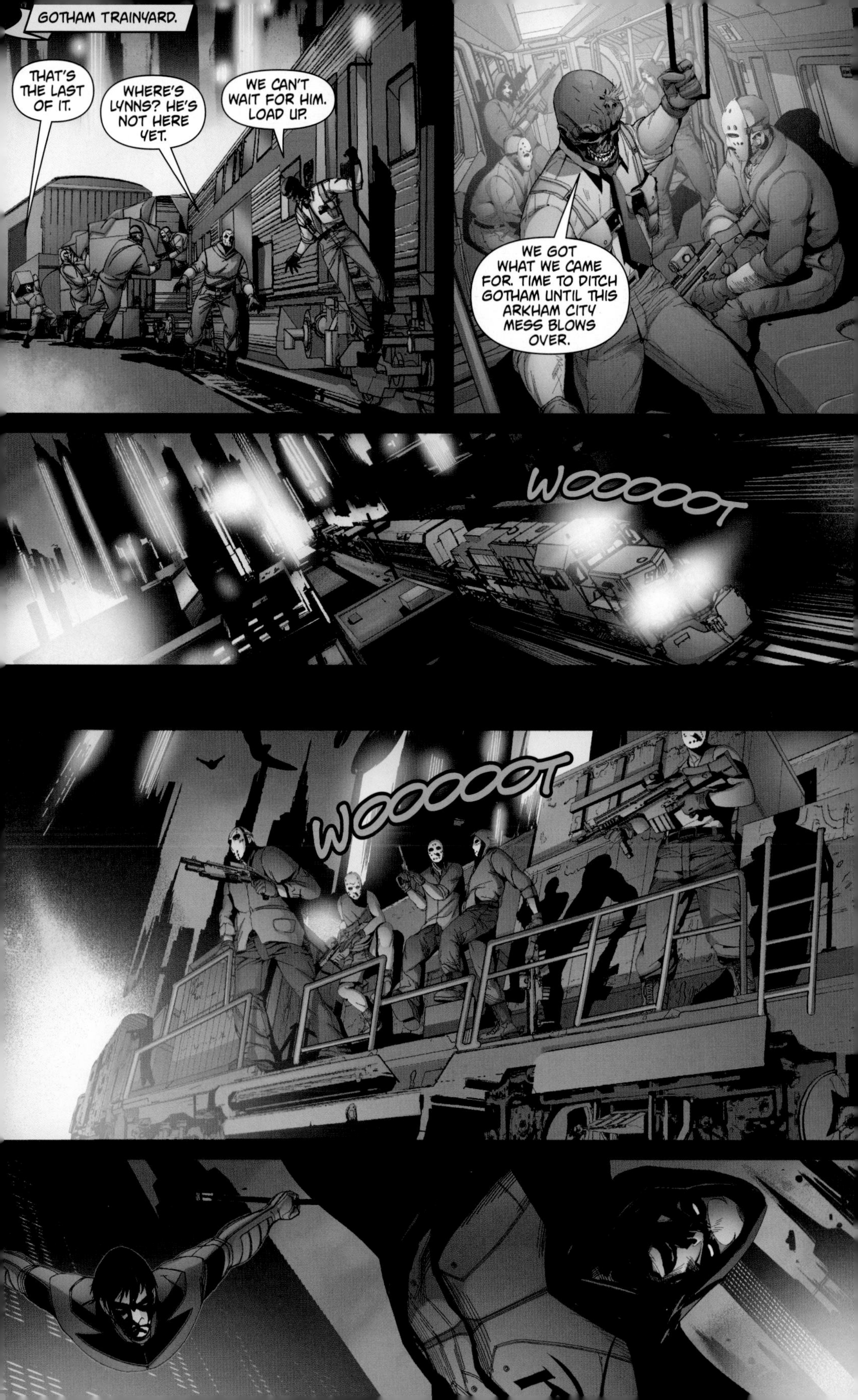
GOTHAM TRAINYARD.
THAT'S THE LAST OF IT.
WHERE'S LYNNS? HE'S NOT HERE YET.
WE CAN'T WAIT FOR HIM. LOAD UP.
WE GOT WHAT WE CAME FOR. TIME TO DITCH GOTHAM UNTIL THIS ARKHAM CITY MESS BLOWS OVER.
WOOOOOOT
WOOOOOOT

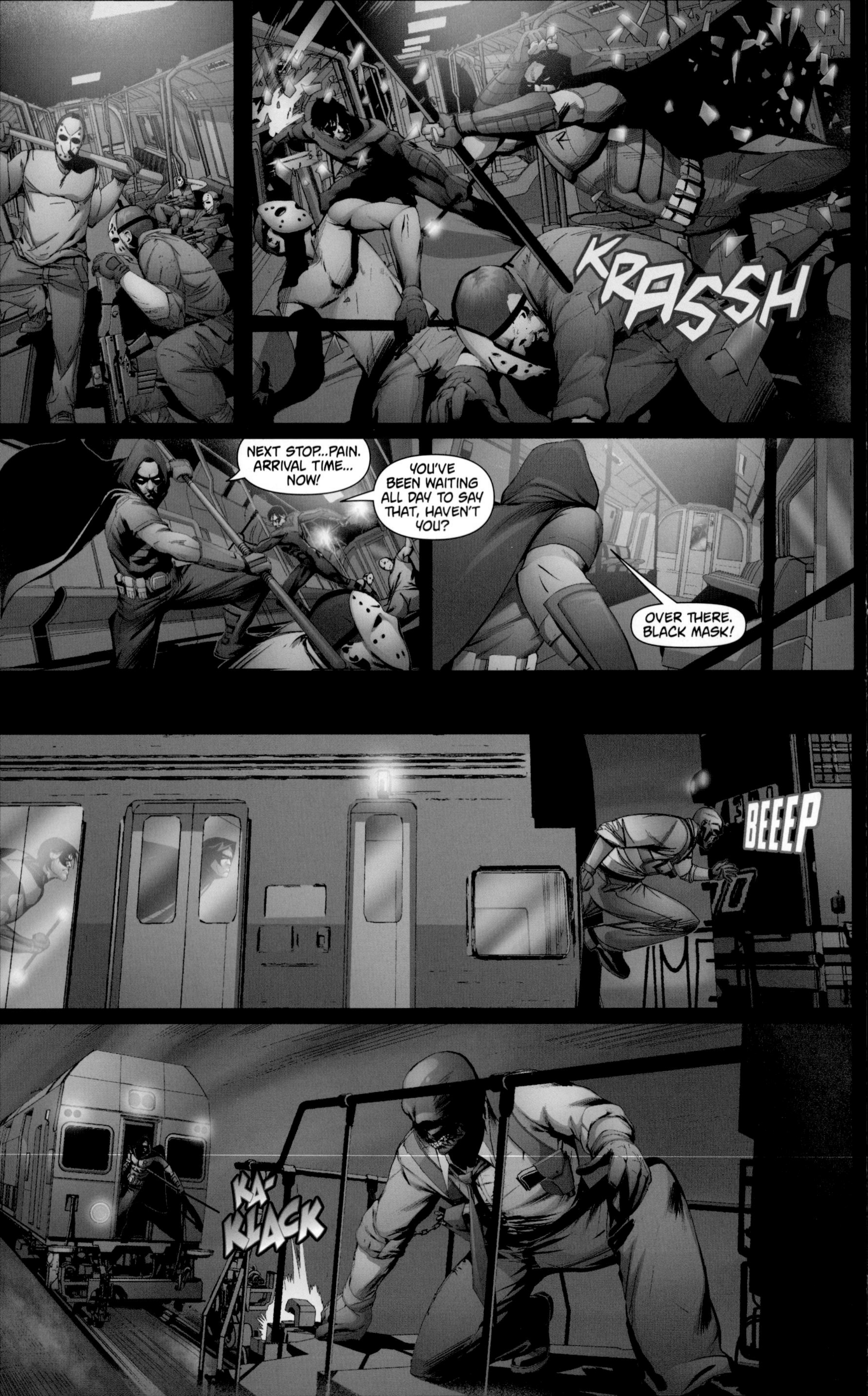
KRASSH
NEXT STOP...PAIN. ARRIVAL TIME... NOW!
YOU'VE BEEN WAITING ALL DAY TO SAY THAT, HAVEN'T YOU?
OVER THERE. BLACK MASK!
BEEEP
KA-KLACK

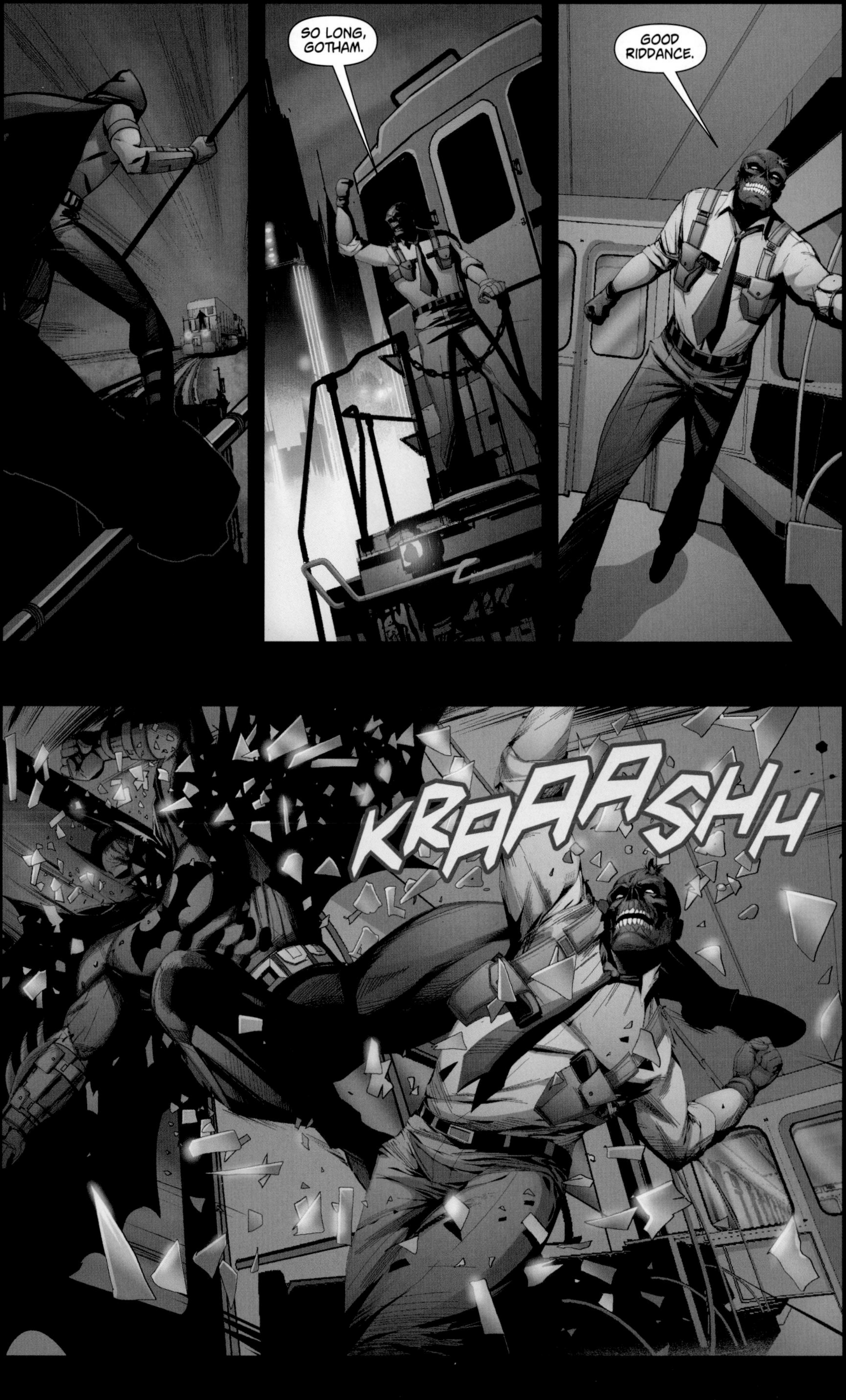
SO LONG, GOTHAM.
GOOD RIDDANCE.
KRAAASHH

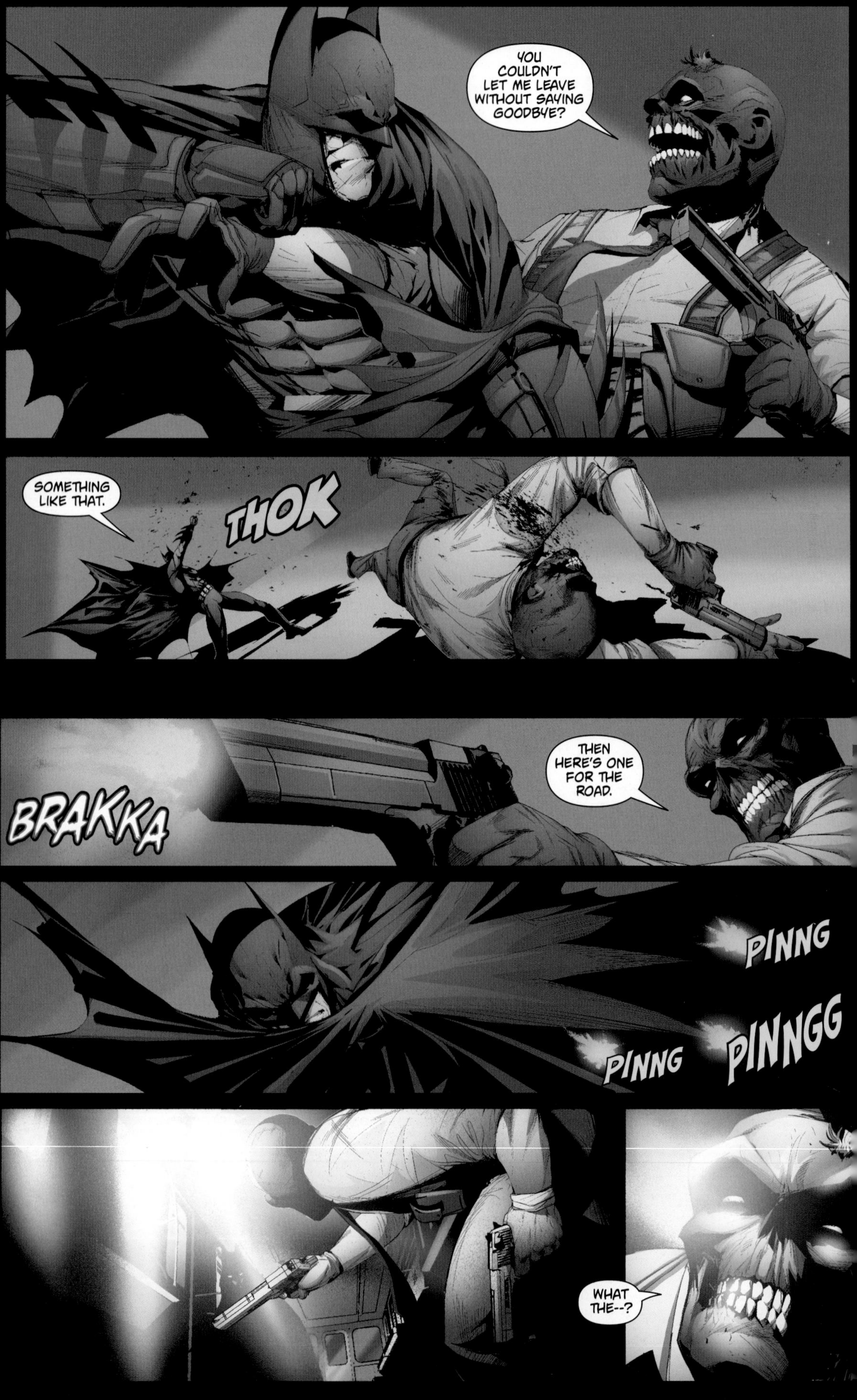
YOU COULDN'T LET ME LEAVE WITHOUT SAYING GOODBYE?
SOMETHING LIKE THAT.
THOK
THEN HERE'S ONE FOR THE ROAD.
BRAKKA
PINNG
PINNG
PINNGG
WHAT THE--?

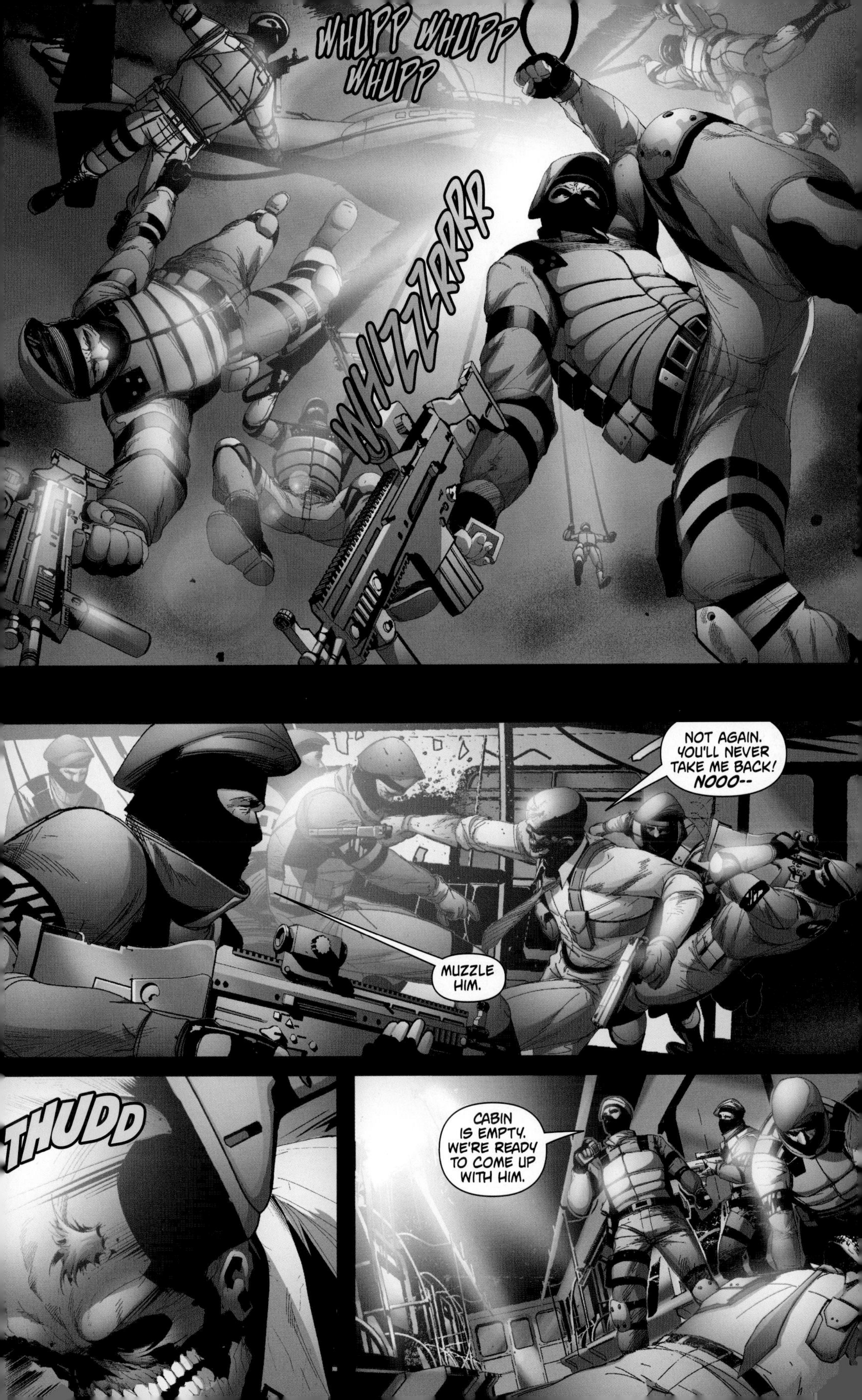
WHUPP WHUPP WHUPP
WHIZZZRRRR
NOT AGAIN. YOU'LL NEVER TAKE ME BACK! NOOO--
MUZZLE HIM.
THUDD
CABIN IS EMPTY. WE'RE READY TO COME UP WITH HIM.

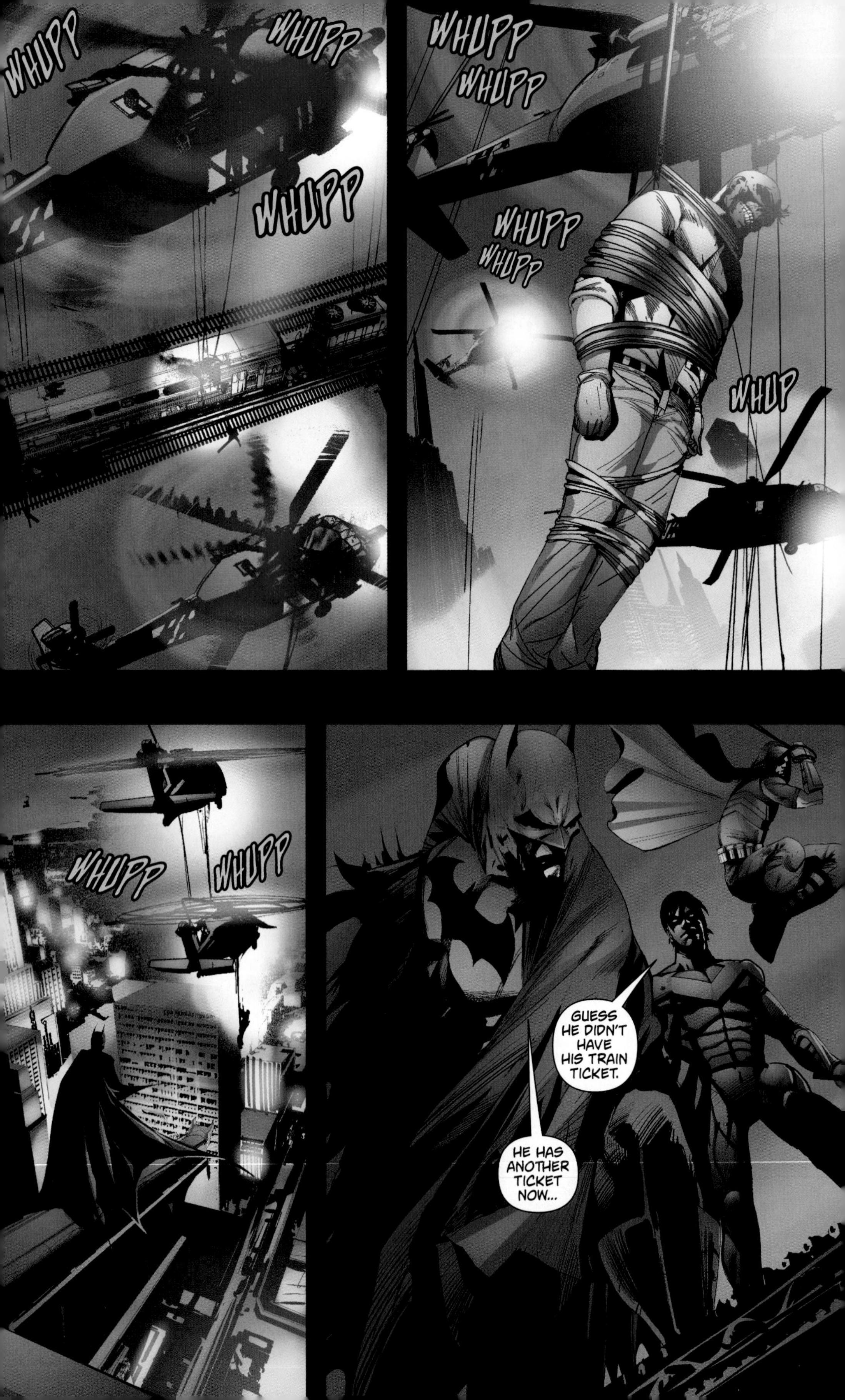
WHUPP
WHUPP
WHUPP
WHUPP
WHUPP
WHUPP
WHUPP
WHUP
WHUPP
WHUPP
GUESS HE DIDN'T HAVE HIS TRAIN TICKET.
HE HAS ANOTHER TICKET NOW...

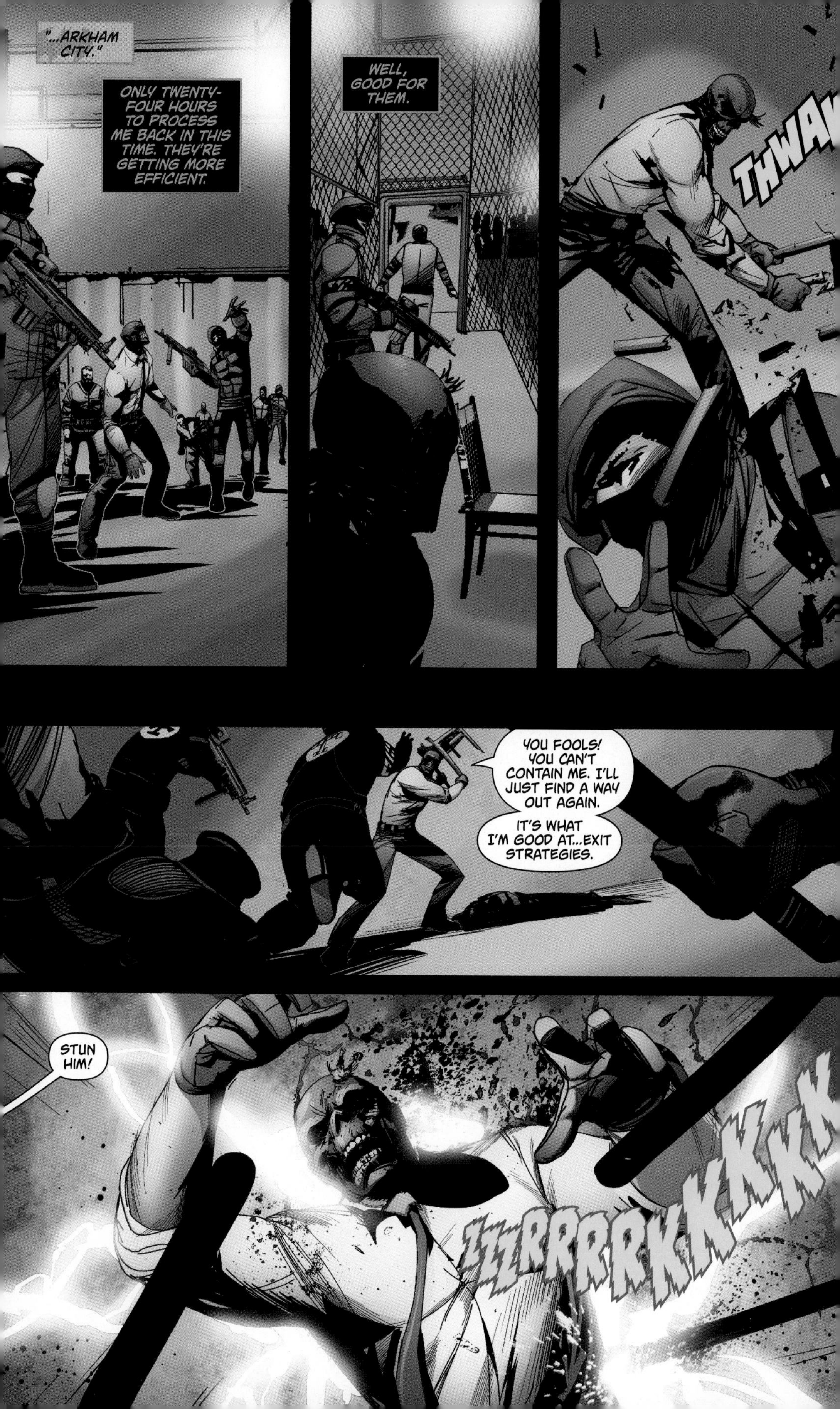
"...ARKHAM CITY."
ONLY TWENTY-FOUR HOURS TO PROCESS ME BACK IN THIS TIME. THEY'RE GETTING MORE EFFICIENT.
WELL, GOOD FOR THEM.
THWAK
YOU FOOLS! YOU CAN'T CONTAIN ME. I'LL JUST FIND A WAY OUT AGAIN.
IT'S WHAT I'M GOOD AT...EXIT STRATEGIES.
STUN HIM!
ZZZRRRRKKKKK

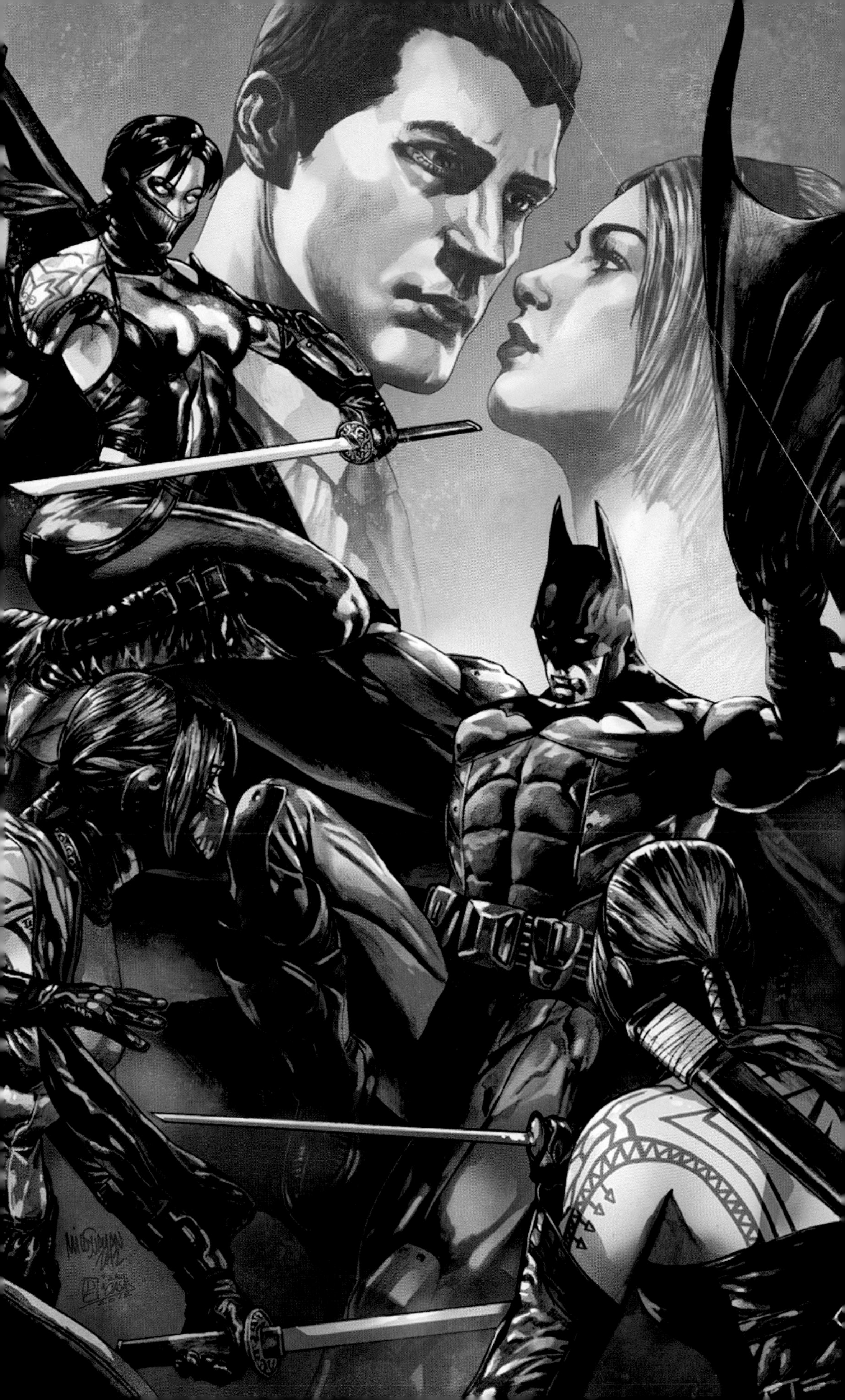

# BELOVED

WRITTEN BY: DEREK FRIDOLFS

ART BY: FEDERICO DALLOCCHIO

COLORS BY: CARRIE STRACHAN

LETTERS BY: TRAVIS LANHAM

COVER ART BY: MICO SUAYAN

COVER COLORS BY: DAVID LOPEZ
& SANTI CASAS OF IKARI STUDIO

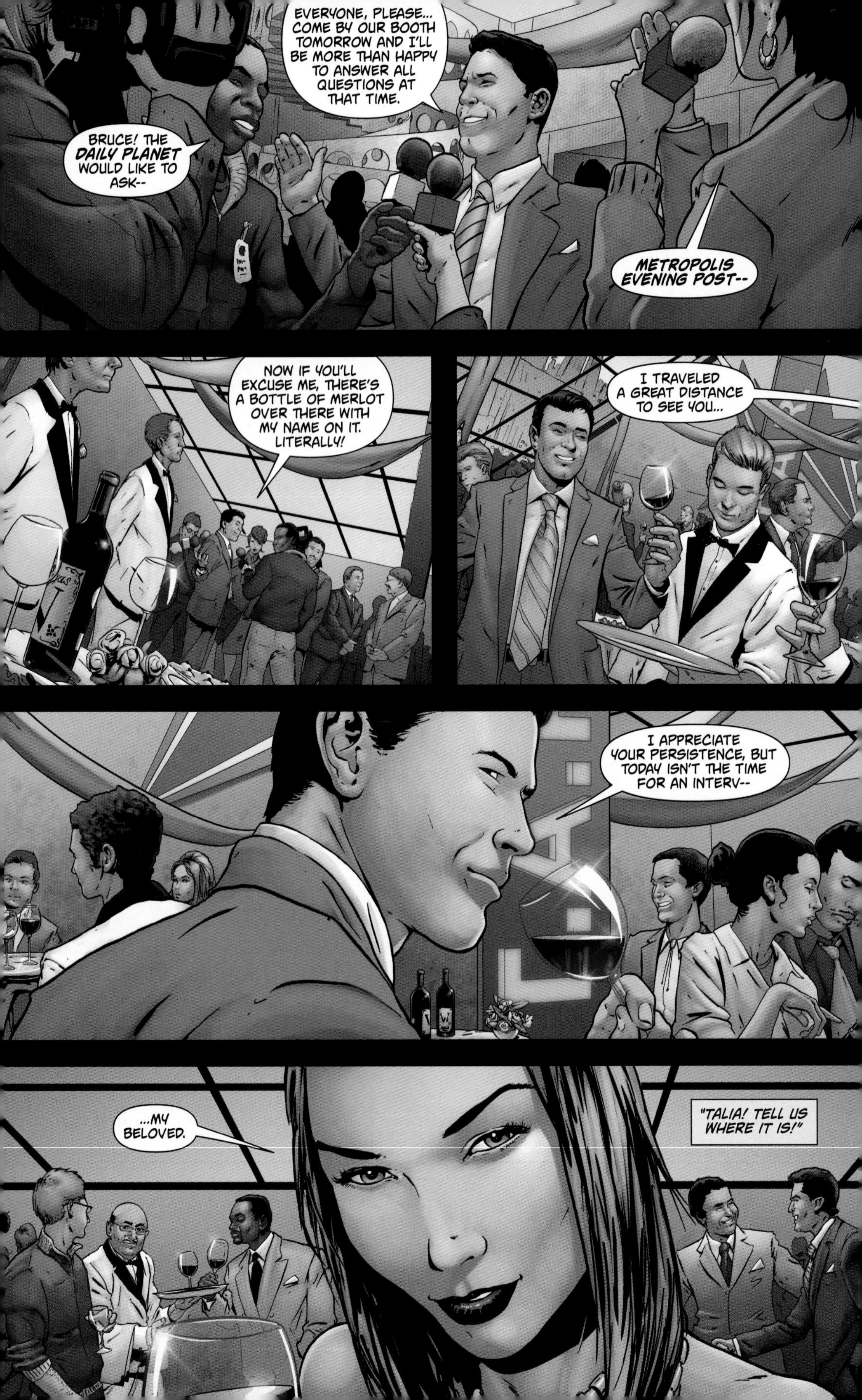
BRUCE! THE *DAILY PLANET* WOULD LIKE TO ASK--
EVERYONE, PLEASE... COME BY OUR BOOTH TOMORROW AND I'LL BE MORE THAN HAPPY TO ANSWER ALL QUESTIONS AT THAT TIME.
*METROPOLIS EVENING POST--*
NOW IF YOU'LL EXCUSE ME, THERE'S A BOTTLE OF MERLOT OVER THERE WITH MY NAME ON IT. LITERALLY!
I TRAVELED A GREAT DISTANCE TO SEE YOU...
I APPRECIATE YOUR PERSISTENCE, BUT TODAY ISN'T THE TIME FOR AN INTERV--
...MY BELOVED.
*"TALIA! TELL US WHERE IT IS!"*

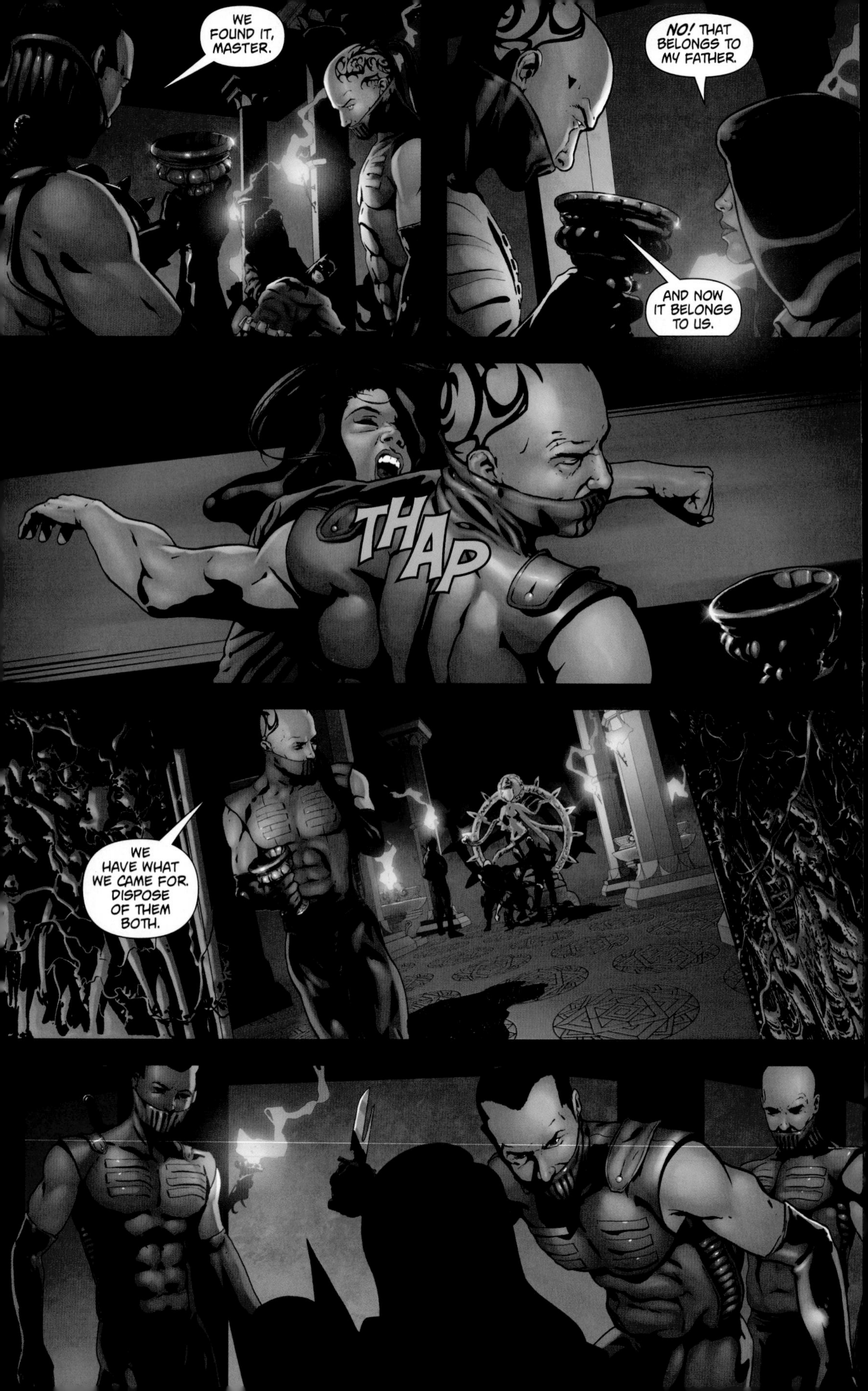
WE FOUND IT, MASTER.
NO! THAT BELONGS TO MY FATHER.
AND NOW IT BELONGS TO US.
THAP
WE HAVE WHAT WE CAME FOR. DISPOSE OF THEM BOTH.

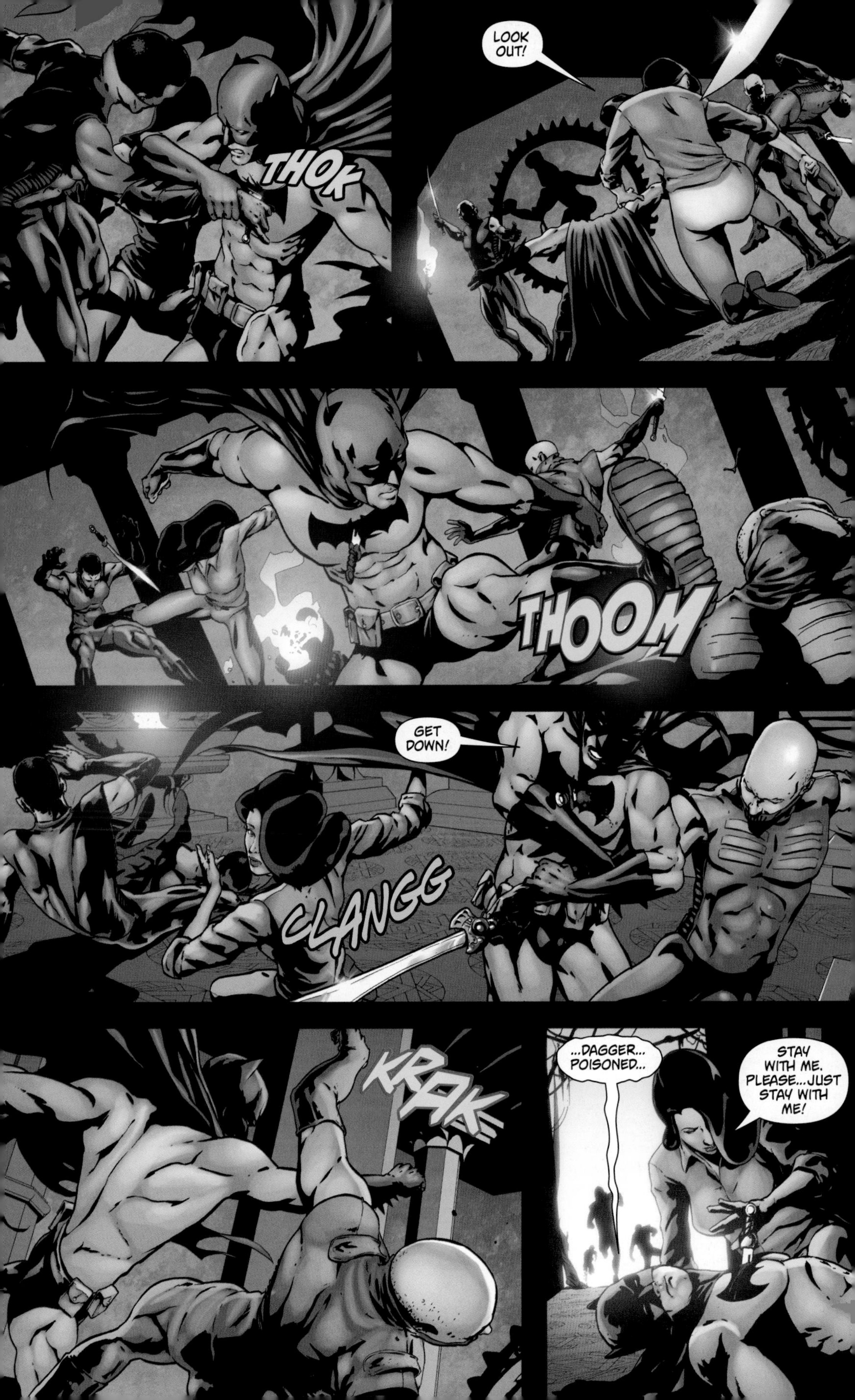
THOK
LOOK OUT!
THOOM
GET DOWN!
CLANGG
KRAK
...DAGGER... POISONED...
STAY WITH ME. PLEASE...JUST STAY WITH ME!

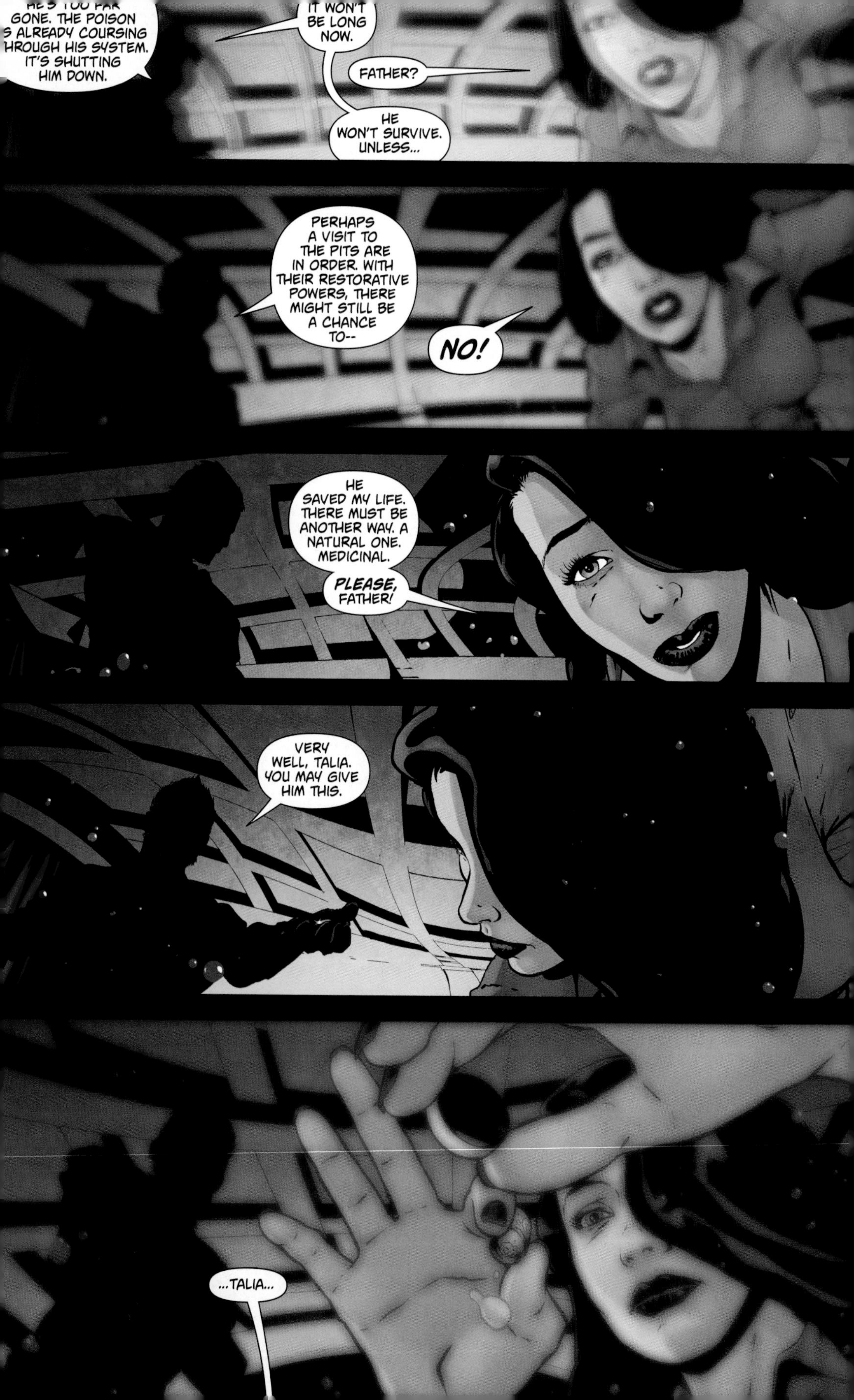
GONE. THE POISON
ALREADY COURSING
HROUGH HIS SYSTEM.
IT'S SHUTTING
HIM DOWN.
IT WON'T BE LONG NOW.
FATHER?
HE WON'T SURVIVE. UNLESS...
PERHAPS A VISIT TO THE PITS ARE IN ORDER. WITH THEIR RESTORATIVE POWERS, THERE MIGHT STILL BE A CHANCE TO--
NO!
HE SAVED MY LIFE. THERE MUST BE ANOTHER WAY. A NATURAL ONE. MEDICINAL.
PLEASE, FATHER!
VERY WELL, TALIA. YOU MAY GIVE HIM THIS.
...TALIA...

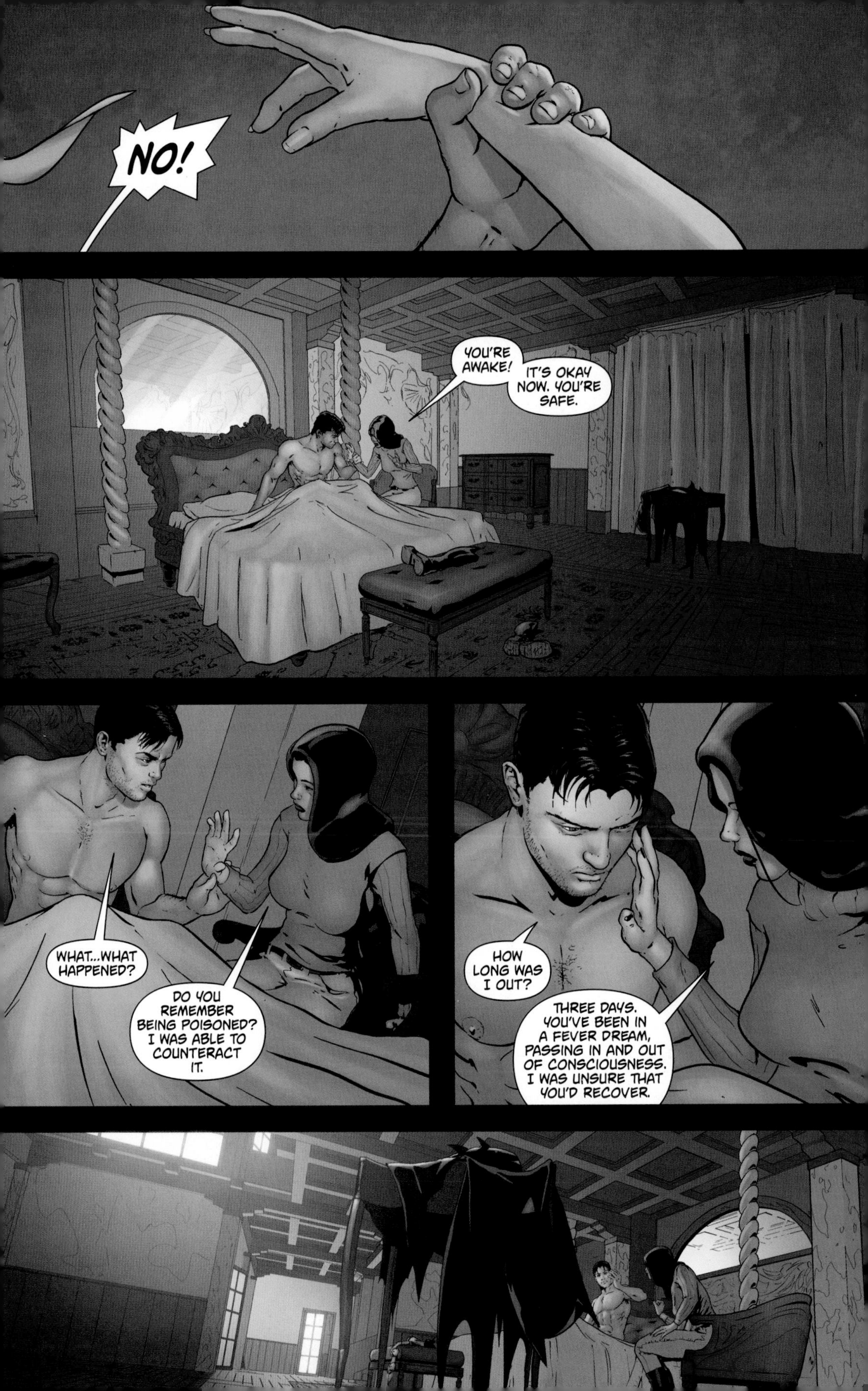
NO!
YOU'RE AWAKE!
IT'S OKAY NOW. YOU'RE SAFE.
WHAT...WHAT HAPPENED?
DO YOU REMEMBER BEING POISONED? I WAS ABLE TO COUNTERACT IT.
HOW LONG WAS I OUT?
THREE DAYS. YOU'VE BEEN IN A FEVER DREAM, PASSING IN AND OUT OF CONSCIOUSNESS. I WAS UNSURE THAT YOU'D RECOVER.

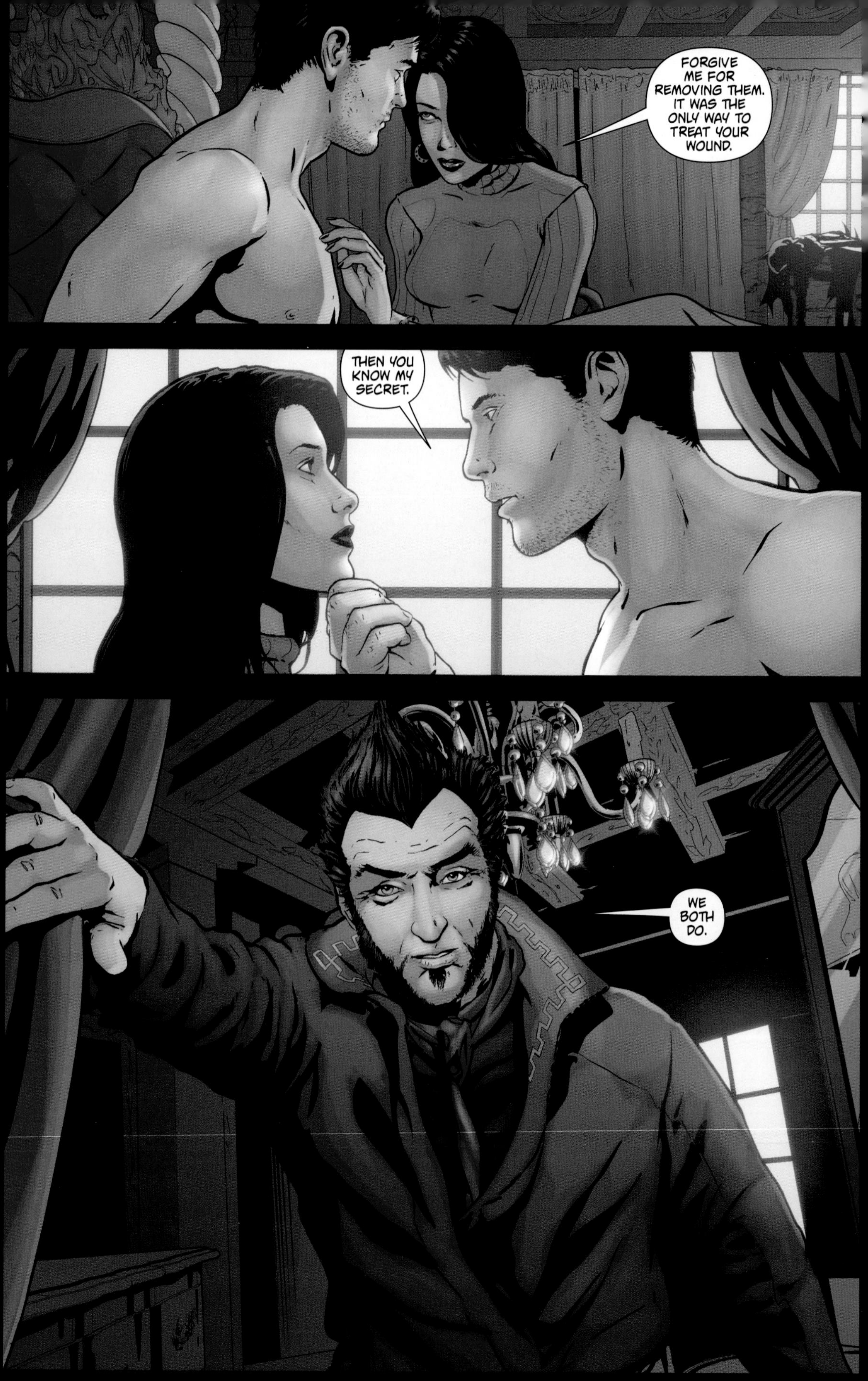
FORGIVE ME FOR REMOVING THEM. IT WAS THE ONLY WAY TO TREAT YOUR WOUND.
THEN YOU KNOW MY SECRET.
WE BOTH DO.

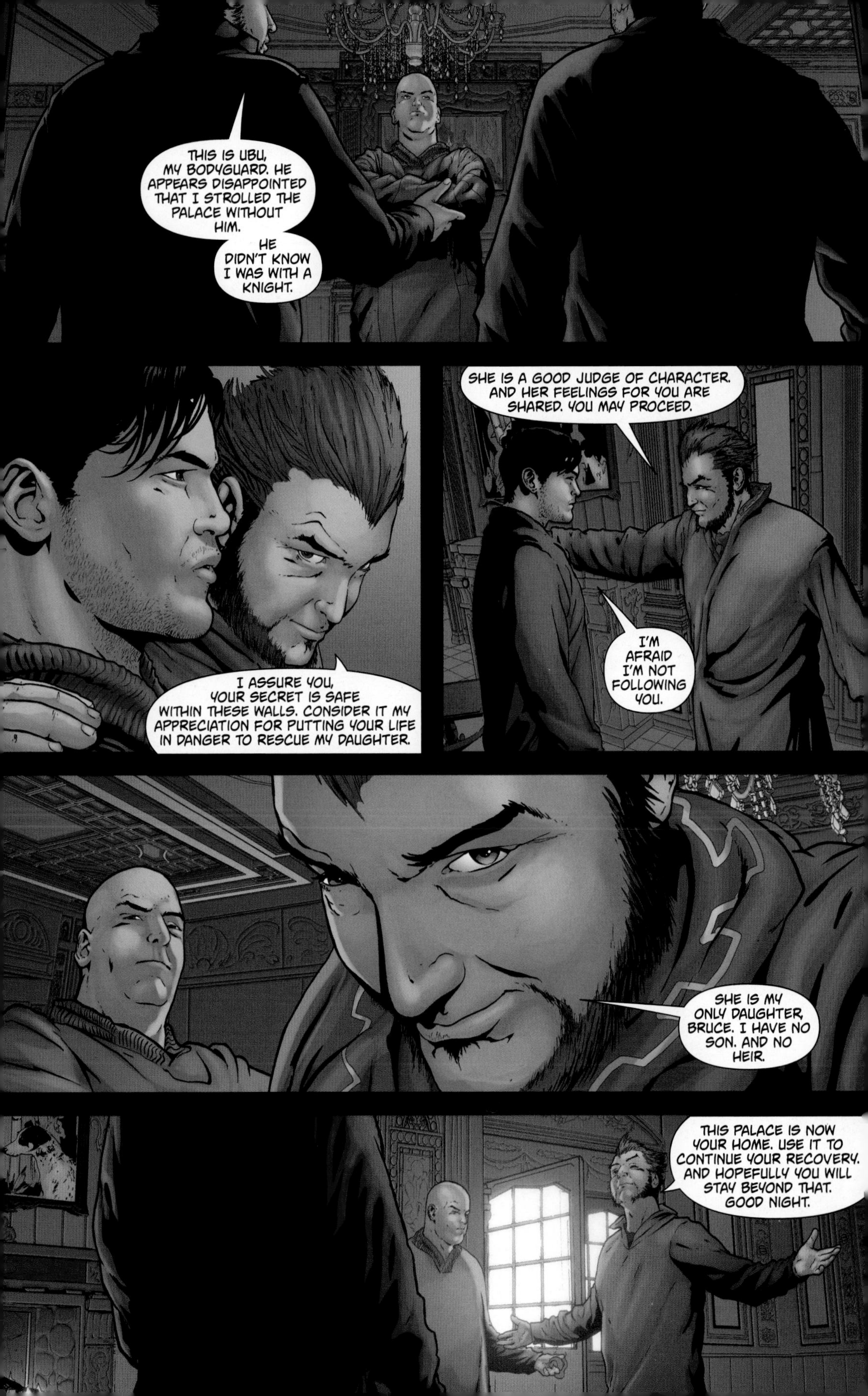
THIS IS UBU, MY BODYGUARD. HE APPEARS DISAPPOINTED THAT I STROLLED THE PALACE WITHOUT HIM.
HE DIDN'T KNOW I WAS WITH A KNIGHT.
I ASSURE YOU, YOUR SECRET IS SAFE WITHIN THESE WALLS. CONSIDER IT MY APPRECIATION FOR PUTTING YOUR LIFE IN DANGER TO RESCUE MY DAUGHTER.
SHE IS A GOOD JUDGE OF CHARACTER. AND HER FEELINGS FOR YOU ARE SHARED. YOU MAY PROCEED.
I'M AFRAID I'M NOT FOLLOWING YOU.
SHE IS MY ONLY DAUGHTER, BRUCE. I HAVE NO SON. AND NO HEIR.
THIS PALACE IS NOW YOUR HOME. USE IT TO CONTINUE YOUR RECOVERY. AND HOPEFULLY YOU WILL STAY BEYOND THAT. GOOD NIGHT.

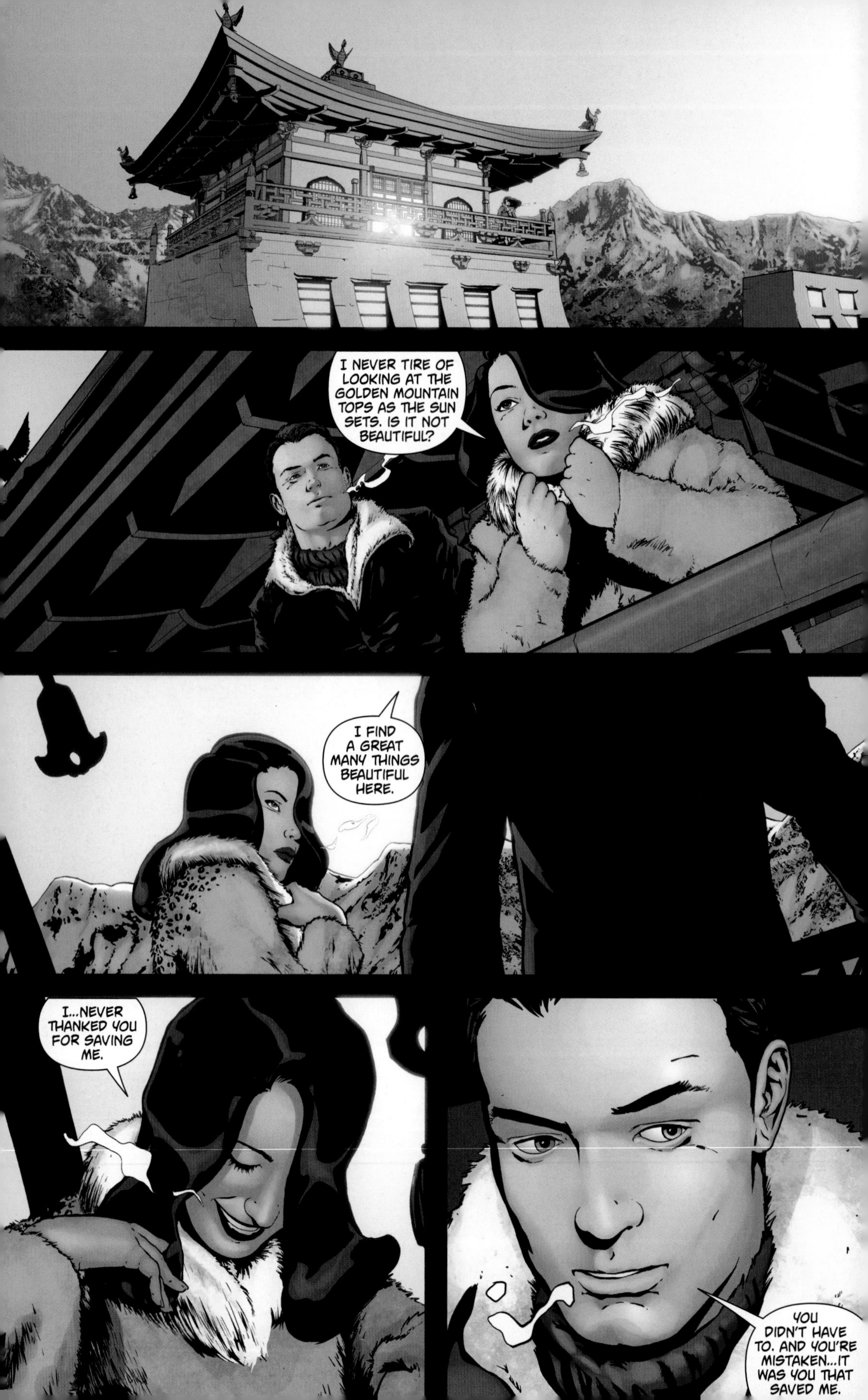
I NEVER TIRE OF LOOKING AT THE GOLDEN MOUNTAIN TOPS AS THE SUN SETS. IS IT NOT BEAUTIFUL?
I FIND A GREAT MANY THINGS BEAUTIFUL HERE.
I...NEVER THANKED YOU FOR SAVING ME.
YOU DIDN'T HAVE TO. AND YOU'RE MISTAKEN...IT WAS YOU THAT SAVED ME.

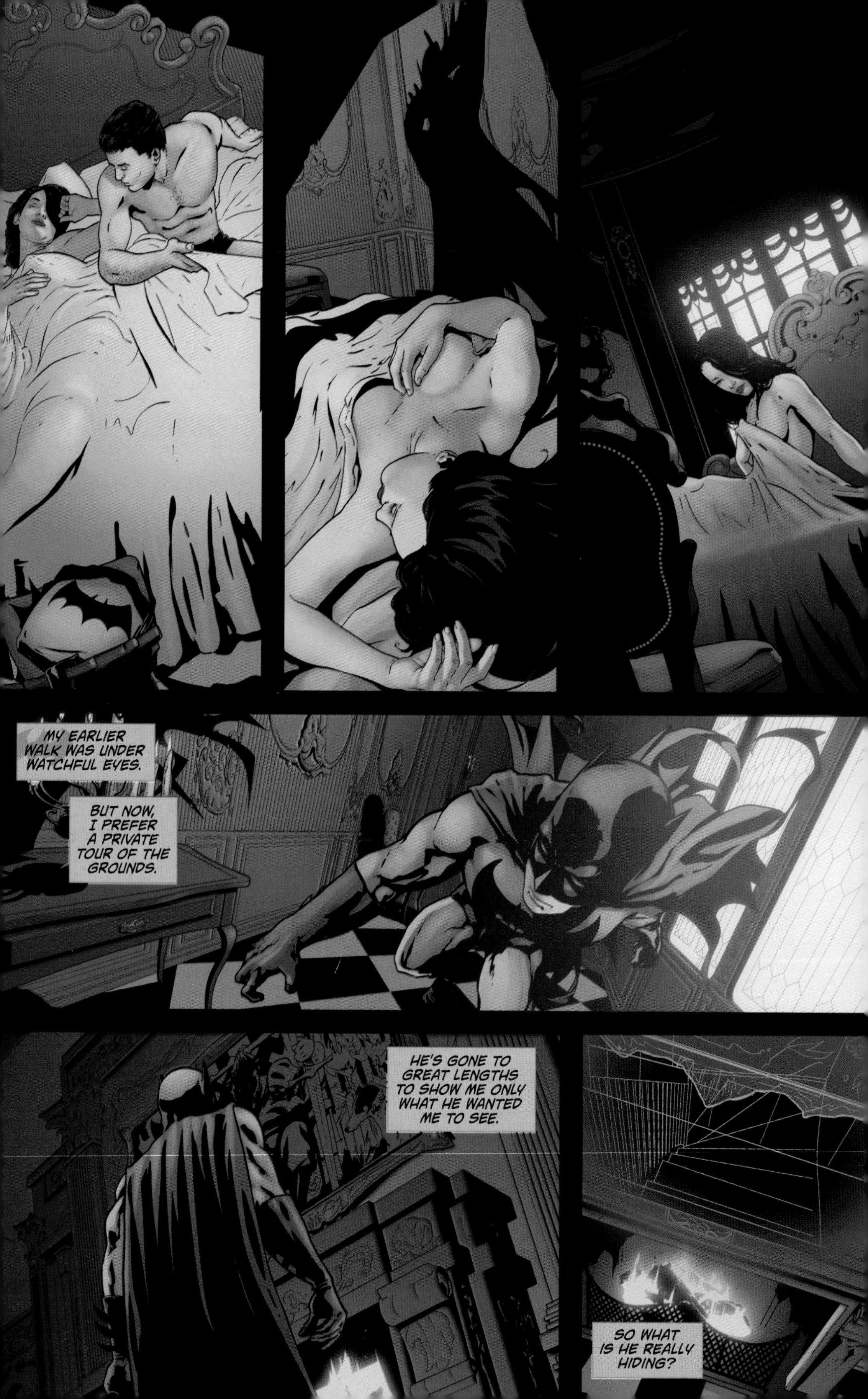
MY EARLIER WALK WAS UNDER WATCHFUL EYES.
BUT NOW, I PREFER A PRIVATE TOUR OF THE GROUNDS.
HE'S GONE TO GREAT LENGTHS TO SHOW ME ONLY WHAT HE WANTED ME TO SEE.
SO WHAT IS HE REALLY HIDING?

**NO!!**

IT'S NO COINCIDENCE MY SOCIETY OF SHADOWS ATTACKED WAYNE ENTERPRISES AROUND THE GLOBE TO DRAW YOU OUT. YOU MIGHT SAY IT WAS DESTINY.

WHAT KIND OF FATHER ATTACKS HIS OWN DAUGHTER TO GET AT ME? OR WAS SHE IN ON THIS AS WELL?

AND YOUR SICKNESS!

SIMPLY PUT...BECAUSE NO ONE ELSE WILL, IT IS MY RIGHT TO DO SO.

WHY DO YOU GET TO MAKE THE DECISION WHO LIVES AND DIES?

AND THE ONLY WAY TO PURIFY IT--TO HEAL IT-- IS TO CUT THE DISEASE OUT: TO REMOVE ALL THE BAD SO THAT THE GOOD WILL THRIVE.

OUR PLANET IS POLLUTED, NOT ONLY FROM THE AILS OF THE WORLD, BUT IT GOES MUCH DEEPER, TO HUMANITY ITSELF.

SO THIS IS WHAT IT MEANS TO "CURE THE WORLD?" MASS GENOCIDE?

WELL PLAYED, DETECTIVE.

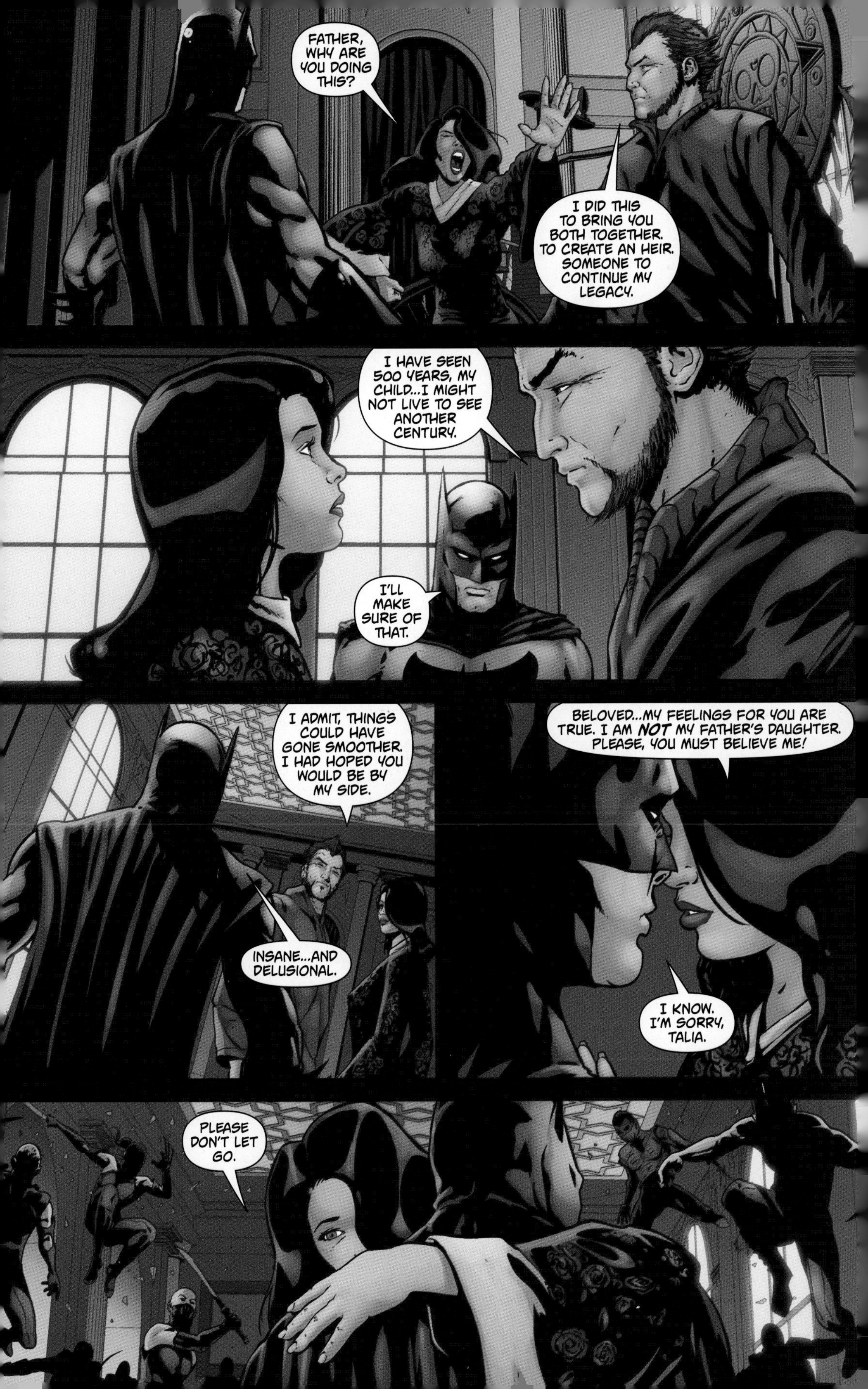
FATHER, WHY ARE YOU DOING THIS?
I DID THIS TO BRING YOU BOTH TOGETHER. TO CREATE AN HEIR. SOMEONE TO CONTINUE MY LEGACY.
I HAVE SEEN 500 YEARS, MY CHILD...I MIGHT NOT LIVE TO SEE ANOTHER CENTURY.
I'LL MAKE SURE OF THAT.
I ADMIT, THINGS COULD HAVE GONE SMOOTHER. I HAD HOPED YOU WOULD BE BY MY SIDE.
INSANE...AND DELUSIONAL.
BELOVED...MY FEELINGS FOR YOU ARE TRUE. I AM ***NOT*** MY FATHER'S DAUGHTER. PLEASE, YOU MUST BELIEVE ME!
I KNOW. I'M SORRY, TALIA.
PLEASE DON'T LET GO.

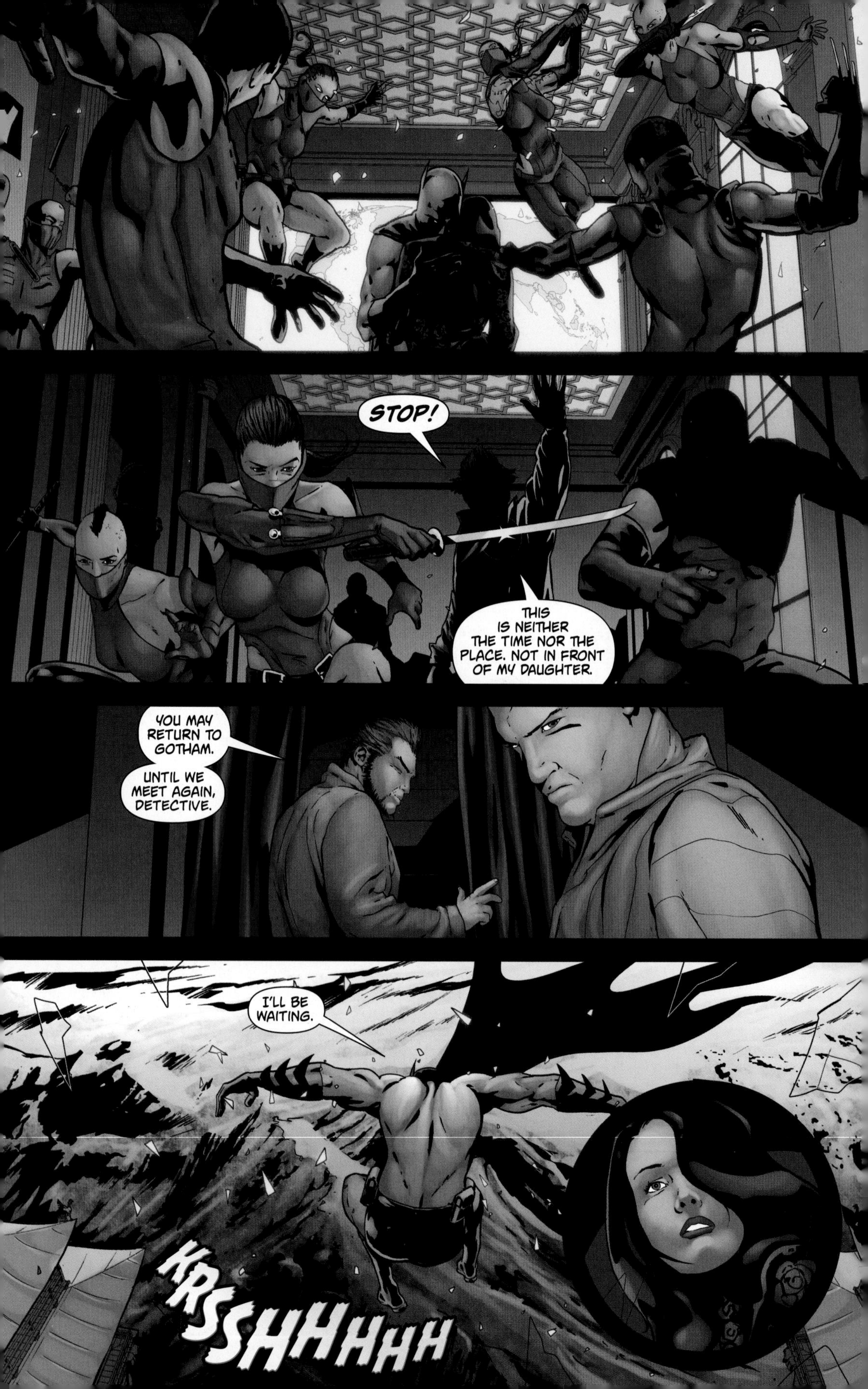
STOP!
THIS IS NEITHER THE TIME NOR THE PLACE. NOT IN FRONT OF MY DAUGHTER.
YOU MAY RETURN TO GOTHAM.
UNTIL WE MEET AGAIN, DETECTIVE.
I'LL BE WAITING.
KRSSHHHHH

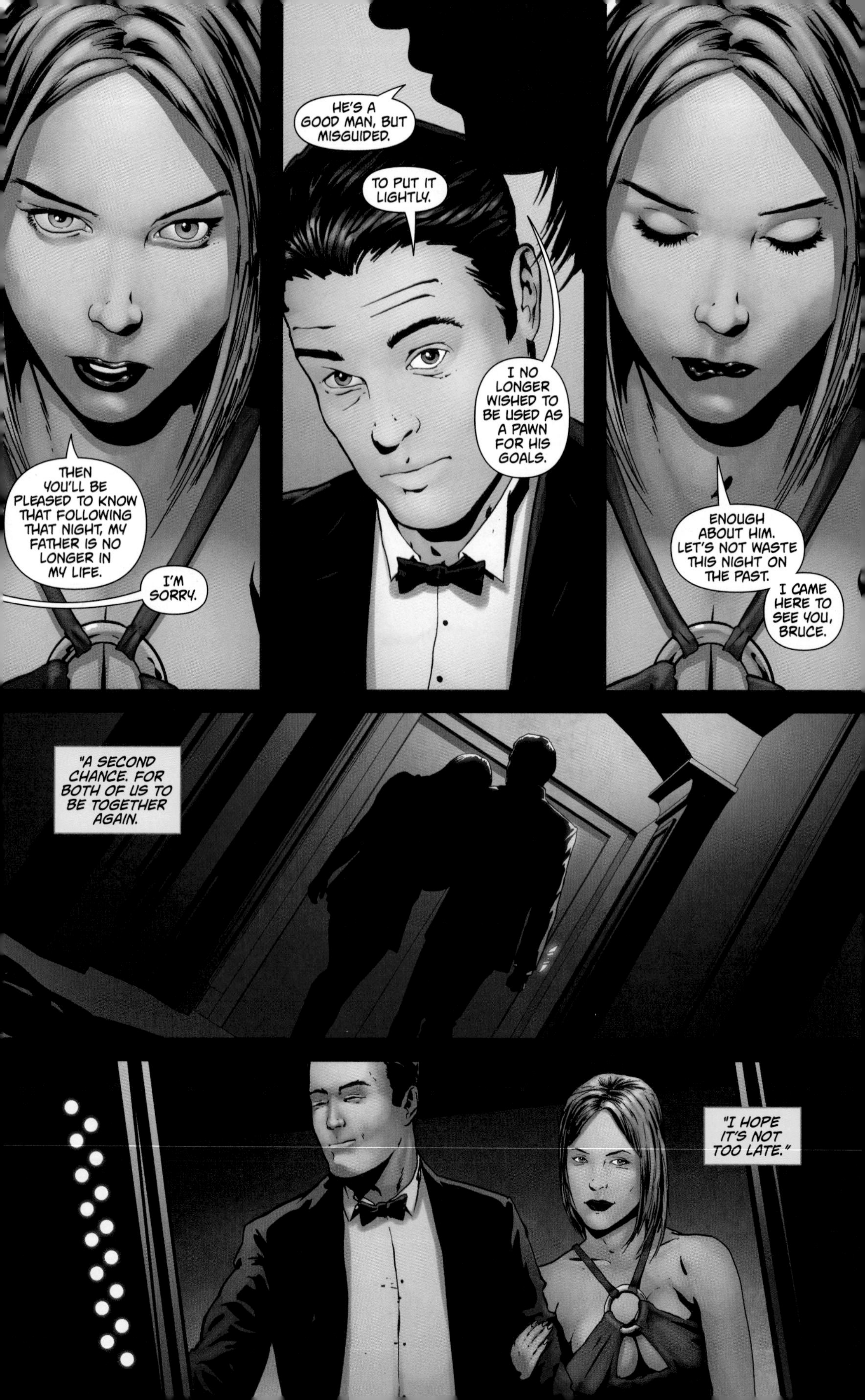
THEN YOU'LL BE PLEASED TO KNOW THAT FOLLOWING THAT NIGHT, MY FATHER IS NO LONGER IN MY LIFE.
I'M SORRY.
HE'S A GOOD MAN, BUT MISGUIDED.
TO PUT IT LIGHTLY.
I NO LONGER WISHED TO BE USED AS A PAWN FOR HIS GOALS.
ENOUGH ABOUT HIM. LET'S NOT WASTE THIS NIGHT ON THE PAST.
I CAME HERE TO SEE YOU, BRUCE.
"A SECOND CHANCE. FOR BOTH OF US TO BE TOGETHER AGAIN.
"I HOPE IT'S NOT TOO LATE."

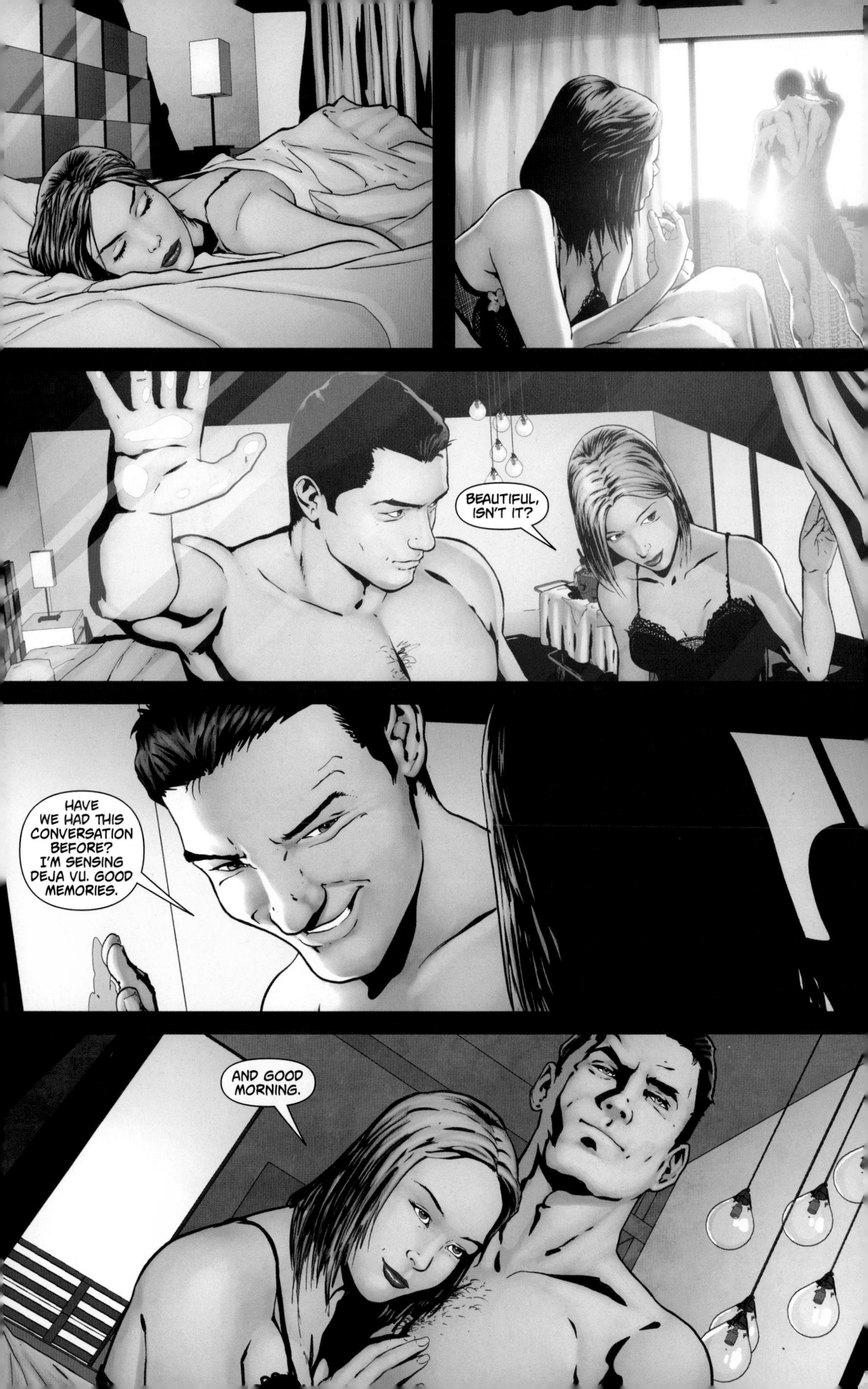
BEAUTIFUL, ISN'T IT?
HAVE WE HAD THIS CONVERSATION BEFORE? I'M SENSING DEJA VU. GOOD MEMORIES.
AND GOOD MORNING.

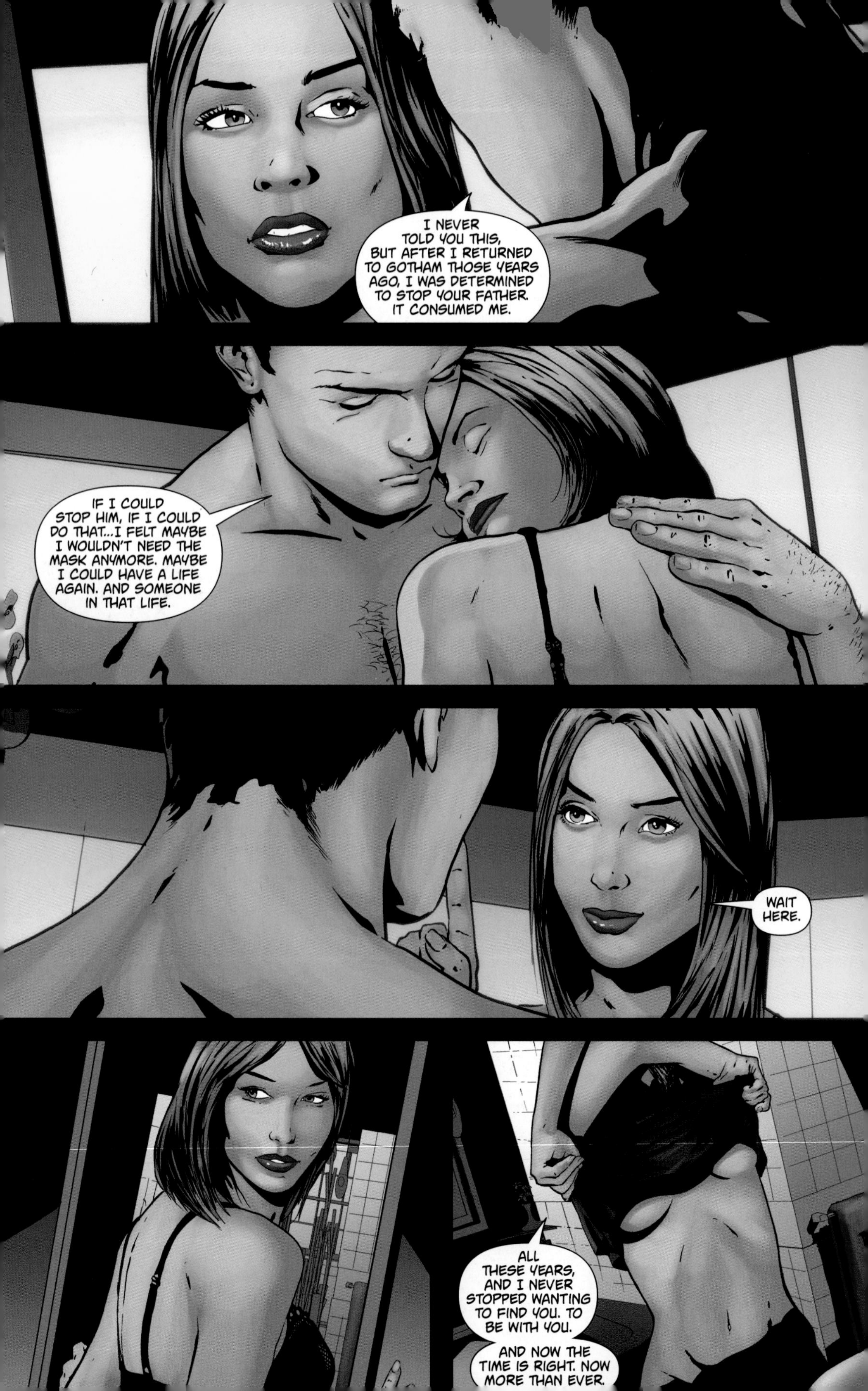
I NEVER TOLD YOU THIS, BUT AFTER I RETURNED TO GOTHAM THOSE YEARS AGO, I WAS DETERMINED TO STOP YOUR FATHER. IT CONSUMED ME.
IF I COULD STOP HIM, IF I COULD DO THAT...I FELT MAYBE I WOULDN'T NEED THE MASK ANYMORE. MAYBE I COULD HAVE A LIFE AGAIN. AND SOMEONE IN THAT LIFE.
WAIT HERE.
ALL THESE YEARS, AND I NEVER STOPPED WANTING TO FIND YOU. TO BE WITH YOU.
AND NOW THE TIME IS RIGHT. NOW MORE THAN EVER.

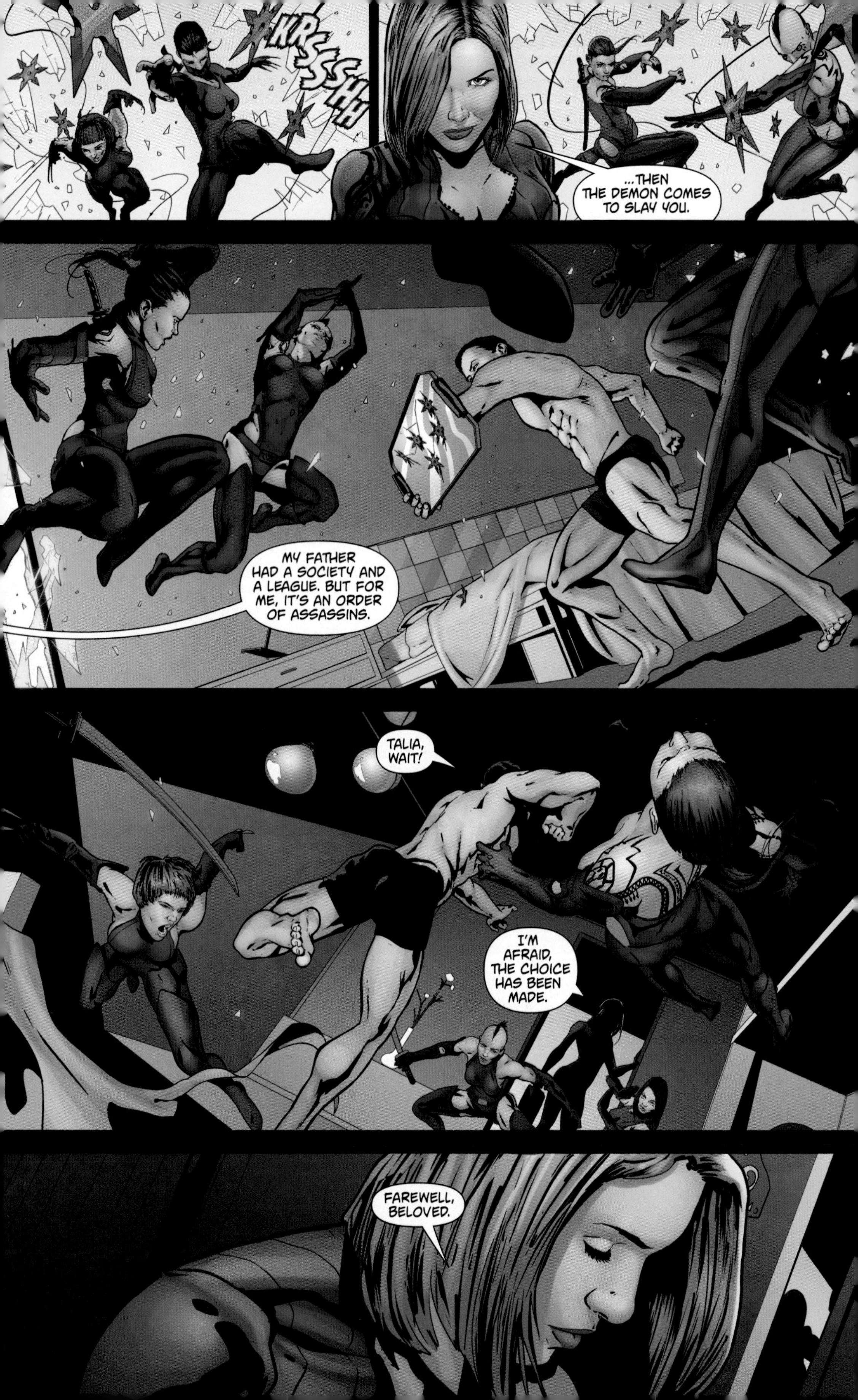
KRSSHH
...THEN THE DEMON COMES TO SLAY YOU.
MY FATHER HAD A SOCIETY AND A LEAGUE. BUT FOR ME, IT'S AN ORDER OF ASSASSINS.
TALIA, WAIT!
I'M AFRAID, THE CHOICE HAS BEEN MADE.
FAREWELL, BELOVED.

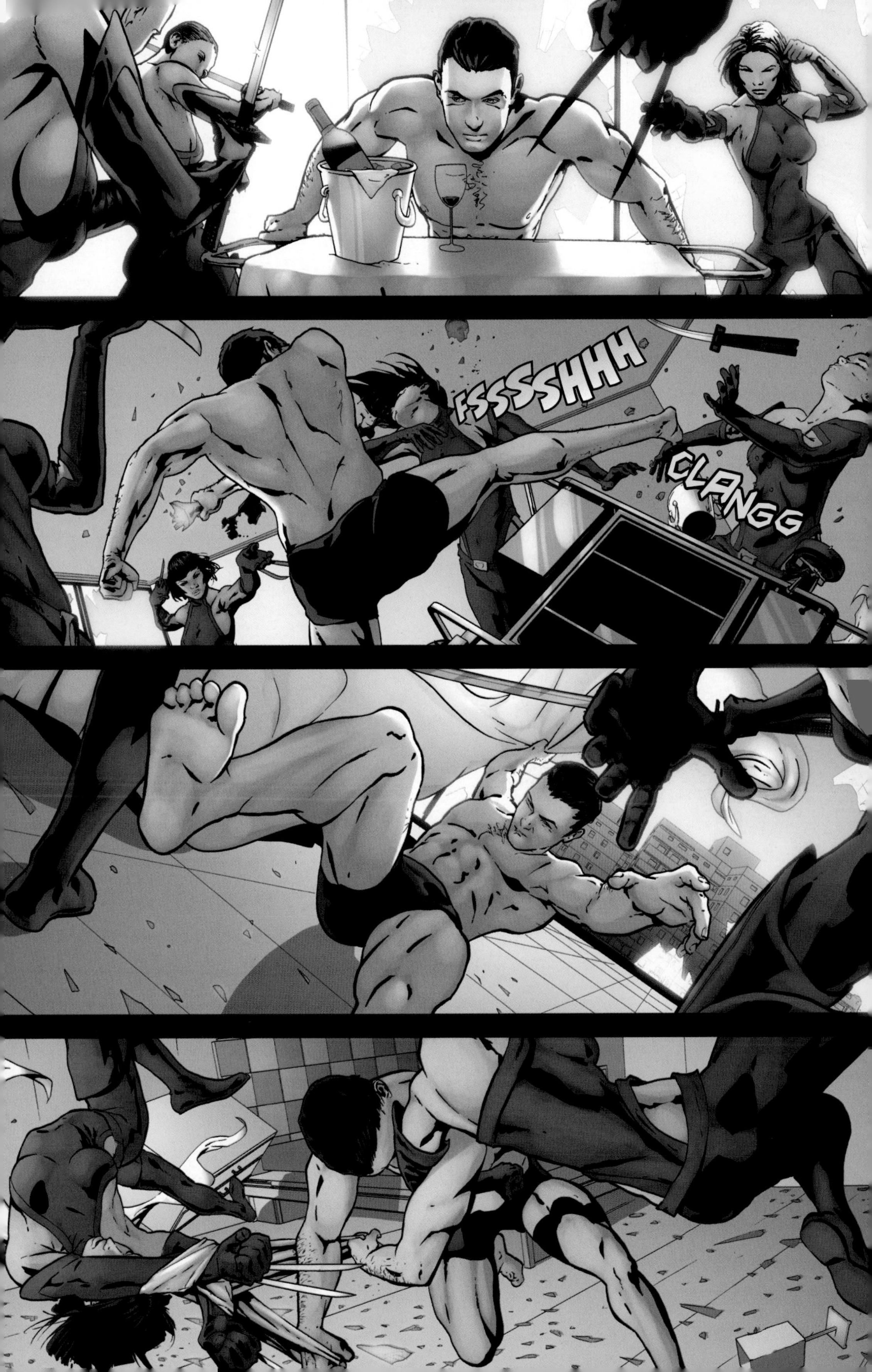
FSSSSHHH
CLANGG

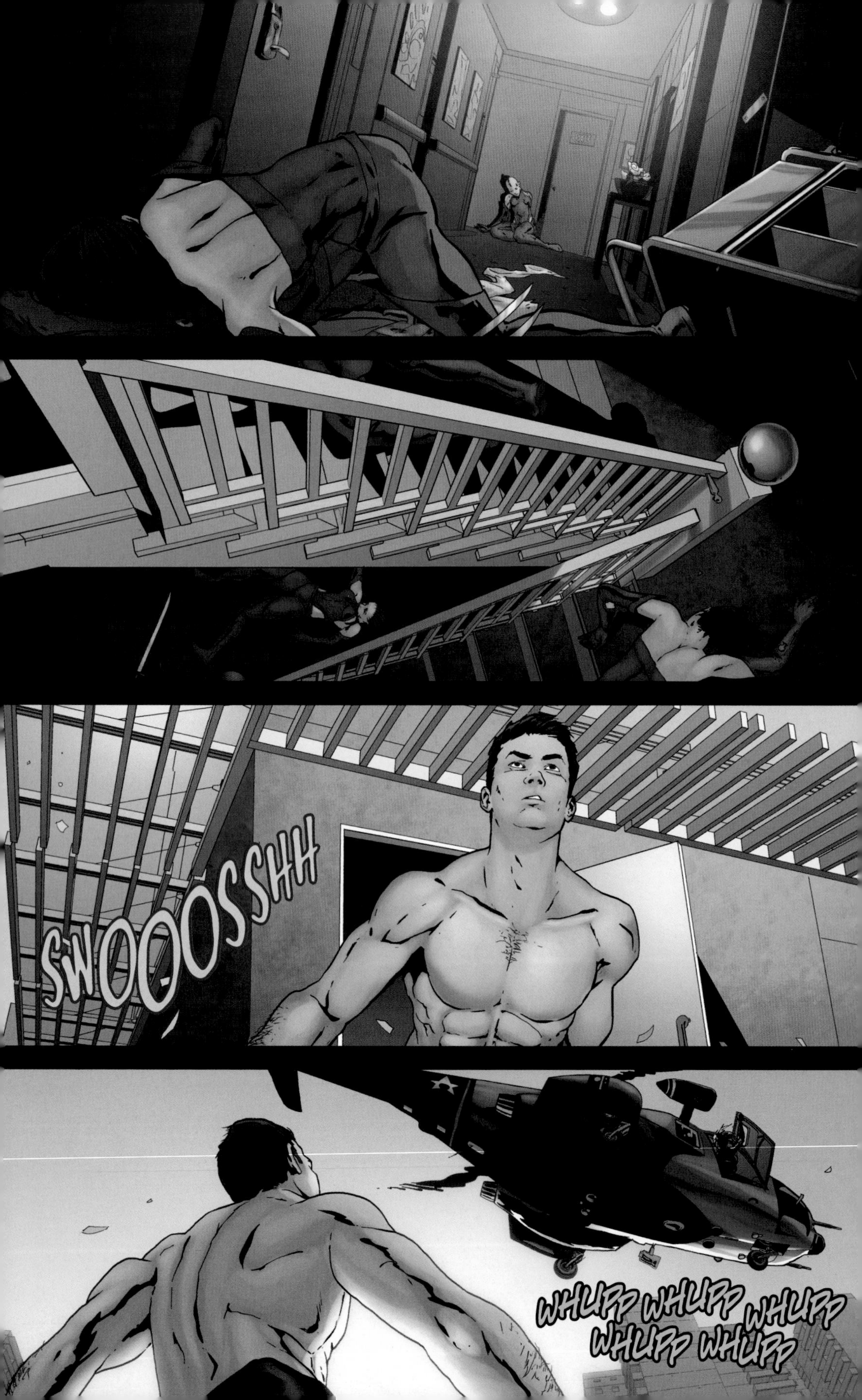
SWOOOSSHH
WHUPP WHUPP WHUPP
WHUPP WHUPP

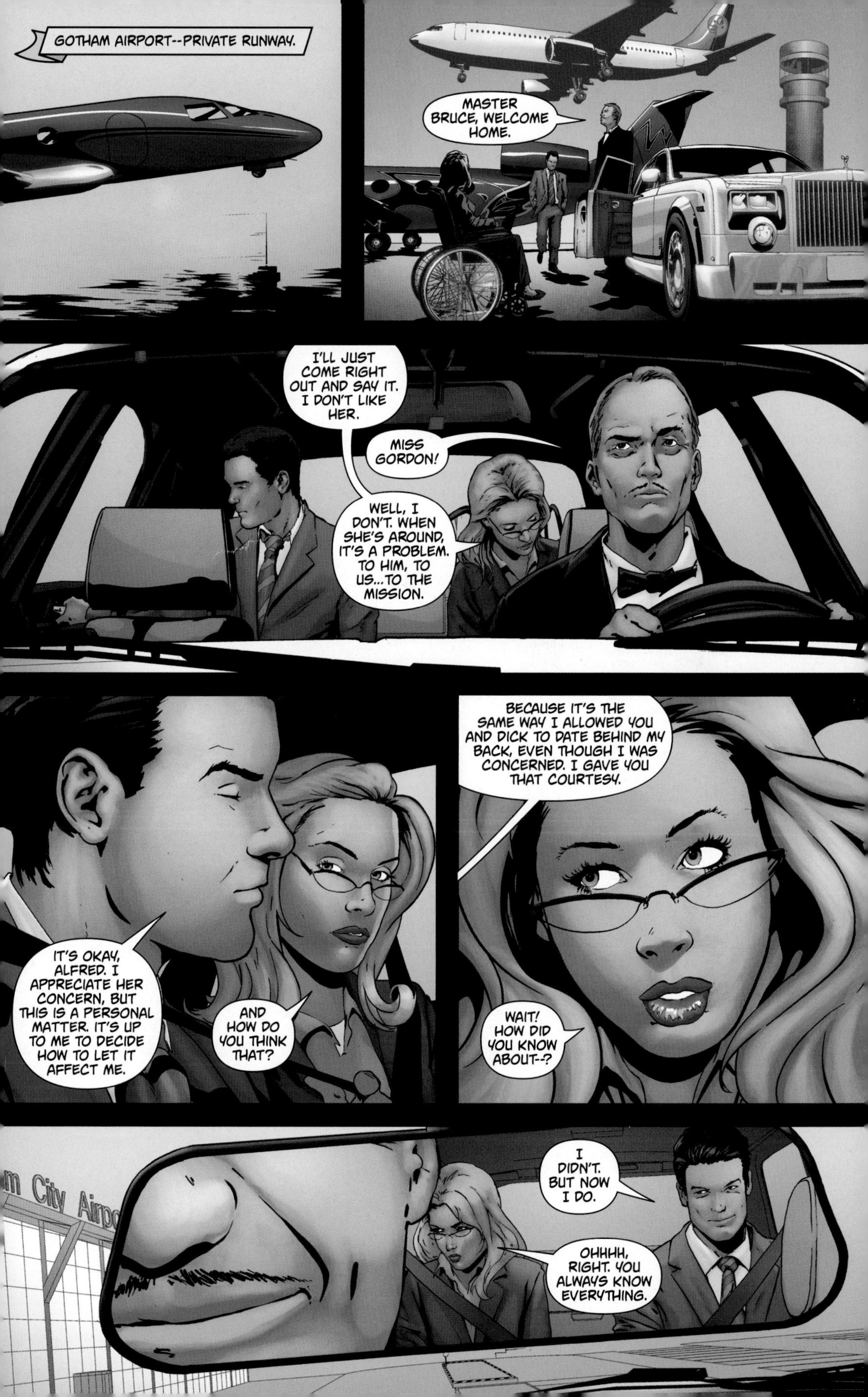
GOTHAM AIRPORT--PRIVATE RUNWAY.
MASTER BRUCE, WELCOME HOME.
I'LL JUST COME RIGHT OUT AND SAY IT. I DON'T LIKE HER.
MISS GORDON!
WELL, I DON'T. WHEN SHE'S AROUND, IT'S A PROBLEM. TO HIM, TO US...TO THE MISSION.
IT'S OKAY, ALFRED. I APPRECIATE HER CONCERN, BUT THIS IS A PERSONAL MATTER. IT'S UP TO ME TO DECIDE HOW TO LET IT AFFECT ME.
AND HOW DO YOU THINK THAT?
BECAUSE IT'S THE SAME WAY I ALLOWED YOU AND DICK TO DATE BEHIND MY BACK, EVEN THOUGH I WAS CONCERNED. I GAVE YOU THAT COURTESY.
WAIT! HOW DID YOU KNOW ABOUT--?
I DIDN'T. BUT NOW I DO.
OHHHH, RIGHT. YOU ALWAYS KNOW EVERYTHING.

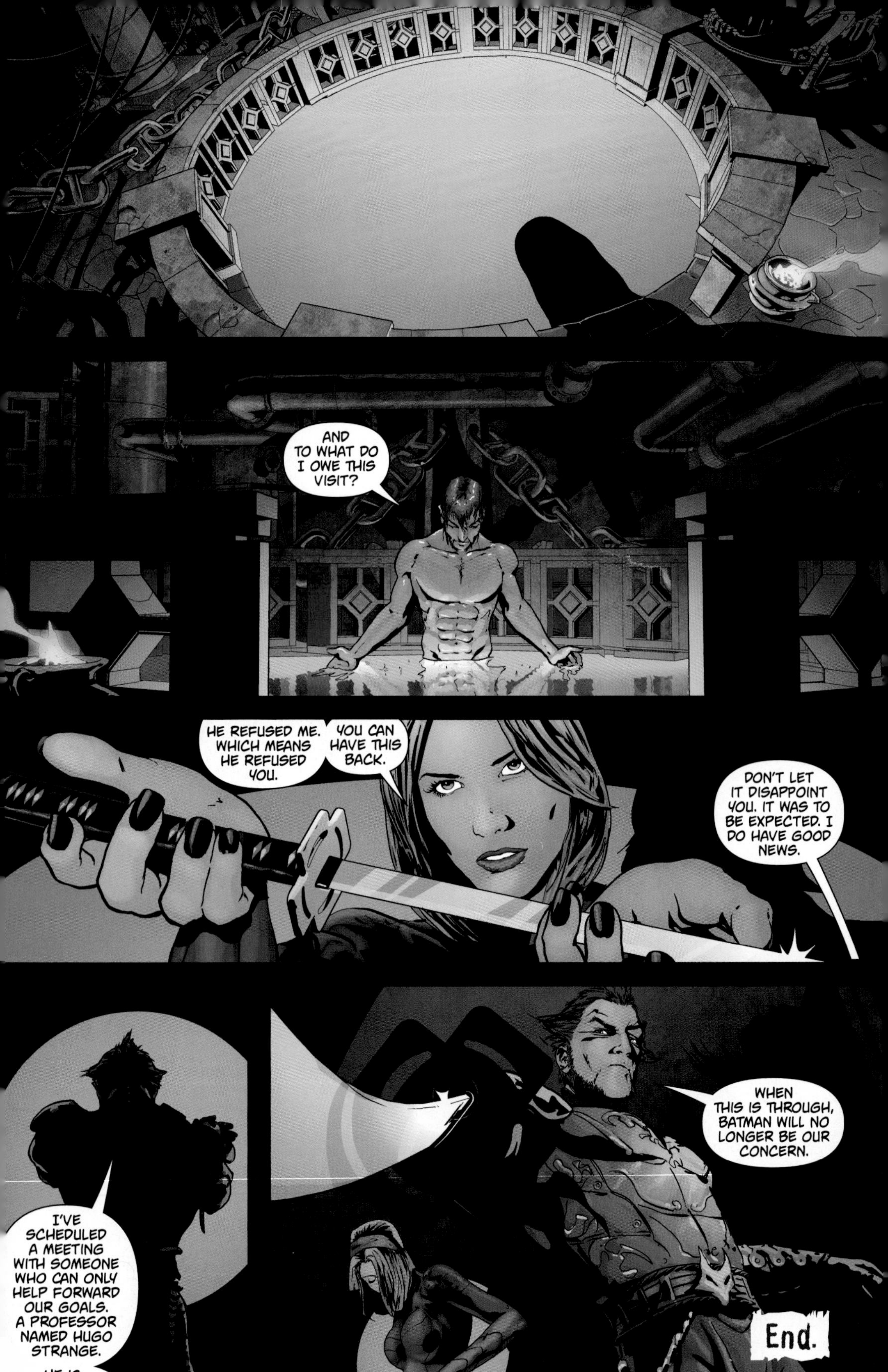
AND TO WHAT DO I OWE THIS VISIT?
HE REFUSED ME. WHICH MEANS HE REFUSED YOU.
YOU CAN HAVE THIS BACK.
DON'T LET IT DISAPPOINT YOU. IT WAS TO BE EXPECTED. I DO HAVE GOOD NEWS.
WHEN THIS IS THROUGH, BATMAN WILL NO LONGER BE OUR CONCERN.
I'VE SCHEDULED A MEETING WITH SOMEONE WHO CAN ONLY HELP FORWARD OUR GOALS. A PROFESSOR NAMED HUGO STRANGE.
HE IS SOMEONE WE CAN USE TO OUR BENEFIT.
End.

The story of Talia and Ra's continues in the Batman: Arkham City videogame

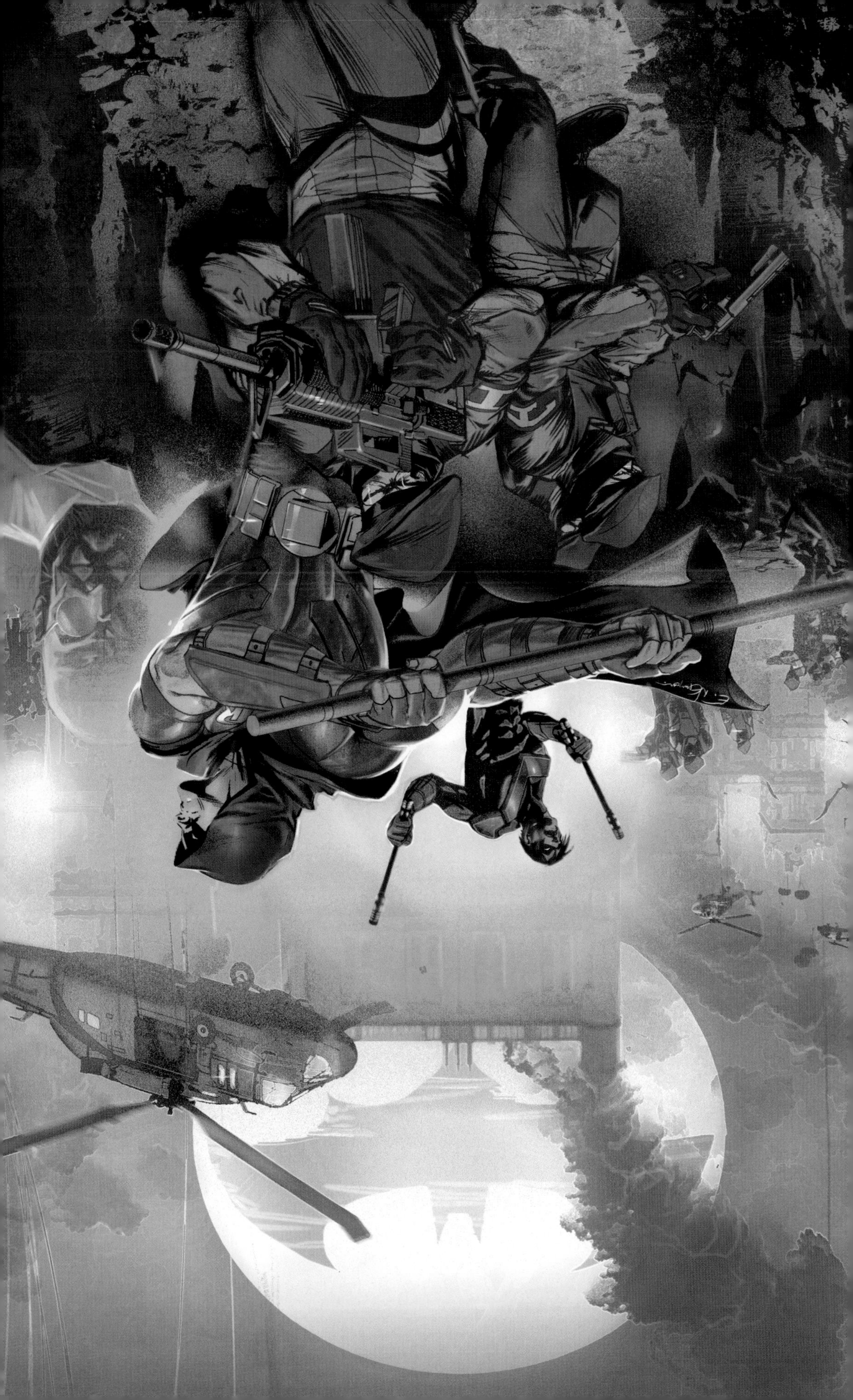

# UNINVITED GUESTS

WRITTEN BY: DEREK FRIDOLFS

ART BY: DAVIDE FABBRI

COLORS BY: ALEJANDRO SANCHEZ

COVER ART BY: ERIC NGUYEN

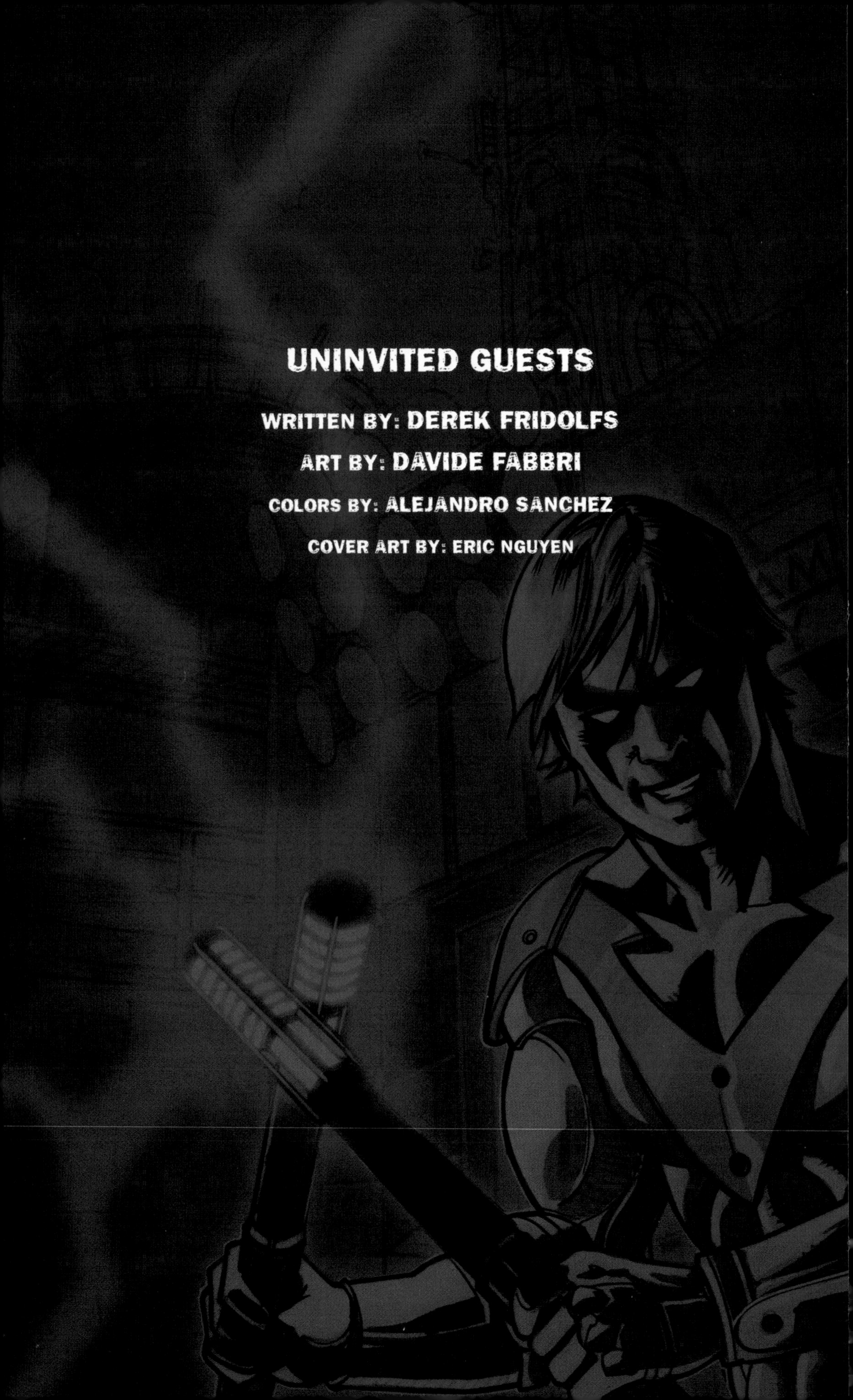

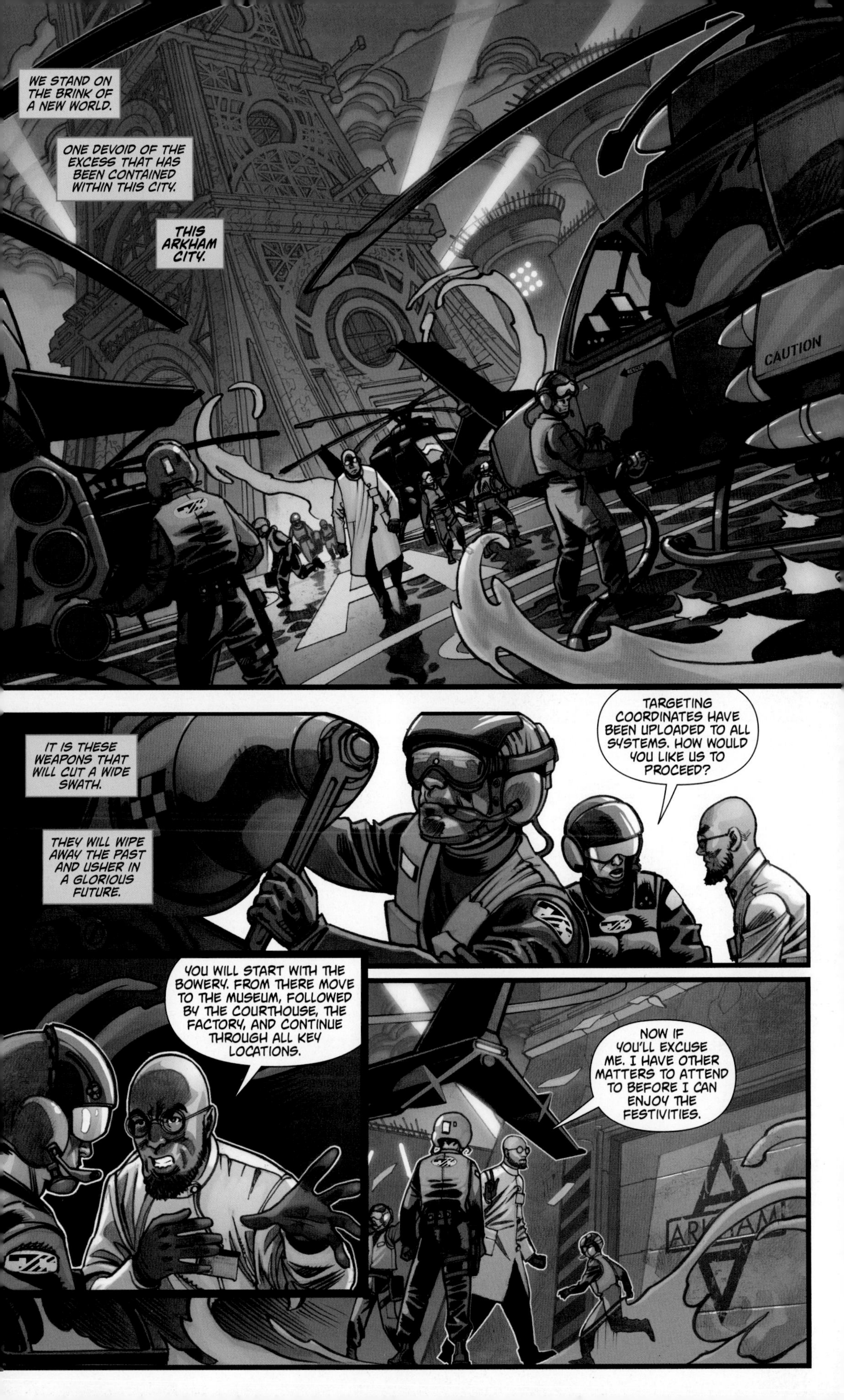
WE STAND ON THE BRINK OF A NEW WORLD.
ONE DEVOID OF THE EXCESS THAT HAS BEEN CONTAINED WITHIN THIS CITY.
THIS ARKHAM CITY.
CAUTION
IT IS THESE WEAPONS THAT WILL CUT A WIDE SWATH.
THEY WILL WIPE AWAY THE PAST AND USHER IN A GLORIOUS FUTURE.
TARGETING COORDINATES HAVE BEEN UPLOADED TO ALL SYSTEMS. HOW WOULD YOU LIKE US TO PROCEED?
YOU WILL START WITH THE BOWERY. FROM THERE MOVE TO THE MUSEUM, FOLLOWED BY THE COURTHOUSE, THE FACTORY, AND CONTINUE THROUGH ALL KEY LOCATIONS.
NOW IF YOU'LL EXCUSE ME. I HAVE OTHER MATTERS TO ATTEND TO BEFORE I CAN ENJOY THE FESTIVITIES.

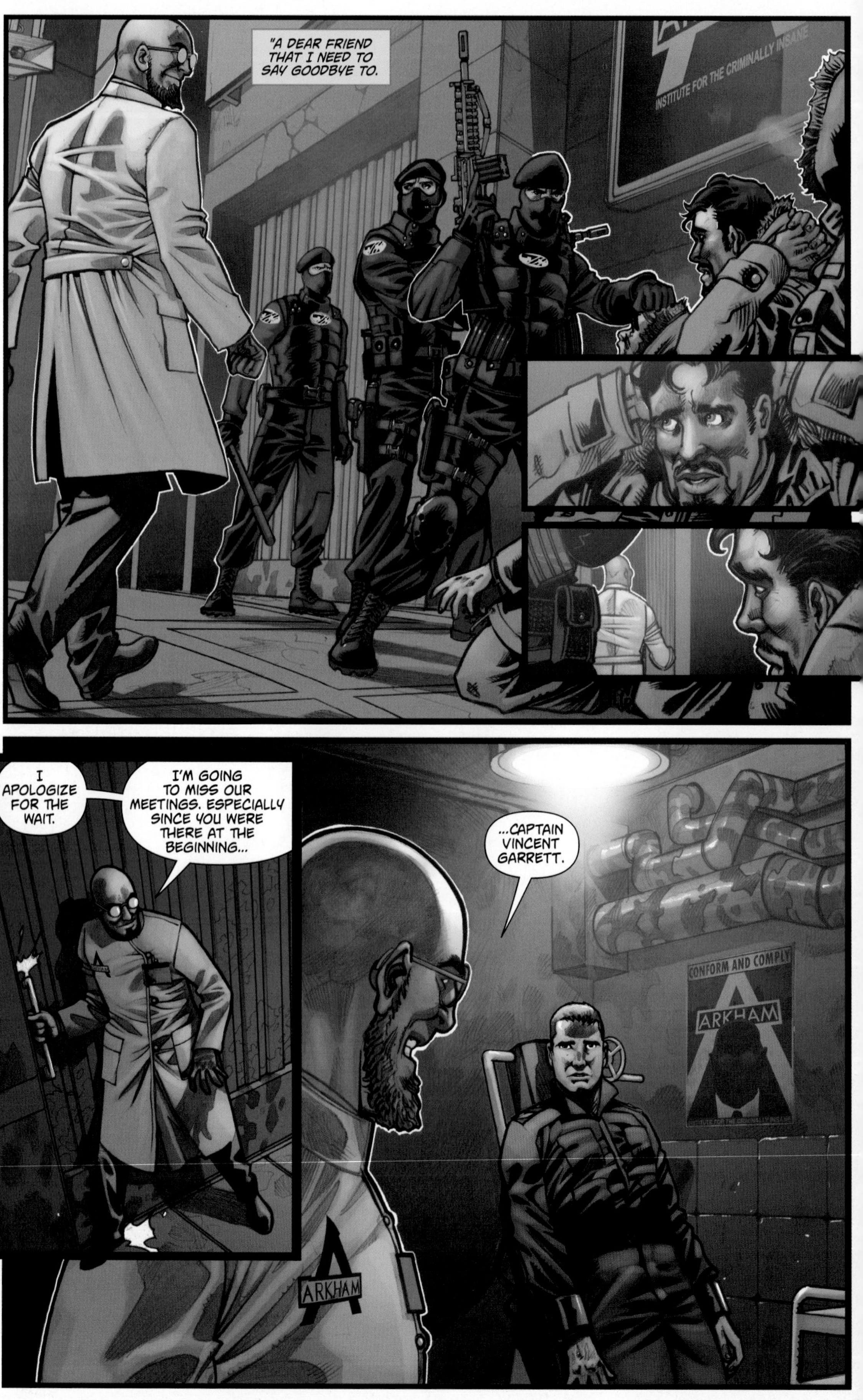
"A DEAR FRIEND THAT I NEED TO SAY GOODBYE TO.
INSTITUTE FOR THE CRIMINALLY INSANE
I APOLOGIZE FOR THE WAIT.
I'M GOING TO MISS OUR MEETINGS. ESPECIALLY SINCE YOU WERE THERE AT THE BEGINNING...
...CAPTAIN VINCENT GARRETT.
CONFORM AND COMPLY
ARKHAM
ARKHAM

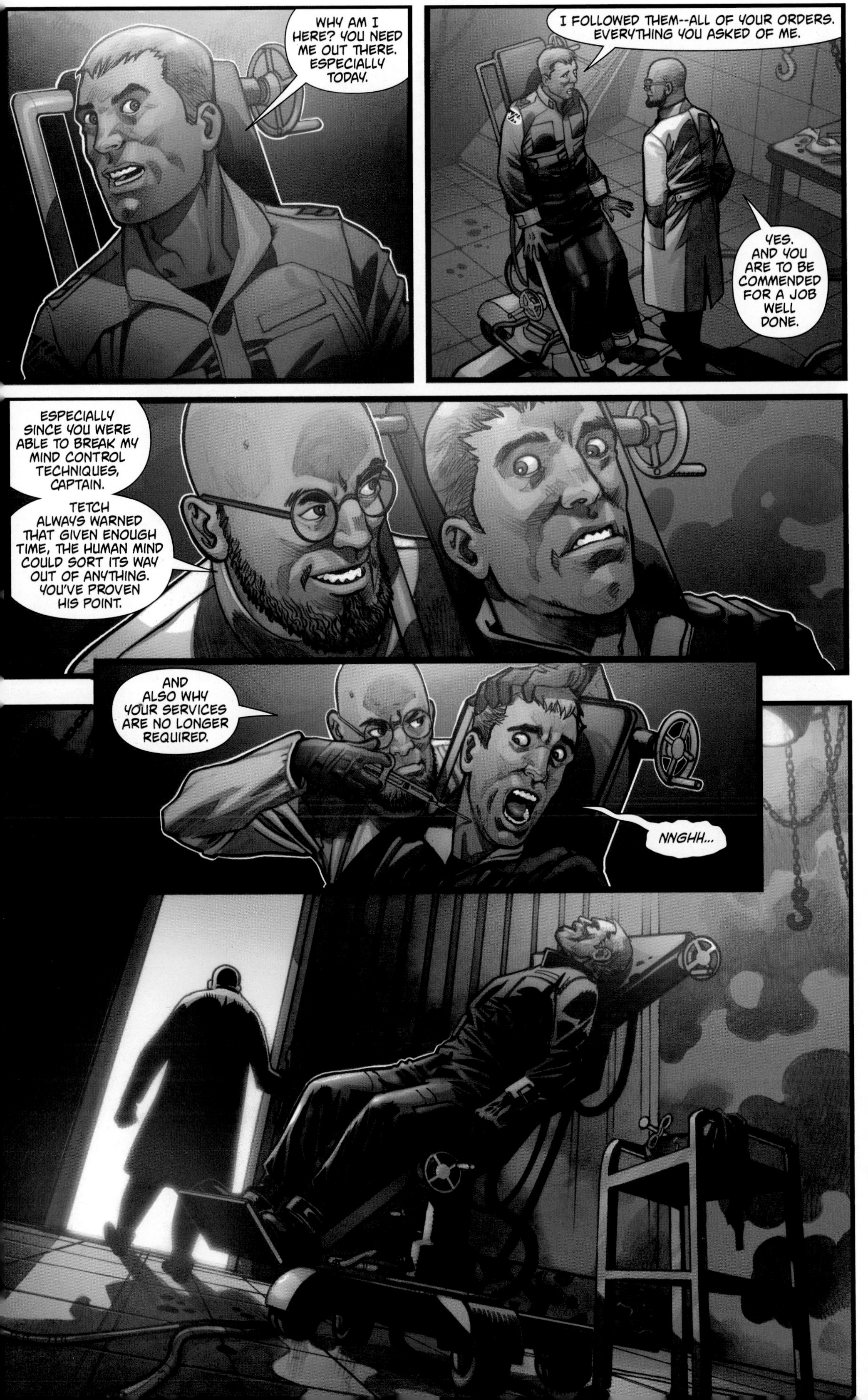
WHY AM I HERE? YOU NEED ME OUT THERE. ESPECIALLY TODAY.
I FOLLOWED THEM--ALL OF YOUR ORDERS. EVERYTHING YOU ASKED OF ME.
YES. AND YOU ARE TO BE COMMENDED FOR A JOB WELL DONE.
ESPECIALLY SINCE YOU WERE ABLE TO BREAK MY MIND CONTROL TECHNIQUES, CAPTAIN.
TETCH ALWAYS WARNED THAT GIVEN ENOUGH TIME, THE HUMAN MIND COULD SORT ITS WAY OUT OF ANYTHING. YOU'VE PROVEN HIS POINT.
AND ALSO WHY YOUR SERVICES ARE NO LONGER REQUIRED.
NNGHH...

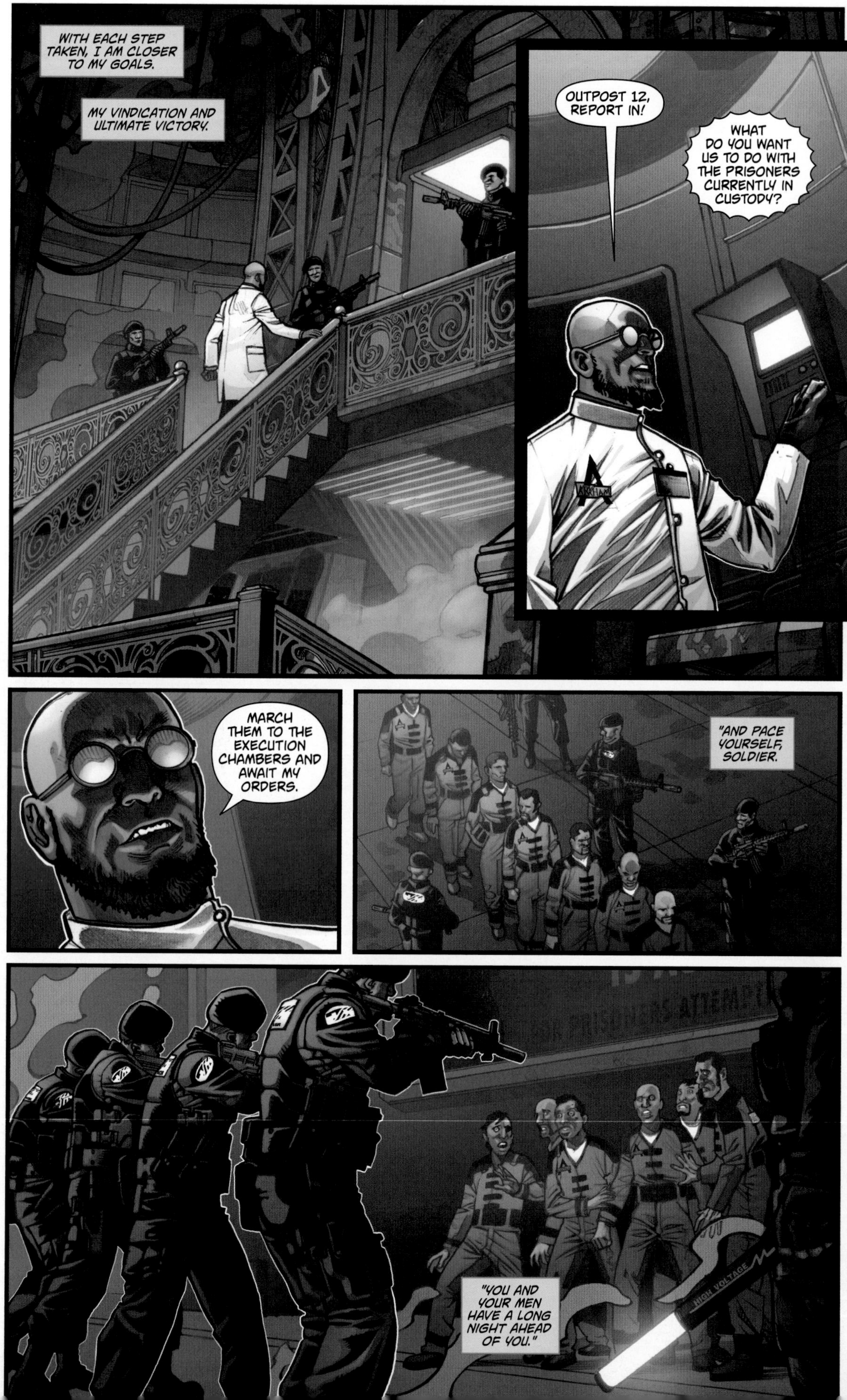
WITH EACH STEP TAKEN, I AM CLOSER TO MY GOALS.
MY VINDICATION AND ULTIMATE VICTORY.
OUTPOST 12, REPORT IN!
WHAT DO YOU WANT US TO DO WITH THE PRISONERS CURRENTLY IN CUSTODY?
MARCH THEM TO THE EXECUTION CHAMBERS AND AWAIT MY ORDERS.
"AND PACE YOURSELF, SOLDIER.
"YOU AND YOUR MEN HAVE A LONG NIGHT AHEAD OF YOU."
HIGH VOLTAGE

BREAKOUT
AT STRYKER'S ISLAND!
INMATES RUN FREE

THREE LOCATIONS TO START, AND MANY MORE PLANNED.

METROPOLIS.

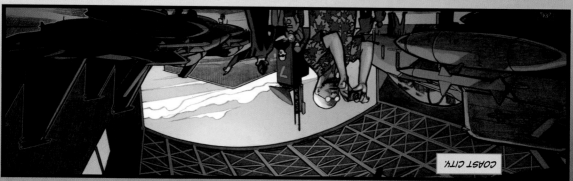

COAST CITY.

KEYSTONE CITY.

SCOUTING OTHER LOCATIONS PROVED TO BE A SIMPLE TASK.

AFTER ARKHAM CITY, OTHER CAMPS COULD BE SET UP ELSEWHERE.

OR THE WRONG PERSON.

OF COURSE, MAYBE I'M ASKING THE WRONG QUESTIONS,

WILL YOU MISS THIS EVENT OR BE PART OF IT?

WHERE WILL YOU BE WHEN EVERYTHING CHANGES?

WHERE ARE YOU, BATMAN?

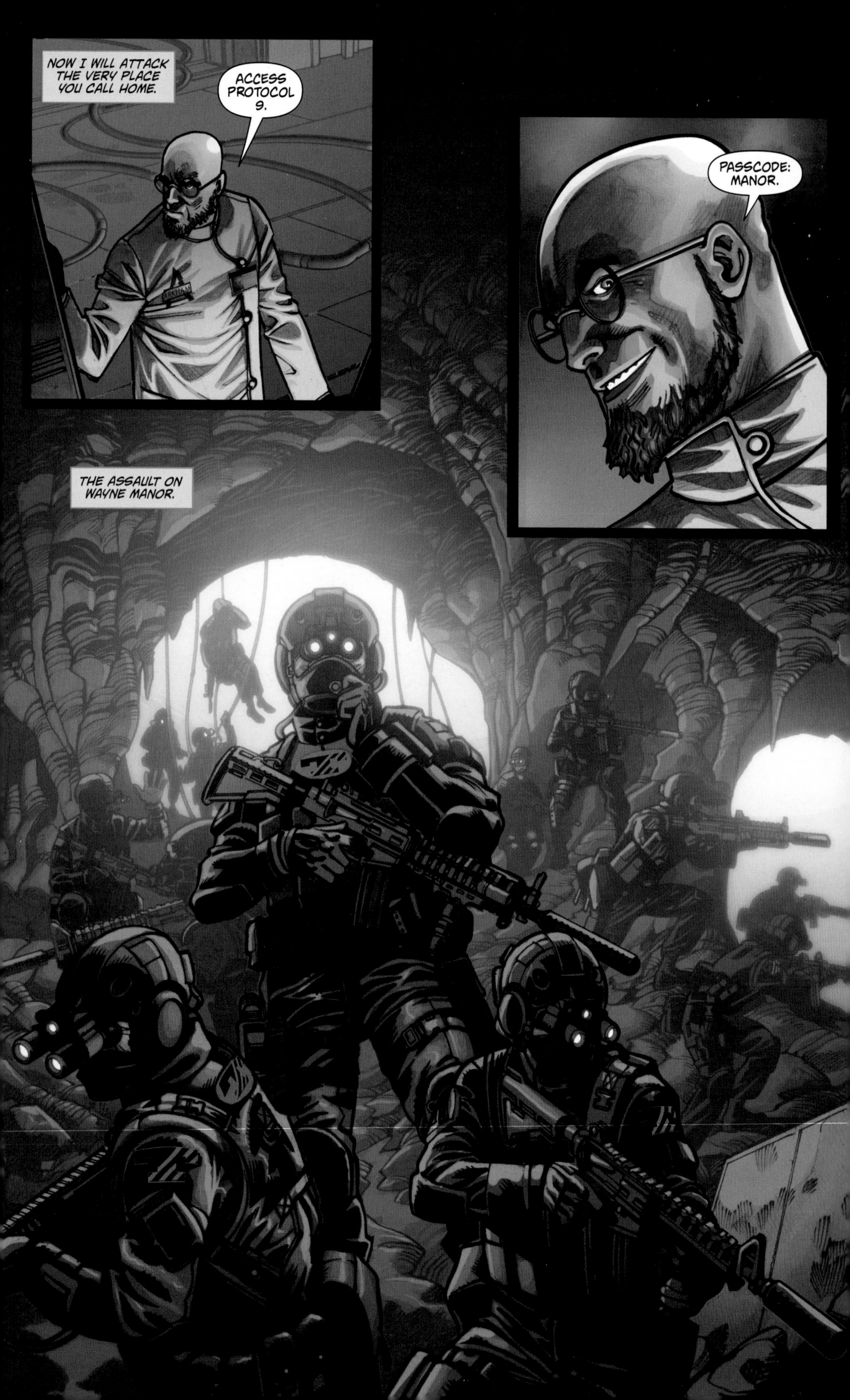
NOW I WILL ATTACK THE VERY PLACE YOU CALL HOME.
ACCESS PROTOCOL 9.
PASSCODE: MANOR.
THE ASSAULT ON WAYNE MANOR.

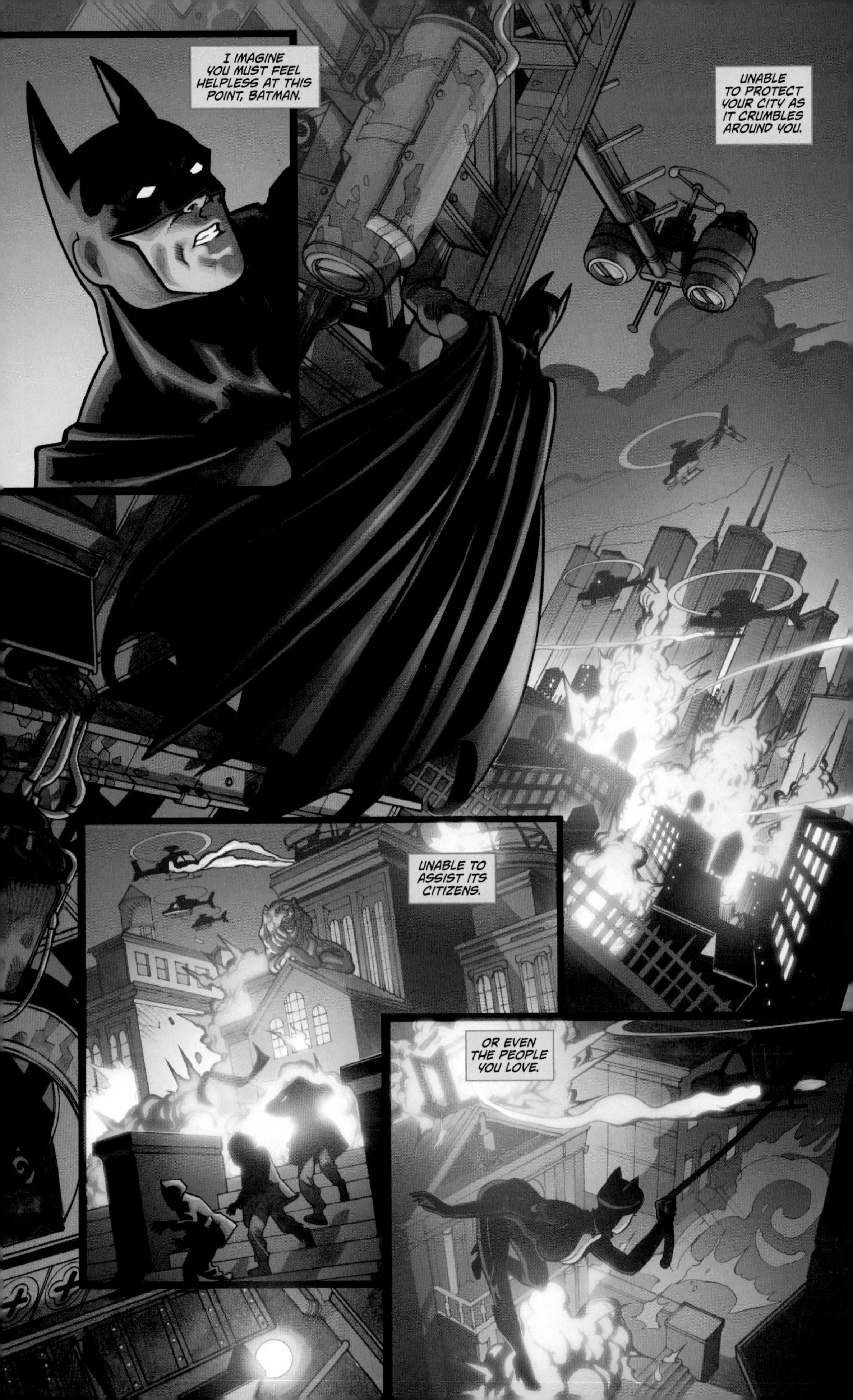

I IMAGINE YOU MUST FEEL HELPLESS AT THIS POINT, BATMAN.
UNABLE TO PROTECT YOUR CITY AS IT CRUMBLES AROUND YOU.
UNABLE TO ASSIST ITS CITIZENS.
OR EVEN THE PEOPLE YOU LOVE.

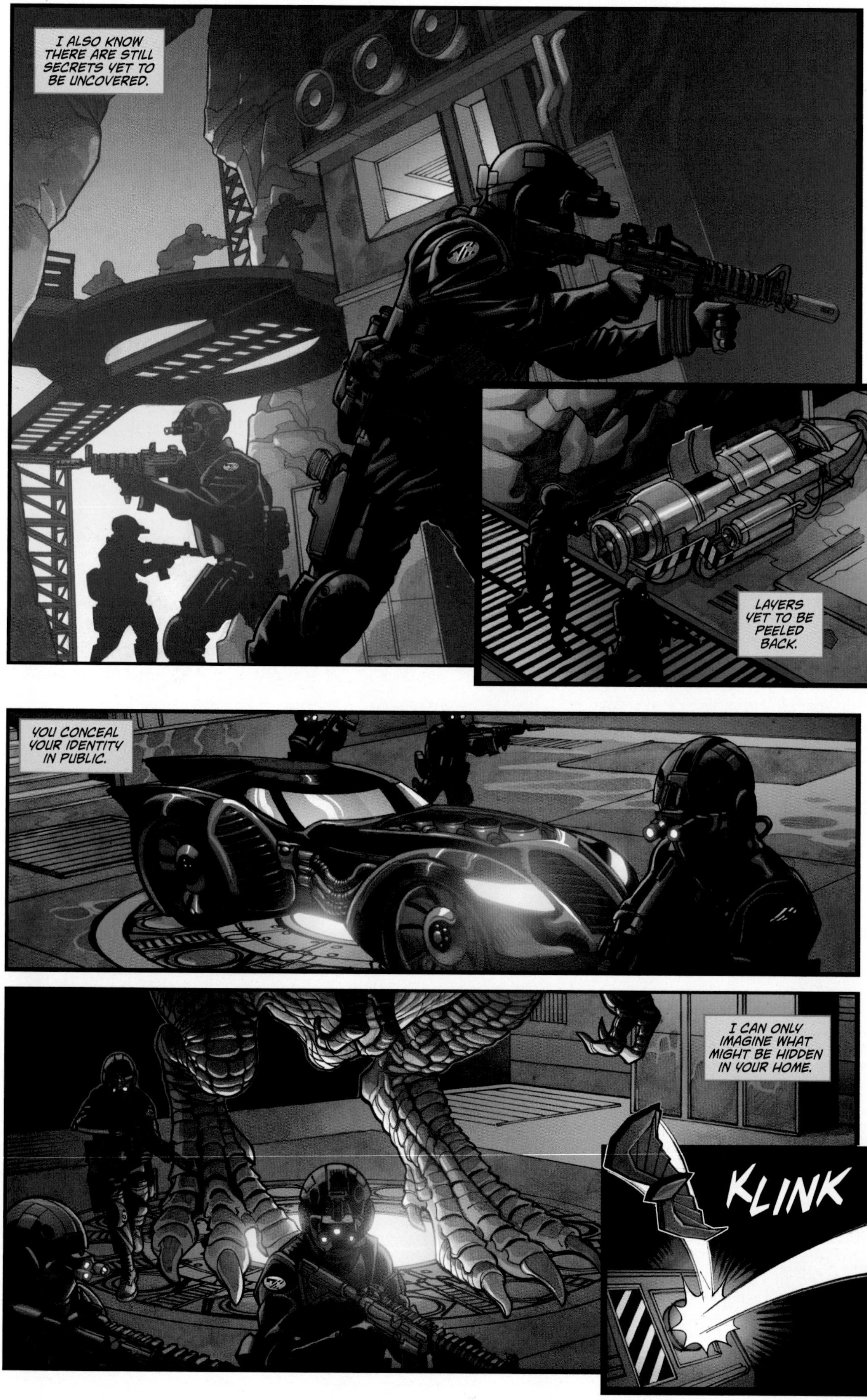
I ALSO KNOW THERE ARE STILL SECRETS YET TO BE UNCOVERED.
LAYERS YET TO BE PEELED BACK.
YOU CONCEAL YOUR IDENTITY IN PUBLIC.
I CAN ONLY IMAGINE WHAT MIGHT BE HIDDEN IN YOUR HOME.
KLINK

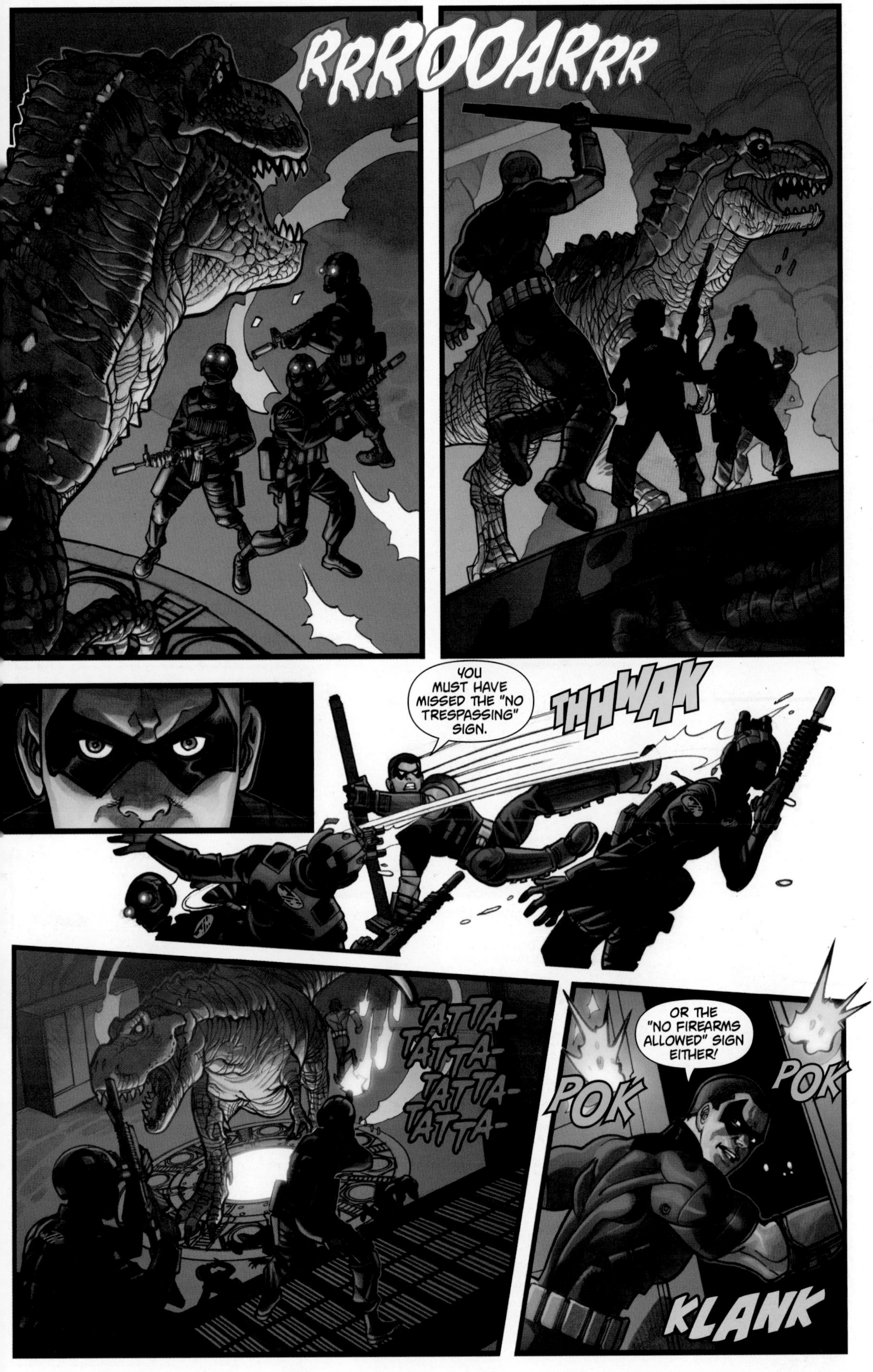
RRROOARRR
YOU MUST HAVE MISSED THE "NO TRESPASSING" SIGN.
THHWAK
TATTA-TATTA-TATTA-TATTA-
OR THE "NO FIREARMS ALLOWED" SIGN EITHER!
POK
POK
KLANK

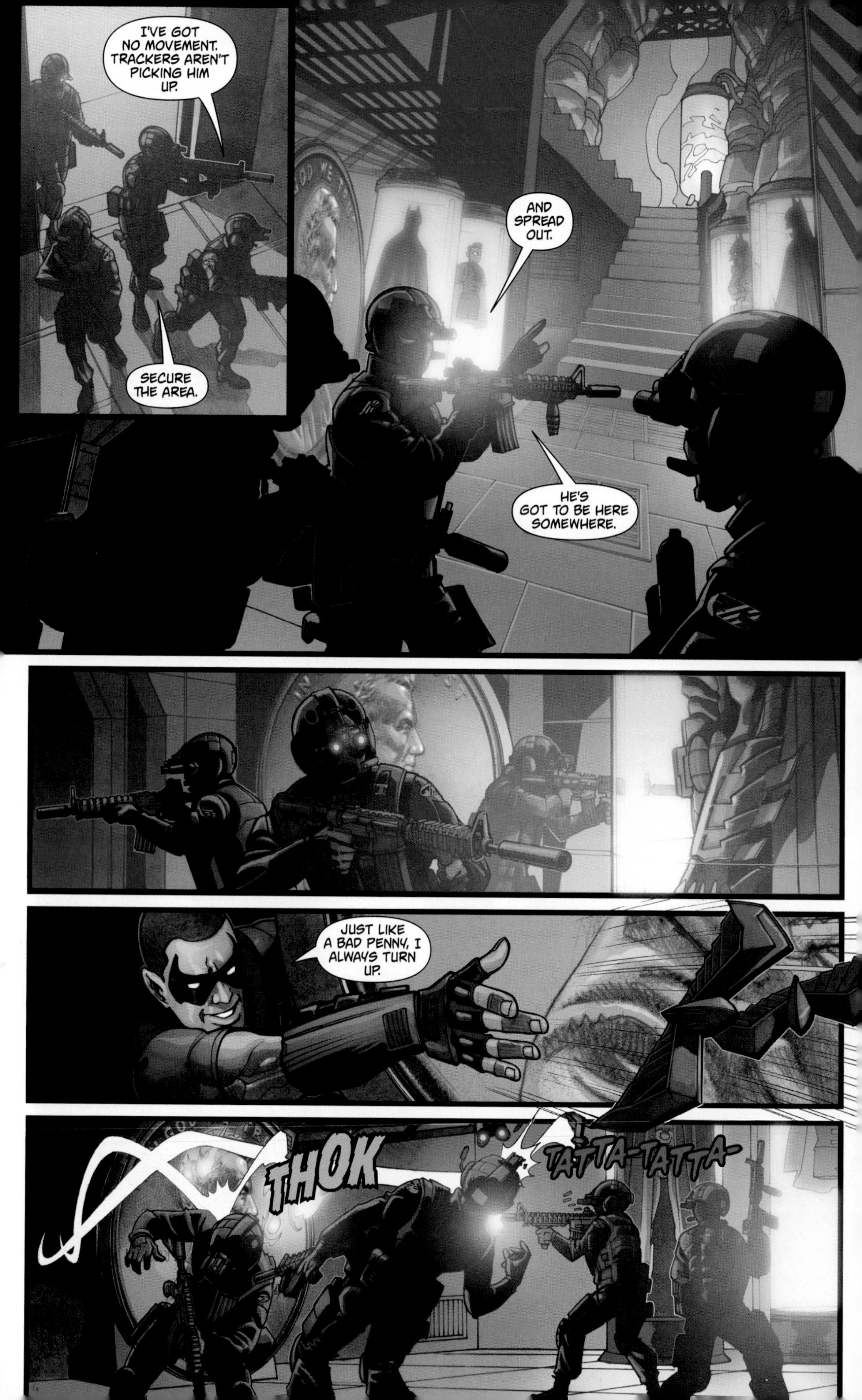
I'VE GOT NO MOVEMENT. TRACKERS AREN'T PICKING HIM UP.
SECURE THE AREA.
AND SPREAD OUT.
HE'S GOT TO BE HERE SOMEWHERE.
JUST LIKE A BAD PENNY, I ALWAYS TURN UP.
THOK
TATTA-TATTA-

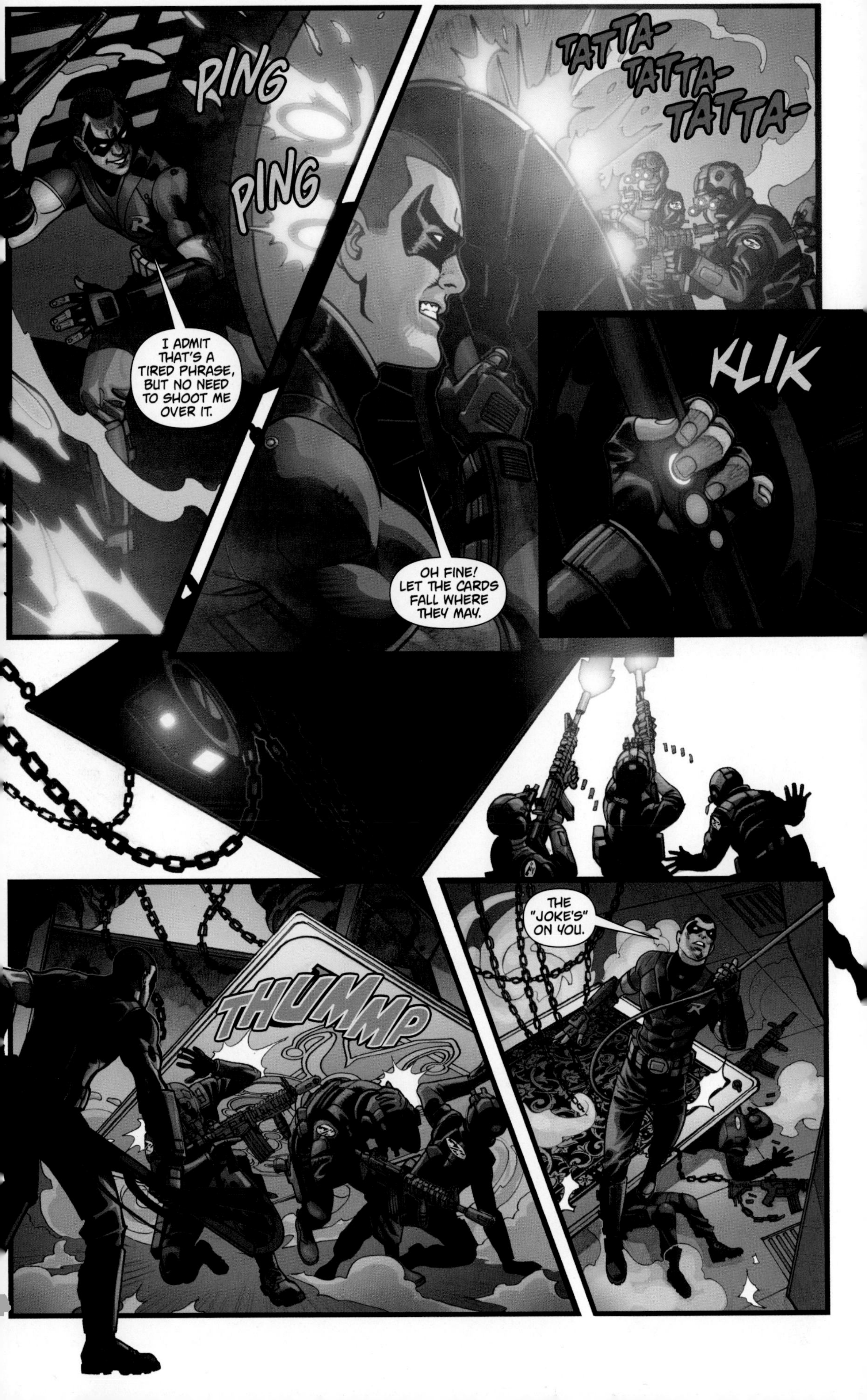
PING
PING
I ADMIT THAT'S A TIRED PHRASE, BUT NO NEED TO SHOOT ME OVER IT.
TATTA-
TATTA-
TATTA-
OH FINE! LET THE CARDS FALL WHERE THEY MAY.
KLIK
THUMMP
THE "JOKE'S" ON YOU.

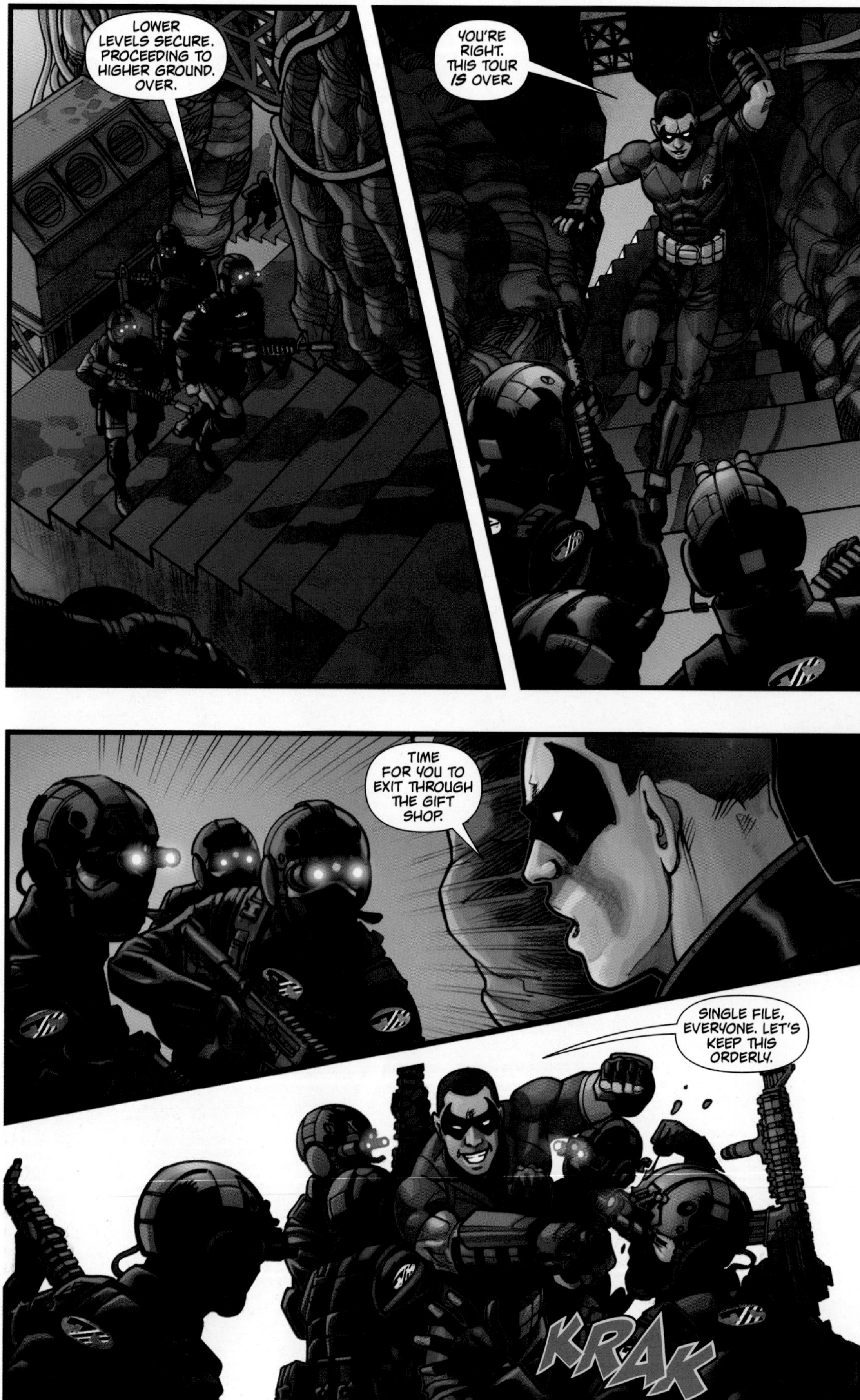
LOWER LEVELS SECURE. PROCEEDING TO HIGHER GROUND. OVER.
YOU'RE RIGHT. THIS TOUR *IS* OVER.
TIME FOR YOU TO EXIT THROUGH THE GIFT SHOP.
SINGLE FILE, EVERYONE. LET'S KEEP THIS ORDERLY.
KRAK

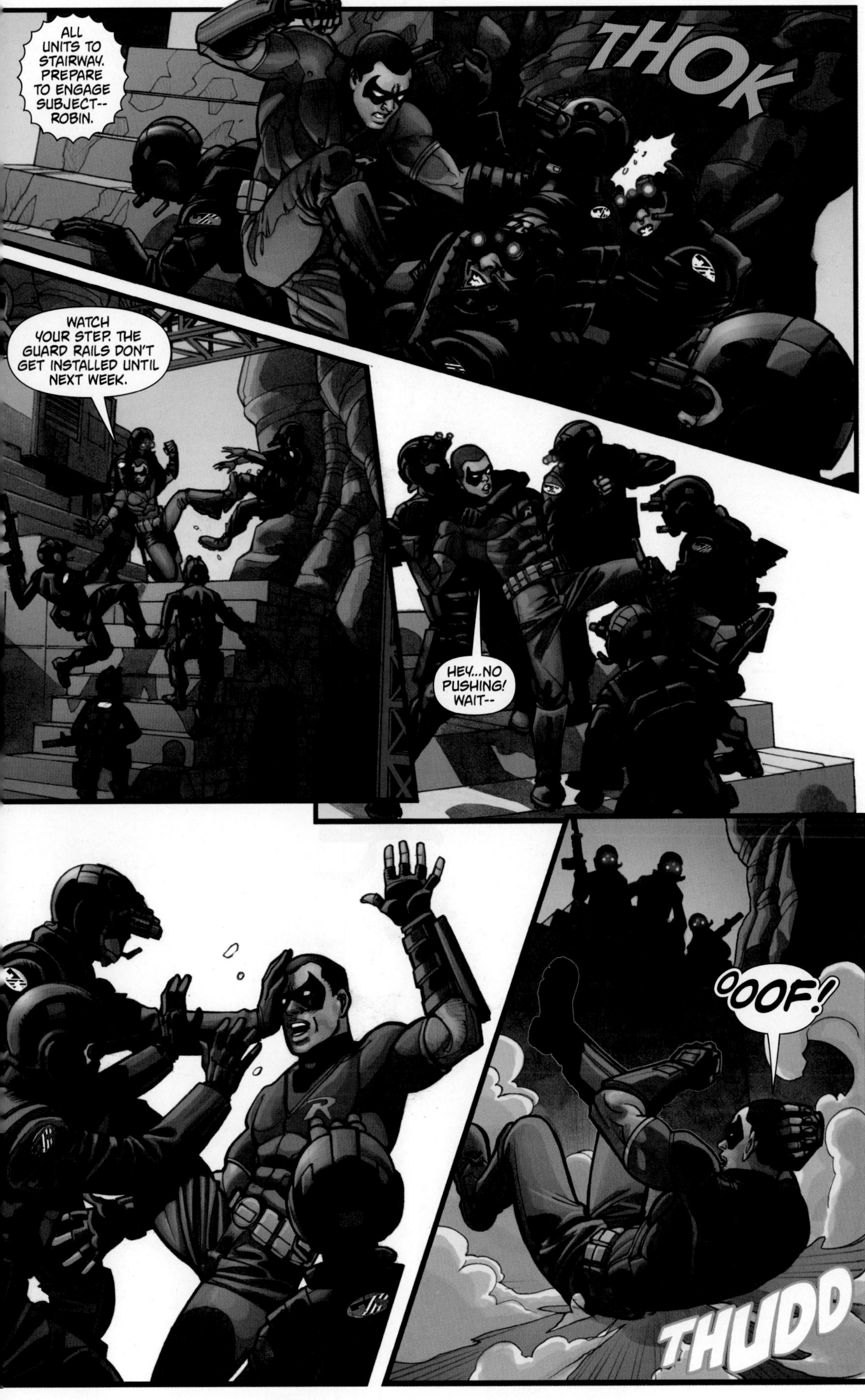
ALL UNITS TO STAIRWAY. PREPARE TO ENGAGE SUBJECT--ROBIN.
THOK
WATCH YOUR STEP. THE GUARD RAILS DON'T GET INSTALLED UNTIL NEXT WEEK.
HEY...NO PUSHING! WAIT--
OOOF!
THUDD

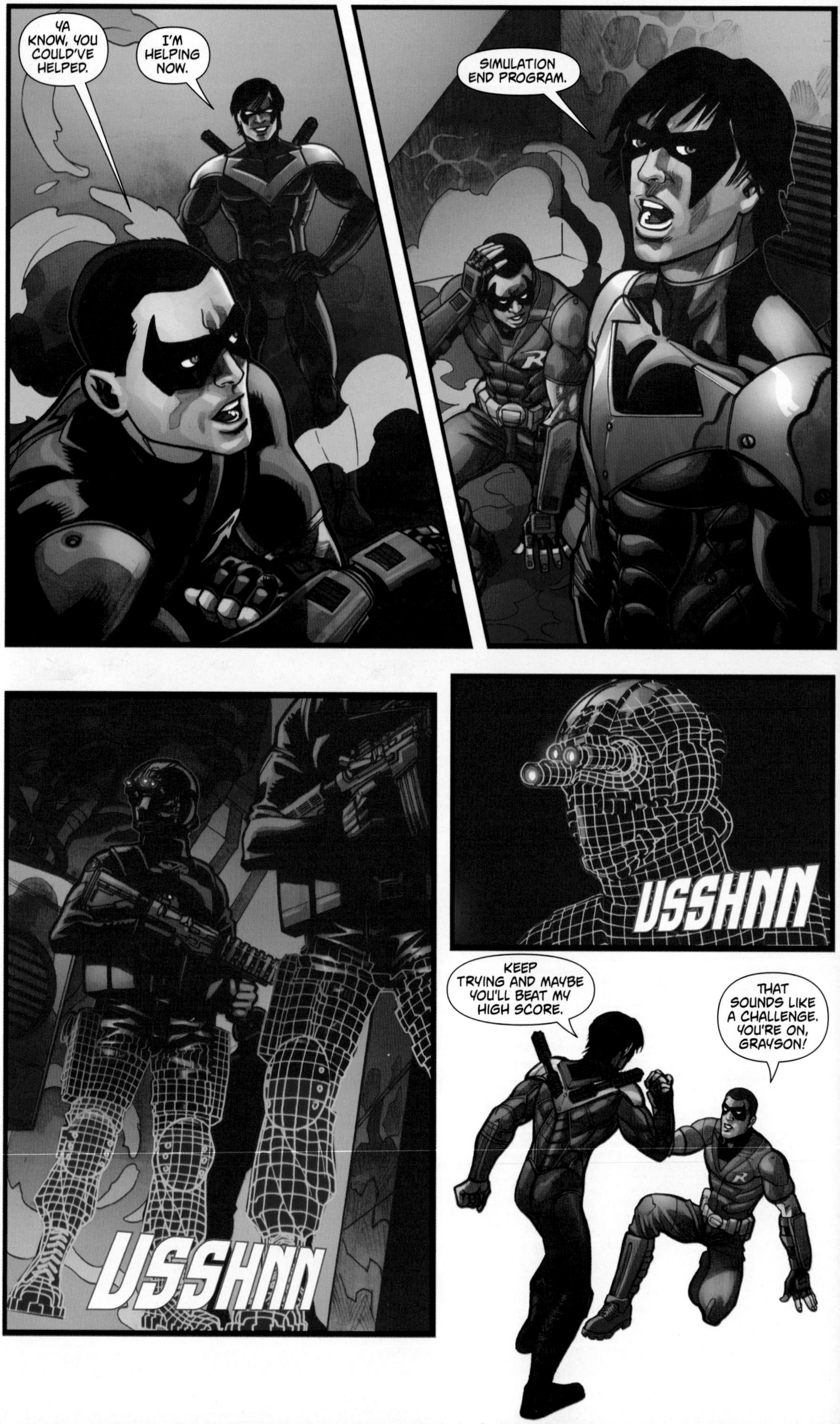
YA KNOW, YOU COULD'VE HELPED.
I'M HELPING NOW.
SIMULATION END PROGRAM.
USSHNN
USSHNN
KEEP TRYING AND MAYBE YOU'LL BEAT MY HIGH SCORE.
THAT SOUNDS LIKE A CHALLENGE. YOU'RE ON, GRAYSON!

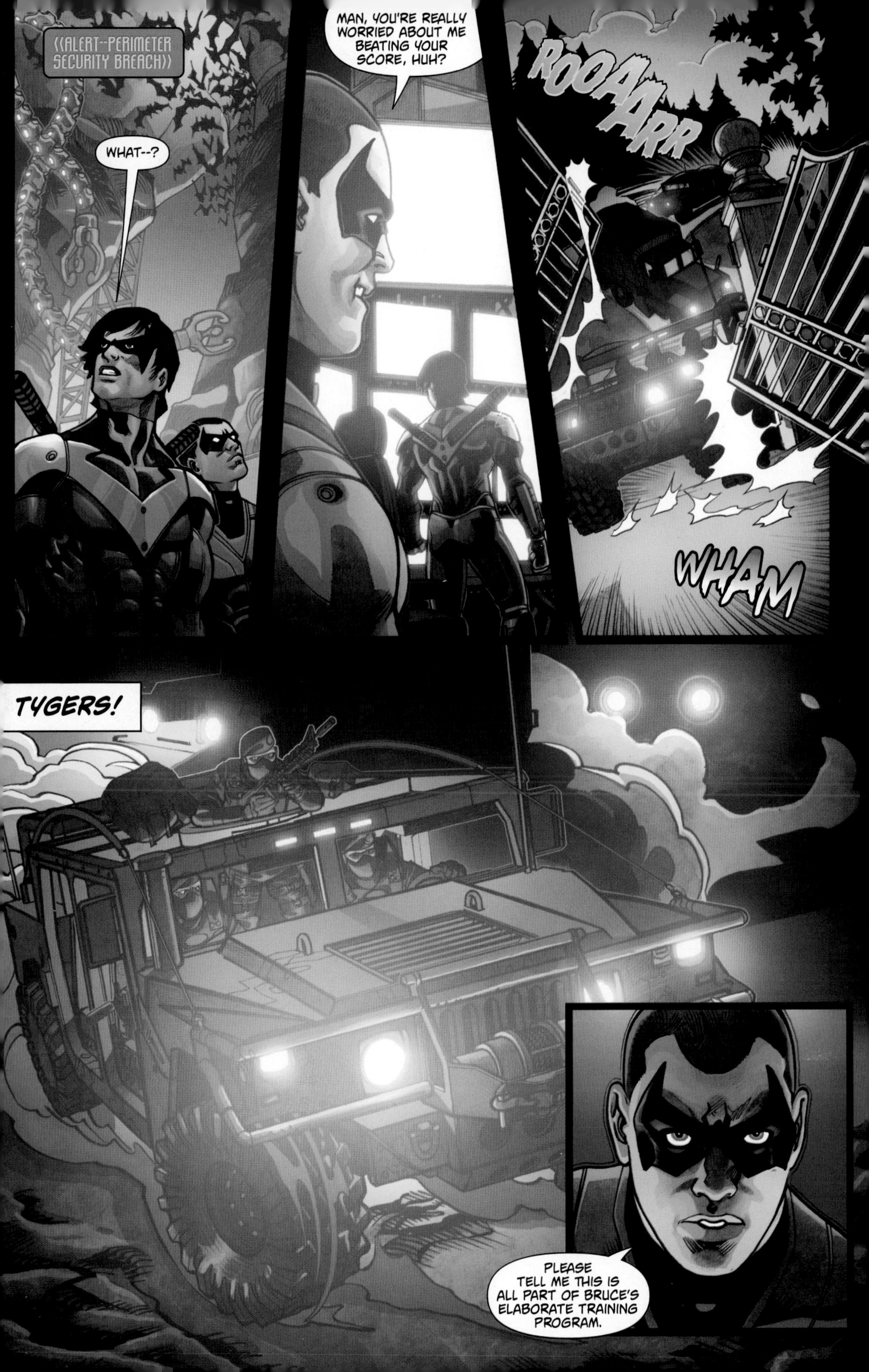
((ALERT--PERIMETER SECURITY BREACH))
WHAT--?
MAN, YOU'RE REALLY WORRIED ABOUT ME BEATING YOUR SCORE, HUH?
ROOAAARR
WHAM
TYGERS!
PLEASE TELL ME THIS IS ALL PART OF BRUCE'S ELABORATE TRAINING PROGRAM.

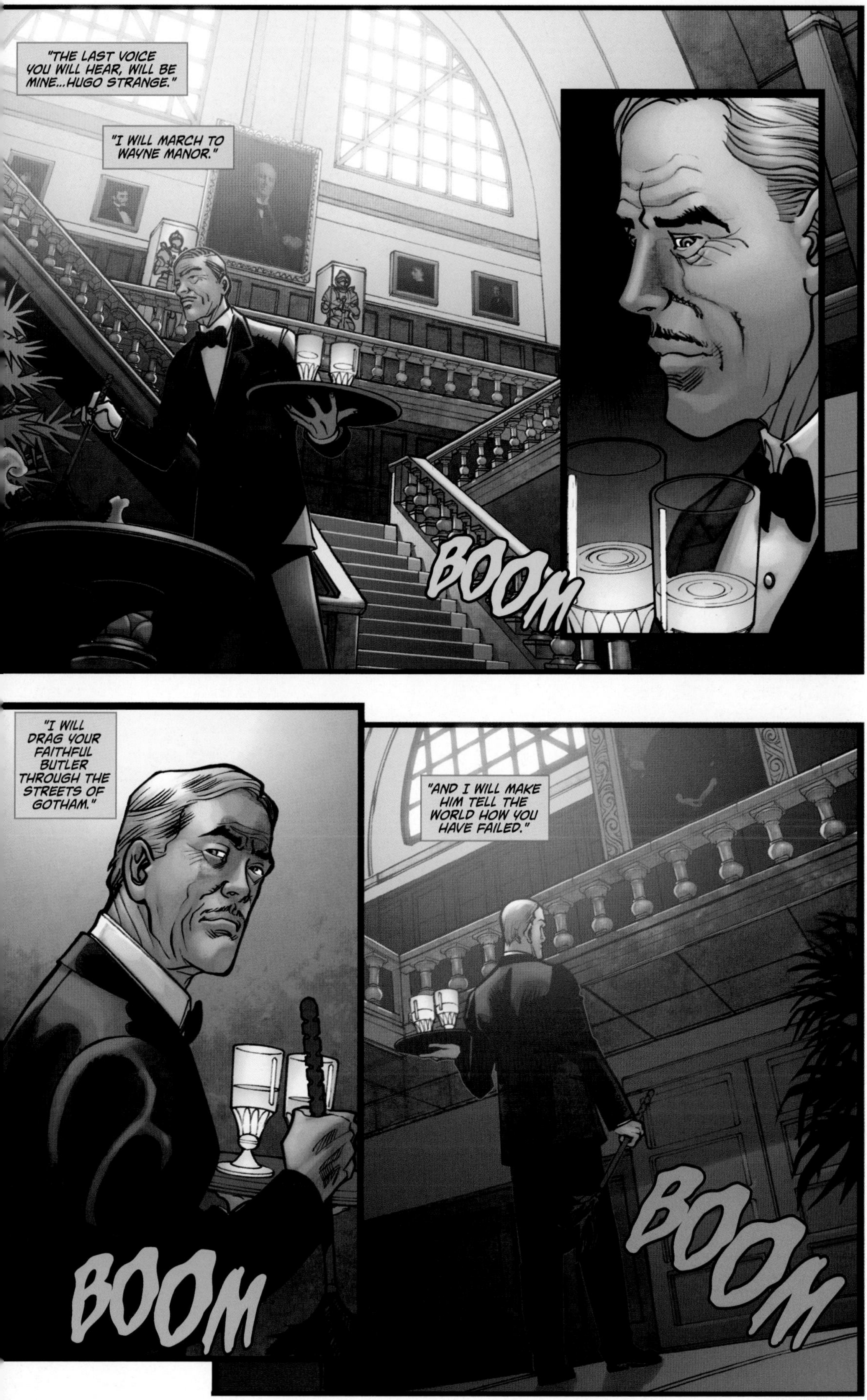
"THE LAST VOICE YOU WILL HEAR, WILL BE MINE...HUGO STRANGE."
"I WILL MARCH TO WAYNE MANOR."
BOOM
"I WILL DRAG YOUR FAITHFUL BUTLER THROUGH THE STREETS OF GOTHAM."
BOOM
"AND I WILL MAKE HIM TELL THE WORLD HOW YOU HAVE FAILED."
BOOM

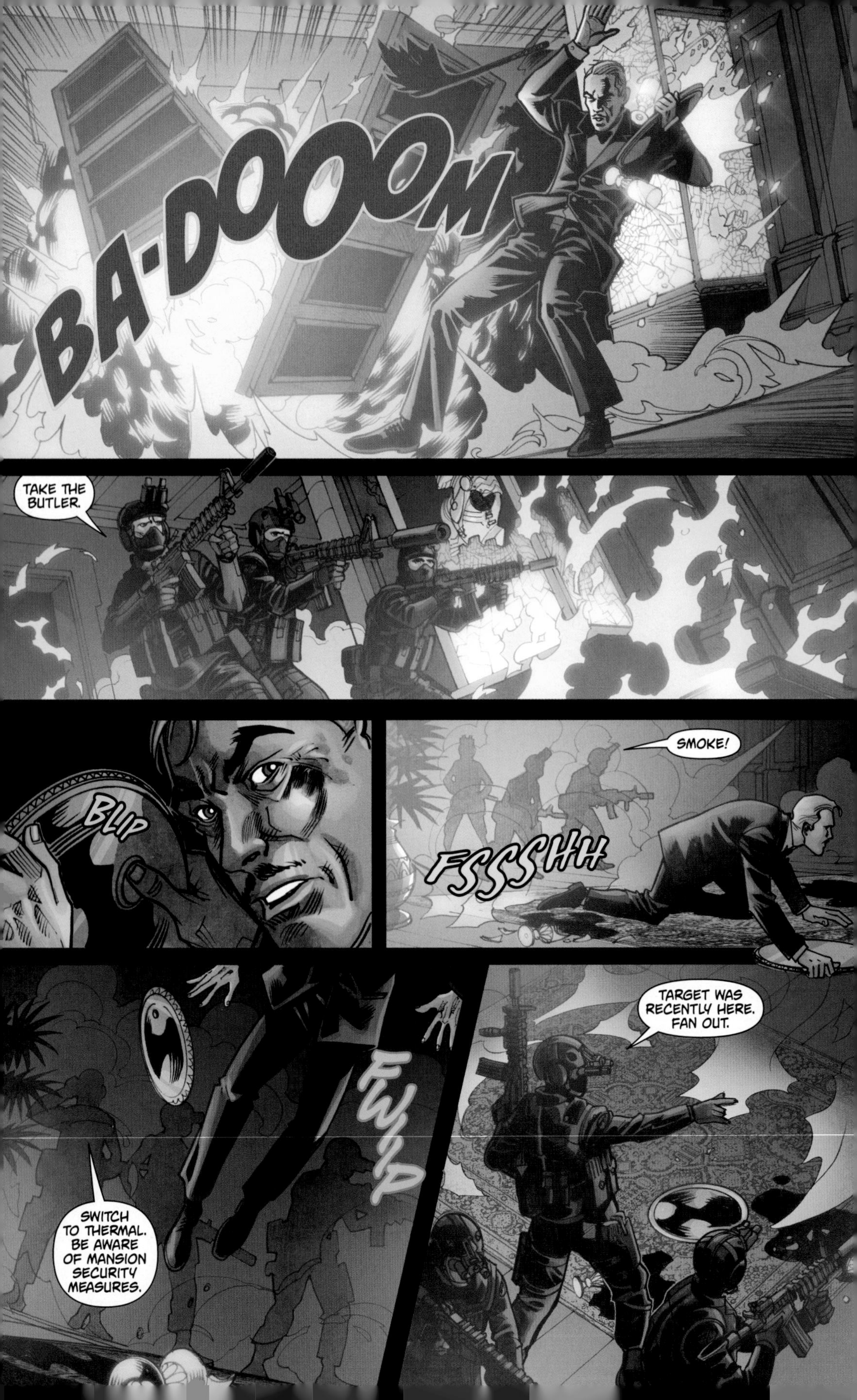
BA-DOOOM
TAKE THE BUTLER.
BLIP
SMOKE!
FSSSHH
FWIP
SWITCH TO THERMAL. BE AWARE OF MANSION SECURITY MEASURES.
TARGET WAS RECENTLY HERE. FAN OUT.

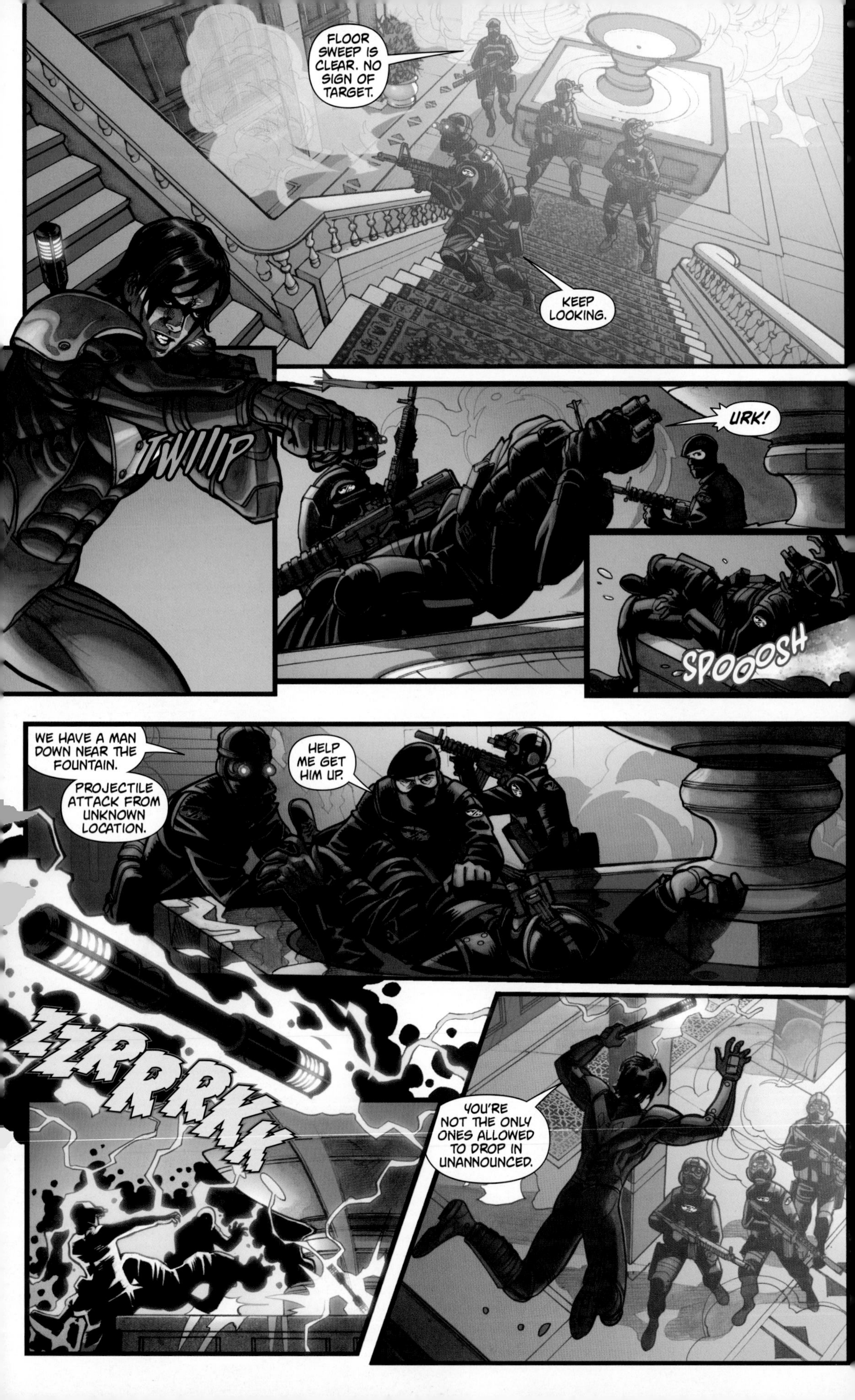
FLOOR SWEEP IS CLEAR. NO SIGN OF TARGET.
KEEP LOOKING.
TWIIIP
URK!
SPOOOOSH
WE HAVE A MAN DOWN NEAR THE FOUNTAIN.
PROJECTILE ATTACK FROM UNKNOWN LOCATION.
HELP ME GET HIM UP.
ZZRRRKK
YOU'RE NOT THE ONLY ONES ALLOWED TO DROP IN UNANNOUNCED.

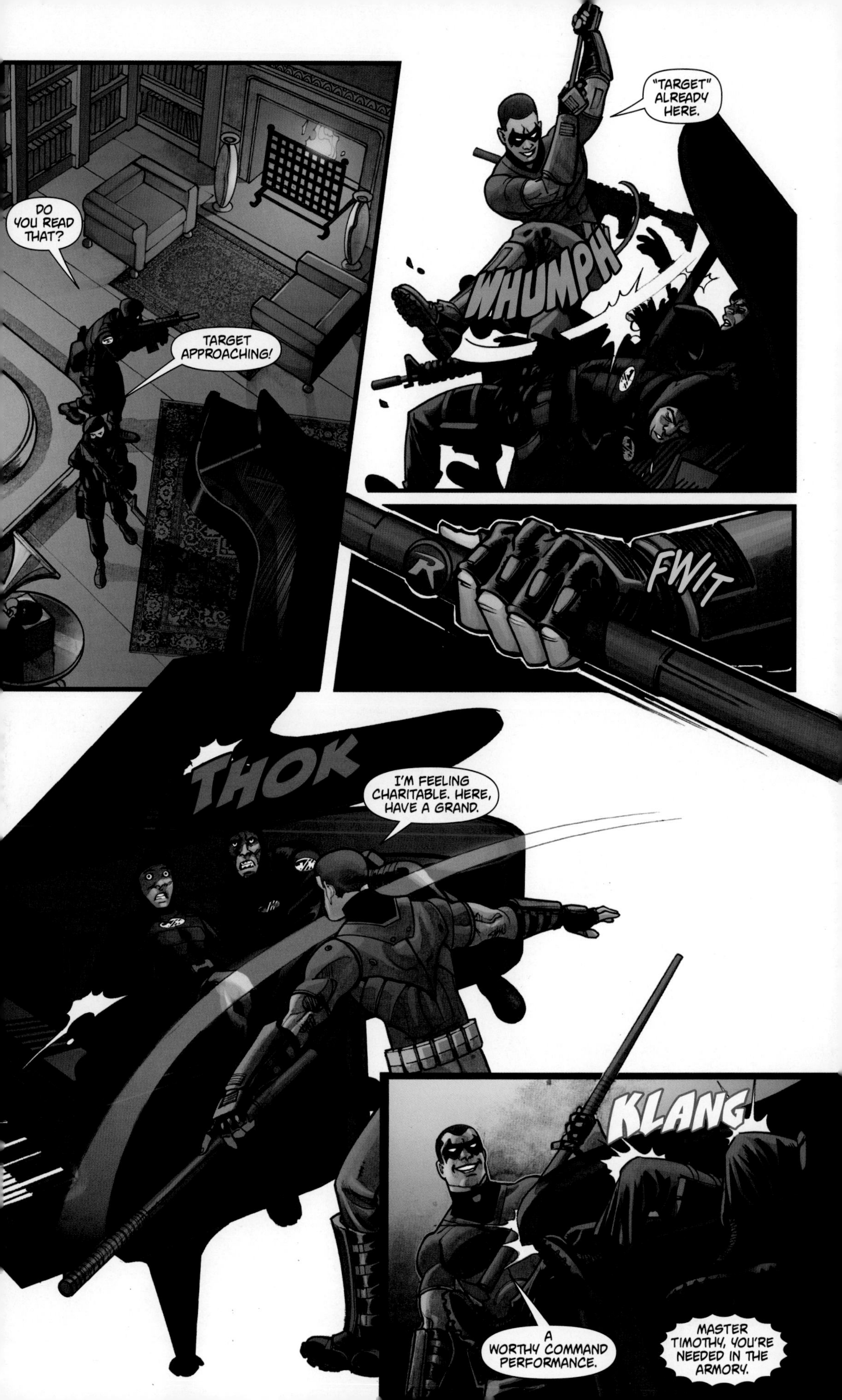
DO YOU READ THAT?
TARGET APPROACHING!
"TARGET" ALREADY HERE.
WHUMPH
FWIT
THOK
I'M FEELING CHARITABLE. HERE, HAVE A GRAND.
KLANG
A WORTHY COMMAND PERFORMANCE.
MASTER TIMOTHY, YOU'RE NEEDED IN THE ARMORY.

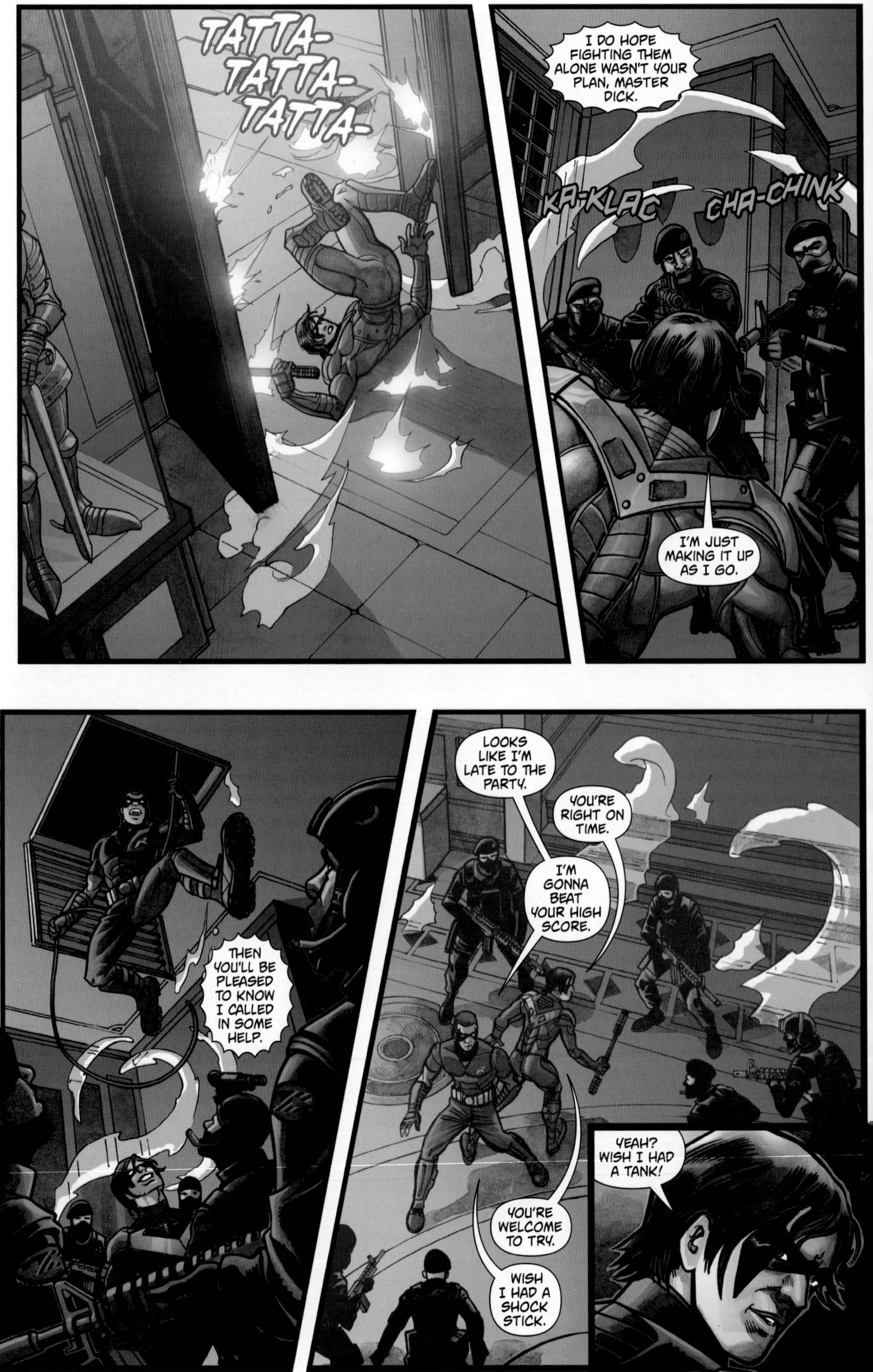

TATTA-TATTA-TATTA-
I DO HOPE FIGHTING THEM ALONE WASN'T YOUR PLAN, MASTER DICK.
KA-KLAC
CHA-CHINK
I'M JUST MAKING IT UP AS I GO.
THEN YOU'LL BE PLEASED TO KNOW I CALLED IN SOME HELP.
LOOKS LIKE I'M LATE TO THE PARTY.
YOU'RE RIGHT ON TIME.
I'M GONNA BEAT YOUR HIGH SCORE.
YOU'RE WELCOME TO TRY.
WISH I HAD A SHOCK STICK.
YEAH? WISH I HAD A TANK!

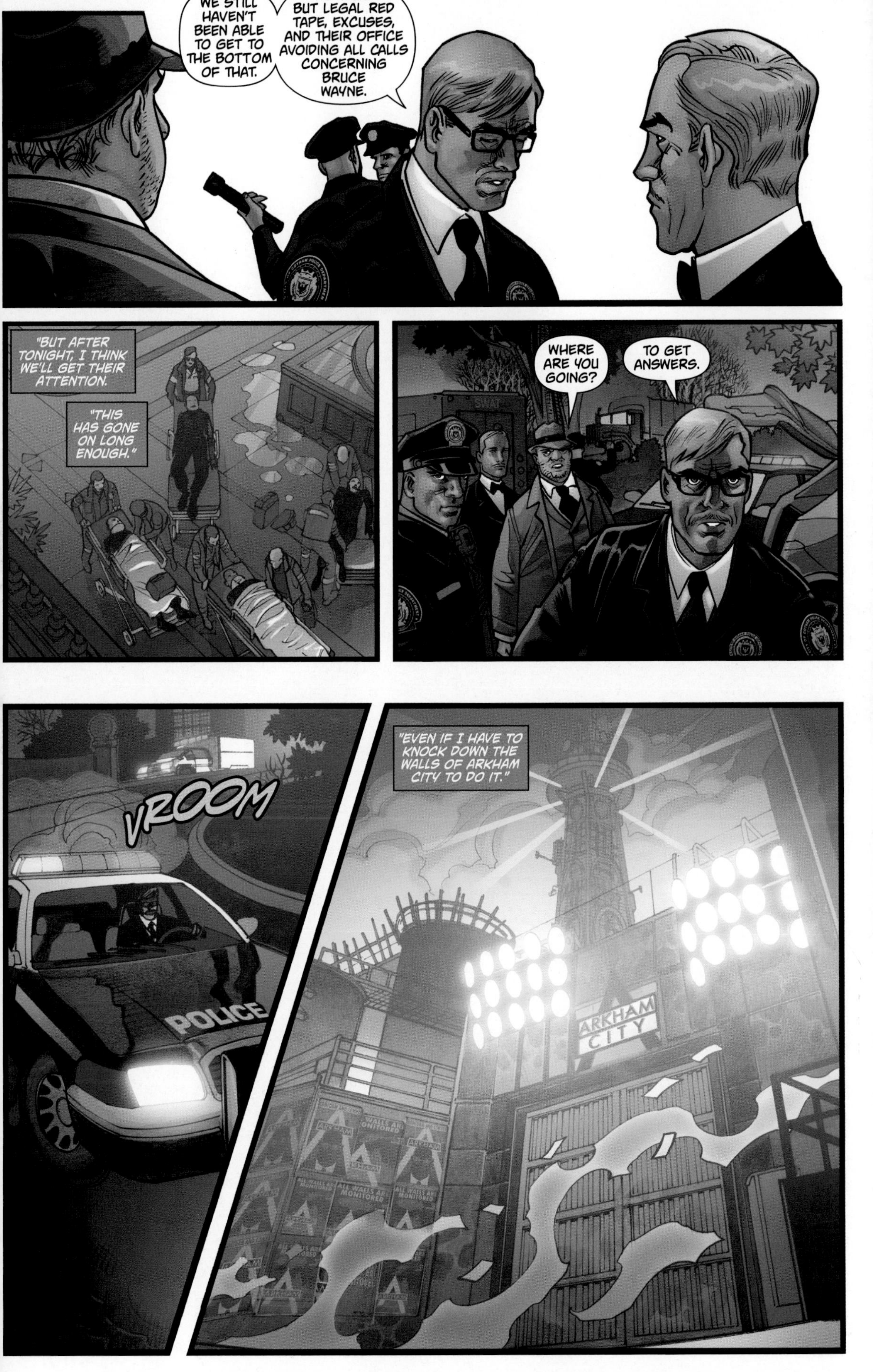
WE STILL HAVEN'T BEEN ABLE TO GET TO THE BOTTOM OF THAT.
NOTHING BUT LEGAL RED TAPE, EXCUSES, AND THEIR OFFICE AVOIDING ALL CALLS CONCERNING BRUCE WAYNE.
"BUT AFTER TONIGHT, I THINK WE'LL GET THEIR ATTENTION.
"THIS HAS GONE ON LONG ENOUGH."
WHERE ARE YOU GOING?
TO GET ANSWERS.
VROOM
POLICE
"EVEN IF I HAVE TO KNOCK DOWN THE WALLS OF ARKHAM CITY TO DO IT."
ARKHAM CITY
ALL WALLS ARE MONITORED

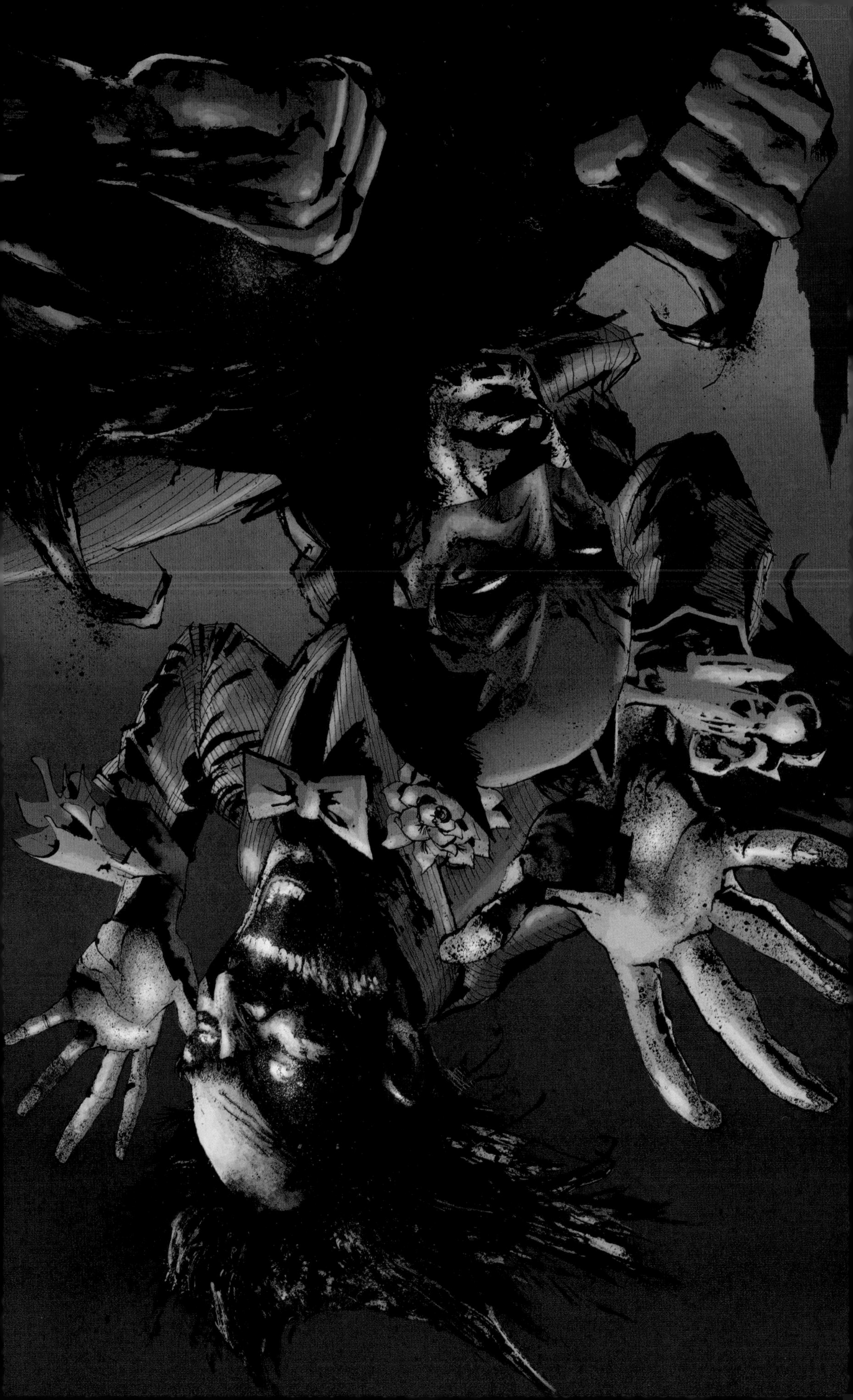

# END GAME

WRITER: DEREK FRIDOLFS
ARTIST: JASON SHAWN ALEXANDER
COLORIST: LEE LOUGHRIDGE
LETTERER: TRAVIS LANHAM
COVER ART BY: JASON SHAWN ALEXANDER
COVER COLORS BY: LEE LOUGHRIDGE
VARIANT COVER PENCILS BY: PAT GLEASON
VARIANT COVER INKS BY: DEREK FRIDOLFS
VARIANT COVER COLORS BY: GABE ELTAEB

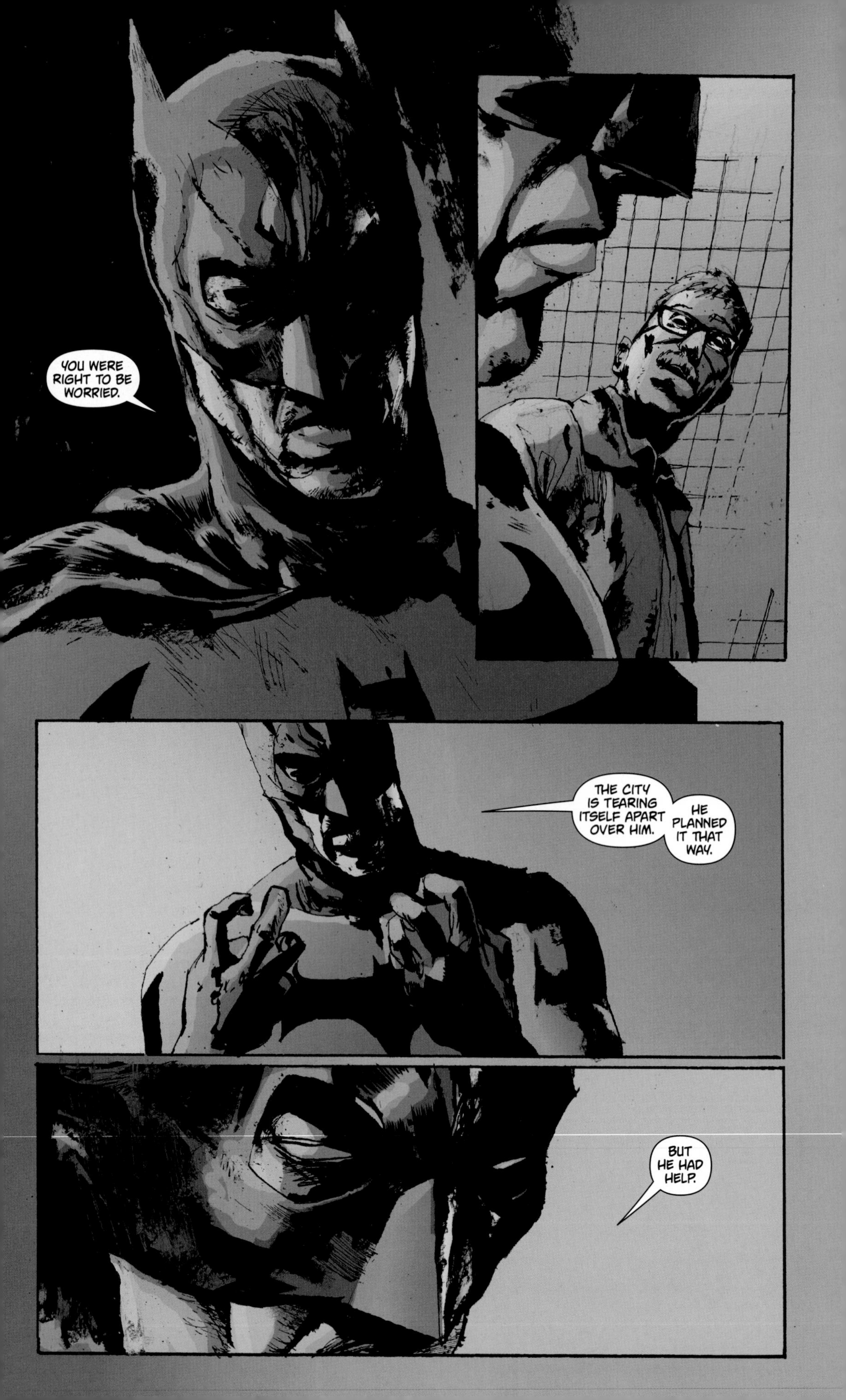
YOU WERE RIGHT TO BE WORRIED.
THE CITY IS TEARING ITSELF APART OVER HIM.
HE PLANNED IT THAT WAY.
BUT HE HAD HELP.

THOK

BANG

LONG LIVE THE JOKER!

"...BUT THEY DON'T.

THERE IS NOW!

YA GOT ME, JOHN LAW, I SURRENDER...

DROP THE WEAPON, NOW!

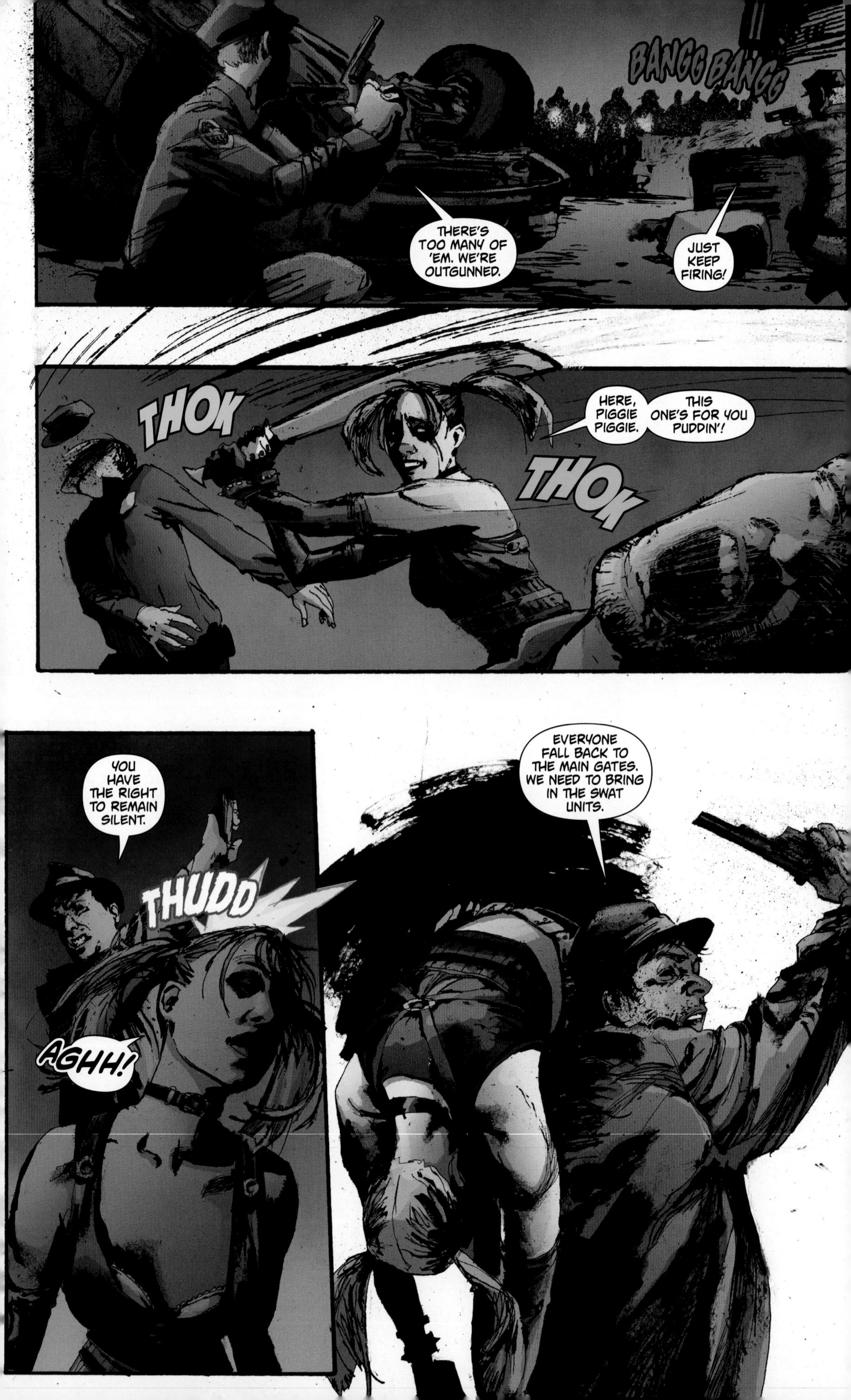
BANGG BANGG
THERE'S TOO MANY OF 'EM. WE'RE OUTGUNNED.
JUST KEEP FIRING!
THOK
HERE, PIGGIE PIGGIE.
THIS ONE'S FOR YOU PUDDIN'!
THOK
YOU HAVE THE RIGHT TO REMAIN SILENT.
THUDD
AGHH!
EVERYONE FALL BACK TO THE MAIN GATES. WE NEED TO BRING IN THE SWAT UNITS.

MY CAPTURE BY HARLEY DELAYED ME. I WOULDN'T SEE WHAT JOKER HAD IN STORE FOR GOTHAM FOR ANOTHER TWO DAYS.

THIS TOWN'S NOT BIG ENOUGH FER THE BOTH OF US.

PUT 'EM UP!

AND NOW
ONE OF YOU
CAN BE THE LUCKY
RECIPIENT.

SO I MAKE
THIS CHALLENGE
TO ALL OF
YOU.

THE ONE
THAT FINDS MY
BODY AND RETURNS
IT, CARE OF ONE HARLEEN
QUINZEL, WILL BE REWARDED
TO THE TUNE OF ONE
HUNDRED MILLION
DOLLARS.

THAT'S
TAX-FREE,
FOLKS! SET UP
IN AN OFFSHORE
ACCOUNT OF YOUR
CHOOSING.

I'VE
BEEN SQUIRRELING
AWAY MONEY OVER THE
YEARS. SEEMS I'VE BEEN
QUITE THE SUCCESSFUL
ENTREPRENEUR.

YES, I'M
AFRAID IT'S TRUE.
YOUR ESTEEMED
CLOWN PRINCE OF
CRIME HAS MET HIS...
M..."UNTIMELY DEATH,"
BUT HOW RARE IS IT
THAT I CAN PROVIDE
MY OWN EULOGY?

HELLO,
GOTHAM! I'M
COMING AT YOU
DEAD FROM
INSIDE ARKHAM
CITY.

AND RATHER
THAN MY LOUSY
OUTLAW IN-LAWS AND
RELATIVES GETTING MY
INHERITANCE, I THOUGHT
IT BEST TO REWARD THE
CITIZENS OF GOTHAM
INSTEAD.

THAT IT HAPPENED ON THIS NIGHT MADE IT EVEN MORE SUSPICIOUS.

GOTHAM WAS CUT OFF AND IN THE DARK.

NOT JUST BUILDINGS AND STREETLIGHTS. ANYTHING ELECTRICAL WAS AFFECTED, INCLUDING VEHICLES.

GOTHAM HAD EXPERIENCED A TOTAL BLACKOUT. THE RESULT OF A MASSIVE ELECTRICAL STORM.

INDEPENDENCE DAY.

JULY FOURTH.

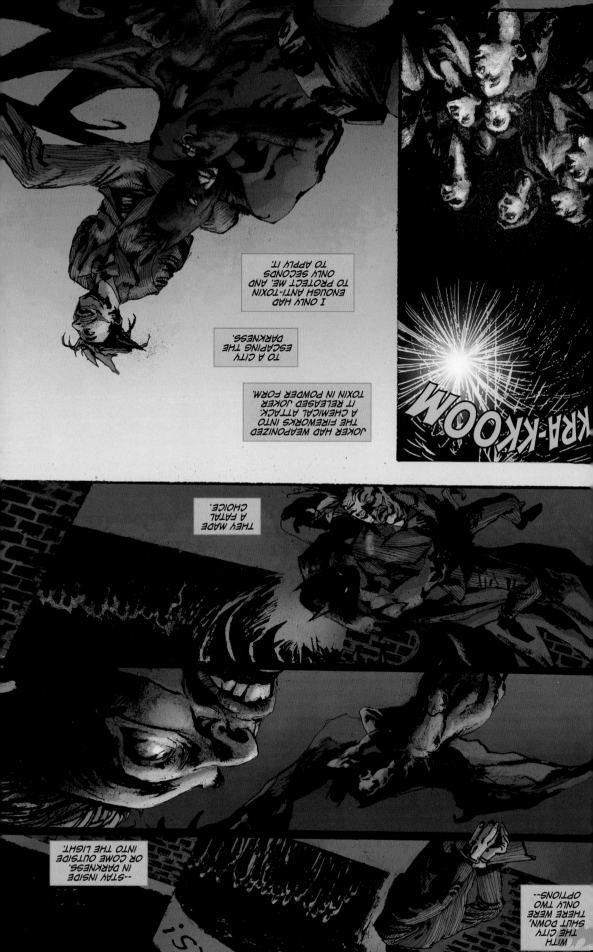

HEH
HEH
HEH
HEH
HEH
HEH
HEH

KLANK

*WAIT!* ONE MORE QUESTION, WHAT AM I SUPPOSED TO DO DOWN HERE?

WRITE A BOOK.

CRREEEEEAK

CLOSING THAT DOOR SOLVES NOTHING, BATMAN. NO MATTER WHAT HAPPENS... I'M NEVER GOING AWAY. YOU AND ME TOGETHER, WE'RE JUST MEANT TO BE.

YOU'RE IN SOLITARY FOR A REASON. I DON'T NEED TO REMIND YOU WHY.

*HA!* AND I THOUGHT *I* WAS THE COMEDIAN?

THE PIPE COMING OUT OF THE WALL TO YOUR RIGHT WILL SUPPLY FOOD AND WATER. THE HOLE IN THE FLOOR TO YOUR LEFT IS YOUR TOILET. GET TO KNOW WHERE EACH IS LOCATED. YOU WON'T BE ABLE TO SEE THEM AFTER THIS DOOR CLOSES, AND WITHOUT LIGHT, YOU DON'T WANT TO MISTAKE ONE FOR THE OTHER.

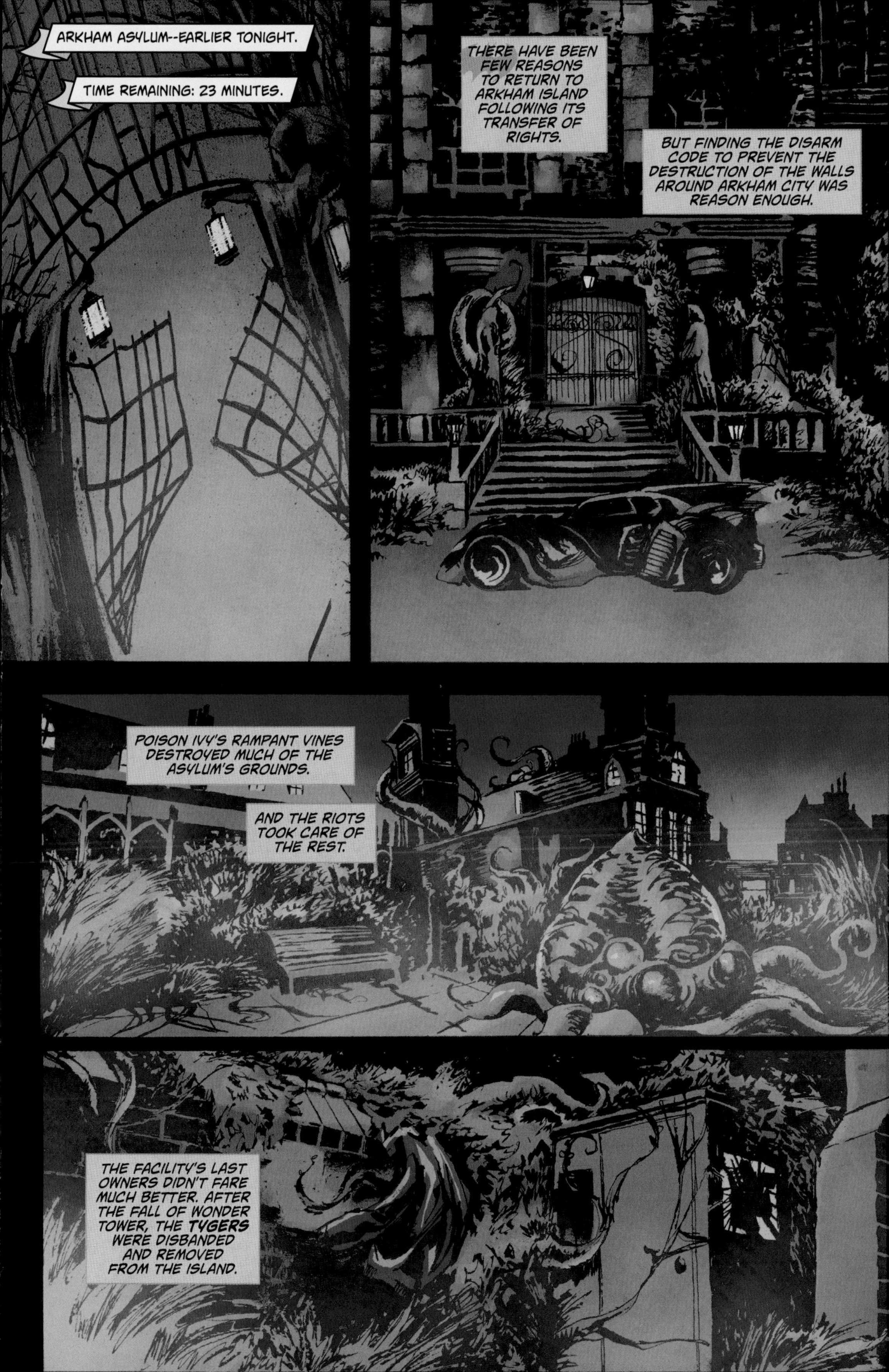
ARKHAM ASYLUM--EARLIER TONIGHT.
TIME REMAINING: 23 MINUTES.
ARKHAM ASYLUM
THERE HAVE BEEN FEW REASONS TO RETURN TO ARKHAM ISLAND FOLLOWING ITS TRANSFER OF RIGHTS.
BUT FINDING THE DISARM CODE TO PREVENT THE DESTRUCTION OF THE WALLS AROUND ARKHAM CITY WAS REASON ENOUGH.
POISON IVY'S RAMPANT VINES DESTROYED MUCH OF THE ASYLUM'S GROUNDS.
AND THE RIOTS TOOK CARE OF THE REST.
THE FACILITY'S LAST OWNERS DIDN'T FARE MUCH BETTER. AFTER THE FALL OF WONDER TOWER, THE TYGERS WERE DISBANDED AND REMOVED FROM THE ISLAND.

WHERE OLD
GHOSTS
GO TO DIE.

ALL PATHS
END HERE.

A DESCENT
INTO DARKNESS.

IT'S REMAINED
A SHELL OF ITS
FORMER SELF.

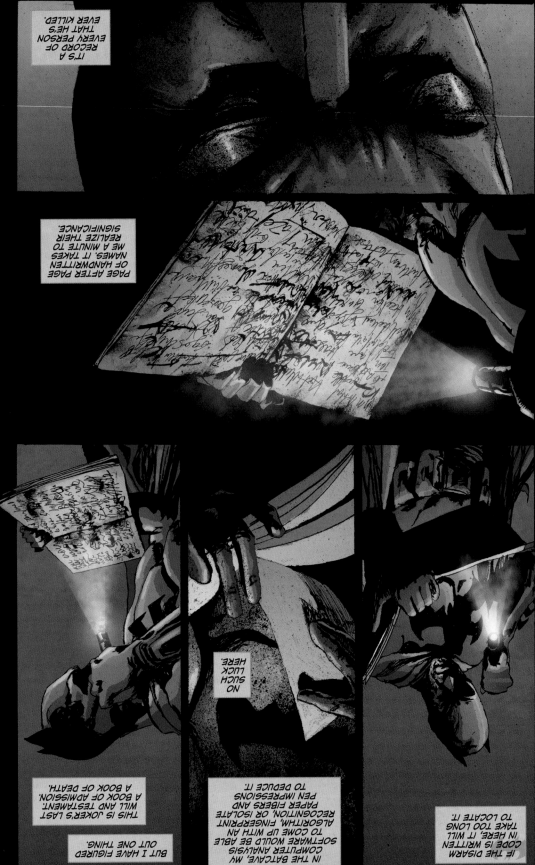

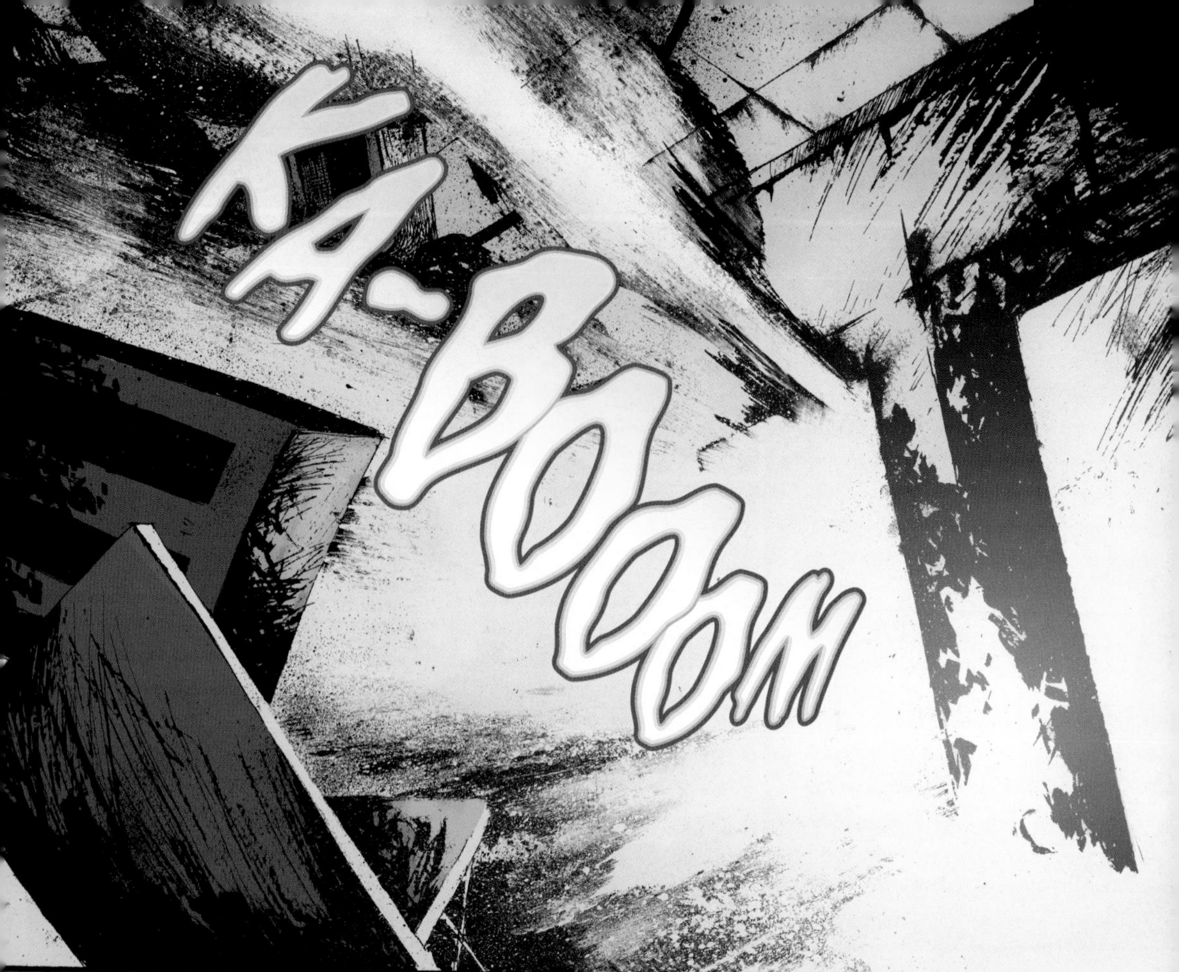
KA-BOOOM
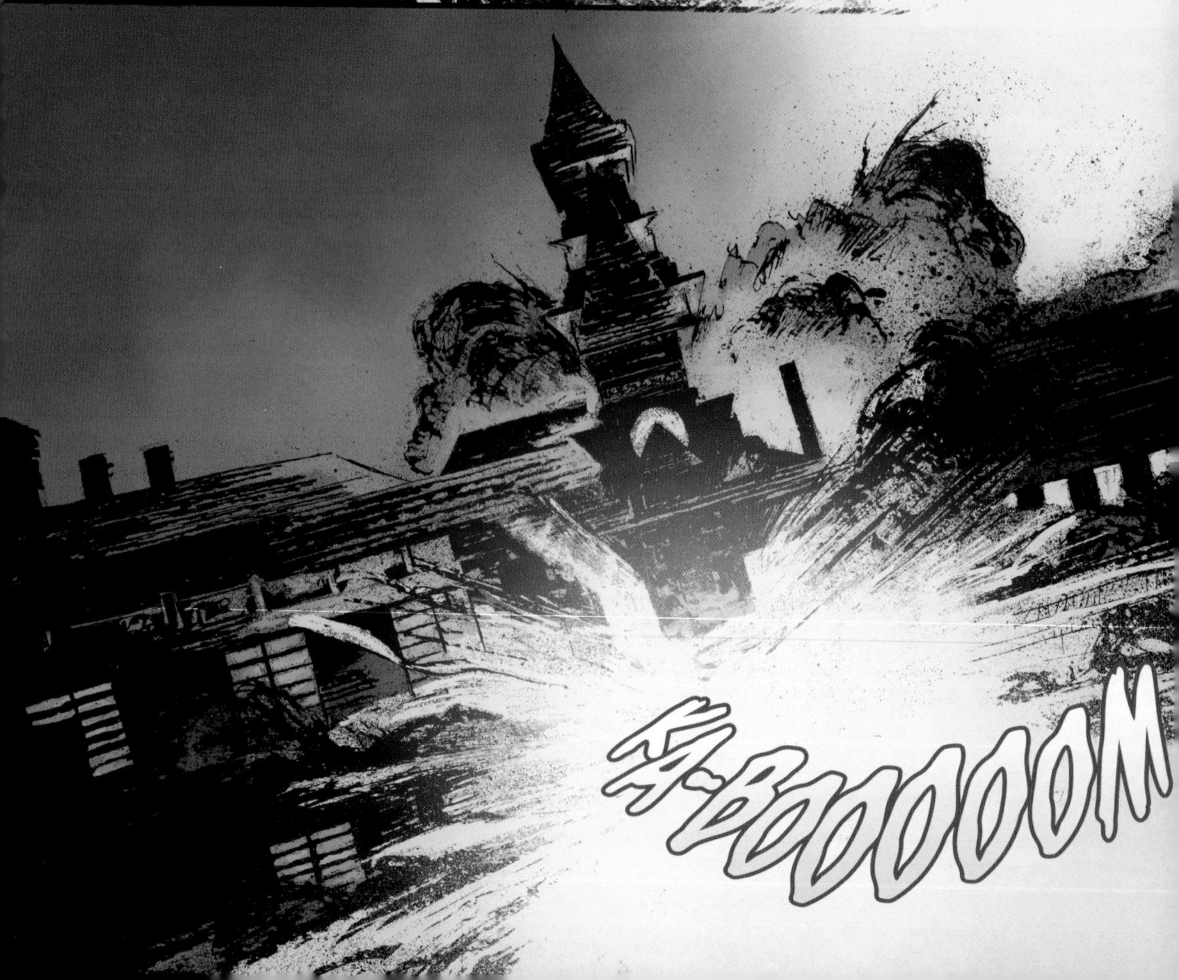
KA-BOOOOOM

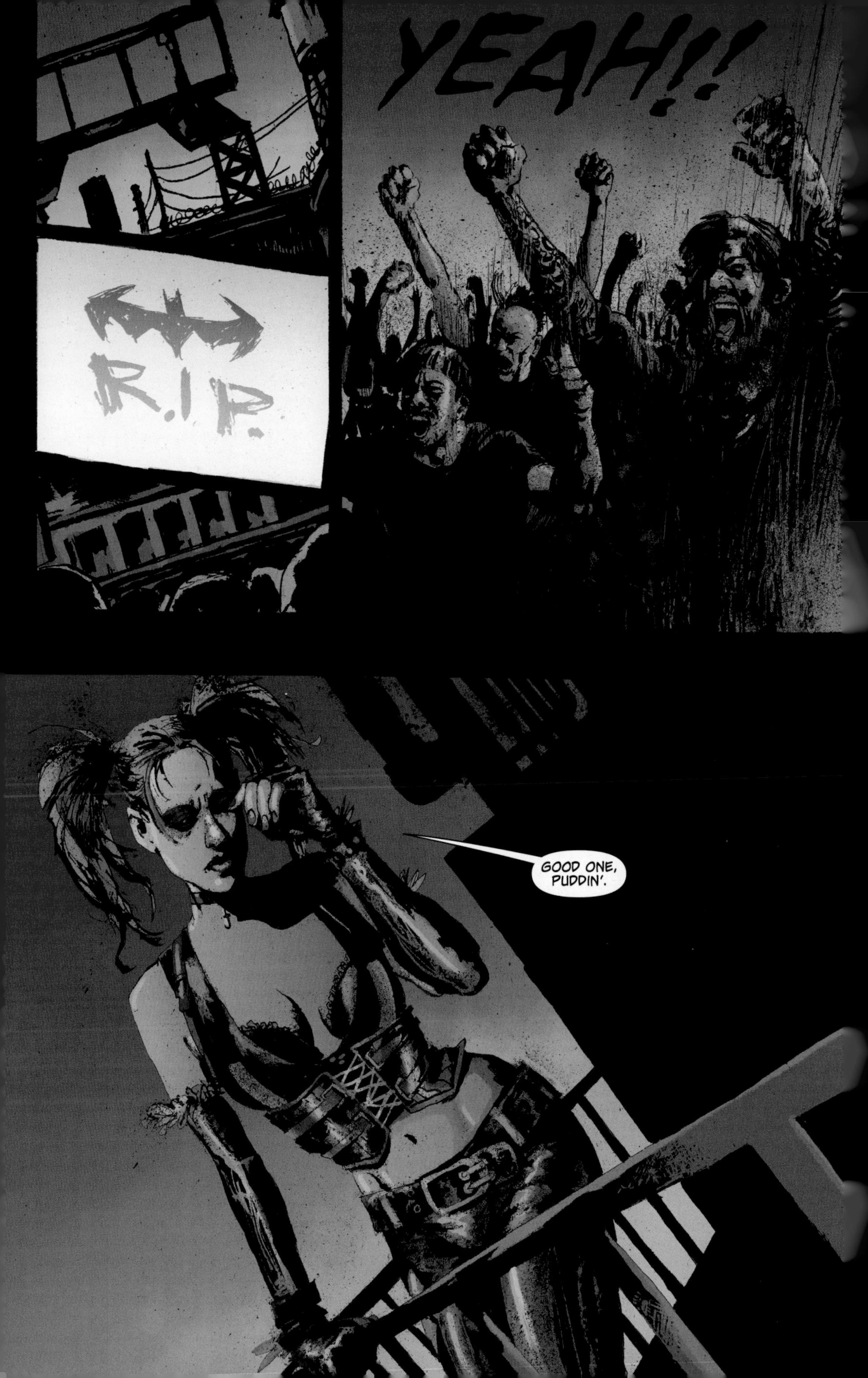
R.I.P.
YEAH!!
GOOD ONE, PUDDIN'.

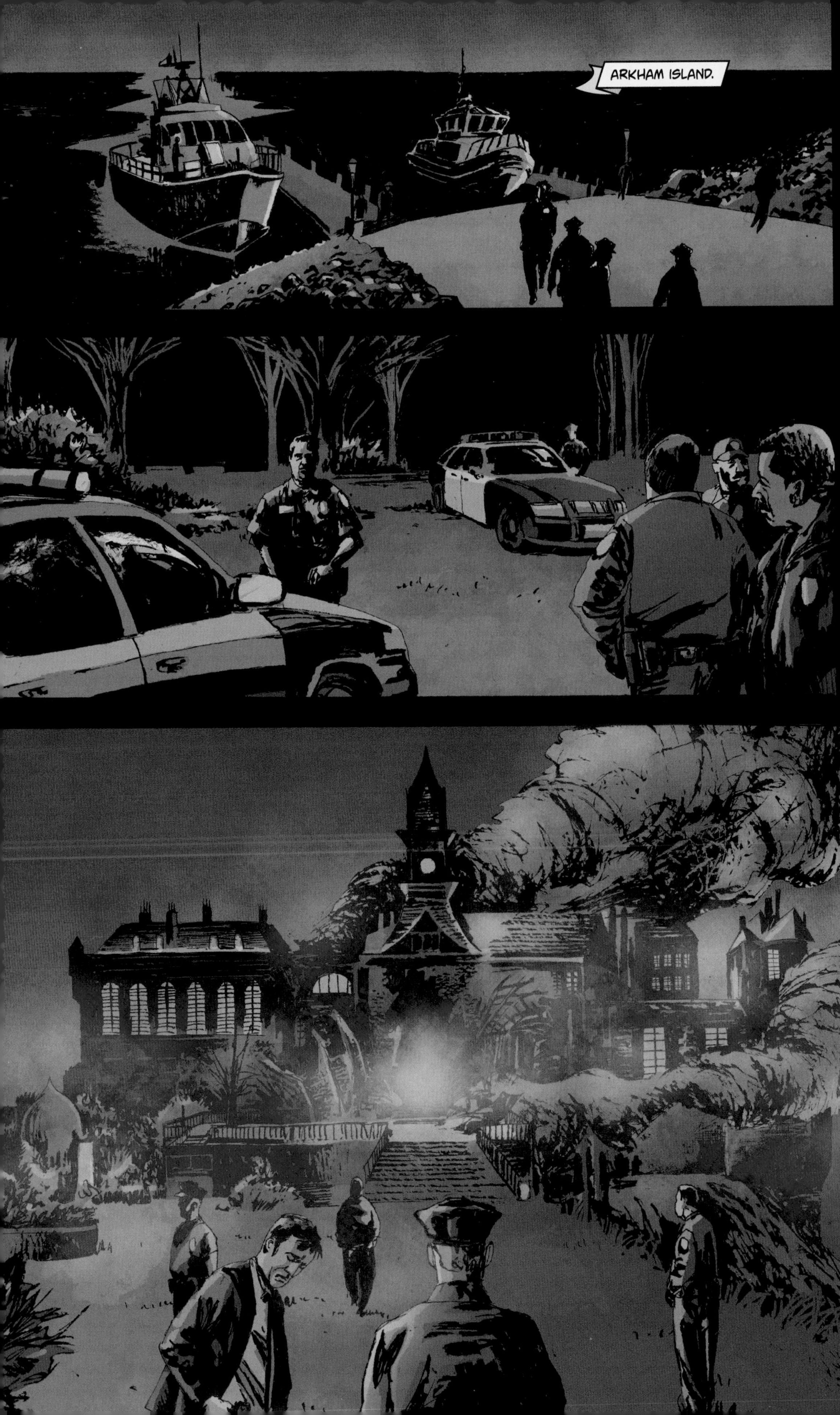
ARKHAM ISLAND.

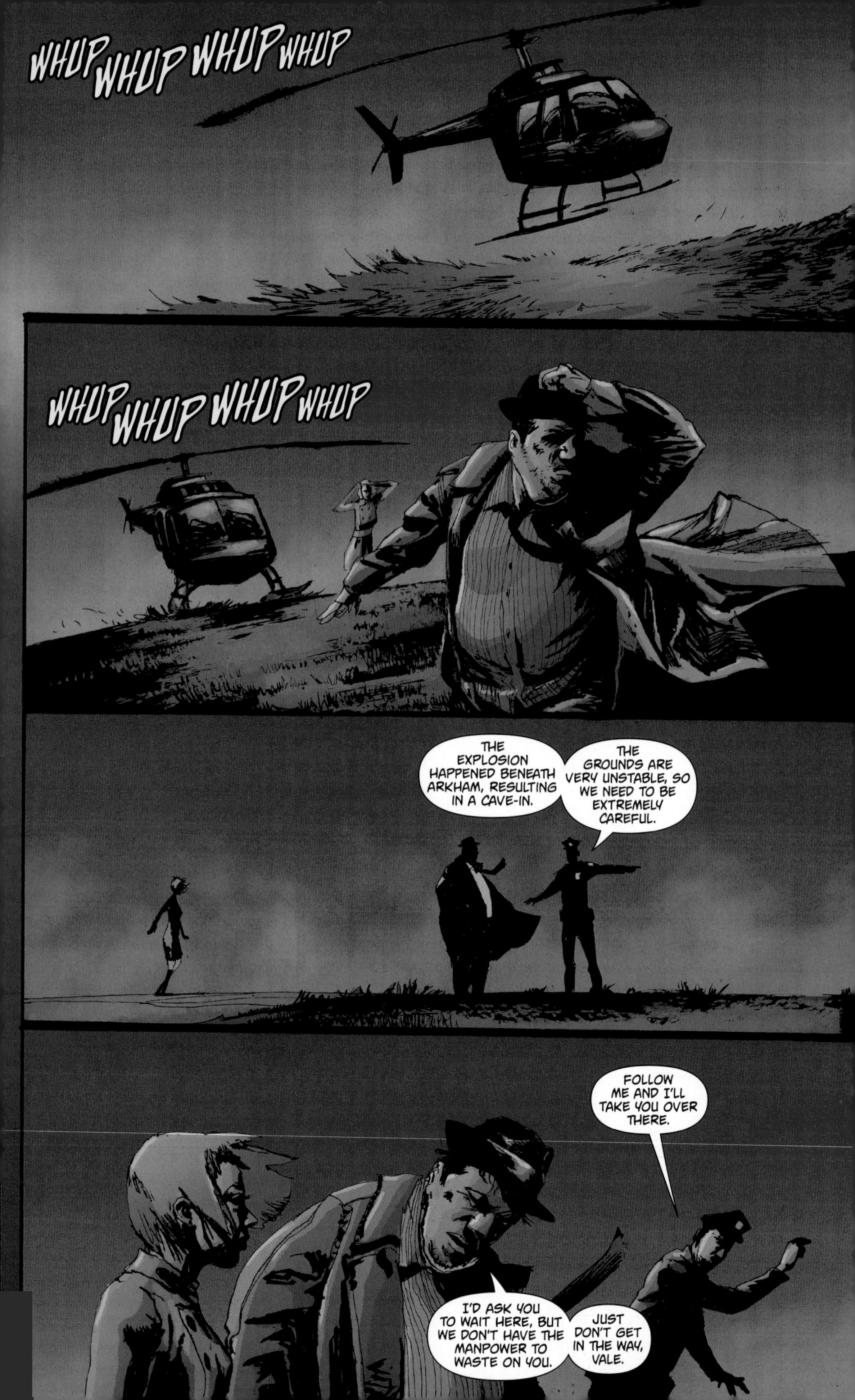
WHUP WHUP WHUP WHUP
WHUP WHUP WHUP WHUP
THE EXPLOSION HAPPENED BENEATH ARKHAM, RESULTING IN A CAVE-IN.
THE GROUNDS ARE VERY UNSTABLE, SO WE NEED TO BE EXTREMELY CAREFUL.
FOLLOW ME AND I'LL TAKE YOU OVER THERE.
I'D ASK YOU TO WAIT HERE, BUT WE DON'T HAVE THE MANPOWER TO WASTE ON YOU.
JUST DON'T GET IN THE WAY, VALE.

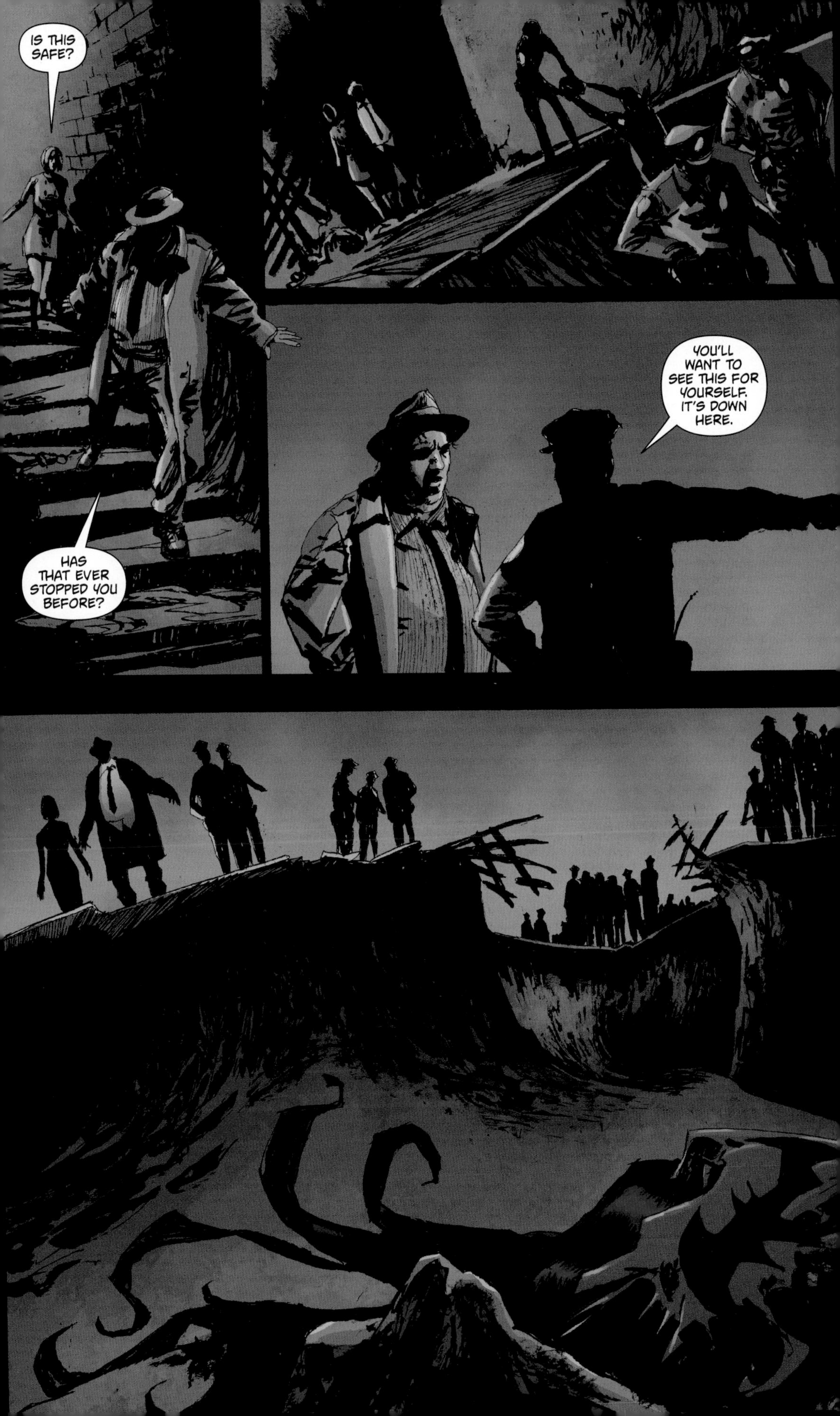
IS THIS SAFE?
HAS THAT EVER STOPPED YOU BEFORE?
YOU'LL WANT TO SEE THIS FOR YOURSELF. IT'S DOWN HERE.

JIM, IT'S TIME TO MEET.

(THIS IS GORDON, WHO IS THIS?)

RIIING RIIING

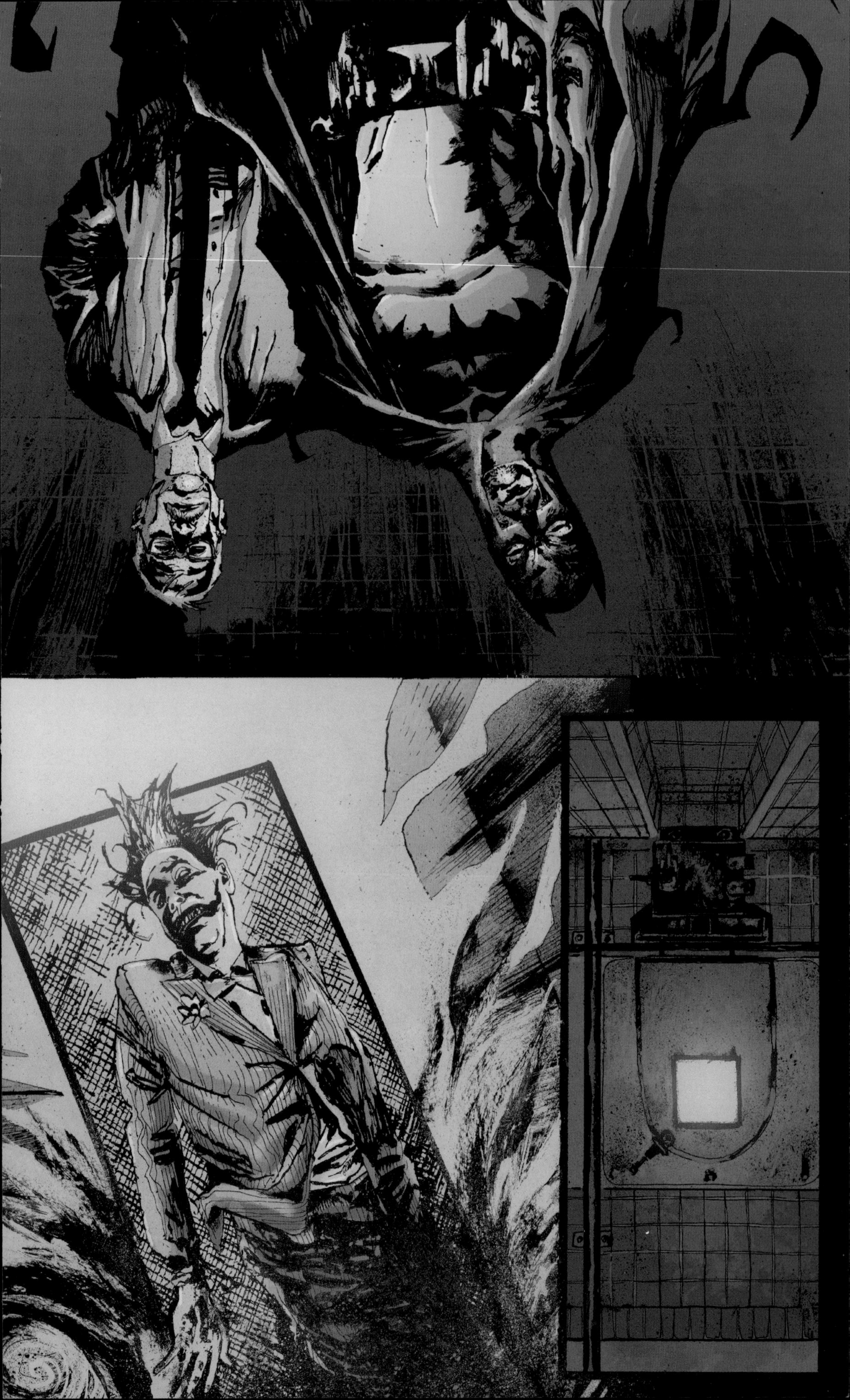

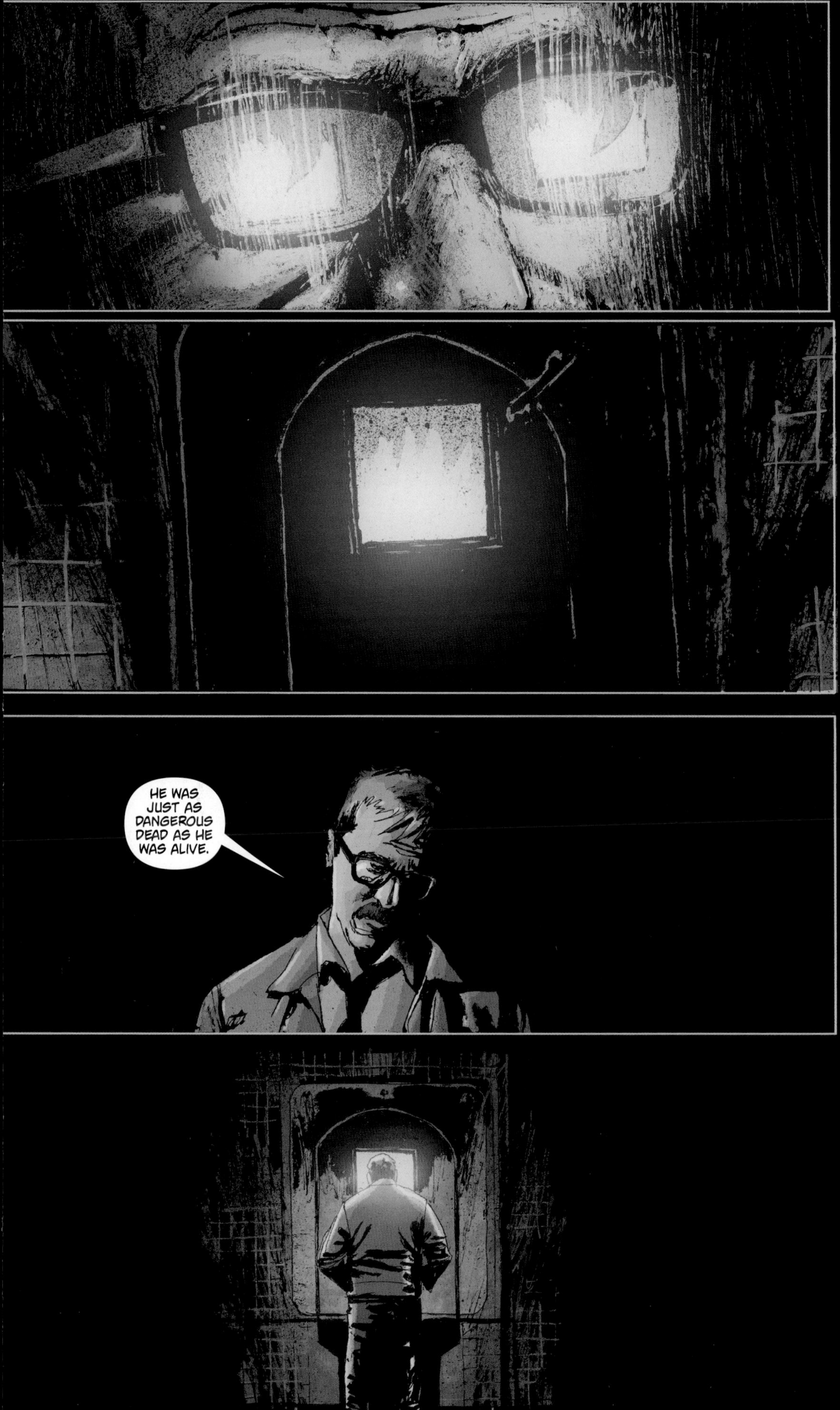
HE WAS JUST AS DANGEROUS DEAD AS HE WAS ALIVE.

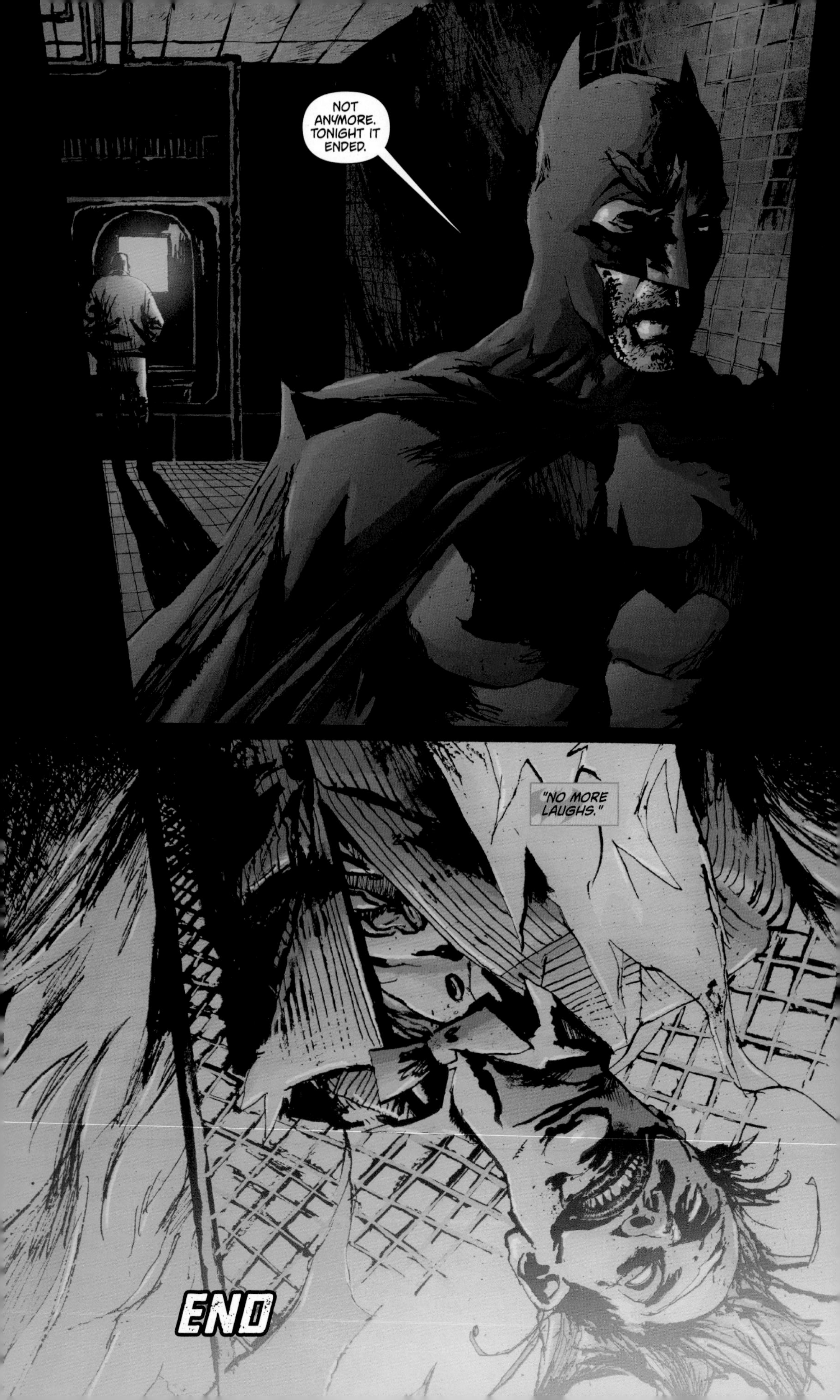
NOT ANYMORE. TONIGHT IT ENDED.
"NO MORE LAUGHS."
END

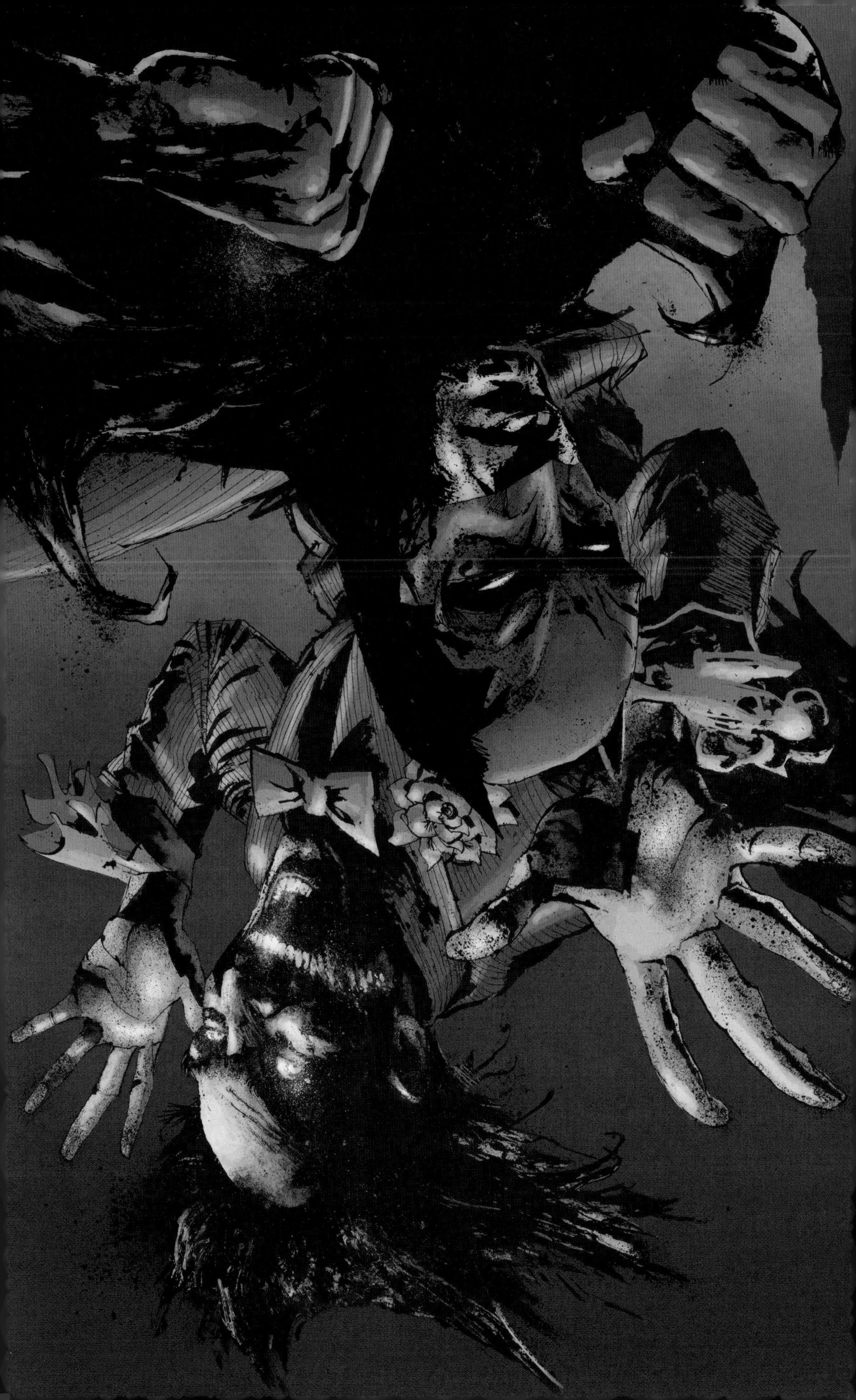

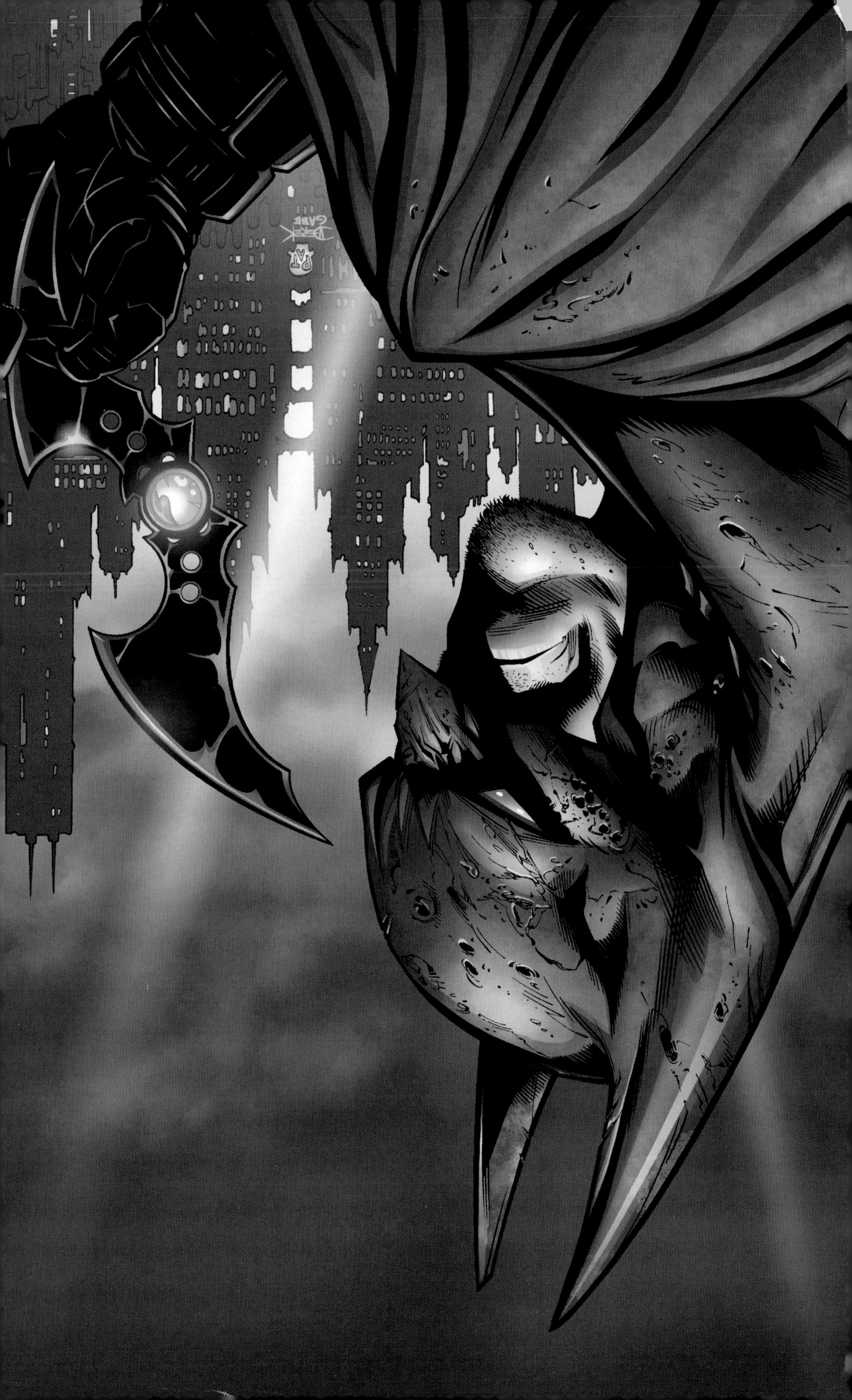

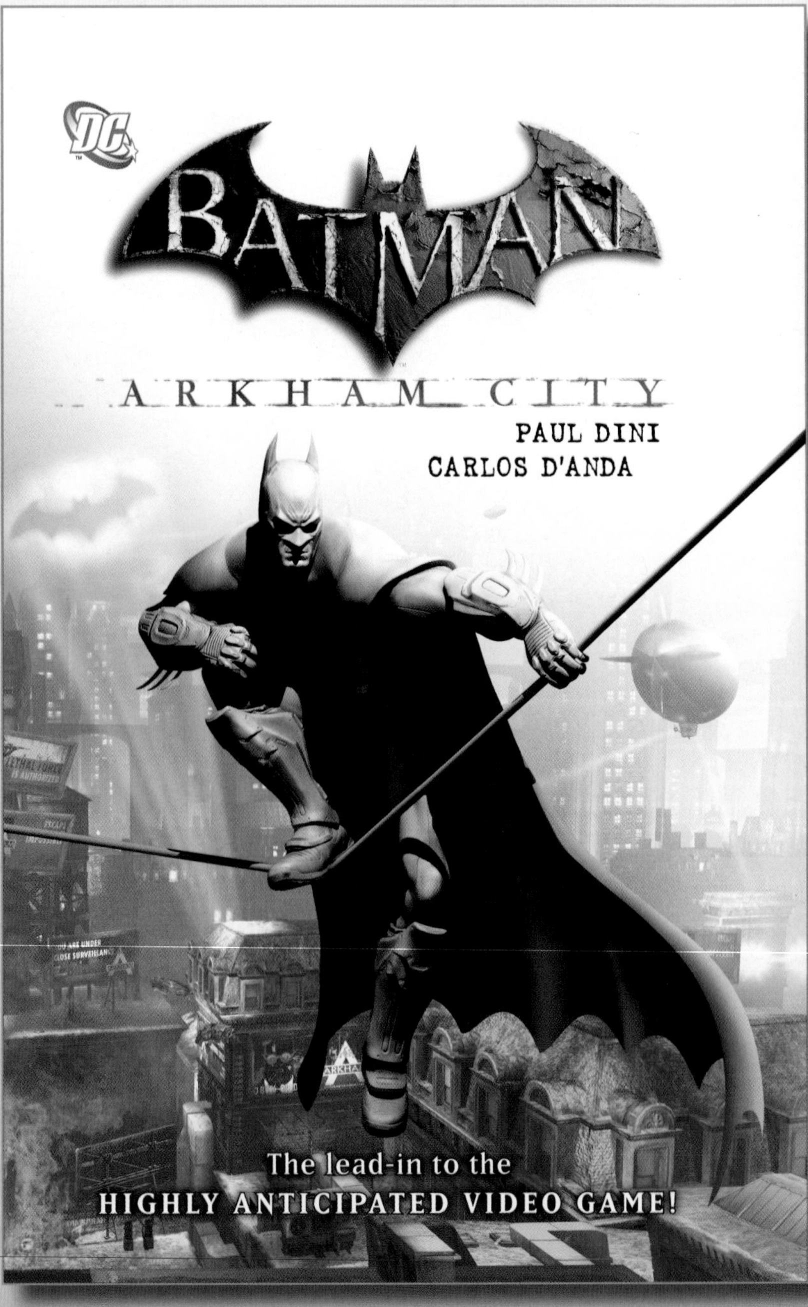

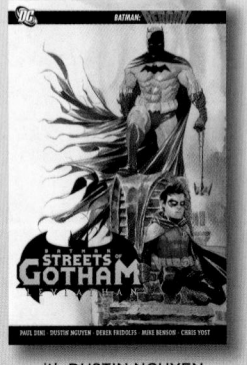